General John Burgoyne

University of Delaware Press Award
General John Burgoyne (Richard J. Hargrove, Jr.)

General John Burgoyne, by Sir Joshua Reynolds, 1766. Copyright the Frick Collection, New York.

General John Burgoyne

Richard J. Hargrove, Jr.

Newark: University of Delaware Press
London and Toronto: Associated University Presses

Associated University Presses, Inc.
4 Cornwall Drive
East Brunswick, N.J. 08816

Associated University Presses Ltd
27 Chancery Lane
London WC2A 1NF, England

Associated University Presses
Toronto M5E 1A7, Canada

Library of Congress Cataloging in Publication Data
Hargrove, Richard J., Jr., 1941–
  General John Burgoyne.

  Bibliography: p.
  Includes index.
    1. Burgoyne, John, 1722–1792.   2. United States—
History—Revolution, 1775–1783—British forces.
3. United States—History—Revolution—1775–1783—
Campaigns and battles.   4. Generals—Great Britain
—Biography.   5. Great Britain. Army—Biography.
I. Title.
DA67.1.B8H37   973.3′41′0924 [B]   80-54788
ISBN 0-87413-200-2   AACR2

Printed in the United States of America

To my parents,
Richard J. Hargrove, Sr.,
and
Grace W. Hargrove,
with love and gratitude

Contents

List of Illustrations

List of Maps

Acknowledgments

In the course of historical training, and especially in the preparation of a book-length manuscript, a writer incurs numerous obligations to those people and institutions who assisted him. The author accordingly here wishes to thank Messrs. Harold L. Gavin and Arthur Hughes, formerly of Brooklyn Preparatory School, who introduced him to the study of history; the late Professor Chester L. Barrows, Professors Irving Mark and Birdsall S. Viault, formerly of Adelphi University, and Professor Robert Ernst, currently of that institution, whose lectures in early American history informed and inspired; and especially Dr. John R. Alden, James B. Duke Professor Emeritus in the Department of History of Duke University, in whose seminars this study began to take shape, and from whom the author has learned much about teaching, research, and scholarship. He thanks Professors R. Don Higginbotham of the University of North Carolina at Chapel Hill and George A. Billias of Clark University, both of whom kindly read and critiqued the manuscript and offered valuable suggestions for improvement. His wife, Dr. Anne C. Hargrove, unfailingly offered sustenance and support, patiently proofread the manuscript with him, and their small son, Andrew, provided periodic and comic relief from such chores.

The author also wishes to thank the following people for assistance of various sorts: Professor Joel Colton, Emeritus Professor John S. Curtiss, Professors Robert F. Durden, Arthur B. Ferguson, Harold T. Parker, Theodore Ropp, Richard L. Watson, Jr., and Robert H. Woody of the Department of History of Duke University; Professor Ian R. Christie of the University of London; Professors Larry T. Balsamo, Spencer H. Brown, William L. Burton, George E. Hopkins, Nicholas C. Pano, and John M. Werner of the Department of History of Western Illinois University; Alice W. Mielke of New York University; Dr. David Irwin of the University of Aberdeen; the late Earl Spencer, Althorp, Northamptonshire; Paul David Nelson of the Department of History of Berea College, and Anne Hebenstreit of Associated University Presses.

The Graduate School and Department of History of Duke University, the Woodrow Wilson National Fellowship Foundation of Princeton, New Jersey, the Research Council of Western Illinois University, and the University of Delaware Press provided scholarships, fellowships, travel grants, and cash awards that helped the author to defray expenses incurred in the preparation of this study. He is most grateful to these institutions for their generosity.

Finally, the writer desires to thank the librarians of the following institutions for their assistance during the course of research: the British Public Record Office, London; the Reading Room and Manuscripts Room of the British Library, London; the Institute of Historical Research of the University of London; the House of Lords Record Office, London; Bedford County Record Office; Buckinghamshire Record Office; Lancashire Record Office; the University of Nottingham Library; Sheffield City Libraries; William L. Clements Library, University of Michigan; the New-York Historical Society; the Manuscripts Division, Rare Books Division, and especially the staff of the American History Room, New York Public Library; the Massachusetts Historical Society; the American Philosophical Society; the Library of Congress; the Chicago Historical Society; the Boston Public Library; Houghton and Widener Libraries, Harvard University; William R. Perkins Library, Duke University; Memorial Library, Western Illinois University; Leon Swirbul Library, Adelphi University; and Parsons Library, London House.

Although all of those mentioned above contributed their talents generously, the author alone accepts responsibility for errors.

Mecklenburgh Square, London

Introduction

Much has been written during the past two centuries about John Burgoyne and the campaign of 1777.[1] Biographers have found a peculiar fascination in the life of the playwright-general who commanded the expedition; writers of patriotic battle pieces have celebrated the triumphs and disasters of Ticonderoga and Hubbardton, Bennington and Saratoga. Academic historians have engaged in extended, and often heated, debate concerning the purpose of the expedition, the conduct of its commander, and the reasons for the catastrophe at Saratoga. Indeed, the Burgoyne literature fills substantial shelves in university libraries. The reader may ask why the author has prepared yet another account of the dashing cavalryman and his ill-fated campaign. To reply that historians must rewrite the past so that it will retain its significance for a new generation is to provide only a partial answer. A brief examination of older works on the subject may reveal other, perhaps compelling, reasons for the appearance of a new study.

Charles Neilson wrote the first detailed narrative account of the Burgoyne expedition in 1844. His work was primarily a memoir based upon the reminiscences of his father, who had lived near Saratoga during the War of Independence. Two newer accounts appeared on both sides of the Atlantic during the one-hundredth anniversary of the expedition. William L. Stone offered in 1877 an edition of the campaign based for the first time upon available source materials.[2] Edward B. DeFonblanque, a historian in the Library of the British War Office, also published an anniversary volume.[3] DeFonblanque's work was the first essentially biographical study of General Burgoyne. Commissioned by the estate of the officer's family to undertake the project, DeFonblanque was understandably partial to his subject. Two further studies, written by English and American authors, appeared during the sesquicentennial celebration of the campaign. Francis J. Hudleston, a successor to De Fonblanque in the Library of the War Office, offered a witty biography in 1927.[4] Spicing his account with wry anecdotes for the entertainment of the reader, Hudleston based his study almost entirely upon the work of DeFonblanque. In America, Hoffman Nickerson prepared a sober, richly detailed study of the campaign of 1777.[5] Nickerson's study was the most comprehensive account, but it is unfortunately of little use to the scholar; the author refused to document any of his material. Harrison Bird presented a recent study of the Burgoyne campaign in 1963.[6] It is less accurate than the work of Nickerson, not as well documented as that of Stone. During the last decade, several popular biographies of Burgoyne have been published, none of them based upon research in manuscript sources.[7] Conscious of such a historiographical legacy, the writer of a new study would seem obligated to prepare in one volume a scholarly biography of the general as well as an accurate, documented account of the 1777 expedition. It is hoped that the study presented herein will fulfill that need.

Notes

1. For additional pertinent historiographical information, see Paul D. Nelson, "British Conduct of the American Revolutionary War: A Review of Interpretations," *Journal of American History* 65 (1978): 623–53.

2. Charles Neilson, *An Original, Compiled, and Corrected Account of Burgoyne's Campaign and the Memorable Battles of Bemis Heights* (Albany, N.Y.: J. Munsell, 1844); William L. Stone, *The Campaign of Lieut. Gen. John Burgoyne and the Expedition of Lieut. Col. Barry St. Leger* (Albany, N.Y.: J. Munsell, 1877).

3. Edward B. DeFonblanque, *Political and Military Episodes in the Latter Half of the Eighteenth Century Derived from the Life and Correspondence of the Rt. Hon. John Burgoyne, General Statesman, Dramatist* (London: Macmillan, 1876).

4. Francis J. Hudleston, *Gentleman Johnny Burgoyne: Misadventures of an English General in the Revolution* (Indianapolis, Ind.: Bobbs-Merrill, 1927).

5. Hoffman Nickerson, *The Turning Point of the Revolution; or, Burgoyne in America* (Boston: Houghton Mifflin, 1928).

6. Harrison Bird, *March to Saratoga: General Burgoyne and the American Campaign, 1777* (New York: Oxford University Press, 1963). See also Rupert Furneaux, *The Battle of Saratoga* (New York: Dial, 1971), and John S. Pancake, *1777: The Year of the Hangman* (University, Ala.: University of Alabama Press, 1977).

7. Noel Gerson [Paul Lewis, pseud.] *The Man Who Lost America* (New York: Dial, 1973); Michael Glover, *General Burgoyne in Canada and America: Scapegoat for a System* (London: Gordon and Cremonsi, 1976); James Lunt, *John Burgoyne of Saratoga* (London: Macdonald and Jane's, 1976); Gerald Howson, *Burgoyne of Saratoga* (New York: Times Books, 1979).

General John Burgoyne

1
Young Burgoyne

The circumstances of young John Burgoyne's arrival in 1722 created much speculation and have continued to puzzle scholars to the present time.[1] He was born in London on February 4, 1722, probably at the town house of his parents in Park Prospect, Westminster, and baptized the next day at Saint Margaret's, Westminster.[2] One of the young child's sponsors, Robert Benson, Lord Bingley, was a distinguished friend of the family, having served as a chancellor of the exchequer and ambassador to Spain.[3] Bingley, who later joined with Lords Dartmouth, Carnarvon, Harcourt, Bathurst, and Castleton to build Cavendish Square in London, lived in close friendship with the Burgoynes.[4] In fact, Lady Bingley believed that her husband's relationship with Mrs. Burgoyne was too affectionate. A woman of "ungovernable temper and malignancy of disposition," according to one observer, Lady Bingley disliked John's mother and "raised a story to poor Mrs. Burgoyne's disadvantage, which, at a later period, in some minds gained a footing."[5] Lady Bingley insinuated that her husband had fathered Mrs. Burgoyne's child, and her charge was thought credible because Lord Bingley left a substantial estate to Anna Maria Burgoyne in his will.[6]

Bingley died on April 9, 1731, when Burgoyne was nine years of age. The will, written in 1729 and proved four days after Bingley's death, provided for Mrs. Burgoyne the ownership of his house in Park Prospect, Westminster as well as title to "The Nunnery," his estate in Cheshunt, Hertfordshire.[7] In addition to whatever silver plate and jewelry Mrs. Burgoyne might find at the two houses, Bingley left her an annuity of four hundred pounds "for her separate use, over which her husband shall have no control," although Captain John Burgoyne was forgiven past debts. He also provided security for his own wife, for legitimate heirs, and for an illegitimate daughter. In default of legitimate heirs, Bingley intended the remains of his estate for "the use of my godson, John Burgoyne . . . (which godson I desire may take the name of Robert Benson if my estate comes to him), for the term of his natural life." As it happened, Bingley's legitimate heirs had issue.[8] Consequently Burgoyne did not receive the portion of Bingley's inheritance that was conditionally reserved for him.[9] By the inclusion of such a provision in his testament, however, Bingley lent support to his wife's charge of infidelity. Furthermore, Lord Bingley's acknowledgment of the existence of an illegitimate daughter can be interpreted as evidence of previous and unarguable infidelity. Although the Burgoynes did not commit to paper any opinions concerning the matter, the evidence of both Lord and Lady Bingley is sufficient to indicate that the child, although legally a legitimate son of John Burgoyne, was in fact a natural son of Lord Bingley.

The charge of illegitimacy was repeated frequently during Burgoyne's lifetime, upon the occasion of his death, when his writings were published, and during the hundredth anniversary of his birth in 1823. Upon the latter occasion, the *London Morning Herald* observed that "neither the time, place or circumstance of his birth are known. Even his parentage is doubtful. He is said, though upon what authority does not appear, to have been a natural son of Lord Bingley." The newspaper report disturbed Miss Warburton, daughter of Burgoyne's sister-in-law, Lady Elizabeth Warburton, and the offended descendant wrote to Caroline Parker, one of Burgoyne's daughters, to vent her rage concerning the insinuation of illegitimacy in the *Morning Herald* article. Of the character of Anna Maria Burgoyne, she quoted the recollections of a friend, Mrs. Carr, whose mother had known well the Bingleys and the Burgoynes. Writing one hundred years after the controversial event, Miss Warburton and Mrs. Carr offered the first favorable testimony concerning the question of Burgoyne's parentage. On balance, it is to be suspected that young John Burgoyne was conceived as a result of extramarital relations between Anna Maria Burgoyne and Lord Bingley. However, there is no question of illegitimacy.[10]

Of greater importance than the known facts of the case are the questions: at what age did Burgoyne first become aware of such gossip, and how did it affect him? George Bancroft wrote about Burgoyne's "darling object of effacing the shame of his birth by winning military glory with rank and fortune."[11] If the young Burgoyne's temperament was as romantic and optimistic as it later became, he might have congratulated himself for the noble blood that he inherited from Lord Bingley. But Burgoyne's puzzling passivity from time to time as he made his way in the world might well have resulted from the uncertainty of his birth and fear of public censure. Although doubts concerning his parentage did not bar him from an education, or from careers in several professions, Burgoyne's ambition—his desire to create for himself a career that the world would value—was of an intermittent sort. Anxiety concerning his origins, possibly exacerbated in later years by the attacks of those who envied or disliked him, may account in part for the sporadic nature of his ambition.[12]

No records concerning John's first ten years have survived; possibly none were kept. It is known that he was sent to Westminster School at the age of eleven.[13] His parents may have detected in the young man a potential for high achievement, or more likely, the Burgoynes expected their son to attend a good school as a matter of course. Westminster, one of the most distinguished of England's public schools, was founded as early as 1340.[14] The influence of the college was a good one, as many distinguished Westminsters attested. The class lists included Sir Christopher Wren, John Dryden, and John Locke among Burgoyne's predecessors; he was succeeded by Warren Hastings and Edward Gibbon, among others. Two students who later distinguished themselves in America, Thomas Pinckney and Arthur Middleton, read the classics at Westminster.

When young John presented himself at the school in May 1733, he met Headmaster John Nicoll, who was beginning the first year of his two decades of service to the college.[15] That Burgoyne was not troubled unduly by the headmaster appears likely, for Nicoll, a master of Latin and Greek, was well known as a tolerant scholar.[16] The curriculum, devoted exclusively to the classical languages, included grammar books written by Richard Busby, who had directed the destiny of the school for fifty-seven years until his death in 1695. These volumes remained a part of the curriculum until the nineteenth century.

Master John Burgoyne's first days settling into the routine of the college must have been busy ones. Not being a King's Scholar, he was required to lodge in one of the private boarding houses owned by elderly widows or spinsters. In each house resided a master and several assistants who were expected to maintain discipline. In practice, however, the older boys kept order. At times the students were unruly. A visitor to the school in 1753 observed that "being once combined, no porters or gatekeepers would dare to withhold them, and when they sallied out they would strike Terror thro' the whole Neighbourhood."[17] In 1733, over four hundred students attended the college, which was divided into five, possibly six, forms.[18] The amenities were lacking; Burgoyne had to do without heat in winter, and many students recalled skating across ice on the floor of the common room during the cold months.[19] In the evenings, Burgoyne probably joined other young scholars to read by flickering candlelight. Westminster boys were privileged to have their own library, opened in 1695 when Headmaster Busby left his personal collection, "one of the school's most treasured possessions."[20] Burgoyne probably studied there with an assigned tutor, who prepared him for matriculation.[21]

Although young John was only eleven years old, he was expected to master quickly the essentials of Greek grammar and literature. The intellectual strain was considerable during the period of examination, which lasted six to eight weeks. Burgoyne did not attend the school the following year, 1734. Perhaps he was not yet able to adjust to the rigid pattern of life at a public school; possibly there was financial trouble at home. But he did return to classes in 1735 and remained at school until 1738.[22]

Burgoyne met some of his classmates again later in life. Francis Bernard became a royal governor in Massachusetts; Thomas Gage, two years Burgoyne's senior, assumed the duties of commanding officer in the same colony four decades later; Welbore Ellis for a short while served as secretary at war. Two other students, the earl of Dartmouth and Lord George Germain, acted successively as secretaries of state.[23] The marquis of Rockingham became prime minister twice. Most of these scholars were members of England's ruling class. Burgoyne, only twice removed by birth from the gentry, was as much an aristocrat as Ellis or Bernard; perhaps even more so if the rumors of his parentage are true. It is not known whether he was acquainted with Gage or the others at Westminster, but he did develop a friendship with James Stanley Smith, later Lord Strange, who was the son of the earl of Derby.

The Derbys were then, and remain today, the preeminent family of Lancashire. Knowsley, the family seat at Prescott, and town houses in Preston and London were but a part of the extensive holdings which the Derbys acquired over the centuries. With the development of their properties and lands, the earls of Derby exerted powerful social and political influence over the county, and eventually in Parliament.[24] In 1733, young Smith was completing his fourth year at Westminster School.[25] He would soon be elected a knight of the shire, the first of many offices in which the future Lord Strange held during his lifetime. Smith was seventeen years of age when he met Burgoyne for the first time.[26] The two young men became the best of friends. Burgoyne, at the age of eleven, was probably delighted, doubtless impressed, that so lofty a figure recognized him. One year later Smith left Westminster for the University of Leyden, but his friendship with Burgoyne lasted a lifetime.

Since there is no evidence to indicate that he attended a university, it may be safely concluded that Burgoyne completed his formal education in 1738. He had acquired among other things the etiquette of an English gentleman, manners which became so well known that they helped to earn for him the appellation "Gentleman Johnny" in later years. Furthermore, he absorbed the style if not the wisdom of the Latin and Greek classics, as his later public speeches, studded with quotations from Virgil, Caesar, and Ovid, so vividly attested. He probably learned the rudiments of argumentation, for Burgoyne's polished debating techniques later brought him a measure of recognition in the House of Commons. His sense of drama, frequently displayed in poetry, military dispatches, political speeches, and the plays he himself wrote, doubtless owed much to literary training at Westminster. Most important, perhaps, his friendship with Lord Strange led to opportunities for a career in the army and marriage to a daughter of the earl of Derby.[27]

Notes

1. Edward B. DeFonblanque, *Political and Military Episodes in the Latter Part of the Eighteenth Century Derived from the Life and Correspondence of the Rt. Hon. John Burgoyne, General, Statesman, Dramatist* (London: Macmillan, 1876), pp. 5–7; Hoffman Nickerson, *The Turning Point of the Revolution; or, Burgoyne in America* (Boston: Houghton Mifflin, 1928), pp. 561–62.

2. Joseph S. Chester, ed., *The Marriage, Baptismal and Burial Registers of the Collegiate Church, or Abbey of St. Peter, Westminster,* Publications of the Harleian Society (London: Harleian Society, 1876), 10:331–32; the year of birth is Old Style.

3. "Robert Benson," *Dictionary of National Biography*, hereafter abbreviated as *DNB*.

4. Charles H. Baker and Muriel I. Baker, *Life and Circumstances of James Brydges, First Duke of Chandos* (Oxford: Clarendon Press, 1949), p. 265.

5. September 23, 1823, Miss Warburton to Caroline Parker, *London Morning Herald;* DeFonblanque, *Episodes,* pp. 6–8, 9–10.

6. "Robert Benson," *DNB*.

7. A summary of the will, dated June 27, 1729, and a codicil, dated March 9, 1730, proved April 13, 1731, appear in Chester, ed., *Registers*, pp. 331–32.

8. May 12, 1738, "Minute of Probate, Last Will and Testament of Robert Benson, Lord Bingley," British Library Additional Manuscripts, 36,046, f. 162. This collection is hereinafter cited as B.L., Add. MSS.

9. October 5, 1777, Horace Walpole to the Rev. William Mason, in Wilmarth S. Lewis, et. al., ed., *The Yale Edition of the Correspondence of Horace Walpole*, 40 vols. (New Haven: Yale University Press, 1937–74), 28:336–37, in which Walpole reported that "the entail [for Burgoyne] was cut off." The title, which lapsed at the death of Bingley, was revived in 1762 for the husband of his legitimate daughter; DeFonblanque, *Episodes*, p. 5, note 1.

10. September 23, 1823, Miss Warburton to Caroline Parker, DeFonblanque, *Burgoyne*, pp. 6–8. As DeFonblanque wrote, "if any scandal had attached to his mother, it must necessarily have been of that nature of which the law does take cognizance, and which can under no circumstances sustain the public charge of illegitimate birth. It does not appear, however, that his parents ever lived upon other than affectionate terms." DeFonblanque, *Episodes*, p. 6.

11. George Bancroft, *A History of the United States from the Discovery of the American Continent*, 6 vols. (Boston: Little, Brown, 1837–85), vol. 5, cited by DeFonblanque, *Episodes*, p. 5, note 2.

12. See, for example, October 5, 1777, Horace Walpole to the Rev. William Mason, Walpole, *Correspondence*, 28:336–37. Walpole had no doubt Burgoyne was a "natural son of Lord Bingley."

13. George F. R. Barker and A. H. Stenning, eds., *The Record of Old Westminsters*, 2 vols. (London: Chiswick Press, 1928), 1:143.

14. 1339–40, Chamberlain's Roll, Chapter Muniments, cited by Barker and Stenning, eds., *Old Westminsters*, 1: v.

15. Barker and Stenning, eds., *Old Westminsters*, 2:692, 1082.

16. J. D. Carleton, *Westminster* (London: Blackie, 1938), pp. 26–27, 33.

17. Ibid., pp. 30–31.

18. In 1733, there were 40 King's Scholars, or scholarship students. In addition, 169 nonscholarship students attended the upper school, and 203 regular pupils were enrolled in the under-school, a total of 412 in all divisions; Barker and Stenning, eds., *Old Westminsters*, 2:1094.

19. Carleton, *Westminster*.

20. Ibid., p. 18.

21. Carleton, *Westminster*, pp. 62–63.

22. Barker and Stenning, eds., *Old Westminsters*, 1:143.

23. John R. Alden, *General Gage in America: Being Principally a History of His Role in the American Revolution* (Baton Rouge, La.: Louisiana State University Press, 1948), p. 12; Barker and Stenning, eds., *Old Westminsters*, 1:370.

24. DeFonblanque, *Episodes*, p. 11.

25. Barker and Stenning, eds., *Old Westminsters*, 2:877.

26. Ibid.; Smith was born January 7, 1716.

27. George Wrottesley, *Life and Correspondence of Field Marshal Sir John Burgoyne, Bart.*, 2 vols. (London: R. Bentley, 1873), 1:2.

2

Marriage and the Army

Whether John entered the army of his own accord or through the influence of friends and family, the young man did follow the footsteps of the senior Burgoyne. While he was completing his final year of study at public school, John obtained a commission as sub-brigadier to a troop in the earl of Albemarle's Third Regiment of Horse Guards.[1] Such an appointment at the age of fifteen was not considered remarkable; the future general Charles Lee purchased an ensigncy at an even earlier age.[2] The assignment was highly prized, for the regiments of Horse Guards when combined with the Life Guards and Foot Guards formed the household army of the king.

When Burgoyne first entered military service in 1737, the army was not considered a promising career for ordinary British subjects. The quality of the rank and file was poor, and morale was low. Private soldiers were flogged without mercy and often without justice. Although military life was dreary and unprestigious for the common soldier, the army appeared to be a respectable and even privileged profession for sons of the nobility and landed gentry. Candidates from Britain's leading families paid for their commissions by purchase rather than earning them by merit, and those who wished to rise through the ranks on their ability rather than their wealth found little opportunity to do so. But with sufficient money, influence, and suitable genealogical credentials, a young man of good family could lead a comfortable life as an officer in the army. He needed to have no theoretical or practical knowledge of military affairs, but if he was ambitious and wealthy he could purchase the command of his own regiment and perhaps win recognition on the field of battle. Such, in part, may have been the aspirations of John Burgoyne when he left Westminster School.[3]

None of Burgoyne's early commissions is accurately recorded, since he was first appointed to an army position just before annual lists were preserved.[4] At some time between 1740 and 1743, he became a cornet in a troop of the Thirteenth Regiment of Light Dragoons: mounted infantrymen who charged the enemy in battle, effecting a shock as they turned a weak flank or broke through a line. No military academies existed in Britain then—Sandhurst was the creation of a later age—and Burgoyne learned the tasks of an officer after he purchased his commission. It was his duty as cornet to carry the colors of the regiment, and he did so when the corps was posted at Preston, Lancashire, near the ancestral seat of the Derby family.

It is not known how Burgoyne purchased those early commissions. Burgoyne's father, if he was still alive, had little money, Lord Bingley was dead, and there is no evidence to indicate that John's uncle, Sir Roger Burgoyne, assisted the young man.[5] It appears likely that Lord Strange, Burgoyne's prospective brother-in-law, bought these early appointments for him, especially in view of the help which he and his father provided from time to time in subsequent years. During 1743, Burgoyne frequently visited Knowsley, where Lord and Lady Derby lived with their large family. The earl's six daughters undoubtedly interested the officer, who had recently ended an unsatisfactory relationship with the daughter of Sir Francis Poole, of Poole Hall, Cheshire.[6] When Frances Poole married Lord Palmerston two decades later, Burgoyne sent several verses to the bridegroom, in which he described his first love:

> 'Twas mine to see each opening charm,
> New beauties rise—new graces charm;
> 　'Twas mine to feel their power;
> Nature and morals just and pure,
> For that has made the fruit mature
> 　Since I adored the flower.

But soon Burgoyne found a new interest:

> After hard conflict passion cool'd;
> Discretion, reason, honour ruled
> 　O'er the subsiding flame;
> Till Charlotte to my vacant breast,
> With kindred charms and virtues blest,
> A sweet successor came.[7]

Lady Charlotte Stanley, only fifteen years of age, was the youngest of Lord Derby's daughters. Her charms grew upon Burgoyne, who was not, however, seen by the Derby family as a good match for their daughter.[8] Consequently, the couple eloped in 1743, probably to London, where Lord Strange occupied a family town house in Grosvenor Square.[9] Derby, believing that his daughter had made a poor choice, begrudgingly gave Lady Charlotte a small dowry, but refused to receive her or her husband.[10] An earlier writer may have reflected the nobleman's own opinion when he called the marriage "an imprudent and unequal one."[11] Perhaps Lord Derby had observed in his son-in-law the over-fondness for gambling which had ruined Burgoyne's father; the selection of an untitled army captain in the cadet branch of a baronetcy probably disappointed the socially and politically prominent earl; furthermore, Derby may have been disturbed by gossip concerning Burgoyne's parentage.

Unwelcome at Knowsley, Burgoyne and his bride remained in London, where Burgoyne used his wife's dowry to purchase a lieutenancy in 1745 and a captaincy later the same year.[12] The young officer and his wife doubtless enjoyed a pleasant life in the capital. Ambition dormant, Burgoyne did not take part in the War of the Austrian Succession, nor did he fight in the battles of the 'Forty-five in Scotland. He preferred to spend his time in London's gambling clubs, where young noblemen won, lost, and sometimes won back fortunes in a matter of hours. More often than not, they incurred serious debts which became difficult to pay. Burgoyne's finances, weakened by such debts, collapsed in 1747.[13] The captain was forced to sell his commission to pay obligations, and shortly thereafter he and Lady Charlotte went to Europe.[14] They settled in France near Chanteloup in Touraine, the seat of François Joseph, duc de Choiseul, grand chamberlain of France and duke of Lorraine, and his heir, Etienne François, comte de Stainville, a lieutenant general who in 1758 became minister of foreign affairs.[15] Learning, not entirely successfully, to write and speak French, Burgoyne studied military literature in that language and observed European political life.[16] In 1750 when Stainville married Louise Honorine Crozat, granddaughter of the marquis de Chatel, a wealthy financier and war contractor, the new couple and the Burgoynes journeyed to Rome where the English ex-captain, now twenty-eight years of age, sat in the studios of Allan Ramsay, who later became portrait painter to George III.[17] The Ramsay painting revealed a handsome, proud, fashionable gentleman who must have enjoyed the tour of Europe. The Burgoynes and Stainvilles concluded their travels in 1753 when the French aristocrat, with the assistance of Madame de Pompadour, became ambassador to the Vatican. The following year, Lady Charlotte was delighted to present her husband a daughter, Charlotte Elizabeth, who lived only ten years.[18] In 1755, the Burgoynes observed the Anglo-French political antagonisms that soon led to armed clash and they decided, perhaps reluctantly, to return to Great Britain, where a family reconciliation took place.[19]

When Lady Charlotte's father at long last opened the gates of Knowsley to his son-in-law, he opened them wide. Lord Derby promised to leave his daughter twenty-five thousand pounds—well over half a million dollars by 1981 standards of purchasing power—and an annuity of four hundred pounds. Through the nobleman's intervention, Burgoyne was reinstated in the army.[20] Such a revival of fortune for a soldier who had been retired nine years was rare; it is doubtful that Burgoyne could have returned to the service without the earl's assistance. The reconciliation made the Burgoynes financially secure. During 1756, Burgoyne was gazetted captain of a troop in the Eleventh Regiment of Dragoons.[21] His rank was one grade higher than the position of junior captain in the Thirteenth Regiment that he held before retirement. The appointment was conferred with a view to further advancement, for Burgoyne in 1757 began to display for the first time a yearning desire for promotion, and he lost no time demanding an improvement of his fortunes in the Eleventh Regiment. Writing to Major George Warde, his commanding officer, Burgoyne

General John Burgoyne, after Allan Ramsay, ca. 1756. Reproduced by permission of the National Portrait Gallery, London.

hoped that he "should not long continue a captain."[22] Complaining that he was uncomfortable serving under so many officers whom he had commanded before retirement, Burgoyne told Warde that conditions were so disagreeable that he "should not have suffered any application to be made" for his reinstatement had he not been given assurances of promotion. Burgoyne expected "as many indulgences as could be made consistent with the good of the service," and invoked the support of the Derby family to make his claim more secure. The captain's request was not immediately granted; in fact, he had to wait two years for his promotion. When he got it, Burgoyne was doubtless pleased to discover that he was restored to the prestigious Household Guard, for in May 1758 he moved up two ranks and became lieutenant colonel in the Coldstream Regiment of Foot. Three months later, Burgoyne saw his first active service when the Coldstreamers were sent to Cherbourg and Saint-Malo.[23]

On August 7, 1758, the British fleet moved to Marais Bay, near Cherbourg.[24] As the light cavalry and guns proceeded ashore, the advance upon Cherbourg began in earnest. The troops, in high spirits, destroyed and ravaged the countryside, disregarding the orders of their commander, who forbade such pillaging.[25] Britain's officers in charge, disgusted, ordered the troops to embark and left Cherbourg on August 16.

Although successful, the exercise was a pointless one, marred by the depredations of the soldiers. However, Burgoyne may have learned the importance of maintaining the respect of one's soldiers.

On August 31, Burgoyne sailed toward a second military encounter. Four days later he landed in the vicinity of Saint-Malo.[26] Located on the Brittany coast south of Jersey, Saint-Malo lies about halfway between Brest on the west and Cherbourg to the east. The town was above insult, said the duke of Marlborough, who estimated that a month of siege work would be necessary to reduce it.[27] Bad weather forced the British troops out of the Saint-Malo area, and the army moved westward toward Matignon in the countryside.

The march to Matignon was arduous, unpleasant, and time-consuming. Burgoyne and his colleagues lacked food, advance scouts, and outposts. Heavy rains marred the clay paths. Many soldiers became ill, and morale declined. Armed French peasants and small military parties killed some of Britain's soldiers. Time was lost while the troops waited for the high water to recede at one of their river crossings. Eventually, all the soldiers arrived at Matignon and camped there, three miles east of Saint-Malo. Soon the French pushed to a point only three miles distant from the British troops.[28]

Burgoyne described in detail the ensuing engagement. Britain's soldiers approached a semicircular bay, about a mile in length, bounded on the right by "a steep hill, with a village on the top," and on the left by a range of high rocks "which stretched a considerable distance into the sea." A cannonproof breastwork, built during the previous war, extended along the beach from the hills to the rocks. A flat plain stretched a quarter mile beyond the breastworks, leading to the village of Saint-Cas, two works, and another range of hills. The French soldiers clambered to the top of these hills just as the guards and grenadier companies took the beach. Burgoyne remained with these men, who were expected to safeguard the evacuation. The rest of the army marched to the ships as quickly as possible. The guards and grenadiers dug in behind the breastworks, forming a line in close formation which extended the length of the beach. Burgoyne reported that "all the frigates gave [the enemy] their broadsides, and from this moment it was a continual fire till the whole affair was over." Within an hour of the first shots, the French managed to mount cannon atop the hill, but they inflicted little damage upon the British troops.

Presently Burgoyne observed a column of French troops pushing to his right in a flanking movement. Although he did not yet realize it, this diversion was the right prong of a pincers formation. Burgoyne requested orders, but no specific directions were forthcoming although his commanding officer asked for a general counterattack. Burgoyne felt "obliged to determine upon our own authority to wheel the divisions we commanded so as to front the enemy." Orders were sent at last and Burgoyne led three hundred men up the hill, but the orders were "countermanded before I had got forty yards."

Now the lieutenant colonel was told to take position upon the rocks in order to halt the left French flank. Burgoyne held out for some time but abandoned his position when the French at last broke through the breastwork. French troops poured down from the village of Saint-Cas, from the rocks, and from the hill, despite the continuing fire of the British frigates, bomb ketches, and grenadier companies. The latter soon depleted their ammunition and had to return to the ships. Confusion reigned as Burgoyne and the first regiment, eighteen hundred strong, marched to the fleet. At the same time, the grenadiers continued their struggle toward safety. Not surprisingly, six hundred British soldiers were killed. The army had landed only three wagons to rescue ten thousand men, and as Burgoyne remarked, "the sick and wounded alone could not have been properly contained in a dozen" wagons. Four hundred more were held prisoner. By one o'clock in the afternoon when the opposing forces ceased fire, the French had lost only five hundred.[29]

Burgoyne emerged from the throes of battle with sorely needed experience. He displayed courage and restraint in the field—valuable qualities which he would retain for the rest of his life. Upon his return, he was appointed lieutenant colonel of the Second Regiment of Foot Guards.[30]

Notes

1. The commission was dated August 9, 1737, and provided rank in the troop but not in the army; army list for 1745, manuscript, Public Record Office, London, Ind. 5437, ff. 3–4.

2. John R. Alden, *General Charles Lee: Traitor or Patriot?* (Baton Rouge, La.: Louisiana State University Press, 1951), pp. 3–4.

3. Sir John W. Fortescue, "The Army," in Arthur S. Turberville, ed., *Johnson's England: An Account of the Life and Manners of his Age*, 2 vols. (Oxford: Clarendon Press, 1933), 1:26–27; see

also Edward E. Curtis, *The Organization of the British Army in the American Revolution* (New Haven, Conn.: Yale University Press, 1926), pp. 51–80.

4. The sources list the following dates for Burgoyne's commission as cornet: 1740, "John Burgoyne," *DNB;* July 14, 1743, Barker and Stenning, eds., *Old Westminsters,* 1:143; 1744, Sir Lewis Namier and John Brooke, eds., *The History of Parliament: The House of Commons 1754–1790,* 3 vols. (London: Oxford University Press, 1964), 2:141–45; 1744, DeFonblanque, *Episodes,* p. 9.

5. The author has found only occasional references to John Burgoyne by his more noble relations. Sir Roger Burgoyne, sixth baronet, named John Burgoyne in the entails of his estate; Sir John Burgoyne, seventh baronet, appointed John Burgoyne his executor. DeFonblanque, *Episodes,* pp. 5–6, note 3.

6. DeFonblanque, *Episodes,* p. 8.

7. Edward W. Harcourt, ed., *The Harcourt Papers,* 14 vols. (Oxford: privately printed, n.d.), 8:156–57.

8. Chester, ed., *Registers,* p. 422.

9. David T. Pottinger, "John Burgoyne: Politician, Dandy, and Man of Letters," *Proceedings of the Cambridge Historical Society* (Cambridge, Mass.: Cambridge Historical Society, 1937), 22:29–45; Horace Walpole, *The Last Journals of Horace Walpole during the Reign of George III,* ed. by A. Francis Steuart, 2 vols. (London: J. Lane, 1910), 1:202, note 1; Namier and Brooke, eds., *Commons,* 2:141–45; DeFonblanque, *Episodes,* pp. 8–9.

10. "John Burgoyne," *DNB.*

11. DeFonblanque, *Episodes,* p. 9.

12. The sources are contradictory: he became a lieutenant in 1741, according to "John Burgoyne," *DNB;* February 22, 1745, according to Barker and Stenning, eds., *Old Westminsters,* 1:143, and Namier and Brooke, eds., *Commons,* 2:141–45. His captaincy, said the *DNB,* dated from 1743, while Brooke and Barker put it at July 1, 1745.

13. "John Burgoyne," *DNB;* DeFonblanque, *Episodes,* p. 9. The commission was officially sold on October 31, 1751, according to Barker and Stenning, eds., *Old Westminsters,* 1:143.

14. September 23, 1823, Miss Warburton to Caroline Parker, DeFonblanque, *Episodes,* pp. 6–8.

15. "John Burgoyne," *DNB;* DeFonblanque, *Episodes,* p. 10; September 23, 1823, Miss Warburton to Caroline Parker.

16. DeFonblanque, *Episodes,* p. 10.

17. September 23, 1823, Miss Warburton to Caroline Parker, DeFonblanque, *Episodes,* pp. 6–8.

18. Chester, ed., *Registers,* p. 450, note 3.

19. "John Burgoyne," *DNB.*

20. DeFonblanque, *Episodes,* p. 20; "John Burgoyne," *DNB;* Pottinger, "John Burgoyne," stated that the annuity was £300.

21. June 14, 1756, *Army List for 1758,* p. 35.

22. November 23, 1757, Burgoyne to Warde, Namier and Brooke, eds., *Commons,* 2:141–45.

23. May 1758, *Army List for 1759,* p. 43. Burgoyne never held the rank of major. Namier and Brooke, eds., *Commons,* 2:141–45. Barker and Stenning, eds., *Old Westminsters,* 1:143; "John Burgoyne," *DNB.*

24. B. L., Add. MS. 32, 881, Julian S. Corbett, *England in the Seven Years' War,* 2 vols. (London: Longman, 1907), 1:286.

25. "Great Outrages" characterized the undisciplined behavior of the troops, Philip H. Stanhope [Lord Mahon], *History of England from the Peace of Utrecht to the Peace of Versailles 1713–1783,* 7 vols. (London: J. Murray, 1836–54), 4:143.

26. Francis J. Hudleston, "The Misfortune at St. Cas," *United Service Magazine* (January 1908), 29:421–25, quotation p. 422; Corbett, *Seven Years' War,* 1:296.

27. Hudleston, "Misfortune," p. 423.

28. September 1758, Burgoyne to secretary at war, DeFonblanque, *Episodes,* pp. 12–14.

29. DeFonblanque, *Episodes,* p. 14, note 1.

30. Hudleston, "Misfortune," pp. 425–26; DeFonblanque, *Episodes,* p. 14.

3

The Sixteenth Regiment

Late in 1758 John Burgoyne rejoined his wife in London to discover military circles in the capital humming with talk of a royal decision to create a regiment of cavalry for regular use in the British army. The army had previously used cavalry only in a limited way for the protection of the royal family, during the Scots rebellion of 1745, and in the War of the Austrian Succession. Although Frederick II of Prussia and Charles XII of Sweden had proved that such troops could be employed with great success, Britain continued to rely primarily upon the strength of infantry and artillery companies. In 1758 George II at last came to believe that a regular regiment of light cavalry would be a useful addition to the British army. Accordingly, he instructed William Pitt to select a suitable colonel to raise a regiment of dragoons, and Pitt recommended Burgoyne.[1] The selection of a junior officer to raise such a potentially prestigious regiment caused some jealousy among senior officers in the service.[2] Nevertheless, in August 1759, the secretary at war, Viscount Barrington, issued warrants to Burgoyne and also to Lieutenant Colonel Sir Gilbert Elliott to raise two regiments of light horse.[3]

The secretary at war also provided Burgoyne with specific instructions to raise four troops.[4] Burgoyne appointed four captains to recruit soldiers: William Gordon, Edward Walpole, Henry Laws Luttrell, and Sir William Peers Williams.[5] Burgoyne disliked Walpole, a relation to the prime minister of that name, but he counted Williams among his closest friends. Other officers appointed to the Sixteenth included Captains Sir George Osborne and the Hon. William Harcourt, who commanded the regiment in later years after Burgoyne obtained other military assignments. Robert Kingston, first among the lieutenants, became a personal friend of the colonel, with whom he campaigned during the ill-fated expedition of 1777.[6] To assist the recruiting captains in filling the ranks, Burgoyne prepared a flamboyant advertisement which reflected the enthusiasm, bombast, and melodramatic rhetoric later characteristic of his prose.[7] Although it is not entirely certain that Burgoyne wrote copy for the recruiting poster himself, the appearance of a quotation from Shakespeare suggests his influence. "Young men out of employment or uncomfortable," it read, " 'There is a tide in the affairs of men, which, taken at the flood, leads on to fortune': Nick in instantly and enlist." Prospective applicants were assured that they would be "mounted on the finest horses in the world . . . with superb clothing and the richest accoutrements." Volunteers were promised admiration and wealth: "your society is courted; you are admired by the Fair, which, together with the chance of getting switched to a buxom widow, or of brushing with a rich heiress, renders the situation truly enviable and desirable." Their uniforms were splendid and their pay, 12s. 6d. weekly, was far greater than the 3s. 6d. which privates received in ordinary regiments.[8] As was the rule elsewhere, however, the rank and file in Burgoyne's regiment were obligated to pay for their own shirts, shoes, and stockings, which cost about half their first year's salary.[9] Burgoyne was required as colonel to supply them with other necessary garments, including coats, breeches, and cloaks, and he derived an annual profit of £900 from that task.[10] Most of the 352 privates who enlisted were residents of Northampton, where the regiment was to be posted, although numerous Londoners volunteered also, for the regiment was highly regarded in the capital. The war office instructed local magistrates and peace officers in Northampton to assist Burgoyne in finding accommodations for the soldiers, many of whom were lodged in alehouses.

On October 13 the king directed the war office to raise two additional troops for the regiment, bringing its strength to five hundred men.[11] Although there were few problems encountered in recruiting troops and appointing officers, other matters entrusted to the notoriously inefficient agencies in Whitehall slowed the process of organizing the regiment.[12] Henry Fox, Lord Holland, who unethically amassed a fortune as paymaster general and whose son Charles James Fox became one of Burgoyne's political allies, along with the clothing board delayed arrangements for the purchase of such basic equipment as swords, saddles and clothing until as late as January 1760.[13]

At length it appeared that the Sixteenth Regiment was finally ready for active service.[14] The war office wanted Burgoyne's force to join Prince Ferdinand of Brunswick in Europe, and Barrington authorized both Lieutenant Colonel Elliott and Burgoyne to augment each regiment to full strength of 629 men.[15] However, Burgoyne postponed departure for Germany until February because he considered his regiment still unprepared.[16] Burgoyne recalled those soldiers who had already left Northampton for Europe. While the war office preoccupied itself with stoppages, off-reckoning and other administrative details during the spring of 1760, Burgoyne marched his regiment to Scotland for additional training.[17] Plans for embarkation were postponed until midsummer, when it was discovered that half-mountings for regimental horses had still not been delivered. Worse still, almost a year after Burgoyne was ordered to raise the regiment, Barrington disclosed on June 5 that two majors from the horse guards were only then on their way to a goods depot on Fenchurch Street in London, where they jointed "a Taylor, a Gunsmith, a Sadler, and an accoutrement Maker" to inspect clothing and weapons for Burgoyne's soldiers.[18] In light of such circumstances, and because the campaign of 1760 in Europe was virtually over, Barrington ordered a reduction in Burgoyne's force to "the establishment of the reg[iment]s of Dragoon then serving in Germany."[19] Shortly thereafter, the army decided to cancel plans to use the Sixteenth Regiment, and Burgoyne did not serve in combat with that force until the summer of 1761. Whether he shared the blame for the year and a half long fiasco remains a question, although the evidence seems to indicate a failure of the bureaucracy rather than negligence on Burgoyne's part.

Using the pen rather than the sword, Burgoyne prepared a code of instruction for his soldiers, to be regarded not "as the orders of a commanding officer, but as the sentiments of a friend."[20] These notes, as Burgoyne observed, were "partly borrowed and partly formed upon observation and practice." As most of his officers were young and not experienced in warfare, Burgoyne took pains to explain the basic points of discipline and training which he thought might be of use to them.

The colonel discussed promotion from the ranks in traditional terms. He did not believe that private soldiers should ever be permitted the opportunity to obtain commissions; instead, "the ranks of corporal and sergeant should be considered as the most signal honour and reward that a man from the ranks could attain." Therefore, he urged the greatest discretion in the selection of men for those positions. Almost all educated Englishmen of the eighteenth century held such views; unlettered soldiers seldom if ever complained. Efforts to reform the system were not made for more than a hundred years. In 1760, however, aristocrats continued to purchase their commissions, a procedure which seemed to work because no one thought of objecting to it.

Burgoyne's reflections upon discipline were well tempered and in many respects advanced, even for the Age of Reason. He knew and disliked the severe methods of regimentation that Frederick the Great enforced upon the Prussian army. He was also familiar with the laxity of the French system. He struck a balance that avoided *"training men like spaniels, by the stick"* and *"substituting the point of honour in the place of severity."* Advocating a respect for the reasoning capacities of those even in the lowest ranks of military society, he nevertheless cautioned against "exalting rationality" or arguing "more from speculation than practice." Thus could the British soldier be brought "to perfection." Burgoyne also tried to explain *"why an Englishman will not bear beating so well as . . . foreigners."* The Prussian recruit, he wrote, was "a stranger to the rights of a fellow creature, inured from infancy to slavery, ignorance, and hardship," and thus he verged "upon the state of mere animal instinct" before entering the service. The enlightened attitude in other German states "when the subjects to be operated upon are proper," was, he thought, "by much the most easy and short." In the culturally more advanced society of France, military disciplinarians faced a greater challenge. The French volunteer had to be made oblivious to the ideas of "liberty, custom, ease, and plenty," which had been implanted in childhood. Such a method of training was difficult, wrote Burgoyne, because it required *"both discernment and labour"* to train minds which were to be "wrought upon." Burgoyne abhorred the "mechanical valour" which produced indoctrination, and urged instead the inculcation of "national spirit and personal attachment" to the army. He concluded that English soldiers were to be treated as thinking beings, and recommended "getting insight into the character of each particular man, and proportioning accordingly the degrees of punishment and encouragement." Burgoyne was perhaps the first British officer to perceive the shortcomings of an aristocratic tradition which denied the humanity of private soldiers.

The colonel's concern for the well-being of the rank and file went beyond words or theorizing. He prohibited officers from swearing at privates, and encouraged them to "slacken the reins" during fatigue or stable duty, suggesting that "even a joke may be used, not only without harm but to good purpose, for condescensions well applied are an encouragement to the well disposed, and at the same time a tacit reproof to others." It may be noted that Burgoyne did not suggest a loosening of the boundaries of social classes; he was hardly in a position to do so had he wanted to. He did approve a strict subordination of men to officers when they were on duty.

Of the officers themselves, Burgoyne expected much. He encouraged his staff to read extensively the military literature of the day, and informed them that a short time given to reading each day, if the books were well chosen and the subject properly digested, would furnish a great deal of instruction. Although he encouraged a "serious and assiduous application" in the study of French because "the best modern books upon our profession are written in that language," Burgoyne insisted that an officer "ought to write English with swiftness and accuracy."[21] He encouraged proficiency in mathematics, the study of which "is so well known to be of utility in a military life, that it is needless to enforce it." Likewise a knowledge of engineering would prove useful for the construction of breastworks on battlegrounds; it also "strongly exercises the mind, and common reading becomes a relaxation after it." Burgoyne urged potential cartographers to "practice taking views from an eminence, and to measure distances with the eye."

Nor were the officers to neglect the more minute details of their occupation. If military science "in the course of a long peace had degenerated into the tricks of parade and the froth of discipline," so had the tricks and froth lost smartness. Burgoyne did not confine his critique to the "grace and art of riding." The study of horsemanship "in the large sense comprehends the knowledge of every article that concerns the horse or the rider." He deplored the general lack of attention to the less obvious points of training. Burgoyne condemned rudeness, intellectual apathy, and inadequate training, but he also complimented his men. Although many of his officers were inexperienced and youthful, they were also particularized "by their rank and fortune," the two last wars having "filled the army with excellent officers from the year 1743," he modestly concluded. These "sentiments of a friend," thoughtful, often perceptive and enlightened, illustrate the man's intellectual powers, which were considerable although perhaps not great. They also reflect Burgoyne's awareness of the importance of the new regiment and its potential usefulness in the advancement of his career.

In October 1760, the Sixteenth was alerted for foreign service, but the death of George II on the twenty-fifth halted all military operations temporarily and the new regiment did not receive its baptism of fire until February 1761, when Burgoyne and two troops of the Sixteenth volunteered to join another naval expedition to harass the French.[22] Although Lady Charlotte objected to his leaving, Burgoyne replied in verse:

> Still does my obstinate repine,
>   And reason's voice reprove;
> Still think him cold who would combine
>   Philosophy with love.
> Try then from yet a nobler source
>   to draw thy wished relief;
> Faith adds to reason double force,
>   And mocks the assaults of grief
> . . . .
>   And when the happy hour shall come,
>   (Oh! speedy may it be!)
> That brings thy faithful soldier home
>   To love, content, and thee;
> Pure may our gratitude ascend
>   To Him who guides our days
> And whilst He gives with bounteous hand,
>   Accepts our bliss for praise![23]

Thus elegantly consoled, Lady Charlotte bid farewell to the colonel, who soon arrived at Belle Ile, a small island off the southern coast of Brittany. Possession of the island would strengthen Britain's position with France at the bargaining table; should it not be conquered, at least British forces would have been placed in a position to attack Spain in the event that country declared war, which it was threatening to do.[24] Major General John Hodgson, a former aide-de-camp to the duke of Cumberland, assumed the duties of commander in chief of the expedition, while Augustus Keppel, later viscount and first lord of the admiralty, led a naval contingent. On April 6 the entire British fleet anchored at Palais, the principal town and chief fortification of the island. By five o'clock in the afternoon, the British held all of Belle Ile except Palais. Keppel, stationed with his fleet in the waters between Belle Ile and Normandy, prevented the duc d'Aiguillon from leaving the mainland to assist his beleaguered colleagues on the island. Hodgson besieged Palais on June 8, and drove the last French troops out.[25] Of the six thousand British soldiers engaged at Belle Ile, eighteen hundred were killed or wounded.[26] Burgoyne survived unscathed, although Captain Williams, who had commanded a company in the Sixteenth

Regiment, lost his life.[27] For his work, Robert Kingston, Burgoyne's friend and future aide-de-camp, was promoted to the rank of captain.[28] William Howe, later one of Burgoyne's colleagues on the American staff of the British army, also fought in the campaign.[29] Although no personal account of his adventures is known to exist, it is safe to surmise that Burgoyne fought with the courage and determination which characterized Britain's troops in that highly successful operation. After the depredations at Cherbourg and the failures of Saint-Malo, the lieutenant colonel was doubtless pleased to have been associated with a highly polished, successful regiment in a victorious campaign. He returned to England in August 1761.[30]

Notes

1. [ca. 1788–89] Burgoyne to William Pitt, DeFonblanque, *Episodes*, p. 452.

2. DeFonblanque, *Episodes*, p. 14.

3. August 4, 1759, Barrington to Burgoyne, Public Record Office, War Office files, 26.24, f. 18. In subsequent citations, the abbreviations A.O. (Audit Office), C.O. (Colonial Office), F.O. (Foreign Office), T. (Treasury), and W.O. (War Office) refer to manuscript collections in the P.R.O. (Public Record Office, London).

4. August 4, 1759, Barrington to Burgoyne, W.O. 26.24, f. 18.

5. Henry Graham, *History of the Sixteenth, The Queen's Light Dragoons (Lancers)* (n.p., 1912), p. 2.

6. Ibid., p. 3.

7. Ibid., p. 2.

8. December 20, 1759, "Estimate of the Charge of Two Troops added to Lieut. Colonel Burgoyne's Regt. of Light Dragoons," W.O. 4.59, f. 444. Captains received £5:8:6 per week; lieutenants £3:3:0, cornets £2:16:0, quartermasters £1:18:6, sergeants 19s. 3d., corporals and drummers 15s. 9d., privates 12s. 6d. The figure of 3s. 6d. per week for privates in other regiments is taken from Curtis, *Organization of the British Army in the American Revolution* (New Haven, Conn., 1926), p. 22.

9. Bounties as high as £16 offset clothing costs, which with other stoppages, reduced their annual pay to £8:14:0; Graham, *Sixteenth*, p. 4.

10. Ibid.

11. October 13, 1759, Barrington to Burgoyne, W.O. 4.59, f. 134; October 27, 1759, Barrington to Burgoyne, W.O. 4.59, f. 211; February 6, 1760, Barrington to Burgoyne, W.O. 4.59, f. 678.

12. August 7, 1759, Barrington to Farquier, W.O. 4.55, f. 332.

13. January 19, 1760, Barrington to Burgoyne, W.O. 26.24, f. 91; August 9, 1759, Barrington to Burgoyne, W.O. 4.58., f. 343; September 21, 1759, Thomas Tyrwhitt to Henry Fox, T. 1.387, ff. 34–37.

14. December 12, 1759, Barrington to Burgoyne.

15. January 26, 1760, Barrington to Elliott, Barrington to Burgoyne, W.O. 4.59, f. 599, in which Burgoyne was advanced an additional £1,000.

16. "John Burgoyne," *DNB;* January 30, 1760, Tyrwhitt to Burgoyne, W.O. 4.59, f. 628.

17. Graham, *Sixteenth*, p. 4; February 23, 1760, Barrington to Burgoyne, W.O. 26.24, ff. 127–28; May, 1760, Barrington to Burgoyne, W.O. 26.24, ff. 185–86.

18. June 5, 1760, Barrington to Lieutenant Colonel Gallatin, W.O. 4.61, f. 214.

19. Ibid.

20. Burgoyne's "code of instruction" may be consulted in DeFonblanque, *Episodes,* pp. 16–21.

21. Burgoyne's views on the French language and military literature were shared rather widely in the British army; see Ira D. Gruber, "British Strategy: The Theory and Practice of Eighteenth Century Warfare," in Don Higginbotham, ed., *Reconsiderations on the Revolutionary War: Selected Essays* (Westport, Conn.: Greenwood Press, 1978), p. 18.

22. Graham, *Sixteenth,* p. 5; DeFonblanque, *Episodes,* p. 23.

23. DeFonblanque, *Episodes,* p. 24.

24. Ibid., p. 23.

25. Ibid., pp. 151–67.

26. Ibid.

27. May 29, 1761, "Return of the Loss of the Troops Employed on the Expedition . . .," W.O. 17, f. 1317[1].

28. June 4, 1761, J. Hodgson to C. Townshend, W.O. 1.165, ff. 355–58.

29. July 19, 1761 and August 16, 1761, Caroline Howe to Georgiana, Countess Spencer, Manuscripts of the Rt. Hon. The Earl Spencer, Althorp, Northamptonshire, hereinafter designated "Spencer MSS."

30. November 30, 1761.

4

Campaigning in Portugal and Spain

The Seven Years' War in Europe showed no signs of diminishing, although many prominent Englishmen wished to end it. In fact, the conflict expanded during August 1761, when Charles III of Spain and his Bourbon cousin Louis XV entered into a family compact designed by the comte de Stainville, now duc de Choiseul and minister of foreign affairs in the French cabinet. Ironically, the nobleman who a decade earlier offered Burgoyne hospitality and friendship now unintentionally provided him an opportunity to win glory by fighting against Choiseul's newly acquired ally.[1]

Burgoyne was the only British lieutenant colonel to receive a promotion to brigadier general in Portugal.[2] Like the other local ranks assigned, it was a temporary appointment which lasted only so long as he served in that country.[3] But the honor did not satisfy him. He sent a petition to Lord Bute in April 1762 requesting promotion from lieutenant colonel to a full colonelcy in the British army.[4] The earl could not oblige Burgoyne and reminded him that there were a great many lieutenant colonels senior to him in the army.[5] Burgoyne contained his ambition for promotion for the time being and prepared to leave for Portugal early in May. Lady Charlotte's protest at their last separation had effect, for Burgoyne obtained permission to bring his wife with him.[6] In addition, because of his new rank he was qualified to lead the Sixteenth, as well as about two thousand Portuguese soldiers, twenty-seven hundred soldiers in all.[7]

Burgoyne's dragoons were the elite corps of the British force in Portugal. Captain Robert Kingston, Major Henry Luttrell, and Lieutenant Colonel Hugh Somerville continued to serve on his staff.[8] Major Charles Lee, now a lieutenant colonel in Portugal, also gained experience with the British army there.[9] In all, Burgoyne commanded 35 commissioned officers, 28 noncommissioned officers, and 500 rank and file soldiers.[10] Because of bureaucratic inefficiency, however, not all of the regiment was available for duty. When Burgoyne arrived in Lisbon late in May 1762, fully 25 percent of his men were missing.[11] Those soldiers still at Belle Ile and Portsmouth finally arrived in Portugal during June, bringing the dragoons to their full strength.[12]

Burgoyne, in a difficult assignment, issued general orders for his troops.[13] He had to subject the local soldiers to the routine of discipline, keep Anglo-

Portuguese relations in balance, and prevent British soldiers from plundering the countryside. Depending upon the nature of the offense, punishments varied from three days' work without pay to summary execution.[14] Meanwhile, England's foe prepared to invade Portugal.

Determined to keep the divisions of the enemy's army from combining, Portuguese commander in chief La Lippe decided to avoid pitched battle with them, and chose Burgoyne to execute the delaying tactics. Burgoyne marched his men to Estremadura, hoping to attack the Spanish in their own territory. He chose for an initial target the fortified frontier town of Valencia de Alcantara, a large supply and ammunition base for the Spanish army. If all went well there Burgoyne could penetrate further to Ponte San Piero and Xenova to block Spanish communication with Badajoz.[15]

On July 27, in secrecy, Burgoyne led the soldiers quickly over forty-five miles of road through the mountains of Castel Danida. However, he was not met by the auxiliary force that he had expected, so he reluctantly but sensibly abandoned his initial hope of penetrating to San Piero.[16] Instead, he concentrated only upon his immediate objective, the town of Valencia de Alcantara, which was reportedly not well guarded. He marched the soldiers in two columns to the border, then ordered Major Henry Luttrell to lead a detachment of grenadiers into Spain, encircle the town as a diversionary measure, and "cut to pieces, or make prisoners any patrols they might meet." Armed Portuguese peasants and irregular infantry covered the flanks and seized the entrance to Valencia in preparation for the main attack.

Burgoyne planned a "brisk gallop" to take the town by surprise. He led the dragoons at three-quarter speed toward Valencia. The advance guard found the entrance to the city unoccupied, and "pushed into the town sword in hand."[17] The raid was a great success; Burgoyne and his men occupied the town at once, killing or seizing Spanish soldiers before they had an opportunity to use their guns. He dealt severely with the inhabitants.[18] Fortunately, the potential holocaust never developed; the people saw "their error, and all was quiet." Consequently, Burgoyne chose to be lenient. He "brought away hostages for the good attendance and safe delivery of my wounded, and for the payment of a year's king's revenue for sparing the convents and town."[19] Large numbers of captured Spaniards, often accompanied by livestock, streamed into Valencia from the countryside under the direction of Burgoyne's troops. His men also captured the colors of three Spanish regiments, innumerable officers, including a Spanish major general, and quantities of ammunition.[20]

Burgoyne exulted in his success. Concerning a victorious report written by a subordinate officer, the brigadier general observed to the secretary of war: "believe me, my Lord, this is no exaggeration of the Colonel, but real fact."[21] La Lippe was delighted to have news of the victory. Burgoyne himself expressed to the field marshal "the highest pleasure," which, he observed with unwonted modesty, was mingled with "confusion." La Lippe's approbation "gratifies my ambition," he wrote, "but at the same time I am conscious that the chief merit of the success was due to the admirable, though not uncommon valour and activity of the troops."[22] Burgoyne especially praised Colonel Somerville's "judgment, his spirit, and humanity; and I do not know for which of those qualities he deserves most commendation." During August Burgoyne continued to receive compliments. He was thanked publicly in general orders for his "glorieuse conduite," which every soldier in the army might well imitate.[23] Words of praise greeted him from even higher quarters. The Portuguese prime minister told La Lippe that the king was edified by Burgoyne's "sagesse et de la bravoure avec lesquelles il a conduit la même affaire."[24] The monarch, in appreciation, presented to Burgoyne a diamond ring, which Prime Minister Pombal brought to him "comme un petit souvenir de l'action de Valence, que vous avez si bravement conduite; et comme une marque de son affection Royal à votre égard."[25] La Lippe wrote warmly of Burgoyne's "remarkable valour, conduct, and presence of mind" in a letter to Lord Bute.[26] "Burgoyne," he said, "carried the place first with his own regiment sword in hand." For the Portuguese, Valencia was a moral victory; for Burgoyne, it was a small, bright feather in his cap. He had displayed to advantage a talent for organization and leadership in his first independent venture.

Burgoyne's exploits on the continent were not yet concluded. The Sixteenth remained posted near the border during August and September, and prevented the enemy from crossing into Portugal. However, Spanish forces edged slowly toward La Lippe's army.[27] During September, they invaded Portugal and took the strategic post of Castello Branco on the Tagus.[28] The security of Villa Velha, a town near the Spanish frontier, was weakened by this movement. Burgoyne learned that the town was carelessly guarded and that it contained munitions and other stores. Early in October he made plans to capture Villa Velha and on the evening of the fifth, he sent Colonel Charles Lee across the Tagus with 250 British grenadiers and 50 cavalrymen. At two in the morning, Lee's grenadiers burst into the camp from the rear, charging with their bayonets, while the light horse dispersed the weak Spanish resistance. Lee's soldiers destroyed the Spanish stockpile of arms; captured booty, pack animals, and prisoners; and killed a major general. The British army had scored a second triumph in Spain.[29] Lee was nominated for a promotion, although Burgoyne also received much credit. Spanish losses at Valencia and Villa Velha were considerable, and Burgoyne's successful leadership brought the Portuguese campaign to a victorious end by the time the autumnal rains commenced in November 1762. The Seven Years' War was virtually over. La Lippe departed for winter quarters and the Spanish withdrew from Portugal as Burgoyne sailed for England.[30]

Before his departure from Portugal he had again applied for promotion to the rank of full colonel.[31] In August, during the lull between the battles at Valencia and Villa Velha, he had written a letter on that subject to Charles Townshend, who was then secretary at war.[32] Unhappy that Henry Clinton and others had received promotions (announced in the *Gazette*), the frustrated lieutenant colonel told the secretary that his "disappointment in being left out of the late promotion of Colonels becomes doubly severe by the apprehension that I have forfeited the friendship you did me the honour to profess toward me."[33] Burgoyne based his claim upon family connection: "upon any other [support] I should blush to ask it." He boasted of "family weight," pressed "the honour of Lord Strange's application," and intimated that failure to promote him "will give me more pain as a slight to my patron, than as a disappointment to myself." Although he appreciated the rank of brigadier general which he held in Portugal, he continued to wish for "the great, substantial point of all military pursuits—rank in England." Townshend replied that he had already presented Burgoyne's petition to the king, and that Lord Strange had also spoken to George III in his behalf. "If [Lord Strange] had in any degree, suggested to me, that he saw the promotion, and his Majesty's answer to him, in the light you do," wrote Townshend, "I should not have suffered one day to have passed, without acting upon his remonstrance."[34] Burgoyne's complaint offended Townshend, who asked the colonel to assure Lord Strange he was "not cold in any interest or to any person he recommends and loves; my life and conduct will be a full answer to that charge." Nevertheless, Townshend indicated that persistence might secure the promotion, for he encouraged Burgoyne to enlist "the interest of those whom you believe most able, and think most willing to support your claims."

Taking the advice to heart, Burgoyne obtained La Lippe's endorsement, and his campaign for advancement was ultimately as effective as his recent military campaign.[35] In November 1762 the earl of Bute sent him news of his promotion to full colonel in the British army, noting that "His Majesty very readily consented to" the nomination, "out of regard to Lord Strange, and your own merit," although he added that La Lippe's reports were "of no small use in procuring what [you] so much wished."[36] Bute praised Burgoyne's "very brilliant" victory and "gallant behavior" at Valencia.

Several months after his appointment Burgoyne in turn exerted influence to obtain a promotion for one of his subordinates. In March 1763, he supported the cause of Colonel Somerville of the Sixteenth, which brought upon Burgoyne the "ill will of the war office." The colonel asked Lord Liverpool to "lay my letter before Lord Bute at a moment when he has leisure to attend to it & could wish that it might be this evening or tomorrow morning."[37] It was the first of a host of letters that Burgoyne continued to write during his lifetime on behalf of friends, subordinates, and their families. His enemies might call him importunate, but perhaps it would be fairer to suggest that Burgoyne's sense of justice at times exceeded his sense of politics.

In the last analysis, the exploits of the British army in Portugal and Spain were of little consequence although years later Burgoyne recollected in an exaggerated fashion that "the whole force of Spain was to be contended with."[38] Likewise, his belief that "the salvation of Portugal depended upon [himself] and Count La Lippe only" was unrealistic. The campaign was of importance to

Burgoyne, who for the first time received widespread favorable comment and recognition. No longer young at the age of forty, Burgoyne had lost time and rank as a result of his frequent gambling. For one whose ambitions were soaring, the expeditions to the peninsula were indeed gratifying. Although the war came swiftly to an end with the Peace of Paris in February 1763, Burgoyne had already taken steps to build a second career.

Notes

1. [n.d., 1762] "General and Staff Officers in Portugal under Lord Tyrawley," W.O. 1.165, ff. 613–16.

2. February 13, 1762, *Army List for 1764* p. 16.

3. [1762] Questions a demander a Monsr. de Mello envoye extraordinaire de La Majestie le Roi de Portugal, W.O. 1.165, ff. 597–98, sixteen questions concerning promotions. [n.d., 1762] De Mello's reply, W.O. 1.165, ff. 601–4.

4. April 1762, Burgoyne to Bute, DeFonblanque, *Episodes*, p. 46.

5. April 12, 1762, Bute to Burgoyne, ibid., p. 46.

6. May 9, 1760, Townshend to Tyrawley, W.O. 1.165, ff. 629–36. June 26, 1762, Burgoyne to Barrington, W.O. 1.165, ff. 693–96.

7. The War Office authorized 5,110 soldiers, but only 3,500 were fit for duty in April 1762; W.O. 17.1317[1].

8. *Army List for 1763*, p. 40.

9. February 14, 1762, "State of His Majesty's Forces Destined to Serve in Portugal," W.O. 1.165, ff. 559–76.

10. [n.d., 1762] W.O. 1.165, ff. 577–80.

11. March 31, 1762, Townshend to Loudoun, W.O. 1.165, f. 653; May 9, 1762, Townshend to Tyrawley, W.O. 1.165, ff. 629–36; May 1, 1762, Lambert to Townshend, W.O. 1.165.

12. June 24, 1762, W.O. 1.165, ff. 681–84; 849 rank and file active; 149 sick; 46 missing.

13. "John Burgoyne," *DNB*; DeFonblanque, *Episodes*, p. 35.

14. DeFonblanque, *Episodes*, p. 35.

15. Alden, *Lee*, p. 39.

16. "I perceived with much dissatisfaction that my guides had greatly deceived me with regard to the distance" wrote Burgoyne. He had anticipated an additional hour of darkness, but "found the day coming on fast." DeFonblanque, *Episodes*, p. 41.

17. July 1762, Burgoyne to the War Office, DeFonblanque, *Episodes*, pp. 39–43.

18. Ibid.

19. Ibid., pp. 39–40.

20. Ibid.; Graham, *Sixteenth*, pp. 6–7.

21. Ibid.

22. Ibid.

23. August 29, 1762, Ordres de Jour, DeFonblanque, *Episodes*, pp. 43–44; Graham, *Sixteenth*, p. 7.

24. September 2, 1762, Pombal to La Lippe, DeFonblanque, *Episodes*, p. 44.

25. September 6, 1762, Pombal to Burgoyne, DeFonblanque, *Episodes*, pp. 44–45. For Burgoyne's defense of La Lippe, see his "Observations and Reflections upon the present Military State of Prussia, Austria, and France," 1766, printed in DeFonblanque, *Episodes*, pp. 62–88.

26. [1762] La Lippe to Burgoyne, ibid., pp. 45–46.

27. DeFonblanque, ibid., p. 50.

28. Ibid.

29. Ibid.; Alden, *Lee*, p. 22; "John Burgoyne," *DNB*.

30. Ibid. Of Villa Velha, La Lippe wrote: "So brilliant a stroke speaks for itself and there is no occasion to lengthen this letter with the well deserved applause due to Brigadier-Gen. Burgoyne as well as to Colonel Lee and the British troops." Graham, *Sixteenth*, p. 7; no citation.

31. DeFonblanque, *Episodes*, p. 46.

32. August 10, 1762, Burgoyne to Townshend, W.O. 1.165, ff. 465–68.

33. August 10, 1762, Burgoyne to Townshend, W.O. 1.165, ff. 465–68.

34. September 19, 1762, Townshend to Burgoyne, DeFonblanque, *Episodes*, pp. 47–49.

35. October 8, 1762, Burgoyne was commissioned a colonel, with army rank. He was placed 111th on a list of 116 colonels; *Army List* (1763), pp. 8, 40. He achieved regimental rank of colonel commandant on March 18, 1763.

36. November 2, 1762, Bute to Burgoyne, DeFonblanque, *Episodes*, p. 49.

37. March 23, 1763, Burgoyne to the earl of Liverpool, B.L. Add. MS. 38,200, f. 278.

38. May 26, 1778, "Notes of General Burgoyne's Speech to the House of Commons," Historical Manuscripts Commission, *Report on the Manuscripts of Mrs. Stopford-Sackville of Drayton House, Northamptonshire*, 2 vols. (London: H. M. Stationery Office, 1904–10), 2:110–15, quotation p. 111.

5

A Career in Parliament

The Portuguese campaign brought Burgoyne's military career to a temporary though successful halt. He did not again serve actively in the army for thirteen years, since the Treaty of Paris assured a period of stability and tranquillity for Great Britain and Western Europe. Doubtless reluctant to disappear from public view after such strenuous efforts to win notice and approbation, Burgoyne must have been pleased to know that he had a seat in the House of Commons when he returned to England in September 1762.

From the death of George II in 1760 until the election polls closed in March 1761, Sir William Peers Williams worked as a tireless campaign manager for the absent Burgoyne. Williams was an extravagant young man, not unlike Burgoyne in some respects. The son of a Sussex baronet, educated at Winchester, Eton, and Clare College, Cambridge, the young officer worked with great diligence in his home county on Burgoyne's behalf.[1] Initially, he proposed Burgoyne's candidacy for the Borough of Midhurst to the duke of Newcastle, who disapproved the idea. But Hans Stanley, a mutual friend of Williams and Burgoyne, informed the duke that Burgoyne would "honorably and steadily adhere to every assurance he gives your Grace on this occasion."[2]

Stanley's support was decisive, for Newcastle had experienced difficulties with politicians in Midhurst. At length Newcastle, Holland, Lord Fitzmaurice, and Lord Bute intervened in order to avoid a contested election. When one of the candidates agreed to withdraw, Stanley and Williams were assured that both Burgoyne and William Hamilton would be returned unopposed.[3] Thus Burgoyne won the election and represented Midhurst until the legislature was dissolved in 1767. Parliament thanked Burgoyne for his services in Portugal when he took his seat in 1762, but otherwise paid little attention to the new and inexperienced politician for several years.[4]

The Parliament that Colonel Burgoyne joined on November 25, 1762, included sixty-three other military officers, among them William Howe, Charles Cornwallis, Lord Granby, Henry Seymour Conway, Robert Clive, and Field Marshal Lord Ligonier.[5] It had already experienced a crisis in leadership, the first of a seemingly endless series of ministerial reconstructions during George III's early years. While Burgoyne was still in Portugal during October 1761, the duke of Newcastle had joined the earl of Bute in a coalition ministry which the king managed to undermine in such a way that Newcastle was quickly forced to resign and Bute thereafter acted as first lord of the treasury and prime minister for ten months. Although he actively sought ministerial employment, Burgoyne made no speeches of importance during that administration, nor did he contribute significantly to the debates of the Grenville ministry, which succeeded the Bute regime.[5] However, he did write a note to George Grenville concerning a projected vote on general warrants.[6] Shortly thereafter Burgoyne temporarily lost interest in political debates, for his ten-year-old daughter Charlotte Elizabeth died on March 7, 1764.[7] She was buried in the North Cloister of Westminster Abbey three days after her death.

In 1765 Burgoyne's fate and that of the American colonies crossed paths for the first time. Grenville's ministry fell, and in the subsequent reconstruction the marquis of Rockingham emerged as first lord of the treasury. Burgoyne voted against repeal of the Stamp Act, and also joined a majority of members who supported a Declaratory Act that would state clearly the fact of British parliamentary sovereignty on North America. Burgoyne delivered a lengthy and emphatic speech on that subject on February 3, 1766. He chose a hard and, conveniently, popular line of argument concerning the American colonies.[8]

Had he been a more persistently ambitious man, one might suspect him, as early as 1766, of preparing a part for himself in the crown's quarrels with the American colonies. However, Burgoyne instead directed his considerable energy in a rather diffuse way during the period between the Seven Years' War and the American Revolution. Content at first to be a favorite at Court he gradually expanded his scope of activities, drilling and parading the Sixteenth Regiment, enjoying life in London, preparing a tour of military bases in Europe, and finally contesting another election for parliament. Eventually he participated in the major political debates of the age, but ten years were to elapse before that time.

After his coronation in 1761, George III had looked with particular interest and favor upon the Fifteenth and Sixteenth Light Horse.[9] When Burgoyne's dragoons returned triumphant from Spain they benefited from the meticulous attention which their leader lavished upon them.[9] In March 1763, Burgoyne was appointed colonel-commandant of the Sixteenth Regiment, and he continued to train them so well that their reputation for polish became widespread.[10] Although the force was reduced in 1763 along with other regiments returning to peacetime budgets, their reputation remained brilliant, for the king inspected Burgoyne's cavalrymen upon numerous occasions, most significantly in February 1766 at Wimbledon Common when he made the Fifteenth and Sixteenth Regiments royal units.[11] Thereafter, the force was officially designated the Queen's Light Dragoons, a signal honor which ended speculation that the regiment would be disbanded. George III continued the practice of personal review until well into the 1770s.[12]

Royal approbation made Burgoyne and Lady Charlotte, who now lived at

"The Oaks," near Epsom in Surrey, a popular couple in London society.[13] When they attended the races at Salisbury and at Newmarket the Burgoynes continued their friendships with the wealthy and prominent in politics, arts and letters, and the military.[14] Burgoyne joined the brilliant society that Georgiana, Countess Spencer entertained at Devonshire House in Saint James.[15] Charles James Fox, Lord North, Lord Strange, George Selwyn, the earl of March and Queensbury, and the duke of Devonshire welcomed the colonel to the gaming table, where he displayed his talent to such good effect that gentlemen in Brooks Club and White's Club soon watched him at their tables.[16] Charles James Fox, Richard Sheridan, Edmund Burke, and Sir Joshua Reynolds became particular friends, the latter meeting Burgoyne occasionally at the Green Room in Drury Lane or at the Star and Garter near Reynolds's home in Richmond.[17] In fact, Burgoyne sat for his portrait in Reynolds's studio.[18]

Such pleasant activities occupied the greater part of Burgoyne's life for several years. When the Rockingham ministry fell in 1766, however, Burgoyne was glad to find William Pitt at the helm of the remodeled ship of state. He secured from the newly created earl of Chatham a letter of introduction to Prince Ferdinand of Brunswick in preparation for a second tour of Europe.[19] Burgoyne's tour of 1766 was not entirely for pleasure, as he had an opportunity to examine for the ministry the military bases of Europe's leading powers.

Arriving on the continent during the summer of 1766, Burgoyne visited the headquarters of the Bohemian army at Teutchbrod in September. At Brunswick he met Prince Ferdinand, "who is well informed," he wrote, "on everything that passes at the academy."[20] Burgoyne observed lectures in mathematics and language at the Brunswick Military Academy, which he noted were of high quality. His mind active and alert, Burgoyne walked enthusiastically about the battlefields of central Europe, speaking with what he termed "the principal actors on both sides." Burgoyne was already describing the "stage" of battle, as though even then he had begun to picture in his mind's eye the events of life in terms of the playwright he was later to become.[21] His "Reflections" for the cavalry, his dispatches from France and Spain, and his account of the tour of Europe all contain rather theatrical prose. In a surprising episode in Prague Burgoyne actually donned a disguise, the garb of an actor, in order to enter a secret army base of the emperor of Austria. "By a little intrigue, a good deal of perseverance, and perhaps more assurance than I ought to boast of," Burgoyne wrote, he managed to pass through the lines incognito. His disguise was effective and he was able to witness the drill parades of the Bohemian and Moravian armies. Burgoyne admired the precision of those maneuvers, and wrote to Colonel Elliott that the infantry, cavalry and general officers were all first class.[22]

In addition to the imaginative capacity which the colonel displayed in abundance, he was also an observant man, and he wrote an intelligent series of detailed "Observations and Reflections" for the earl of Chatham. Burgoyne admired Frederick the Great's personal supervision of Prussia's military machine, he wrote to Chatham, and he especially noted that Frederick continued "to superintend every branch of the service, and by his presence and unremitted attention invigorates and supports a system which can hardly be any longer improved."[23] Not surprisingly, Burgoyne's most accurate observations concerned the regiments of cavalry that he observed. Prussia's horse soldiers did not meet with his approval, for they were "not highly mounted nor well appointed." Although Frederick required "extraordinary velocity in the movements of his cavalry," Burgoyne did not think the Prussian dragoons were prepared for such excellence. They lacked the "mechanical valour of the infantry resulting from order, regularity, and subordination." The colonel found warm words, however, for the large and capable artillery.

Burgoyne's fondness for the theatrical did not lead him to forgive the indecorous. He found the dress of the Prussian troops absurd, and imagined the costumes to have been introduced "not by error, but by design, to amuse and mislead the observations of strangers." Although the uniforms of the rank and file did not hinder their performance, the officers adopted "the fopperies as the essentials," and made everything give way to them. Burgoyne admired, however, Prussian economy of movement, training, and "the finest discoveries and improvement in tactics."

Burgoyne's appraisal of the rank and file and of the officers was mixed. He did not have a high opinion of the private soldiers, a third of whom he said were "strangers, deserters, prisoners and enemies, of various countries, languages, and religions." Burgoyne concluded that Prussian soldiers could not fight from principles of national patriotism, and therefore he believed that the policy of the Prussians "to sink and degrade all intellectual faculties, and to reduce the man as nearly as possible to mere machinery" was a wise one. Such a task was not difficult, "as nature has formed the bulk of the King of Prussia's native subjects." Nevertheless, the Prussian attitude differed from Burgoyne's own belief that soldiers should be treated as human beings.

It is not surprising that on balance he found the Prussian system inferior to that of Great Britain. On the other hand, Burgoyne found that the first Prussian maxim, "not to reason, but to obey," made officers precise and alert. However, most of the great generals who fought in the Seven Years' War were, by this time, dead or retired. Burgoyne was critical of their replacements who, it seemed to him, were concerned only with the routine of parade, and suffered from shallow educations. The noncommissioned officers, he thought, were the best in the world. Burgoyne did not expect the excellence of the Prussian establishment to last indefinitely. The king made the army, and Burgoyne believed that Prussian military expertise might decline after Frederick died. The extraordinary expense necessary to maintain such a splendid army was a burden to the people, he noted, and diverted capital from other important national interests.[24] In the long view, Burgoyne thought Prussia would not be a threat to Great Britain. Unfortunately for Great Britain, Burgoyne's prediction was shortsighted. Frederick's system endured through the ensuing two centuries and Prussian militarism engulfed a united Germany. For the span of Burgoyne's life, however, his judgment was correct. Prussia did decline temporarily as a military power after Frederick's death, and caused Britain no trouble for some time.[25]

Burgoyne found the Austrian military establishment more to his liking, and possibly for that reason he overestimated its power. He saw in the Austrian force all that was lacking in the Prussian army. But the splendor of the Austrian army did not seem to him as great as it should have been, because of domestic political difficulties and "mismanaged pomp." Nor were the private soldiers well trained and well equipped. The Austrian army, however, was "always respectable" during the Seven Years' War, and Burgoyne believed that it would improve again. The new emperor, Joseph II, wrote Burgoyne, seemed intent upon establishing the greatest military power in Europe." Burgoyne believed Joseph II to be able and ambitious, a judgment not confirmed by history. He found the officer staff competent and admired the "detail and precision" of the troops. Burgoyne inspected the arsenal at Vienna, to which the emperor had devoted a great deal of attention. He was pleased with the troops' uniforms, observing that in every instance innovations were undertaken "to unite as much as possible, lightness, warmth, and ease." The Austrians, Burgoyne judged, were "not yet arrived at the extraordinary steadiness" of the Prussians, nor were they equal to their neighbors in discipline. But he believed that they could someday surpass the Prussians in both respects. In his interpretation of military affairs in Austria, Burgoyne was not accurate.

The colonel was least enchanted with the army of France, Britain's recently vanquished foe.[26] Burgoyne's appraisal of his former neighbor and now the French Foreign Minister, the duc de Choiseul, was only partly flattering. He observed in him "lively talents and sanguine temper," but though he acknowledged Choiseul's vigilance and enterprise, he faulted him for his secrecy, ambition, and for "activity often resembling precipitancy, and perseverance that may sometimes be termed obstinacy." Furthermore, he suggested in his letters to the prime minister that Choiseul was motivated by private pride as well as patriotism and that he dreaded more the loss of honor than the "expense of blood, of treasure, or of dominion." Almost uncannily, Burgoyne described all of his own faults that the world would discern during his conduct of the expedition of 1777. More immediately apparent was his lack of discretion concerning Choiseul, who had befriended Burgoyne and his wife for several years. Perhaps Burgoyne considered such disclosures to be in the national interest.

He praised highly the talents of the young officers of the French army, but complained of "not only the prejudices, but the judgment of age" with which these officers had to contend. Choiseul's zeal, he thought, might overcome bureaucratic hindrance, "but the attempt is so far bold and hazardous, that should it fail, the affairs of the army will probably be in worse condition than they were before it was made, as the relapse is usually more desperate than the original disease." Burgoyne discerned a need for reform of discipline and an improvement of the French cavalry. Modern generals who neither understood the purpose of the cavalry nor how to use it were responsible for the dormant state of France's dragoons. Military schools labored assiduously to train horse soldiers all over France; some of them had achieved a distinct superiority. But concerning the larger picture, Burgoyne was less than enthusiastic.

Burgoyne perceived accurately that France had the potential to threaten Great Britain, but he did not believe that her infantry, senior officers, or methods of administration were of sufficient quality to cause alarm. He did not understand that France was Britain's greatest enemy, that she was preparing herself for an opportunity to secure her revenge for the humiliations of the last war. Moreover, he neglected to analyze Britain's inadequate military structure. He noted only that British horses and officers were of such a quality as to "enable the cavalry of Great Britain not only to retain its present superiority, but to rise far beyond any strength it has yet shewn."

For John Burgoyne, then, war in the future would be war with Europe. He saw a continent "in arms, or at least intently occupied either in precautionary or hostile preparations." Unfortunately for the colonel, his observations were not of great assistance to the war office, nor would they help him in his own career. The North American colonies were the "stage" of the next war, but Burgoyne did not visit them. He was not alone, for few of Britain's military or political leaders gave much attention to the rising storm across the Atlantic. In the immediate future, Burgoyne's next battle, a political one, would be fought in an unlikely place: the county palatinate of Lancaster.

Notes

1. Namier and Brooke, eds., *Commons*, 3:645.
2. October 21, 1760, Stanley to Newcastle, B.L., Add. MS. 32,913, f. 257, cited by Namier and Brooke, eds., *Commons*, 1:395–96.
3. [n.d.] John Roge to Newcastle, B.L., Add. MS. 32,910, f. 417, cited in ibid.
4. DeFonblanque, *Episodes*, pp. 54–55.
5. January 28, 1764, George Grenville to Burgoyne, in John R. G. Tomlinson, ed., *Additional Grenville Papers, 1763–1765* (Manchester: Manchester University Press, 1962), pp. 79–80. Although Burgoyne failed to obtain the appointment (as secretary to Lord Northumberland), he obtained warm praise from Grenville, a close political associate of Lord Strange; ibid., pp. 270–72.
6. Sir Lewis Namier, *The Structure of Politics at the Accession of George III* (London: Macmillan, 1929), p. 25; February 16, 1764, Burgoyne to George Grenville, in Tomlinson, ed. *Additional Grenville Papers, 1763–65* p. 86.
7. Chester, ed., *Registers*, p. 404 and note 1.
8. Namier and Brooke, eds., *Commons*, 2:141–45.
9. Graham, *Sixteenth*, p. 8; DeFonblanque, *Episodes*, p. 15.
10. The commission was dated March 18, 1763; *Army List for 1764*, p. 40.
11. May 26, 1763, Ellis to Holland, W.O. 4.72, ff. 491–92; May 29, 1766, Barrington to Burgoyne, W.O. 4.79, f. 576. Lieutenant Colonel George Elliott of the Fifteenth Regiment re-

ceived a similar honor, as his force was designated "The King's Own Dragoons." See also November 10, 1766, W.O. 4.1044, ff. 99–100.

12. June 18, 1764; May 20, 1766; May 25, 1767, 1769, 1770, 1771, 1774; Graham, *Sixteenth*, pp. 8–9, and appendix I, p. 239.

13. June 10, 1765, Burgoyne to earl of Liverpool, B.L., Add. MS. 38,204, f. 265.

14. June 4, 1763, Welbore Ellis to Burgoyne, W.O. 4.71, f. 419.

15. Pottinger, "John Burgoyne," pp. 37–38. For entertaining glimpses of the Burgoynes' milieu during the years 1767–74 as well as repeated references to Lady Charlotte's gambling habits, see Lady Mary Coke, *The Letters and Journals of Lady Mary Coke*, 4 vols. (Bath, Eng.: Kingsmead Reprints, 1970) 2:29, 200, 250–51, 274, 283, 326, 344, 373, 432, 3:16, 78–80, 135, 142, 148, 260, 263, 266, 270–71, 274, 282, 297, 422, 432, 436, 438, 439, 442, 4:96, 98, 113–14, 125, 128, 132, 135, 141, 148, 151, 157, 163, 180, 365, 375, 413, 438.

16. The membership roll at White's included Lord John Cavendish, the earl of Shelburne, the duke of Richmond, Henry Dundas, Charles Jenkinson, Admiral Keppel, Fox, and others. William B. Boulton, *The History of White's*, 2 vols. (London Algernon H. Bourke, 1892), 1:113. Volume 2:37–39, the "Betts Book," contains some of the colonel's wagers.

17. Charles R. Leslie and Tom Taylor, *Life and Times of Sir Joshua Reynolds*, 2 vols. (London: J. Murray, 1865), 2:99.

18. Ibid., 1:266.

19. July 1, 1766, Pitt to Burgoyne, DeFonblanque, *Episodes*, p. 56.

20. December 9, 1766, Burgoyne to Elliott, ibid., pp. 59–61.

21. Visiting the camp of the king of Prussia, Burgoyne wrote: "I passed some days in these mountains, tracing with extreme amusement the positions and marches of both armies during different periods of the late war."

22. December 9, 1766, Burgoyne to Elliott, DeFonblanque, *Episodes*, pp. 59–61.

23. June 27, 1766, Burgoyne to Pitt, W. S. Taylor and J. H. Pringle, *Correspondence of William Pitt*, 4 vols. (London: Murray, 1838–40), 2:429–32, and August 21, 1766, Burgoyne to Pitt, ibid., 3:41–45; DeFonblanque, *Episodes*, pp. 62–88.

24. Ibid.

25. Burgoyne found Frederick the Great's military observations of great interest, and preserved in his own handwriting copies of Frederick's correspondence with La Motte Fouquet, some of which was later printed in *Les Oeuvres Militaires de Frédéric II;* DeFonblanque, *Episodes*, p. 82 and appendix A, pp. 469–82.

26. Burgoyne, "Observations and Reflections," DeFonblanque, *Episodes*, p. 82.

6

A Contested Election

The earl of Chatham read with polite enthusiasm Burgoyne's account of European armies, counting the minutes "while indispensable business deprives me the pleasure of seeing you."[1] The elder statesman wrote in December 1766, shortly before he became ill. Burgoyne was granted an interview. Although he may have enjoyed his conversation with the old war hero and perhaps learned from him, his career did not benefit directly, for Pitt's indisposition deprived Burgoyne of a patron and the ministry of an effective leader. Parliament was dissolved during the summer of 1767, and writs authorizing new elections were issued. Burgoyne's tenure for Midhurst was at an end, but he immediately engaged Lord Strange's support and presented himself as a candidate for the borough of Preston, in Lancashire.

Burgoyne had already entrenched himself in Preston. He had built a house in Walton-le-Dale, the site of a Roman military station, and not far distant from Patten House, where Lord Strange resided when he was not in London or Knowsley.[2] Burgoyne, who designed the plan for the structure, called the house Cooper Hill, and according to tradition it was the first in England to include the lightning rods invented by Benjamin Franklin.[3] Since Lady Charlotte's parents also lived nearby at Knowsley, the Burgoynes were able to maintain close ties with her family. Lord Strange, who controlled the Whig political interest in Preston, soon exerted himself on behalf of his brother-in-law and friend of thirty years. His task was a difficult one for the Tories had dominated the political life of the city since 1741, and they were loath to relinquish it.[4]

Burgoyne encountered difficulty from the first. His candidacy roused the Tories, who had put forward two stalwarts of their party, Sir Peter Leicester and Sir Frank Standish. Lord Strange perceived that Burgoyne, still considered an outsider by the inhabitants of Preston, might have difficulty winning votes. A few weeks before the election he decided to nominate for the second seat Sir Henry Houghton, sixth baronet of Houghton Tower, in order to enhance Burgoyne's prospects.[5]

Heretofore a fashionable cavalry officer and court favorite, Burgoyne soon became an unpopular man, even a hated one, as he plunged into the depths of an acrimonious controversy. The borough election at Preston, like others held in Great Britain during that period, was fought not on national issues, but on local matters; there were no discussions of John Wilkes, Lord Chatham, or foreign policy. It was a battle for local power in Preston, fought between the corporation of that borough and the Derby family. The first canvass for eligible electors was held in June 1767.[6] By February 1768, public passions were at a high pitch as incidents of bribery, bloodshed, and rioting created general disorder. "The Tumults, the Insults, the Violences, the Barbarities exercis[e]d against the Persons and Properties of my Friends during that Period," wrote Burgoyne at a later date, were "unprovoked, unreturn'd, unrestrain'd, and unparalle'd [sic]."[7] Few observers doubted that gangs of toughs were brought into Preston to force constituents to support a particular candidate.[8] Both Burgoyne and Lord Strange were among those whose tactics were called dubious, or worse, illegal.

Trouble of one sort or another had begun even before Burgoyne's arrival in the city. During February 1768 he hesitated to present himself in such an atmosphere, but urged by his friends, he at length set out for Preston as "a Reluctant Visitor." On the road to the city he was assailed by a mob. "Venting their Spleen, in Abusive Language, or throwing a little Dirt," the attackers seemed to have followed a prearranged plan, for it was "totally Dark, the ground calculated and judiciously chosen for Ambuscade and Mischief."[9] Several bystanders seized bricks and stones, hurling them at Burgoyne's chaise. He managed to arrive at Preston unscathed, but "found the state of the Town Surpass'd the description I had rec[eive]d of it." Who had caused such a commotion to take place? Burgoyne believed that a trained, disciplined corps of opponents who had achieved "absolute rule" among his constituents had subverted the municipal government and the magistracy through "Uproar and Violence, Sedition and Treason." A debate concerning voting rights— specifically, the qualifications of freemen—apparently caused the unrest.

The officers of Preston corporation, fearful of Strange and aware that they were disregarding custom as frequently as the Whigs, employed legal specialists to watch carefully the activities of their opponents. When the Tories threatened to take action, the Whigs intimidated the corporation with their hired toughs. Burgoyne claimed that the 100 supporters whom he had retained for his own protection against the Tory gang had been influenced by his opponents and were not under his control. He declared that his own supporters feared that he could not overcome force by force. When his life was threatened, he requested all the candidates to gather in committee in order to propose methods for eliminating violence.[10] When the meeting took place, according to Burgoyne, he was joined by only a few supporters, although they were "the most respectable Inhabitants." His friends arrived "without Weapons, without Parade and without Clamour." The Tories, however, were supported by "the known Band of Rioters Arm'd with Bludgeons delivered to them from the Town Hall— which was become an Arsenal for that Purpose—Strip't to the waste [sic] and every way prepared for mischief." Those people marched up to the windows of the meetinghouse and "instantly opposed" Burgoyne's "defenceless few." Burgoyne ascribed the motivation for their "Outrage" to the fact that "the expression of Burgoyne for ever had been herd [sic] in the streets, and that my friends had Orange Cockades in their Hats." An officer of the Lancashire militia finally succeeded in quelling the disturbance.

Relative calm having been imposed, Burgoyne proceeded to offer several suggestions for a permanent improvement in public order. He asked the mayor to appoint special constables from both political factions to patrol the streets in pairs. The plan was approved and the meeting adjourned, but shortly thereafter, Burgoyne received from the mayor a recantation of that agreement. The next day he was subject to insult and ridicule when he canvassed the town. The "Ringleaders shewed me Bludgeons under their coats" and tried to provoke a riot. In the afternoon, they "assaulted the House where I dined in the most Violent Manner." Consequently a second meeting was held to restore order. Burgoyne's opponents charged that he brought nonresidents into town for the election, which he denied. After the second meeting, further violence erupted and was once again quelled by the Lancashire militia. A mob dispersed but regrouped near the marketplace, where "a Barrel of Ale was publickly distributed to them by the agents of the Candidates." Fearing for their candidate's life, Burgoyne's supporters urged him to return to his home in disguise. Instead, he took a gun, and accompanied by two friends and a servant, he walked "thro' the streets Home but not without such an Insult as Demonstrated to all present that the Preservation of my Life depended soley [sic] upon the Pistol I had in my hand."[11] By February 17, the rioting had reached its height and had spread beyond Preston. Burgoyne accused his opposition of having broken every agreement that they made concerning a restoration of the public tranquillity. Dislike for him had reached such intensity that "it became the Universal Opinion that I must quit the Town or probably Die in it."

Two days later a new group of potential voters entered Preston, motivated, according to Burgoyne, not "by the call or by the Promises of the rewards of my friends" but by "General and Voluntary resentment against the Partial and Overbearing conduct of the Corporation and by the Interference and Activity of the whole Popist Interest against me." Burgoyne accepted their support, and later refused to relinquish his undertaking with that group because of what he called the popularity of his cause. When the opposition asked him to leave Preston because he provoked ill feeling and violence, Burgoyne refused to do so. Lacking power to enforce order, Burgoyne said that his absence would "increase the evil and have upon men's minds together with an indelible imputation upon my character the Impressions of miscarriage and Disappointment." The new supporters, whom Burgoyne called a "concourse," acted in self-defense on the afternoon of their arrival to repel an attack by the "Corporation Mob." Burgoyne heard the commotion and left his house, but observing the temper of those in the streets, decided to take refuge at the home of a friend and wait for weapons. After some time, he emerged from the house with a pistol under his arm and another in his pocket. He addressed his critics at the town hall, in coffee houses, and on the streets: "If I had no better security for a free Election than the words of People who had never kept a Promise I sho[ul]d not take pains to remove a set of People who were evidently come there to support my interest."[12]

Finally, the polls opened on March 21, 1768.[13] Guards were posted at doorways of the town hall for the protection of voters. Burgoyne, carrying a loaded pistol in each hand, was the only candidate present.[14] His supporters tried to prevent Tories from voting; the "Corporation Mob" exerted similar pressure upon Whig electors. As soon as the polls had closed on April 1, Tory mayor Robert Moss threw out almost 600 Whig votes for various reasons.[15] However, the mayor did not use the same criteria for counting Tory votes, and he validated all such ballots regardless of residency or religion. Predictably, the Tories won the election by 565 votes to 489. Burgoyne and Houghton, however, claimed that 1,147 electors had voted Whig, against 567 Tory ballots.[16] In November 1768, Lord Strange presented a petition to the House of Commons in favor of Burgoyne and Houghton.[17] Strange argued that the two Whig candidates "were duly Elected by a very great Majority of the persons qualif[ie]d to vote by the Constitution of the s[ai]d Boro[ugh]." However, Mayor Moss, with the assistance of a bailiff, "conducted the poll with the most Appar[en]t Partiality to the Int[erest] of Sir Peter Leicester and Sir Frank Standish, Barts.[,] the other candidates rejected with[ou]t any good reason."[18] Not content with a "false, arbitrary, and illegal Definit[io]n of the R[igh]t. of Election," the mayor also rejected many votes "under the most frivolous pretences." Consequently a very small and clearly illegal majority was obtained for Leicester and Standish, "contrary to the truth of the last Resol[u]t[io]n of this Hon[ora]ble House Concern[in]g the right of Election for the said Boro[ugh] in Defiance of the Laws," concluded Strange. Now it seemed that all might not be lost.

On November 11, the speaker of the House of Commons, Sir John Cust, informed the mayor that a hearing would be held at the bar of the House in three weeks.[19] The mayor was instructed to bring all the polls, charters, and public books pertaining to the election for investigation.[20] The inquiry proved to be a thorough one. The wording of the 1661 charter was examined, and the interpretation of the phrase "all the inhabitants" became the center of discussion. The Whigs had demanded the vote for everyone; in effect, they wanted universal male suffrage. After deliberation, the House virtually gave them that privilege by voiding the mayor's return and declaring Burgoyne and Houghton the rightful representatives. The Commons may have wished to end the disorders in Preston once and for all; possibly the weight of Lord Strange's family influence tipped the balance.[21] In the end, Preston received the broadest franchise ever known in Great Britain, and retained it until the electoral reforms of 1832.[22] The power of the Tory corporation was broken after twenty-seven years as Burgoyne took his seat in Parliament.[23] In view of the fact that Burgoyne's major claim to fame is his attempt to conquer a people who also insisted upon the principle of one man, one vote, there is a certain irony in the circumstances of his election at Preston.

The colonel had been confident of victory. The king was certainly not offended by the Preston election, for on October 9, 1769, he appointed Burgoyne governor of Fort William in Scotland, a sinecure that provided him an additional three hundred pounds per year.[24] Burgoyne was one of the few officers below the rank of general to have obtained such a plum.[25] Indeed, Burgoyne felt sufficiently confident in his victory to discuss the Preston case freely after Lord Strange's petition was accepted, publicly boasting that he had "engaged Government on his side, and [was] sure of success."[26] Burgoyne's statement was indiscreet and partly inaccurate. The Commons had dealt with the constitutional issues, but the question of violence remained to be settled.

On March 23, 1769, at six o'clock in the morning, Burgoyne and others were called to the Court of King's Bench and charged with aiding and abetting the rioters during the election.[27] The hearing lasted thirteen hours, after which the court was adjourned. When it met again in May, Burgoyne delivered a strongly worded, dramatic speech concerning the "Heavy and unexpected Misfortune" of his indictment.[28] Virtually admitting guilt, Burgoyne declared that, "the Duties of Publick Justice will be Tempered, with every consideration that can Justify, excuse, or mitigate the case of an unconscious offender.[29] His argument was one of self-defense. Burgoyne maintained that he was forced to hire his "concourse" in order to combat the violence of the "Corporation Mob." He recapitulated the incidents of the campaign, and twice noted that his life had been threatened. He denied responsibility for the excesses of his supporters, contending that the Tories had gained their allegiance. He also denied the very damaging testimony of one witness for the prosecution who claimed that when the corporation mob refused to come to terms Burgoyne had assured his supporters that they might "level the town."[30] He promised that if his conduct had been "of so Flagitious a Dye that it ought to be distinguished by an example, . . . in a case which has passed untried in almost every contested Election time Immemorial I shall submit with humility and teach myself contrition."[31] Burgoyne's final and probably most effective argument—that he had done nothing worse than anyone else—had some truth in it, but Sir Joseph Yates, the presiding justice, was unmoved. "After a very pathetic and proper speech, wherein he laid it on very hard upon the Colonel," Sir Joseph found Burgoyne guilty, fined him one thousand pounds, but excused him from imprisonment.[32]

A severe personal blow, the judgment made Burgoyne a nationally unpopular figure. One contemporary wrote: "I do think they should have sent the Colonel to keep Mr. Wilkes company as well as the rest, and then every body would have been satisfied; most people think that part was wanting to make the sentence complete.[33]

Just as success had come to him in abundance, now misfortune multiplied for Burgoyne. The duke of Grafton, who had become prime minister, upon Burgoyne's request sold a patent place at Exeter worth thirty-five hundred pounds and gave the proceeds to the colonel as a gesture of compensation for payment of the fine.[34] What would have been considered of no special consequence in other circumstances was characterized an example of Burgoyne's perfidious character. The anonymous pamphleteer Junius,—thought to be Sir Philip Francis, a Whitehall functionary—found Burgoyne's transaction with Grafton a superb matter for ridicule.[35] Junius proclaimed ironically that Grafton arranged the gift "to reward him I presume, for the decency of his deportment at Preston; or to reimburse him, perhaps, for the fine of one thousand pounds. . . . It is not often that the Chief Justice [Sir Joseph Yates] and the Prime Minister are so strangely at variance in their opinions of men and things."[36] Burgoyne's victory at Preston was costly in many respects. Indeed, Junius decided to explore Burgoyne's character in some detail. "No man is more tender of his reputation," exclaimed the man who feared to divulge his identity. He reported that Burgoyne was not above "taking his stand at a gaming-table, and watching, with the soberest attention, for a fair opportunity of engaging a drunken young nobleman at piquet."[37] Since Burgoyne was forced to sell his commission in 1747 because of gambling debts it does not appear likely that he was so cunning; moreover, Junius fed upon gossip.[38] However, twenty years had passed, during which time the colonel had had ample opportunity to improve his skills. Burgoyne's ethics at the gaming table may not have been above reproach, but at no time was he accused of cheating, nor was he ever challenged to a duel.

The storm passed eventually and Burgoyne returned to less sensational matters in the Commons. The commotions of 1768 and 1769, however, shed some light upon his personality. That Junius was right when he said "no man is more tender of his reputation," there can be no doubt. Born into the world amidst rumors and allegations, Burgoyne seemed always to court controversy. His first military career ruined by the gambling which had despoiled his father, Burgoyne had later succeeded in laying the foundations for a second career, a remarkable achievement. Unfortunately, the same ambition that enabled him to accomplish so much also led him to importunacy. He pushed relentlessly even those who were already disposed to help him. In his attempt to force circumstances to favor him at Preston Burgoyne displayed a lack of caution and prudence. His eagerness to win the election led him to actions inappropriate to the event and brought humiliating and long-lasting consequences.

Notes

1. December 14, 1766, Chatham to Burgoyne, DeFonblanque, *Episodes*, p. 83.
2. Winifred Proctor, "The Preston Election of 1768," *Transactions of the Historical Society of Lancashire and Cheshire for the Year 1959* (Liverpool: Historical Society of Lancashire and Cheshire, 1960), 3:93–116.

3. Ibid., pp. 98–99.

4. Ibid., p. 97.

5. Ibid., p. 100.

6. July 10, 1767, Burgoyne to "the Independent Burgesses of the Town of Preston," Lancashire Record Office, DDPr, 131/7, pp. 2–3.

7. 1769, "Substance of Col. John Burgoyne's Speech before the King's Bench, Relative to his Election for Preston, in Lancashire, in the year 1769," Lancashire Record Office, DDPr, 131/7, pp. 66–77.

8. Proctor, "Preston Election," p. 100.

9. 1769, "Burgoyne's Speech," Lancashire Record Office, p. 67.

10. Ibid., p. 69.

11. Ibid., p. 71.

12. Ibid., p. 74.

13. March 21, 1768, "A State of the Poll at the Election at Preston," Lancashire Record Office, DDd 11/51.

14. Proctor, "Preston Election," pp. 101–3.

15. Two polls were taken: one of freemen, one of inhabitants; Namier and Brooke, eds., Commons, 1:319.

16. Proctor, "Preston Election," p. 112.

17. November, 1768, Lord Strange to the Honorable House of Commons of Great Britain in Parliament Assembled, Lancashire Record Office, DDPr 131/8.

18. Ibid.

19. November 11, 1768, Sir John Cust to Robert Moss, Lancashire Record Office, DDPr 131/8.

20. November 16, 1768, William Shaw and John Wilkinson to John Nabb, Lancashire Record Office, DDPr 131/8.

21. Proctor puts forth the first interpretation, "Preston Election," p. 115; Namier and Brooke, eds., Commons, 1:319, suggest the second.

22. Namier and Brooke, eds., ibid.

23. Some writers have condemned the decision of Parliament: H. W. Clemesha, History of Preston (Manchester: Manchester University Press, 1912), pp. 205–6.

24. Army List, 1770, p. 169; Edmund Burke, The Correspondence of Edmund Burke, edited by Thomas W. Copeland et al., 10 vols. (Chicago: University of Chicago Press: 1958–78); 2:99, note 4.

25. DeFonblanque, Episodes, p. 86. He held the post until 1779; Brooke, "John Burgoyne," Namier and Brooke, eds., Commons, 2:141–45.

26. November 10, 1768, Historical Manuscripts Commission, Fourteenth Report, Appendix, part IV, The Manuscripts of Lord Kenyon (London: H. M. Stationery Office, 1894), p. 501.

27. March 24, 1769, George Kenyon, Jr. to George Kenyon, Kenyon MSS., pp. 501–2.

28. 1769, "Burgoyne's Speech," Lancashire Record Office, p. 66.

29. Ibid.

30. Burgoyne contended this statement was made for the first time only two weeks before the hearing; even at war he had exercised more clemency than that; 1769, "Burgoyne's Speech," Lancashire Record Office, p. 76.

31. Ibid., p. 77.

32. May 9, 1769, R. Bradley to George Kenyon, Historical Manuscripts Commission, Kenyon MSS., p. 502.

33. Ibid.

34. October 29, 1768, Duke of Grafton to Lord Granby, Rutland MSS., cited by Brooke, "John Burgoyne," in Namier and Brooke, eds., Commons, 2:141–45; December 1, 1769, Charles Lloyd to Grenville, William J. Smith, ed., The Grenville Papers, 4 vols. (London: J. Murray, 1853), 4:484, and December 19–20, 1769, Whately to Grenville, ibid., 4:493–96.

35. John Cannon, ed., The Letters of Junius (Oxford: Clarendon Press, 1978), pp. 153–54.

36. December 12, 1769, Junius to Mr. H. S. Woodfall, ibid., 358–59; December 12, 1769, Junius to the Duke of Grafton, ibid., 154–59.

37. December 12, 1769, Junius to the Duke of Grafton, Cannon, *Junius*, 154–59.

38. The hostile Walpole called Burgoyne "a fortunate gamester. Junius was thought unjust, as he was never supposed to do more than play very well." October 5, 1777, Walpole to Mason, Walpole, *Correspondence*, 28:336–37.

7

Politics

During the first two sessions of the 1768 Parliament Burgoyne was preoccupied with the repercussions of the Preston election. In January 1770, however, he turned his thoughts to the ministerial reconstruction that had recently
taken place. After a decade of dispute with various coalitions, George III found
in Frederick, Lord North, a prime minister who was also a loyal servant.
Burgoyne, however, did not know North well. He could no longer seek the
favor of Lord Bute, George Grenville, or the earl of Chatham. Nor could he
ask Lord Strange for assistance; his brother-in-law and most loyal patron died
at Bath at the age of fifty-five in 1771.[1] Burgoyne had not developed a political
program nor had he achieved a reputation in Parliament; Walpole called him "a
pompous man whose speeches were studied and yet not striking."[2] Approaching the age of fifty, he could boast only one brilliant military expedition.
Nonetheless, he soon embarked upon a cautiously independent political course
in the House of Commons during the first years of the North ministry, perhaps hoping to make his mark as his own man.

Burgoyne first attempted to break away from his custom of reiterating
ministerial policy early in 1771. The Commons was the scene of a mildly
important debate concerning the Falkland Islands, and Burgoyne chose this
time to present his own ideas on governmental policy.[3] When North asked
Parliament to approve an Anglo-Spanish detente, Burgoyne was prompted to
deliver an emotional speech in the House of Commons.[4] Burgoyne condemned
ministerial restraint and urged the House to declare war against Spain in order
to satisfy British honor. The speech was partly inaccurate, self-interested despite demurrers to the contrary, and somewhat theatrical, although not more
so than usual for a Burgoyne address. The colonel's defection was not un-
noticed by the prime minister's opponents. Edmund Burke told the marquis of
Rockingham that "Burgoyne spoke remarkably well. I know not how we came
to have him."[5] Despite the efforts of Burgoyne and others, however, the Commons ultimately approved the agreement with Spain by a vote of 275 to 157.[6]
The king also noticed Burgoyne's independent vote, and he brought the matter
to North's attention. "The great majority yesterday is very creditable for administration," the king told the prime minister, but "Colonel Burgoyne's name

on the side of the Minority appears so extraordinary that I almost immagine [*sic*] that is a mistake."[7] Burgoyne's decision, apparently calculated, was followed by another departure from ministerial loyalty in 1772.

Parliament was prorogued in May 1771 and did not convene again until January 1772. Shortly thereafter, family problems in the royal household became matters for parliamentary debate and therefore Burgoyne's consideration. The king discovered that two of his brothers, the dukes of Cumberland and Gloucester, had apparently married without informing Parliament or requesting his consent. Moreover, they had married commoners in ceremonies which were considered by some to have been questionable, if not invalid. During the course of the ensuing debate the duke of Richmond characterized the conduct of the duke of Gloucester as an affront to Parliament. However, there were others who did not support the expressed wish of the king that Parliament enact a Royal Marriages Bill, which would permit the sovereign to control the selection of marriage partners and prevent "improper marriages made by adolescent, impulsive princes."[8] The marquis of Rockingham called such proposed legislation an extension of the royal prerogative and he opposed the bill. Edmund Burke made similar objections, and a large number of the opposition followed his lead. Burgoyne at first declared that he could vote for the measure in good conscience. But he later spoke against the preamble of the bill after Charles Fox had denounced it. When Fox was silenced Burgoyne abstained from a preliminary vote on the measure, thus incurring the displeasure of the ministerial whip, who ordered him to vote for the bill during the third reading. The king made it clear that Burgoyne would lose his sinecure at Fort William if he did not comply with administrative instruction.[9] Consequently, Burgoyne voted affirmatively for the measure, which passed into law during March 1772.[10] General Henry Conway, Speaker of the House, "applauded Burgoyne's manly honesty (with a sneer)," wrote Horace Walpole, and said that "there was no rule for an honest man but to act as he felt."[11] Burgoyne's independent career thus ended ignominiously, although Conway was excessively caustic. The monarch's favors were distributed in the expectation of support, and the king had no desire to waste his plums, especially when the fate of legislation of personal importance to him was at stake.

Patronage and its consequences were facts of daily life in British politics, but the king was unable and sometimes unwilling to allow his "gold pills" to silence all controversy. Tales of administrative mismanagement on the Indian subcontinent soon reached Westminster, and when Burgoyne decided to investigate those reports he did not incur the royal wrath; he was promoted in May 1772 to the rank of major general, instead.[12]

Burgoyne's motives for pursuing with such diligence and energy the activities of the East India Company were primarily political, although he denied it.[13] The colonel perceived in the company's difficulties an opportunity to display his political talents and to become familiar with the problems of empire. When Parliament reconvened in January 1772, members conducted a review of the company's activities and discovered that serious administrative and fiscal problems had developed during 1771. They concluded that the company was corrupt; it was plundering India and governing the province badly.

Realizing that decisions soon to be made might not be in the interest of the company directors, friends of the organization—many of whom were also stockholders—introduced a judicature bill in March 1772 to provide for a new charter and improved management. Burke and others in opposition replied that the House needed time to collect information before a debate could take place, and North agreed.[14] While desultory speeches and debates continued through March and April, Burgoyne studied the political and economic activities of the company and at length he submitted his own observations and proposals to the House for consideration. The colonel discussed proposals for reorganization that had already been brought forward by friends of the company.[15] Burgoyne proposed that the company ask its creditors to grant a period of grace so that outstanding loans could be repaid. He also advised the organization to reduce its dividend rate of 6 percent. These measures, Burgoyne believed, would bring the company to a state of solvency and establish good faith and credit on a permanent basis.

However, the colonel cautioned, his economic remedy would be effective only if Parliament checked "the rapacity of the servants abroad and the knavery of the Directors at home." Burgoyne wrote a summary of his political plan, which he showed to several of his colleagues in Parliament.[16] He advised the legislature to add to the charter methods of inspection and control. Although the old charter clearly prohibited the conduct of military operations for the sake of plunder, it did not provide methods for restraining such military operations. Thus, Burgoyne's reform proposal included an economic plan to provide solvency and a political plan to insure good government.

The duke of Grafton and others urged him to present his views to the Commons. The colonel did so at the first opportunity, for the ministry decided on April 13, 1772, to consider the judicature bill proposed in March.[17] After the House considered the substance of the measure Burgoyne rose to deliver a dramatic speech.[18] He condemned the "narrow and rotten" system of government that permitted "the most atrocious abuses that ever stained the name of civil Government." Government, he continued, must "hold up the mirror of truth to the Company." Its economic problems and administrative difficulties resulted from a defective constitution, which was framed in such a manner as to "excite and give play to the vicious passions of men." The instruments of government themselves were not evil; in fact, observed Burgoyne, charters were sacred things and "to touch them with the hands of the Crown, or any other single branch of the legislature would be sacrilege." Since the constitution and administrative structure of the company permitted plunder and pillage to occur, Burgoyne challenged the House to take action.[19] There was but one solution to the problem, Burgoyne concluded: the judicature bill ought to include provision for a select parliamentary committee, which Burgoyne himself would chair, to censure the company and provide recommendations for a new constitution and administrative system.

Burgoyne's speech and proposed amendment received a mixed response. Lord North, confessing that he did not understand the affairs of India, approved Burgoyne's motion, but his endorsement was not a wholehearted one.[20] Nor did Burgoyne receive enthusiastic support from the opposition. Nevertheless, the Commons approved the bill with Burgoyne's amendment to appoint a thirty-one-member investigatory committee. Despite the opposition of several cabinet members, and others, the proposal became law by affirmation after a debate that lasted until eleven o'clock in the evening.[21]

After Parliament recessed for the summer the newly appointed commissioners, including Burgoyne, Lord George Germain, Richard Lord Howe, Sir Gilbert Elliott, Isaac Barré and Charles James Fox, among others, delved into the tangled operations of the company.[22] Immediately before the legislators dispersed, however, the prime minister submitted for consideration his own proposals for resolution of the crisis, including approval of a government loan to the India Company, and the imposition of controls upon the operation of local administration in the subcontinent. North had his own game to play, perhaps independently of Burgoyne.

However, observers noted that North had "cut and shuffled exceedingly" during the debates on India, approving Burgoyne's proposal, submitting his own, pleading ignorance of India's affairs, promising the company a loan then suspending their dividends. At last, in November the prime minister bent under the combined weight of the India lobby and the king, who had warned North that it would be disgraceful to waver.[23] Acting decisively, North proposed to establish a second investigating committee, a secret group directly responsible to the ministry, that would meet independently of Burgoyne's select committee.[24] North announced that such a committee would be more efficient and effective than Burgoyne's. Only a committee that was directly responsible to the ministry could have access to all pertinent information, and keep that information secret. North thus obeyed the king's command for action and at the same time assuaged the fears of the company directors that past mistakes would become public knowledge. Burgoyne, upon hearing North's proposal, immediately objected that a second committee would make his own unnecessary and he strenuously denounced the new scheme.[25] Although North assured Burgoyne that his own committee could be revived, the prime minister did not hesitate to urge Parliament to accept his own proposal, which was ultimately approved with a division.[26]

During the Christmas recess the secret committee met with North at Downing Street. In January the prime minister disclosed to Parliament a number of conclusions reached by the committee.[27] But North did not take action, and during February and March friends of the company continued to exert pressure upon the prime minister to grant a loan. North finally agreed to do so, but he emphasized that Parliament was not obliged to save private enterprises that were foundering. However, on May 3 Parliament enacted further measure for the reform of the India Company. North's program thus succeeded. Burgoyne, not surprisingly, was less than delighted to observe the prime minister and his secret committee push aside his own reports. On May 3, immediately after the approval of the North proposals, he declared that the reforms would mean nothing if the guilty were not identified and punished. Otherwise, he warned, plunderers would be encouraged to continue their program of exploitation in India. Burgoyne chose to reveal the information that his select committee had uncovered. The object of his wrath was Robert, Lord Clive, explorer, adventurer, politician, and chief suspect among the plundering nabobs of India. Burgoyne declared that Clive was guilty of crimes "which . . . shocked human nature to conceive," and he proposed three resolutions to punish him. First, he declared that Clive's considerable fortune belonged to the crown because Clive had obtained it as a company employee using military force. Next, he charged that Clive had extorted very great sums of money from native princes for his own personal emolument and that of other people employed by the company. Finally, Burgoyne stated that Clive had abused his power, betrayed his trust, and illegally acquired the sum of £234,000 "to the dishonour and detriment of the State."[28]

Walpole described dramatically the "bitter invectives" that Burgoyne hurled at Clive. He had recapitulated "treacheries and perfidies in which Clive had almost gloried," declared the diarist. The strongly worded resolutions also encountered the opposition of Alexander Wedderburn, the solicitor general, who fought each one of them. Wedderburn demanded "time, suspense, and sober correction of so large and important a question."[29] North, who at first vacillated, ultimately agreed with Wedderburn that the charges of misconduct were too complex to investigate and settle quickly.[30]

Since the mood of the House encouraged procrastination, the subject was not again discussed for several weeks.[31] Then, on May 19 and 20 the House again debated the Clive resolutions, which Burgoyne brought forward for a second reading. During the interval, the king and North had agreed that Burgoyne's charges were too serious to be ignored, and North voted for the resolution even though Clive had enumerated with "arrogant haughtiness" his services to the crown.[32] Wedderburn and Burke supported the adventurer, but Fox and Thurlow condemned him, the latter offering to prepare an indictment to convict him.[33] The motion was not seconded, although Barré and the Bedfords supported Burgoyne. Despite their opposition to Clive, he was permitted to produce witnesses upon his own behalf, and he was personally acquitted of criminal activities by a vote of 119 to 81. Nevertheless, Burgoyne's first motion passed, and a codicil was added charging that Clive had abused his powers.[34] Wedderburn attempted to soften the impact of the amendment when he moved that Clive did "at the same time render great and meritorious services to his country."[35] The Wedderburn resolution was unanimously carried on May 21, and the House of Commons exonerated the adventurer. In an ironic aftermath, Clive committed suicide eighteen months later.

The conduct of the Burgoyne committee during the debates may have been a decisive factor in the House's final decision to vindicate Clive. The announcements of Burgoyne and of his committee were frequently sensational and usually chaotic. In contrast, North's committee of secrecy acted in an orderly, thorough manner.[36] The voters, in large part composed of ordinary House of Commons men, preferred the restrained, competent judgments of that committee.[37] Although in subsequent years historians praised Burgoyne and called his summation against Clive "the most striking proof of his ability as a statesman," Burgoyne's efforts to censure the adventurer were unsuccessful. That the explorer had been guilty of excess, there was no doubt. But the personal malice displayed in Burgoyne's attack against Clive was not helpful to his cause.[38] Burgoyne's relentless denigration of Clive's character may well have been a method of deflecting public animosity away from the question of his own recent behavior at Preston, which Wedderburn raised again during the course of the India investigation.

Wedderburn quoted the charges of Junius that the election of 1768 was decided by force, to which Burgoyne immediately replied:

> I am now personally marked, and rejoice in the opportunity. I have long groaned in secret for any occasion of venting myself against those scandalous aspersions; and if that wretch Junius is lurking here in any corner of this House, I now tell to his face he is an assassin, a liar, and a coward.[39]

Horace Walpole observed that Junius, whose writings "every man almost had pronounced . . . libels," was hardly an appropriate source for Wedderburn the prosecutor of libels, to quote. "Here was the Solicitor-General," he wrote, "ranking the aspersions of that writer against the tender honour of an officer, an officer that [sic] had distinguished himself, and that was countenanced by the Crown, as matter for parliamentary charge against a member of Parliament!"[40]

During March and April 1774, Parliament became increasingly concerned about reports of renewed riot and violence in the American colonies. After three years of superficial tranquillity, Anglo-American relations deteriorated dangerously as colonial Massachusetts reacted to North's tea scheme for the East India Company. When news of the Boston Tea Party prompted an unsuccessful motion to repeal the tea tax of 1767, Burgoyne censured the colonials severely in a widely noted speech.[41]

> I look upon America to be our child, which I think we have already spoiled by too much indulgence. . . . It is said, if you remove this duty, you will remove all grievances in America: but I am apprehensive that it is the right of

taxation they contend about, and not the tax. It is the independent state of that country upon the legislature of this, which is contended for.

The major general's comments reflected the thinking of king and cabinet as well as the mood of the House, which approved coercive legislation and also the appointment of General Thomas Gage as military governor of the Massachusetts Bay Colony.[42] Burgoyne thus fell in line with ministerial policy; he lacked the qualities of leadership that would have made him a statesman. But his attention to imperial problems waned with the prorogation of the legislature in June and he devoted his time to a new venture.[43]

During the summer of 1774 Burgoyne supervised final preparations for the presentation of his first dramatic effort, a play he composed to celebrate the marriage of Lady Elizabeth Hamilton, daughter of the duke of Hamilton, to Lord Stanley, grandson of the earl of Derby and son of the late Lord Strange.[44] The play, entitled *The Maid of the Oaks*, was performed at "The Oaks" in Surrey in June 1774. Burgoyne appeared as master of ceremonies, greeting the guests as they arrived and conducting them to what he described as a "voluptuous scene" on the back lawn of the estate. He had prepared a "fête champêtre," which included the installation of an orangery, a concealed musical orchestra, ninepins, swings, archery stands, and a large dance floor.[45] The festivities were followed by a sumptuous dinner "on the most costly dishes all hot and tempting." The fête cost £5,000; Horace Walpole speculated that Burgoyne had "bought all the orange trees round London" and thought that the haycocks were "made of straw coloured satin."[46] After dinner the masqueraded guests moved to the theatre, where the plot of Burgoyne's *Maid of the Oaks* unfolded.[47]

At the conclusion of the play, the wedding guests adjourned to the dance floor where the orchestra played minuets and country airs until three in the morning. The program of Burgoyne's "fête" was repeated for five nights after the wedding, and soon word of his two-act comedy spread to London where David Garrick expressed an interest in producing it in the West End.[48] The century's outstanding manager was glad to meet the fashionable cavalryman and parliamentarian, and after a conference, they agreed that Garrick would rewrite the dialogue and stage an expanded version of the play at the Theatre Royal, Drury Lane. The new production opened on November 12, 1774, and ran for several nights.[49] Mrs. Frances Abington, who had played the part of Lady Bab Lardoon in the original company, and who had earlier originated the part of Lady Teazle in *The School for Scandal*, appeared in the London production. Although critics praised her characterization as loving and amusing, the ingenue who played Maria received unkind words. The indefatigible commentator Horace Walpole said, "There is a new puppet show at Drury Lane, as fine as scenes can make it, called 'The Maid of the Oaks,' and as dull as the author could not help making it." Nevertheless, Burgoyne's work became a prototype of a new form of musical comedy, which reflected the influence of middle-class tastes upon dramatic productions.[50]

Refreshed by his summer success, Burgoyne next turned to the question of parliamentary elections, for Lord North announced that Parliament would be dissolved on September 30, 1774.[51] The king, anxiously contemplating American plans for a Continental Congress, wished to consolidate his power in a House of Commons that soon would have to make unpleasant decisions concerning his American empire. During the election campaign which ensued, few real issues were debated or even discussed, and after George III provided generous campaign funds to insure the election of court supporters, Lord North was pleased but not surprised to watch the safe return of a comfortable majority of king's friends. Over seventy members of the 1774 Parliament held court appointments or other ministerial sinecures, and Burgoyne, who was returned for Preston without a contest, was counted among them.[52]

The new Parliament almost immediately became absorbed with the rising storm in America. In January 1775, members received reports of the deliberations of the first Continental Congress, and listened to a speech from the throne that committed the North ministry to a firm, unyieldingly conservative attitude toward the colonial rebellion. Although the aged earl of Chatham offered suggestions for a compromise in late January and early February 1775, the ministry had other plans, and Burgoyne was included in them.[53]

On February 2, the secretary at war called Burgoyne to his office for an interview. Barrington informed him that the government had decided that "everything in America would mend" when Burgoyne "and two other Generals for whom he was to make out letters of service, should arrive there."[54] The other officers, both of whom had been promoted with Burgoyne in 1772 to the rank of major general, were William Howe and Henry Clinton, and both of them accepted the government's assignment to Boston, Massachusetts, to serve as a staff for General Thomas Gage. However, Burgoyne protested that such an appointment would constitute the most disagreeable event of his life, and that, unless the assignment was a royal command, he would decline for professional and personal reasons.[55] Having heard similar protestations from both Clinton and Howe, Barrington assured Burgoyne that the king had decided the issue. The general accepted, convincing himself that he had placed the national interest above personal happiness.

Burgoyne's ambition did not cease, however. He soon arranged an interview with the prime minister. What he wanted was a position similar to General Gage's, and his meeting with North constituted the first step in his plan. Conscious that he had opposed the ministry on numerous occasions, Burgoyne anticipated the meeting with North cautiously. Upon greeting the prime minister, Burgoyne explained that his opposition in the House of Commons was consistent with his independent conduct during previous ministries. Indeed, he had at times voted "even against the sentiments of the late Lord Strange, the man of whose integrity and political judgment I had the highest

veneration, and who was besides my benefactor, my patron, and my friend."[56]
Burgoyne hoped Lord North would look upon his independence with the same
benevolence that had characterized Lord Strange. He emphasized that he sub-
scribed to North's position on America and offered his services to the crown.
He also expressed surprise that William Tryon, governor of New York, had

**Lord North, by Rinke after Dance. Reproduced by permission of the William L.
Clements Library, University of Michigan.**

been absent so long from his post, and he noted that the lieutenant governor,
Cadwallader Colden, was advanced in age. The general made it clear that he
wanted to be appointed military governor of New York, and he asked North
for that assignment, which would allow him to work independently of Gage.
Burgoyne's audacious request, made after his independent career in Parliament, was ill timed and futile. Gage was a veteran of many years of service in
Canada and over ten years of tenure as commander in chief of the British army

in America. Furthermore, Gage was a full general. The prime minister refused to commit himself to Burgoyne's plan, although the interview ended cordially.

Burgoyne persisted in his efforts. He visited the chambers of Charles Jenkinson, Lord George Germain, and Sir Gilbert Elliott.[57] Jenkinson, who had first suggested Burgoyne's nomination and who had first informed Burgoyne of the ministry's intention to send him to America, endorsed Burgoyne's new plan heartily. In fact, he was thought to have wanted Burgoyne appointed commander in chief in America after Howe, Clinton, and Gage were withdrawn. Continuing the canvass, Burgoyne approached Lord George Germain, soon to become secretary of state for the American colonies. He found Germain "communicative and friendly, a sort of behaviour he has shown towards me upon all occasions." Burgoyne considered him spirited and well informed, more so than any member of the ministry. Germain listened to Burgoyne's proposal, agreed that the administration of New York had been neglected, and revealed that he was "in all consultations" upon American measures: "Indeed," wrote Burgoyne, "his warmth had led him almost to offer himself to Lord North."[58] Lord George said he "knew not where they could find a more proper person than [Burgoyne]" to send to New York, but he did nothing to help accomplish that goal.

Burgoyne next approached John Pownall, Dartmouth's secretary and Burgoyne's distant cousin, and requested an interview, whereupon Pownall launched into a "long, formal, and sometimes unintelligible discussion" of the American crisis. The general got along more easily with Dartmouth himself, in whom he observed "*much* politeness and benevolence of mind, *too* much attention to his secretary whose parts appeared to me inferior to his own, and a good deal of caution in committing an opinion upon nice subjects, though not more of it than was excusable in a minister conversing with a perfect stranger."[59] The two old Westminsters chatted amiably, but Dartmouth was reluctant to commit himself to any plan for Burgoyne's advancement in America. The general was not greatly disappointed; he decided to "work [his] own measures through other engines" in order to obtain the New York appointment, "the desirable situation for doing the public service, and acquiring personal credit." Burgoyne again presented his qualifications to the ministers, only to receive again Dartmouth's rejection, which he described "as a mere ministerial put-off; knowing, that according to the secret intention then, Tryon was not, at least not speedily, to return."[60] Burgoyne, meanwhile, informed Howe of his ambitions concerning North America. Wishing himself employed "in some more active station than the mere inspection of a brigade," Burgoyne promised not to interfere with Howe's personal plans but he warned that "New York opened another line of business." Howe rather skillfully avoided Burgoyne's questions concerning New York by denying that he sought to obtain the Boston assignment. Burgoyne said he knew "the reason given publicly by all his friends for that wish was the obligation his family owed to the Bostonians, who had raised a monument to the late Lord Howe, and particularly complimented the general."[61] Howe's real reluctance, however, stemmed from his low opinion of Gage—or so Burgoyne believed.

Burgoyne continued to worry that he would be sent to Boston merely "to make a triumvirate of reputation." He could not remain still, and shortly went to see Sir John Blaquiere, chief secretary to the lord lieutenant of Ireland, who had "a head excellently turned for ministerial intrigue." Burgoyne was well received, being "entrusted with secrets of the most important and most private nature." Blaquiere disclosed that both Lord Dartmouth and Lord Suffolk, secretary of state for the Northern Department, preferred Howe, and were "indefatigably at work" on his behalf, while the king and Lord North were very graciously disposed toward Burgoyne. When Burgoyne attended George III's levee he was the object of royal approbation, and the king again uttered "the most obliging expressions." Time was passing, however, and even Lord George Germain wondered aloud whether the major generals would be called before the cabinet for an interview before Gage's instructions were written.

No formal council was held, but Burgoyne was invited to a series of cabinet dinners. The first of these, at Lord Dartmouth's home, included: Howe; Clinton; Burgoyne; Lord Sandwich, first lord of the admiralty; Viscount Barrington; General Harvey, master general of the ordnance; Governor Hutchinson; Pownall; the earl of Hardwicke; and others. A "motley" assembly, thought Burgoyne, not one to accomplish business. Speaking on behalf of the cabinet, Lord Dartmouth asked Burgoyne for permission to reprint his speech on tea so that it could be distributed in America. Unfortunately for Burgoyne's ambitions, it was Dartmouth's only reference to him or to America, and the general was left once again to speculate upon the part he would play in forthcoming events.

The triumvirate—Howe, Clinton, and Burgoyne—remained totally in the dark concerning plans for the campaign. Burgoyne marveled at his "sacrifice" of leaving family and friends, "only to attain the character of a cypher." Yearning for a high-level appointment in America, he sought Lord North once again, but the prime minister, like Dartmouth, suggested that Gage was the appropriate officer to delegate posts in the military departments of North America. "I shook my head at that insinuation," said Burgoyne, "and requested his Lordship to do me at least the honour to treat me like a man not totally ignorant of the world; that I knew General Howe was using every engine of interest for the preference, and it was preposterous to suppose a private hint would not be given to General Gage where to give it."[62] North admitted the truth of Burgoyne's observations, and said that a promise had been made early and unadvisedly to Howe, but he hoped to reconcile all difficulties. As it happened, neither Howe nor Burgoyne went to New York in 1775; both of them joined Henry Clinton as advisors to Gage in Boston. The general lamented his failure to obtain a high appointment. Burgoyne was junior in rank, if not in age, to

Howe, Gage, Clinton, and most of the other officers with whom he wished to compete or supersede, yet he was one of only three officers who were selected for appointment to the North American staff in 1775. A man less ambitious might have accounted this new position a signal honor. It is possible, though, that the ministry proposed Burgoyne for appointment to America in order to remove him from the political arena of Westminster where the Clive investigation had caused considerable embarrassment. Burgoyne's brash and insistent importunings may betoken his suspicion that such was the case and represent his attempt to get all he could out of the ministry's desire to rid itself of him. Whatever the reasons for his appointment, and despite his expressed discontent, Burgoyne took advantage of the opportunity to return for the first time since 1762 to active military duty.

Notes

1. Burke, ed., *Peerage.*

2. Steuart, ed., *Last Journals of Walpole,* 1:80.

3. DeFonblanque, *Episodes,* 92–93.

4. February 13, 1771, William Cobbett, ed., *The Parliamentary History of England, from the Earliest Period to the Year 1803,* 36 vols. (London: T. C. Hansard, 1806–20), 16:1364–68.

5. February 16, 1771, Burke to Rockingham, Burke, *Correspondence,* 2:199.

6. Lord Weymouth, who had urged the government to declare war, resigned from the Cabinet as a result of the vote.

7. February 14, 1771, the king to North, Sir John W. Fortescue, ed., *Correspondence of King George III from 1760 to December 1783,* 6 vols. (London: Macmillan, 1972–28), 2:218.

8. Steuart, ed., *Last Journals of Walpole,* vol. 1, pp. 26–70.

9. March 12, 1772, the king to North, Fortescue, ed., *Correspondence,* vol. 2, pp. 328–29.

10. Steuart, ed., *Last Journals of Walpole,* 1:53, 55, 69.

11. Ibid., p. 66.

12. May 25, 1772, *Army List for 1772,* p. 3. Promotions for Guy Carleton, Henry Clinton, and William Howe were announced on the same day.

13. April 13, 1772, W. Cobbett, ed., *The Parliamentary History,* 17:453–58.

14. March 30, 1772, East India Judicature Bill, Carl B. Cone, *Burke and the Nature of Politics: The Age of the American Revolution* (Lexington, Ky.: University of Kentucky Press, 1957), p. 235.

15. John Burgoyne, comments on financial condition of the East India Company, DeFonblanque, *Episodes,* pp. 94–96.

16. John Burgoyne, "A Short Account of the Political Conduct of the East Indian Company's Servants," DeFonblanque, *Episodes,* pp. 96–98.

17. Lucy S. Sutherland, *The East India Company in Eighteenth-Century Politics* (Oxford: Clarendon Press, 1952), p. 231.

18. April 13, 1772, Cobbett, ed., *Parliamentary History,* 17:453–58.

19. Ibid.

20. Cone, *Burke,* p. 235.

21. Steuart, ed., *Last Journals of Walpole,* 1:84–85.

22. October 29, 1772, Burke, *Correspondence,* 72:354, note 1; *The Cambridge History of the British Empire: British India,* ed. H. H. Dodwell (Cambridge: At the University Press, 1929), 4:186.

23. November 25, 1772, the king to North, Fortescue, ed., *Correspondence,* 2:407.

24. Steuart, ed., *Last Journals of Walpole,* 1:161.

25. Cobbett, ed., *Parliamentary History,* 17:534–35.

26. Ibid., 17:535.

27. Sutherland, *East India Company,* p. 238; although the company was £9.2 million in debt, he said, there remained assets of £4.7 million. Since the company had requested a loan, the committee proposed that Parliament approve the payment of £1.4 million to the company immediately.

28. Lord Edmond Fitzmaurice, *Life of William, Earl of Shelburne, Afterwards First Marquis of Lansdowne,* 3 vols. (London: Macmillan, 1875–76), 1:447–48; see also Cobbett, *Parliamentary History,* 17:855–56, 872–73, 880–81.

29. Steuart, ed., *Last Journals of Walpole,* 1:199–200.

30. Ibid., p. 200.

31. May 10, 1773, Namier and Brooke, eds., *Commons,* 1:143; Sutherland, *East India Company,* p. 236.

32. Steuart, ed. *Last Journals of Walpole,* 1:200–201.

33. Robert Gore-Browne, *Chancellor Thurlow: The Life and Times of an Eighteenth Century Lawyer* (London: Hamilton, 1953), p. 78.

34. Steuart, ed., *Last Journals of Walpole,* 1:231; May 22, 1773, North to the king, Fortescue, ed., *Correspondence,* 2:490.

35. Cobbett, ed., *Parliamentary History,* 17:882.

36. Sutherland, *East India Company,* pp. 236–37.

37. Ibid.

38. As John Brooke observed, Burgoyne's "revelations had considerable influence on parliamentary operation, but it did not shape government policy: Burgoyne was only the fly on the chariot wheel." Namier and Brooke, eds., *Commons,* 2:141–45.

39. Steuart, ed., *Last Journals of Walpole,* 1:202–3.

40. Ibid.

41. April 19, 1774, Cobbett, ed., *Parliamentary History,* 17:1271. For a detailed examination of North's tea plan, see Benjamin W. Labaree, *The Boston Tea Party* (New York: Oxford University Press, 1964).

42. April 19, 1774, North to the king, Fortescue, ed., *Correspondence,* 3:95.

43. Burgoyne had by 1774 spoken sixty-six times in the House of Commons. P. D. G. Thomas, "Votes in the House of Commons, 1768–1774," *Bulletin of the Institute of Historical Research,* 35:220–26.

44. Leslie and Taylor, *Reynolds,* 2:82; DeFonblanque, *Episodes,* p. 395; "John Burgoyne," *DNB;* Wrottesley, *Sir John Burgoyne,* 1:4.

45. Hudleston, *Burgoyne,* p. 324.

46. Leslie and Taylor, *Reynolds,* 2:82.

47. John Burgoyne, *The Maid of the Oaks* (London: T. Beckett, 1774). The text may be conveniently consulted in John Burgoyne, *Dramatic and Poetical Works,* 2 vols. (London: C. Whittingham, 1808), 1:37–122.

48. Hudleston, *Burgoyne,* pp. 324–25.

49. "John Burgoyne," *DNB.*

50. W. J. Lawrence, "The Drama and the Theatre," in Turberville, ed., *Johnson's England,* 2:169.

51. Cobbett, ed., *Parliamentary History,* 17:1408.

52. Clemesha, *Preston,* p. 207.

53. Burgoyne was included in a list of generals who were to be appointed to commands in North America, written in the king's hand, December 1774, Fortescue, ed., *Correspondence,* 3:162.

54. John Burgoyne, "Private Memorandum," DeFonblanque, *Episodes,* pp. 120–33.

55. Ibid., pp. 121, 123.

56. Ibid., p. 124.

57. Ibid., p. 126.
58. John Burgoyne, "Private Memorandum," DeFonblanque, *Episodes,* p. 126.
59. Ibid., p. 128.
60. Ibid.
61. Ibid., p. 129.
62. Ibid., p. 132.

8

In America with Gage

When Viscount Barrington informed Burgoyne in February 1775 of his assignment to serve with Howe and Clinton in America, the major general had
exclaimed that such an appointment would be the most disagreeable event of
his life. He suffered greatly making a decision about the appointment: "men of
the world are too callously composed to conceive what I endured." Burgoyne
was not a modest man, and it may be concluded that his remarks were nothing
more than standard responses expected of British politicians in his situation. To
be sure, he would miss the comforts of life in London and the companionship
of his wife, to whom he apparently remained devoted. He regretted a separation "for a length of time, perhaps for ever, from the tenderest, the faithfullest,
the most aimiable companion and friend that ever man was blessed with—a
wife, in whom during four and twenty years I never could find a momentary
act of blame!"[1] Burgoyne acknowledged the "levities, the inattentions, and
dissipations of my common course of life," and reflected upon his own un-
worthiness of Lady Charlotte: "to supply the requisites of her rank, to reward
the virtues of her character, I could only bequeath her a legacy of my impru-
dences."[2] Perhaps Burgoyne exaggerated his imprudence; although he spent
considerable sums on gambling, his income from appointments as major general in the army, colonel of the Sixteenth Regiment, and governor of Fort
William exceeded thirty-five hundred pounds annually.[3] Furthermore, he
owned properties in London and Preston, for Lady Charlotte enjoyed the
luxuries of a Mayfair residence in Hertford Street as well as use of country
homes in Lancashire, and Epsom, Surrey.[4] Despite Burgoyne's financial and
sexual improprieties, his love for his wife was evident, at least in his writings,
throughout their married life. Shortly before he departed for America, Burgoyne sent to the king a remarkable letter, not to be opened unless he died in
battle. In that "address from beyond the grave," he implored the monarch to
take Lady Charlotte under the royal protection. "What will be her consola-
tion?" he asked. "Wretched state, when poverty is disregarded, only because it
is the least poignant of our sensations, and the pains of distemper are alleviated
by the hopes that they tend to our dissolution."[5] In conclusion, Burgoyne

asked the king to "smooth her passage through the remains of life."

On February 3, 1775, Burgoyne received official confirmation of his appointment to the American staff.[6] He also obtained permission to return to England for the winter, unless "he should have a separate command, or . . . should be employ'd in any service . . . beyond the common routine of military business."[7] Before his departure, however, Burgoyne participated in a debate that Lord North prompted on February 20 when he disclosed proposals for conciliating the American colonies, including exemption of internal taxation for those provinces which agreed to contribute funds for the administration of civil justice and military defense.[8] During the ensuing debate, which lasted for three days, the opposition branded North's scheme inadequate as well as insincere. Welbore Ellis, Henry Dundas, Edmund Burke, and others (including Burgoyne) spoke against the measure. Burgoyne took the opportunity to clarify his position concerning America. He contended that his participation in debates during 1774 as well as his appearance in certain divisions of the House in 1775 "before I had any knowledge or suspicion of my destination" had led to misrepresentation of his views on America. The "licentious prints," Burgoyne continued, charged that the bloodthirsty Germain had chosen generals who were best equipped to wreak "havock and destruction" across America, while members of the House believed that officers would use their discretion to implement coercive policies then being debated in the Commons. Although admitting that "there is a charm in the very wanderings and dreams of liberty that disarms an Englishman," Burgoyne advocated punishment for the American colonies rather than conciliation: "While we remember that we are contending against brothers and fellow subjects, we must also remember that we are contending in this crisis for the fate of the British Empire." Repeating the argument raised by Major John Acland that Americans would immediately deny British parliamentary authority, Burgoyne warned that the colonists would reject North's conciliatory proposals. Arguing that the British government had perpetrated "great and manifest" errors in colonial policy during the previous ten years, Burgoyne nevertheless refused to debate further questions of real and virtual representation or external and internal taxation "till one's head grows dizzy with distinctions." Agreeing that inquiries were proper at proper times, and that conciliation was an important tactic, Burgoyne concluded that "the refusal of [conciliation] will be as explicitly and decisively declaratory, as any manifesto could express, of the principles upon which they act who continue to resist, and it puts the dispute upon clear ground." Arguing forcefully that parliamentary rights were a cause to "fight for, to bleed and die for," notwithstanding the opposition's recriminations, Burgoyne urged action, "*Now*, this unparalleled moment in English History, when we tamely suffer government to be suspended—when we sit here the mere shadow of authority—The phantom of a Parliament." Otherwise, the officer concluded, Great Britain would "revert to her primitive insignificancy in the Map of the World, and the Congress of Philadelphia" would become the "Legislature to dispense the blessings of Empire."

Ten weeks later—one day before the shot heard round the world was fired—Burgoyne departed with Clinton and Howe for Portsmouth where they embarked upon the frigate *Cerberus* bound for Boston, hub of Massachusetts Bay Colony.[9] After a swift crossing, they reached the American continent on May 25. The inhabitants, emboldened after the battles of Lexington and Concord, greeted the newcomers with derision:

> Behold the Cerberus the Atlantic plough,
> Her precious cargo, Burgoyne, Clinton, Howe,
>   Bow, wow, wow[10]

As the ship edged into Boston harbor, Burgoyne was informed that ten thousand "country people" surrounded Gage's garrison, to which he is said to have replied: "What? Ten thousand peasants keep five thousand of the King's troops shut up? Well, let *us* get in, and we'll soon find elbow-room."[11] When he disembarked, Burgoyne found to his dismay no room at all. A "rabble in arms" had "advanced their sentries to pistol shot of our out-guards."[12] Burgoyne thought the Americans bold and insolent, "a preposterous parade of military arrangement," yet in a state of "stupefaction" and "despondency" which he attributed to the recent clashes at Lexington and Concord.[13] The Americans replied to Burgoyne's rudeness in kind: "Should the boasting General Burgoyne ridicule the simplicity of our American Cincinnatus Putnam and be asked at the same time where his master's orders found *him* when he was commanded to repair to Boston, the answer would most probably be, 'in a gambling house or brothel.' "[14]

In due course the major general met his beleaguered commander in chief, Thomas Gage. Second son of Viscount Gage of Firle, Sussex, Lieutenant General Gage was a veteran of the French and Indian War and held since 1763 the first military post in the colonies. A cautious, decent man, Gage was unpopular in Massachusetts because he became a symbol of the standing army so detested by the inhabitants. He was equally unpopular in London because it was believed he had not acted with sufficient speed or determination to quell the earliest manifestations of discontent in Massachusetts.[15] In fact, the king had considered replacing him in December 1774, but General Jeffrey Amherst had refused to accept the burdens of that office.[16] Now the triumvirate was sent in place of Amherst to bolster Gage's direction of the war and to provide him an administrative staff.

Burgoyne thought well of his commander in chief personally; he bore high respect for his private virtues.[17] Gage had a talent for civil administration "calculated to dispense the offices of justice and humanity." However, Burgoyne resented Gage's higher station: "his mind has not resources for great, and sudden, and hardy exertions, which spring self-suggested in extraordinary

characters, and generally overbear all opposition."[18] Burgoyne criticized severely Gage's hesitation to act before the clashes at Lexington and Concord.
Although Gage was right to seize the rebel stores of arms and ammunition on
April 19, said Burgoyne, "we can only wonder that it was not sooner
adopted."[19] Gage should have captured Samuel Adams and John Hancock; he
should have obtained secret intelligence of enemy plans; he had neglected to
occupy those posts near the British garrison that would have allowed him to
keep open lines of communication with the countryside. Further, he had not
provided ample ammunition for his troops. Burgoyne condemned Gage's plan
for April 19 and his "want of preparation of the consequences": "Thousands"
of rebels were moving from the countryside to Boston every day; they stole
cattle from the pastures adjacent to Boston harbor; they burned houses; they
took away the guns of a British warship "in the view of an admiral and a
lieutenant-general." Burgoyne also found grave deficiencies of funds and supplies, especially wagons and horses.[20] Soldiers were not available in sufficient
numbers to secure anything more than communication between the army camp
and outlying magazines.[21]

Clearly, then, Gage was unequal to the task according to Burgoyne. Admitting that Gage's situation was one "in which Caesar might have failed," he did
not believe that the Roman would have mismanaged finances. When Burgoyne's grant of five hundred pounds for equipage did not arrive, he censured
Gage anew.[22] Burgoyne acknowledged that subordinate departments of the
army in Boston may have been negligent; perhaps the source of the trouble lay
hidden in Whitehall, although he was quick to exonerate Lord North and Lord
Dartmouth of the "dirtiness of office."[23] But the lack of immediate funds
provided Burgoyne with a personal grievance, and he took advantage of it.
Gage, he reported, "cooly advises us to write home to our agents for money to
be remitted in specie."[24] More convinced than ever that Gage was not only
incompetent but was also out of favor in London, Burgoyne continued to
attack the man who in many respects had done nothing worse than obey
orders. Affecting objectivity, Burgoyne damned Gage with faint praise as he
observed that it was "no reflection to say he is unequal to the present situation,
for few characters in the world would be fit for it. It requires a genius of the
very first class, together with uncommon resolution, and a firm reliance upon
support at home," he confided to General Elliott.[25] Obviously Burgoyne imagined himself the genius in whose mind solutions sprang unbidden. Believing
that he could have succeeded where even Caesar failed, Burgoyne took every
opportunity to discredit Gage: "In commenting upon the circumstances of his
public conduct," Burgoyne told Lord Rochford, he found "reason to justify
him in some, to excuse him in others, and to pity him in all."[26] Nor did he
neglect to bemoan continuously his own "humble station," as he described it to
Barrington.[27] And he told Lord North that his "portion of command, in point
of numbers, is inferior to what has often fallen to my lot as Lieut.-Colonel; and
when I look round me, I am persuaded it is not likely to be mended in point of

enterprise."[28] Burgoyne's message was clear: Gage was unequal to his assignment; Burgoyne was superbly qualified, but did not have the authority to act.
Since he could not lead troops in battle, he suggested for himself the role of
peacemaker. Burgoyne asked the prime minister to dismiss him

> from the Army as early as the propriety of any service in which I may then
> be employed will permit—that the Admiral [Samuel Graves] be at the same
> time instructed to facilitate my passage to New York, Philadelphia, or any
> other Province which in my judgement His Majesty's service may call me
> and afterwards to convey me to England.[29]

He wished to confront the Americans not as a warrior, but as "a friend of
human nature." He was certain many colonials would support suggestions for
peace; his observations could become the basis for future government policy.
Although Burgoyne said he desired to act as a private person, he made provision for an official role: "Should it be considered as a measure of state, I beg the
favour of your Lordship to put it in proper train."[30] Burgoyne planned to
return to England in October as his presence was of importance to his private
affairs.[31]

The plan was not approved. The government appointed commissioners of
peace during the following year, but Burgoyne was not among those selected.[32]
Fortunately, he managed to stifle the "regret of being otherwise employed."
Among other things, he composed a proclamation for Gage,[33] who wished to
make known to the American people the decisions of government. The British
crown declared Massachusetts to be in a state of rebellion. Although those who
returned to allegiance were assured of pardon, all others were subject to martial
law. The "flagitious" offenses of John Hancock and Samuel Adams particularly
marked them as leaders of rebellion, and called for "condign punishment." The
proclamation, couched in Burgoyne's "most inflated style," was hardly appropriate to the situation.[34] Nor was it new; Lord George Germain remarked to
General Irwin: "You will see in a moment that Burgoyne composed Gage's
proclamation. It is very like the last speech we heard him make,"[35] and James
Robertson, one of Gage's brigadier generals, observed that people said there
was "more attention paid to style than to policy."[36] Burgoyne's effort did not
deter the Bostonians, nor did the presence of fresh troops.[37] Residents of
Boston sent the major general derisive congratulations, worked with "double
diligence," and on June 17, two months after Lexington and Concord, fought
the king's troops for a second time.

Burgoyne witnessed the conflict at Bunker Hill. Although he had "formed
the Plan" in concert with Gage, Howe, and Clinton,[38] Burgoyne did not
participate actively, as he complained to Lord Rochford: "the inferiority of my
station as youngest Major-General upon the staff, left me almost a useless
spectator, for my whole business lay in presiding during part of the action over
a cannonade to assist the left."[39] The strategy to seize Dorchester Heights,

Sir William Howe, engraving by Rogers. Reproduced by permission of the William
L. Clements Library, University of Michigan.

Sir Henry Clinton, engraving from a miniature by J. Smart. Reproduced by permission of the William L. Clements Library, University of Michigan.

Bunker's and Breed's Hills, was scheduled to be executed on the eighteenth. However, perhaps because Burgoyne spoke indiscreetly, the American patriots discovered British intentions two days early and the plan was not used.[40] Not surprisingly, Burgoyne found on the seventeenth, "at Dawn of day, . . . the enemy had pushed Entrenchments with great Diligence, During the Night, on the Heights of Charles-Town, were there in force, and we evidently saw that every Hour gave them new Strength."[41]

The battle took place a day earlier than Gage expected and the British lost the element of surprise. Howe led two thousand soldiers protected by the fleet anchored nearby to the peninsula. He intended to march up Breed's Hill and take it: "Clinton and myself took our Stand (for we had not a fixed post) in a large Battery directly opposite to Charles Town and commanding it, and also reaching to the heights above it, and thereby facilitating Howe's attack."[42] Howe deployed his men in a formation which Burgoyne called "perfect." However, American soldiers in Charleston opened fire on the troops and the general asked Burgoyne and Clinton to set that town ablaze. "No sooner said than done," reported Burgoyne. "We threw in a Parcel of Shells, and the whole was instantly in flames." Burgoyne's battery, in concert with frigates and ships of the line, kept up "an incessant Fire upon the height." Shortly, Howe attacked again. Although Burgoyne escaped American fire, "except two Cannon Balls that went 100 yards over our heads," Howe's left wing was routed. Clinton, "without waiting for Orders," rushed to rescue two battalions that should have been sent to Howe, but were instead "in Embarrassment, which way to march."[43] Howe and Clinton carried on bravely, but the patriot forces swept them back several more times, inflicting substantial damage. The "Day ended with Glory," wrote Burgoyne, but "the Loss was uncommon in Officers, for the Numbers engaged." He praised Howe, whose conduct "will not want my testimony to do it justice,"[44] and had kind words for the privates, "a very few rascally drafts, and recruits taken out of Irish jails excepted."[45] Admitting that the American defense was "well conceived and obstinately maintained," and that the patriots were brave and skillful, Burgoyne insisted that Bunker Hill "establishes the ascendancy of the King's troops, though opposed by more than treble numbers."[46] Two months after the engagement, Burgoyne repeated that opinion.[47]

Although he admitted that the American retreat was "no flight; was covered with bravery and even military skill," he said the war was a rebellion instigated by men of ill will who could be defeated by the regular army of Great Britain. That was the lesson Burgoyne derived from the battle of Bunker Hill.[48] He would continue to underestimate that force.

Burgoyne soon had a second opportunity to make a mark during his residence in America. General Charles Lee, Burgoyne's former colleague in Portugal who had recently entered the war on the American side, sent the general a propaganda letter.[49] Brilliant but unbalanced, Lee thrived upon controversy. He warned Burgoyne that Britain could not defeat America. Protesting his

General Charles Lee, engraver unknown. Reproduced by permission of the Prints Division, New York Public Library.

esteem and affection for Burgoyne, Lee urged him to leave the British army and join the patriots. He reminded the general of North's "wickedness and treachery" during the investigation of the India Company. Lee contended that America should not be taxed without representation in Parliament. Even if the colonies were represented, he believed that tax collections would not be used "to the purpose of . . . easing the mother country," but would be diverted for "the enormous fund for corruption." The fiery Lee invoked the spirit of liberty and the British constitution, said Gage's mind was "totally poisoned," and urged Burgoyne to resist becoming "infected" by "the same miscreants who have infatuated General Gage."

Burgoyne read the letter for what it was and returned to Lee a similar piece of propaganda.[50] He flattered the former British officer, and hoped he would return to the royal army. Their correspondence was interrupted for a month by the battle of Bunker Hill, but on July 5 Burgoyne, after consultation with Gage, dispatched a second friendly message to Lee.[51] Lee resumed the dialogue in equally cordial terms, sending compliments to Howe and Clinton.[52] After three days of preparation, Burgoyne dispatched a long and dramatic letter to Lee.[53] Confessing "it was my pride to be known for your friend," he attempted to win Lee back to the British army. He contended that the British constitution could be safeguarded only when the supremacy of king in Parliament was guaranteed: "a compound, indefinite, indefeasible power, coeval with the origin of the empire, and coextensive over all its parts."[54] Burgoyne announced that he was no stranger to Locke; he was in fact filled with reverence "almost amounting to idolatry" toward the old Whigs. Nevertheless, he could not support those who charged that the crown misused its power: "I hold that resistance, to be justifiable, must be directed against the usurpation of undue exercise of power; and that it is most criminal when directed against any power itself inherent in the constitution."[55] Burgoyne repeated his belief that the American war was "a struggle for total independency," not merely a wish to be relieved of paying taxes, or a philosophical objection to external or internal tariffs, or a plea for just representation. He did not object to the elimination of imperial taxation, for "it is in the power of the Colonies to put an end to the exercise of taxation immediately, and for ever." But breaking the link of empire was to deny that "the whole of our political system depends upon the preservation of its great and essential parts distinctly, and no part is so great and essential as supremacy of legislation."[56] Burgoyne proposed to meet Lee at a house located in Boston, and promised to obtain a parole of honor for Lee's safe return.

The letter received attention on both sides of the Atlantic. Charles Stuart, son of the earl of Bute, reported an interesting conversation between two army majors that he overheard while on duty. One of the officers observed that "if Gen[eral] Burgoyne had authority from His Majesty to write the Letter, he was certain Congress would be happy to receive the terms he hinted at. I fear the General has said too much, and I think replied to Lee very improperly."[57] On the other side of the ocean, Major Samuel B. Webb told Silas Deane: "A certain something runs through the whole of his letter which shews they [the British] are sick at the stomach."[58] Burgoyne had overstepped his authority when he suggested that the colonists might stop paying taxes, and Webb's suspicion of Burgoyne's sincerity was shared in the Massachusetts Provincial Congress, where Lee delivered the letter on July 8, 1775.[59] Lee hoped that if the Congress approved a meeting with Burgoyne, it would "depute some one gentleman of their body to accompany General Lee, and be witness of the conversation."[60] Congress received the proposal with great caution, at first agreeing to the meeting, then changing its mind.[61] Lee wrote to Burgoyne once again on July 11.[62] He dismissed some of the general's counterarguments, especially those pertaining to conciliation. Lamenting that both he and Burgoyne had made up their minds concerning America, Lee declared there was no reason for a meeting. He was apprehensive that an interview "might create those jealousies and suspicions so natural to a people struggling in the dearest of all causes, that of their liberty, property, wives, children, and their future generation."[63] The correspondence lapsed.

General Gage used these letters for propaganda purposes, as did the Americans. The British commander sent Dartmouth copies, "as it's hoped Gen[era]l Burgoyne's letter will open People's Eyes who are blinded to an astonishing Degree by the Leaders of the Rebellion."[64] Burgoyne himself sent printed copies to the earl.[65] Assuredly, he was moved by "zeal for the public service," he told both the pious Dartmouth and the more pragmatic North. The ambitious officer wrote in different terms to the prime minister. He described Lee in an unflattering way to North and provided another motive for his correspondence. Calling Lee a "late . . . incendiary in the King's service," now a "demagogue in the rebel army," Burgoyne told how Lee "served under me in Portugal, and owed me obligations which in the very overflow of his misanthropy, he has since constantly acknowledged, and we have usually conversed upon a certain style of friendship."[66] Burgoyne's "great object" had been to arrange an interview with Lee, to "cut him short in that paltry jargon of invective," and to refute point by point his arguments for American independence. Burgoyne enclosed the entire correspondence, apologized for the "mild, and as they may appear, friendly terms" in which he wrote to Lee, and hoped that another attempt to meet the American general would become possible.

Burgoyne used Lee's letters to develop ideas of his own. When Lee disclosed that he feared Britain would use Indians during the war, Burgoyne wrote to North that he thought that letter "alone shows the expediency of diligently preparing and employing that engine."[67] Lee also disclosed that the Americans believed France and Spain would "accept the colonies."

Burgoyne seemed excessively eager to impugn Lee's honor. He had already suggested Lee might not be averse to a bribe; if he would not accept it, there were other ways to destroy him, one of them being Burgoyne's attempt to smear Lee's character in letters to North. Perhaps the real pragmatism of the man may be glimpsed here, shorn of glittering rhetoric and appeals to principle. No matter that what Lee and Congress said "should be true"; the important point was to obtain a victory. Later in the same letter to North, Burgoyne returned to his facade. The "leaders of the revolt may refuse . . . to admit me, or any well affected man, amongst them," he disclosed, "It is more than probable they will be as much averse to trust their cause to fair discussion as to the fair field. Distant skirmish, ambush, entrenchment, concealment, are what they depend upon in debate as in arms." Perhaps unwittingly, Burgoyne condemned what he disliked most in his own thinking—deceit. Fear for his honor and a desire to put himself forward may have led him to make insinuations concerning Lee, or he may have merely played the politician's game.

Lee's loyalty was questioned by some, especially when the correspondence was published.[68] On December 1, the quick-tempered American officer wrote a last letter to Burgoyne. Although Americans were not then seeking independence, Lee predicted that patriots would ultimately seek a complete separation from Britain. Time proved Lee correct, although not before he was captured by Burgoyne's Sixteenth Regiment a year later.[69]

During the course of the Burgoyne-Lee correspondence, Lord North confided to Burgoyne that the king disapproved his plan to meet Lee. "If taken," wrote the prime minister, "you would be a valuable hostage."[70] However, even such a flattering compliment could not have been comforting to the energetic Burgoyne, who was again without an assignment of importance. In August Gage kept him busy writing a reply to charges that General Washington had brought against Gage. The American commander in chief accused Gage of throwing American prisoners into a "common gaol appropriated for felons."[71] Washington believed Gage had disregarded the "obligations arising from the rights of humanity and the claims of rank," which were binding in all circumstances of war: "except in cases of retaliation . . . for the future I shall regulate my conduct toward those gentlemen who are or may be in our possession, exactly by the rule which you shall observe towards those of ours who may be in your custody."[72] If Gage practiced "severity and hardship," so would Washington; "kindness and humanity" would be likewise reciprocated. Burgoyne's reply, commissioned by Gage in his name, was as flamboyant as the proclamation Burgoyne had written two months earlier.[73] General Gage's American captives, he maintained, had been "treated with care and kindness—indiscriminately, it is true, for I acknowledge no rank that is not derived from the King."[74] Burgoyne accused Washington of treating British prisoners "like negro slaves to gain their daily subsistence; while others are reduced to the wretched alternative to perish by famine or take arms against their King and country."[75] Burgoyne then counseled Washington to "be temperate," to "give free operation to the truth," and to "punish those who deceive and misrepresent." Americans ridiculed the letter as "bravado."[76] Indeed, Burgoyne's initial public statements outside the House of Commons were inappropriately theatrical.

In September Burgoyne found another channel for his ample energy. Lord Rawdon, later marquis of Hastings, told his uncle "we are to have plays this winter in Faneuil Hall," and added that "General Burgoyne is our Garrick."[77] The general provided a prologue and epilogue for *Zarah*, a burlesque of Puritan Boston.[78] Lord Rawdon delivered the prologue, and the play was apparently a success. Soon Burgoyne decided to bring forth a new production, *The Blockade of Boston*. During the performance the patriots attacked a mill at Charleston, which prompted a sergeant to jump onto the stage and cry: "Turn out! Turn Out!"[79] However, he was mistaken for an actor, and the audience applauded and remained seated until the play was ended. Burgoyne's theatrical successes in Boston were answered by Mercy Otis Warren, who produced *The Blockheads*, and later *The Fall of British Tyranny*, in which Burgoyne became "Elbow Room."[80]

Burgoyne may have also produced *Tamerlane* and several contemporary comedies, although evidence is not conclusive.[81] It is certain that he had the Old South Meeting House converted into a school for cavalry volunteers, to the consternation and disgust of the patriots.[82] Although the versatile general created controversy for and lent color to the British army stationed in Boston, he remained depressed because of his "lowly station." Burgoyne continued to write lengthy letters to ministers in London, hoping to influence the shaping of strategy for the campaign and thereby assure a place for himself in future operations. He had already prepared the groundwork, filing report after report criticizing Gage's generalship. After Bunker Hill Burgoyne continued to assail his chief: "I take with great pleasure," he told Lord Rochford, "this opportunity to do justice to Mr. Gage; and the Admiral must take to himself, and account for, a great share of our inactivity, our disgrace, and our distress."[83] Admiral Samuel Graves received the burden of Burgoyne's wrath during August: "It may be asked in England 'What is the Admiral doing?' I wish I were able to answer that question satisfactorily; but I can only say what he is *not* doing."[84] Graves, whom the king soon removed from command, breathed nothing but "impatience and flame," Burgoyne reported. In September conditions were the same: "Our present situation is a consummation of inertness and disgrace."[85] If Gage was not equal to his task, neither did the subordinate staff escape censure: "The department of Adjutant General is also all peace, parade, and St. James's Park."[86] The "supineness" of the naval command, the "diffidence" of the commander in chief, and the incompetence of the quartermaster generals, adjutant generals, secretaries, and commissaries "will make altogether a mass of inefficiencies that I am afraid would counteract and disappoint the ablest counsels in the world."[87] In such a manner Burgoyne continued to undermine ministerial confidence in the American staff of the British army. He believed that the army must either engage in total war or stop fighting altogether. Any intermediate measure would "be productive of much fruitless expense, great loss of blood, and a series of disappointments." Burgoyne claimed that he spoke "the sentiments of those who know America best, that you can have no probable prospect of bringing the war to a speedy conclusion with any force that Great Britain and Ireland can supply."

Burgoyne appended to the complaints some constructive comments. During his residence in Massachusetts he was able to develop two schemes for strategy that he hoped would impress London as welcome contrasts to the hopeless muddle that Gage and his subordinates had gotten themselves into. Burgoyne sent descriptions of his plans to London often and at great length. He called the army's position at Boston a poor one. Nothing could be accomplished there because of insufficient supplies and troops. To relieve the army in Boston, Burgoyne proposed a diversionary attack upon Rhode Island "where I might entrench." "I would embark this force," he wrote, "and unite to it all the ships of war that can be safely spared from the protection of Boston."[88] Burgoyne wished by his diversion to divide the solid mass of citizenry surrounding Boston. Some of them would move to Rhode Island, others would return to the countryside; still more, lacking the support of the by then diminished American force, would resume their allegiance to the crown. Lines of supply could thereupon be reopened to relieve the starving British army in Boston and at the same time Rhode Island would feel "chastisement."[89] But the diversion had more than merely those purposes: it would "cover and facilitate greater designs." New York was the key to strategy in Burgoyne's mind. It was lost "for want of proper management, and a proper force to second it." He believed it could be reclaimed, and that Long Island should serve as a supply base for larger operations. Lying at the mouth of the Hudson River, the city formed the key element in Burgoyne's plan.[90] He envisioned two armies, one ascending from New York, the other penetrating from Canada. If supplied with mercenary troops, he believed that he could command such an independent operation successfully. He did caution that land equipment and local supplies were scarce in northern New York, but he was convinced that geographical and political advantages of the strategy outweighed the logistical and tactical problems.[91] Burgoyne's vision was grandiose. He would issue a manifesto calculated to subdue the rebels. The British fleet in the Atlantic would cause the "whole coast of America" to be "equally in alarm." The Indians were expected to "awe the southern provinces." Burgoyne reckoned that such a force "might possibly do the business in one campaign."

In fact, what Burgoyne wanted was an independent command for himself. In the summer of 1775, however, he was unable and Gage was unwilling to take precipitate action. Gage did not have sufficient troops to do so. Therefore, the commander in chief considered whether it would be best to move to New York City for the winter. Burgoyne declared that the matter required "very mature reflection" and he "would not be understood to give my opinion."[92] Nevertheless, Burgoyne concluded that both Boston and New York should be retained and declared that he would "be happy to be employed in the execution" of such an operation.[93] However, Lord North informed the calculating officer that only two thousand soldiers were available for the current campaign, thus ending temporarily Burgoyne's dream of an independent command. Although Lord Dartmouth had agreed that New York would be a useful base "to make the Hudson's River the Seat of the War,"[94] Gage decided that the army could safely remain in Boston for the winter.[95]

Burgoyne returned to melancholy: "I begin now to despair of the expedition of which I expressed promising hopes in my last. Enterprise is not ours. Inertness, or what is equal to it, attention to small objects, counteracts or procrastinates undertakings when no visible objection lies to them."[96] His grand strategy postponed, Burgoyne requested permission to return to England where he promised to be a "faithful intelligencer" for Parliament.[97] For some reason, North did not relay the king's permission to return to Burgoyne and it was not until November 1775 that Dartmouth granted permission to return.[98] Burgoyne departed for England in December.[99] The ship's Captain Evelyn, not knowing the ambitious general's many letters and plans for glory remarked of his passenger: "He appears from the line he has taken to have been intended rather as a negociator than to be active in the field. He is a man of great abilities and power of language."[100]

Notes

1. John Burgoyne, "Private Memorandum," DeFonblanque, *Episodes,* p. 122.

2. Ibid.

3. "John Burgoyne," *DNB.*

4. The Hertford Street residence was occupied by the earl of Sandwich before Burgoyne bought it, and by Richard Sheridan after 1792. The Greater London Council has designated the house a site of historic interest.

5. April 18, 1775, Burgoyne to the king, DeFonblanque, *Episodes,* pp. 133–35.

6. February 3, 1775, Barrington to Gage, in Howard H. Peckham, ed., *Sources of American Independence: Selected Manuscripts from the Collections of the William L. Clements Library,* 2 vols. (Chicago: University of Chicago Press, 1978), 1:124–5; February 3, 1775, Barrington to Dartmouth, Historical Manuscripts Commission, *Report on the Manuscripts of the Earl of Dartmouth,* 3 vols. (London: H. M. Stationery Office, 1887–96), 2:266.

7. April 14, 1775, North to the king, Fortescue, ed., *Correspondence,* 3:203; the king to North, ibid., pp. 203–4.

8. John Burgoyne, *The Speech of a General Officer in the House of Commons, February 20, 1775* (London: n.p., 1775), p. 1. See also Cobbett, *Parliamentary History,* 18:353–7.

9. April 15, 1775, Dartmouth to Gage, C.O. 5.92, f. 97; May 25, 1775, Gage to Dartmouth, C.O. 5.92, f. 166.

10. Edmund B. O'Callaghan, ed., *Orderly Book of Lieut.-Gen. John Burgoyne from his Entry into the State of New York until his Surrender at Saratoga, 16th Oct., 1777* (Albany, N.Y.: Munsell, 1860).

11. Richard Frothingham, *A History of the Siege of Boston* (Boston: Little, Brown, 1851), p. 114.

12. June 1775, Burgoyne to Lord Rochford, DeFonblanque, *Episodes*, pp. 142–53.

13. Ibid., and p. 119.

14. 1775, *Pennsylvania Packet*, Hudleston, *Burgoyne*, p. 54.

15. Alden, *Gage*, pp. 234–35.

16. December 18, 1774, the king to North, Fortescue, ed., *Correspondence*, 3:157.

17. June 1775, Burgoyne to Lord Rochford, DeFonblanque, *Episodes*, p. 149; Rochford submitted a copy of this letter to the king, September 8, 1775, Rochford to the king, Fortescue, ed., *Correspondence*, 3:252–53.

18. DeFonblanque, *Episodes*, p. 143.

19. Ibid., p. 143.

20. June 14, 1775, Burgoyne to General Edward Harvey, DeFonblanque, *Episodes*, pp. 140–41.

21. Ibid., p. 180. See Alden, *Gage*, for a sympathetic discussion of Gage's conduct in Boston.

22. July 19, 1775, Howe, Clinton and Burgoyne to Gage, Gage papers, William L. Clements Library, University of Michigan.

23. Ibid., DeFonblanque, *Episodes*, p. 141.

24. Ibid.

25. Ibid., p. 140.

26. June, 1775, Burgoyne to Lord Rochford, DeFonblanque, *Episodes*, pp. 142–53.

27. June 14, 1775, Burgoyne to Barrington, W.O. 1.2, ff. 459–61.

28. June 14, 1775, Burgoyne to North, Historical Manuscripts Commission, *Tenth Report, appendix, part VI, Report on the Manuscripts of the Marquess of Abergavenny* (London: H. M. Stationery Office, 1887), pp. 8–9.

29. Ibid.

30. June 14, 1775, Burgoyne to North, DeFonblanque, *Episodes*, pp. 136–40.

31. June 14, 1775, Burgoyne to Barrington, W.O. 1.2, ff. 459–61.

32. General William and Admiral Lord Howe were selected for the peace commission; Ira D. Gruber, *The Howe Brothers and the American Revolution* (New York: Atheneum, 1972), and Troyer S. Anderson, *The Command of the Howe Brothers during the American Revolution* (New York: Oxford University Press, 1936).

33. June 14, 1775, Burgoyne's Proclamation "drawn up by me at the request of General Gage," DeFonblanque, *Episodes*, p. 136, note 1.

34. Ibid., Peter Force, ed., *American Archives: A Documentary History of the Origin and Progress of the North American Colonies*, fourth series, (Washington, D.C.: M. St. Clarke and P. Force, 1837–53), 2:968–70.

35. July 26, 1775, Germain to General Irwin, Historical Manuscripts Commission, *Stopford-Sackville MSS.*, 1:136.

36. June 13, 1775, James Robertson to ?, Historical Manuscripts Commission, *Dartmouth MSS.*, 2:315.

37. DeFonblanque, *Episodes*, p. 136.

38. June 17, 1775, Burgoyne to ?, B.L., Add. MS. 5, 487, f. 378.

39. June, 1775, Burgoyne to Lord Rochford, DeFonblanque, *Episodes*, p. 145.

40. Allen French, *The First Year of the American Revolution* (Boston: Houghton, Mifflin, 1934), p. 209.

41. June 17, 1775, Burgoyne to ?, B.L. Add. MS. 5,487, f. 378.

42. Ibid.

43. Ibid.; French, *First Year*, p. 243, note 32, has challenged the accuracy of Burgoyne's account of Howe's and Clinton's movements, citing inconclusively the testimony of the latter officers; James Thacher, *Military Journal of the American Revolution from 1775 to 1783* (Hartford, Conn.: American Subscription Publishing House, 1862), p. 24.

44. June, 1775, Burgoyne to Lord Rochford, DeFonblanque, *Episodes*, pp. 142–53.

45. August 20, 1775, Burgoyne to Germain, Germain papers, William L. Clements Library, University of Michigan.

46. June, 1775, Burgoyne to Lord Stanley, DeFonblanque, *Episodes*, pp. 155–56.

47. August 20, 1775, Burgoyne to Germain, Germain papers, Clements Library.

48. Burgoyne is said to have rowed over to look at the body of Dr. Joseph Warren, who was killed during the battle; Esther Forbes, *Paul Revere and the World He Lived In* (Boston: Houghton, Mifflin, 1942), p. 314.

49. June 7, 1775, Lee to Burgoyne, C.O. 5.92, f. 233. Edmond Quincy mistakenly thought Lee's letter would influence Burgoyne to defect; July 22, 1775, Quincy to John Hancock, Peckham, ed., *Sources of American Independence,* 2:460.

50. June 7, 1775, Burgoyne to Lee, Historical Manuscripts Commission, *Dartmouth MSS.,* , 3:337.

51. July 5, 1775, Burgoyne to Lee, cited by Alden, *Lee,* p. 85; *The Kemble Papers* (New York: New-York Historical Society, 1884), p. 146.

52. July 9, 1775, Lee to Burgoyne, [Charles Lee], *The Lee Papers, 1782–1811,* 4 vols. (New York: New-York Historical Society, 1872–6), 1:188–93.

53. July 8, 1775, Burgoyne to Lee, DeFonblanque, *Episodes,* pp. 168–77.

54. Ibid.

55. Ibid., p. 169.

56. Ibid., pp. 170–71.

57. July 24, 1775, Charles Stuart to Lord Bute, Emmaline Stuart-Wortley, ed., *A Prime Minister and His Son* (London: J. Murray, 1925), pp. 66–71.

58. Hudleston, *Burgoyne,* pp. 80–81.

59. July 8, 1775, Lee to Congress, DeFonblanque, *Episodes,* p. 172; Alden, *The American Revolution,* (New York: Harper, 1954), p. 85.

60. July 10, 1775, Lee to Congress, *Lee Papers,* 1:193.

61. July 10, 1775, Congress to Lee, ibid., pp. 193–4.

62. July 11, 1775, Lee to Burgoyne, ibid., 194–5.

63. Ibid.

64. July 24, 1775, Gage to Dartmouth, C.O. 5.92, f. 232.

65. July 26, 1775, Burgoyne to Dartmouth, Historical Manuscripts Commission, *Dartmouth MSS.,* 2:337–38.

66. July 11, 1775, Burgoyne to North, DeFonblanque, *Episodes,* pp. 174–79.

67. Ibid., p. 179.

68. December 1, 1775, Lee to Burgoyne; [Charles Lee], *The Lee Papers,* 1:222–5.

69. In August 1775, Barrington informed Gage that Burgoyne's Light Horse would be augmented and sent to America in the spring of 1776 (August 31, 1775, Barrington to Gage, P.R.O. 30.55.1.27, ff. 1–4). Although Burgoyne remained colonel in chief of the regiment, Lieutenant Colonel William Harcourt assumed command on the battlefield (*Army List for 1775,* p. 44). The Sixteenth Regiment arrived in New York in November, 1775 (Ambrose Serle to Dartmouth, Historical Manuscripts Commission, *Dartmouth MSS.,* 2:427), and one month later Harcourt captured Lee in Morris County, New Jersey (Edward H. Tatum, ed., *The American Journal of Ambrose Serle, Secretary to Lord Howe, 1776–1778* [San Marino, Calif.: The Huntington Library, 1940], pp. 186–87, and letter of 1778, Lee to James Roberson, Clinton MSS., William L. Clements Library).

70. July 31, 1775, North to Burgoyne, Historical Manuscripts Commission, *Abergavenny MSS.,* p. 9.

71. August 11, 1775, Washington to Gage, DeFonblanque, *Episodes,* pp. 184–85, endorsed by Burgoyne: "From Washington, Commander in Chief of the rebel army, to General Gage." Lee may have helped Washington write the letter; Alden, *Lee,* p. 82.

72. Ibid.

73. August 11, 1775, Gage to Washington, DeFonblanque, *Episodes,* pp. 185–86, endorsed by

Burgoyne: "As wrote by me; one sentence which does not appear here was added by the General"; ibid., p. 185.

74. Ibid., p. 186.

75. Ibid.

76. DeFonblanque, *Episodes*, p. 187.

77. October 5, 1775, Francis, Lord Rawdon to Francis, tenth earl of Huntingdon, Historical Manuscripts Commission, *Report on the Manuscripts of the Late Reginald Rawdon Hastings, Esq. of the Manor House, Ashley de la Zouch*, 4 vols. (London: H. M. Stationery Office, 1928–47), 3:159–60.

78. [n.d.] playbill, *Zarah*, Massachusetts Historical Society.

79. Thacher, *Military Journal*, pp. 360–61.

80. Hudleston, *Burgoyne*, p. 53.

81. Pottinger, "John Burgoyne," p. 38.

82. Frothingham, *Siege*, p. 328, citing "Deacon Newell's Diary."

83. July 11, 1775, Burgoyne to Lord Rochford, DeFonblanque, *Episodes*, pp. 180–83. Yet Burgoyne publicly continued to sit with Gage in committee and approve the general's decisions. See, for example, August 2, 1775, minute of a meeting held at Gage's, Clinton papers, William L. Clements Library, University of Michigan.

84. August 20, 1775, Burgoyne to Germain, Germain papers, Clements Library.

85. September 1775, Burgoyne to [Elliott?], DeFonblanque, *Episodes*, pp. 202–3; Historical Manuscripts Commission, *Dartmouth MSS.*, 2:357.

86. DeFonblanque, *Episodes*, p. 203.

87. August 20, 1775, Burgoyne to Germain, Germain papers, Clements Library.

88. Ibid.

89. Ibid.

90. Thynne Manuscripts, American Affairs, nos. 21–22 in papers of Lord Weymouth, Marquis of Bath Estate, Longleat (copy of Burgoyne's reply to questions from Gage, supplied to Lord Rochford), cited by Piers G. Mackesy, *The War for America 1775–1783* (Cambridge, Mass.: Harvard University Press, 1964), p. 59.

91. Hoffman Nickerson, *The Turning Point of the Revolution; or, Burgoyne in America* (Boston: Houghton Mifflin, 1928), pp. 48–56, argued for the soundness of the Lake Champlain–Hudson River–Mohawk route.

92. July 11, 1775, Burgoyne to Lord Rochford, DeFonblanque, *Episodes*, p. 181.

93. Ibid., p. 182.

94. August 2, 1775, Dartmouth to Gage, C.O. 5.92, ff. 196–201.

95. October 1, 1775, Gage to Dartmouth, C.O. 5.92, ff. 290–91.

96. July 11, 1775, Burgoyne to Rochford, DeFonblanque, *Episodes*, p. 180.

97. August 20, 1775, Burgoyne to Germain, Germain papers, Clements Library.

98. November 1775, Dartmouth to Burgoyne, DeFonblanque, *Episodes*, p. 206

99. December 3, 1775, William Feilding to Earl of Denbigh, in Marion Balderston and David Syrett, eds., *The Lost War: Letters from British Officers during the American Revolution* (New York: Horizon Press, 1975), pp. 55–56.

100. Hudleston, *Burgoyne*, p. 94.

9

In Canada with Carleton

Burgoyne returned to his town house in Mayfair on December 28, 1775.[1] Horace Walpole, who noted his arrival, wrote caustically to the countess of Upper Ossory in Ireland: "Fresh, very fresh news! General Carlton is not come, but General Burgoyne is, though not yet landed in town. He is to bring very good accounts from Boston; but as he does not yet know what, till he is told by those he is to tell; and as I am too scrupulous to send any news before it is born, you will excuse my [not] mentioning the particulars."[2] Others in London were more genuinely glad to see Burgoyne, especially his wife, whose parents had been ill. On February 23, 1776, the earl of Derby died at Knowsley at the advanced age of eighty-seven; his grandson, the son of Lord Strange, succeeded him as the twelfth earl.[3] Two days later, Lady Derby followed her husband to the family grave at Ormskirk, where they were both buried on March 11.[4] Subsequently, the health of Lady Charlotte Burgoyne weakened, and in March the king inquired "anxiously" about her.[5] Lord George Germain told Burgoyne he hoped he did not mislead the king in telling him that she was slightly improved. However, the news of her favorite sister's sudden death caused Lady Charlotte's condition to worsen, and Burgoyne asked Germain for permission to remain with his wife rather than return at once to America. "Her piety, resignation, and fortitude," he wrote, "of which no woman ever had more, are not proof at once, and her body not at all, against these combined sorrows, and in my soul I believe that my immediate separation, against which, however, she would not say a word, would convey her to the family grave before it is closed."[6] He considered resigning his commission in consequence of such "extraordinary calamities," and declared that he would "even relinquish all I hold or could ever hold from the Crown, rather than forsake the duty I owe to a wife who through the space of twenty-four years has never given me a moment's pain, except upon a bed of sickness or in an hour of parting." Nevertheless, Burgoyne felt a "sense of duty to the King and of attachment to the cause in which he is so gloriously exerting himself," which superseded "every private consideration." Burgoyne perhaps took advantage of the situation to obtain his coveted advancement. Leaving the ailing Charlotte, Burgoyne departed for America from Portsmouth on April 7.[7] Two months later his wife died in Kensington at the age of forty-eight.[8] Germain hoped that his letter of sympathy would find Burgoyne "superior to every private misfortune, after exerting every effort which reason, judgment, and above all resignation to the will of Providence could suggest," and he assured the general that he had "no friend who has felt more sincerely for you than I have done."[9] Horace Walpole, less sympathetic, snapped: "[Burgoyne] pretended grief for his wife's death, which was laughed at."[10] The event, however, had an impact upon Burgoyne. Whether from grief or regret, he informed Henry Clinton in July that his wife was the "truest friend, [most] aimiable companion, tenderest, best of women."[11] Her virtues, he confessed, grew upon him, "as do every fault I ever committed toward her. (They are not, indeed, many; and even those are unknown to her.)" Not wishing to distress Clinton, Burgoyne considered destroying the letter, for, he said, he knew "too well your mind to think you can read it without pain." Months later, Burgoyne still brooded over her death, at least in public, and told Clinton that he was "an unconnected cypher in the world—the partner lost which made prosperity an object of solicitude—my prospects are closed—Interest, ambition, and animation of life is over."[12] Lady Charlotte was buried on June 14, 1776, in the north cloister of Westminster Abbey with her daughter Charlotte-Elizabeth.[13] Burgoyne apparently ordered John Deare of the workshop of Thomas Carter in Piccadilly to construct a monument to install at her grave, but the project was, perhaps significantly, never completed.[14]

Germain, who consoled Burgoyne upon the loss of his wife, had seemingly become a reliable acquaintance. The earl of Shelburne once observed that Germain's "Westminster connection never failed to advise and support him underhand, even when he was most pressed."[15] Germain supported Burgoyne's attempts to obtain an important post in New York for 1775. While he was in Boston and before Germain became secretary of state, Burgoyne kept him fully informed, and often indulged in flattery: "Your Lordship's insight into men and things will make my reflections equally superfluous upon the part of our present dilemma imputable at home."[16] On leave in London in 1776, Burgoyne continued to praise the secretary both publicly and privately. He told the earl of Huntingdon "when I consider the resolution with which I find he is supported from the throne, I derive great confidence in the prospect of the next campaign."[17]

However, Germain, who succeeded the ineffectual earl of Dartmouth as secretary of state for the colonies on November 10, 1775, was an unpopular minister.[18] During the reign of George II he had been cashiered from the army for disobedience in battle and was subsequently barred "forever" from the king's court. Nonetheless by pulling strings he became vice treasurer for Ireland and was restored to the Privy Council although not to the hearts of his peers.[19] Burgoyne's flattering phrases were doubtless welcome to the new secretary of state, and it is perhaps not coincidental that Burgoyne and Major General William Howe, whom Germain also favored for a time, were ap-

Lord George Germain, by Sir Joshua Reynolds. Reproduced by permission of the William L. Clements Library, University of Michigan.

pointed to active commands while Carleton and Clinton, seniors in rank respectively to Howe and Burgoyne, languished in unimportant posts.[20] In one of his first administrative decisions, Germain announced early in 1776 a major change in the structure of the American staff, the purpose of which may well have been to isolate Carleton and reward Howe. The secretary divided the North American theater of war into two departments, each with its own commander in chief. Germain sent Howe his commission in March 1776,

Sir Guy Carleton, engraving by Ritchie. Reproduced by permission of the William L. Clements Library, University of Michigan.

confirming his appointment as commander in chief of the major department, the thirteen colonies. Guy Carleton, still senior to Howe and military governor of Canada, was also promoted to the rank of general in America, but he was instructed to remain in the less strategically important department of Canada. Burgoyne, while not obtaining an independent command, was assigned to work under Carleton during 1776.[21]

Although there is little evidence that Carleton and Clinton blamed their fellow officers for their plight, there is no doubt that they resented Germain's treatment of them. Despite the fact that he was senior in rank to all but Gage, Carleton received not only a minor command, but also the unwelcome news that he would not be appointed to the peace commission, which provided the Howe brothers five thousand pounds per year each. Carleton complained at length to Germain, stating that he had been subjected to "every kind of Slight, Disregard and Censure."[22] Clinton, who had seniority, was chagrined that Burgoyne was given a superior post, and late in 1776 made his complaints known in London.[23]

The root of the problem is clear: Germain was unable or unwilling to make persistent efforts to get along with his military subordinates. Germain's malice toward Carleton was long-standing. In every other instance, Germain began to construct a positive relationship with a particular officer only to end the association with recriminations. This pattern may be obeserved in his relationship to the Howes, to Clinton, and, in the end, to Burgoyne. Burgoyne was particularly adept at manipulating Germain's propensity to pick quarrels with his officers. By directing Germain's fire against his own peers, Burgoyne assured for himself Germain's favor and thus perhaps guaranteed for himself a major role in the campaigns of 1776 and 1777. To sum up, the problem was not one involving officers pitted against other officers; instead, what developed was a pattern of recrimination initiated by Germain, and subsequently spread through the network of command.

Because Germain did not promote Burgoyne over Carleton in 1776, the foregoing theory may not appear completely convincing. However, opposing interpretations are even less valid. For example, the assumption that Burgoyne was instructed to succeed Carleton early in 1776 is clearly wrong.[24] Although rumors circulated in London early in March of 1776 that Carleton had been recalled and that Burgoyne was to take his place, such rumors were at that time untrue.[25] According to carefully designed instructions, Burgoyne was specifically instructed to take command of the reinforcements scheduled for Canada only until he met Carleton.[26] If Burgoyne found that Carleton had retained control of Quebec, he was to place himself under Carleton's command at once. If Quebec had fallen, then Burgoyne was instructed to keep his troops in a safe place "until General Carleton is informed of your arrival, and shall have given directions with regard to your future proceedings."[27] After all, Carleton's position with the king was secure, and such approbation from on high made even Germain hesitate to harm him. Germain also provided for the ultimate contingencies: "In case of his death or absence (in either of which cases the command in Canada is to devolve upon you) [You must keep the troops aboard ship] until you shall have formed your own Opinion of what further Steps it may be proper to take."[28] It is clear from these orders that Burgoyne was given independent command of the reinforcements only until he had reached the Isle aux Coudres, at which point Carleton would give Burgoyne directions with regard to his future proceedings. Only if Carleton died or was absent could Burgoyne assume command. It is also clear from Germain's orders to Carleton of the same date that he expected Carleton, at least during March 1776, to lead the expedition across Lake Champlain and then south to meet General Howe.[29] A copy of the orders for Carleton was given to Burgoyne.[30] The orders seem clear enough.[31] Although Germain wished to replace Carleton, and did so in August 1776, he did not remove him from active command in March of that year. The friction that did develop involved officers complaining about Germain, rather than officers attacking each other. Almost every general who served in the American war came to dislike Germain. Late in 1776, however, Burgoyne was on good terms with his chief and with his fellow officers.

Although successful in obtaining a high appointment, Burgoyne was not in excellent spirits when he left for America in April 1776. He had not been appointed to the position he coveted on the peace commission; nor had he obtained an independent command. Then, his wife lay ill. However, Burgoyne turned his thoughts from disappointment and sorrow to the affairs of Canada, which demanded his immediate attention.[32] When reports of the American advance upon Canada reached Germain in February 1776, he sent early reinforcements, providing additional troops when Burgoyne sailed in April.[33] Burgoyne himself arrived in Canada later in May, aboard the *Isis*.[34] His troops found Quebec "safe and sound," much to Burgoyne's chagrin, it may be suspected.[35] He had hoped to engage immediately in battle, and boasted to Germain that not one American would have escaped had the captain of his convoy permitted him to press ahead with twenty of his fastest ships.[36] Nevertheless, his ambition was satisfied in part once he joined with Carleton, who had gone "up the river . . . with a few troops to keep the Rebels in Awe."[37] He presented Germain's instructions to the governor, and then on May 30 followed Carleton's column to Trois Rivièrs, a town on the St. Lawrence River about halfway between Montreal and Quebec.[38]

Benedict Arnold had by this time retired to Montreal, but Congress had sent 5,300 reinforcements northward earlier in May for a second attack on Quebec. American Brigadier General Thompson had sailed his best soldiers in fifty bateaux north to Trois Rivières via the Sorel and landed at Point au Lac. On June 8 the British troops there were exceedingly surprised to see 2,000 patriots marching toward them.[39] "Nothing was more unexpected than this Visit of the Rebels," wrote Burgoyne's aide-de-camp at Trois Rivières.[40] The Americans were even more confounded when it was reported that Burgoyne's entire force lay a few hundred yards away in Trois Rivières. Burgoyne ordered his men to cut off Thompson's force, which fled in disarray to Saint John's on June 9 and 10 after a short skirmish. The British pursued the Americans for six miles, but, as Clerke told Lord Polwarth in England, "very few of them ventured out of the woods, and as soon as they perceived our Troops were so eager to give them a warm Reception, they hastily retired back again."[41]

Only a few rounds were fired, one British sergeant killed, and eleven or twelve soldiers wounded. Among American soldiers, Thompson was captured along with three hundred others who were taken prisoners.[42] The remaining Americans marched back down to Sorel. Burgoyne followed with the three columns under his command.[43] As Clerke described it, "the Troops were all racing up the River in their Transports, and some of the first having outrun their Wind, were proceeding by land, very eager."[44] Several days were lost because of adverse winds; Burgoyne finally sailed on the thirteenth and arrived two days later in Sorel. The Americans decamped and moved further south to Saint John's, where Sullivan, their leader, expected to meet Arnold who was evacuating his men from Montreal. Burgoyne wished to intercept Sullivan's force on the Richelieu before they joined with Arnold. "We began our chace with might and main," remarked Clerke, who observed that the "nimble heel'd Rebels" were retreating in such haste that they did not destroy any of the "innumerable small bridges over the broad gullies that the Snow Water makes in the Spring." Carleton, however, cautioned Burgoyne not to press the Americans too quickly. Arnold and Sullivan joined forces at Saint John's and immediately marched their troops southward toward the lakes. Burgoyne and Carleton reached Saint John's an hour after the American evacuation, only to find the town in flames. The patriots had fled to Isle aux Noix, thence to Crown Point and safety, and as Clerke commented, "left us at a non-plus."[45]

The American patriots lost their bid for Canada, but did gain a year's grace before the British invasion of New York could take place. The British retained Quebec, and succeeded in driving all the American troops from Canada. Burgoyne was satisfied with his effort. In a general order he complimented his troops, who were already in good spirits, encamped at Chambly.[46] Burgoyne had long been popular with the soldiers under his command and the Canadian force was no exception.[47] Burgoyne reported his success to Germain,[48] who replied that "the willingness which the Soldiers shewed, fully justifies all you have said in Parliament about their zeal and spirit in acting on the present contest."[49] Germain, perhaps implying that he was happy Carleton did not receive the king's praise for the conduct of the Canadian operation, said he was glad that Burgoyne commanded the column that forced the Americans from the Richelieu River to Lake Champlain, and he told him that "everybody does justice to your conduct upon that occasion. The King expressed himself upon that subject in a manner that gave one great pleasure, as it did you so much honour."[50] On the very day Burgoyne wrote to him, Germain had tried to thwart an attempt by the cabinet to award Carleton the Order of the Bath for his defense of Quebec.[51] Lord North, however, upheld Carleton and said that, "even if some parts of his conduct were doubtful, good policy required them. . . . The Red Ribband was thought a very proper mark of his Majesty's approbation."[52] The king himself did not like Germain's attitude, and wrote immediately to North: "I think you ought to write . . . to M[ajor] G[eneral] Carleton my approbation of his conduct and that Lady Mary will be the bearer of the Red Ribband."[53] Carleton got his reward despite Germain, who remained annoyed.[54] Although there is no evidence that Carleton resented Burgoyne, it is clear that Germain wished to prejudice Burgoyne against his own commander in chief. He opposed the Red Ribbon for Carleton because he personally disliked him.[55]

As if to assure Carleton's failure, Germain sent him few reinforcements. That was not the least of Carleton's troubles. Before he could continue his pursuit of the American army he had to organize a fleet so that his force could cross Lake Champlain, which was once again held by America.[56] Only then could he and Burgoyne lead an invasion force to New York to meet Howe. But, having few ships, he was not equipped for naval action and was forced to rely upon local craftsmen to build a fleet for him.[57] While they labored to construct ships during June, July, August, and September, Burgoyne found himself without immediate occupation. William Howe, stationed in New York City after successfully forcing out Washington's army, did not face a similar interlude of inactivity.[58] The taciturn commander pondered the consequences of a junction with Carleton, which he thought possible that year "if the Canadians are hearty."[59] Junior to Carleton, Howe worried that the projected junction would imperil his command. He wrote to Germain in May and June, complaining that Carleton's entrance into the territory of the American department would interfere with his command.[60]

Germain made three attempts to get orders to Carleton, but the ships carrying them were blocked by adverse winds. Carleton did not read the secretary's instructions until May 6, 1777.[61] Unaware that he had been superseded, he began to organize his newly constructed fleet during October 1776, in order to get control of the lakes and then join with Howe.[62] On October 4, Carleton and Burgoyne led the British expedition down the Richelieu River into the blue waters of Lake Champlain.[63] Arnold moved to action immediately and halted Carleton's progress at Valcour Island on October 11.[64] Carleton beat Arnold, but the American general had gained time for the colonial cause. Carleton resumed his drive into New York and occupied Crown Point, an abandoned military outpost near Fort Ticonderoga. Major Generals Horatio Gates, Philip Schuyler, and Thaddeus Kosciusko had fortified Ticonderoga with nine thousand soldiers.[65] Aware that the generals were securely entrenched, and fearful of the onset of a severe winter, Carleton hesitated.[66] Burgoyne was convinced that an attack upon Fort Ticonderoga would be successful. His old colleague of the Portuguese campaigns, artillery Major William Phillips, supported Burgoyne and urged at least a strong feint against the fort.[67] But Carleton decided to return to Crown Point, which he did on October 15.[68] After a week's stay there, Carleton concluded that the damaged fortifications at Crown Point were not suitable for long-term occupation.[69] Moreover, his gunboats, newly constructed of green timber, were unseasoned.[70] Sir Guy decided on October 23 to abandon the expedition and return to Quebec.[71] Artificers were evacuated from Isle aux Noix and Saint John. Phillips and Burgoyne did not challenge Carleton's decision openly, although the latter maintained privately that Crown Point could have been held had Carleton called in "his own good sense to direct the fortification without being guided by the drawings and technical reasonings of dull, formal, methodical, fat engineers."[72] By November 1, Burgoyne's first brigade was at Montreal and Carleton had gone into winter quarters at Quebec with the second regiment.[73] The campaign of 1776 had aborted.[74]

Burgoyne sent a heated letter to Clinton in November, in which he openly criticized Carleton for the first time.[75] He maintained that Sir Guy's decision "jeopardized the fruits of our summer's labor and autumn victory," leaving the entire campaign to be repeated in the spring:

> I must honour Carleton's abilities and judgment, I have lived with him on the best terms and bear him friendship. I am therefore doubly hurt that he has taken a step in which I can be no otherwise serviceable to him than by silence.[76]

Carleton had rejected all of Burgoyne's suggestions during the campaign. Now in November Burgoyne joined Germain in opposition to Carleton. His motivation for doing so, as always, was his desire for power. That he hoped to supersede Carleton in the near future may be inferred from Phillips's letter to him expressing "most sincerely [the] hope you will come out to us."

Meanwhile Burgoyne began to arrange passage to return home.[77] Claiming to Germain that his health had deteriorated and that the affairs of his late wife demanded attention, he confided to Clinton the most important reason for his wish to leave: "a secondary station in a secondary army is at no time agreeable."[78] Carleton granted Burgoyne leave and he departed for London in mid-November.[79] One month later, Burgoyne wasted no time representing to the king and Germain the considerable criticisms of Carleton that he and Phillips had made.

Notes

1. January 5, 1776, Germain to Howe, C.O. 5.243, f. 107.

2. December 27, 1775, Walpole to Lady Ossory, *Correspondence*, 32:286.

3. Brydges, ed., *Collins' Peerage of England, Genealogical, Biographical and Historical*, 9 vols. (London: Rivington, 1812), 3:102; DeFonblanque, *Episodes*, p. 81, note 1.

4. G. E. C[okayne], *The Complete Peerage of England, Scotland, Ireland, Great Britain, and the United Kingdom*, 13 vols. (London: St. Catherine Press, 1912–40), 4:217–8.

5. March 1, 1776, Germain to Burgoyne, DeFonblanque, *Episodes*, pp. 212–13; March 3, 1776, Burgoyne to Germain, Germain papers, Clements Library; Brydges, ed., *Collins' Peerage*, 3:99.

6. March 1, 1776, Germain to Burgoyne, DeFonblanque, *Episodes*, pp. 212–13.

7. April 6, 1776, Burgoyne to ?, C.O. 5.93, ff. 383–85.

8. June 7, 1776, Chester, ed., *Registers*, p. 422; Edmund Lodge, ed. *Lodge's Peerage, Baronetage, Knightage and Companionage of the British Empire for 1912* (London: Kelly's Directories, 1912), p. 393; Brydges, ed., *Collins' Peerage*, p. 3:102, records her death on June 9.

9. August 23, 1776, Germain to Burgoyne, Historical Manuscripts Commission, *Stopford-Sackville MSS.*, 2:39.

10. Steuart, ed., *Last Journals of Walpole*, 1:592.

11. July 7, 1776, Burgoyne to Clinton, William B. Willcox, *Portrait of a General: Sir Henry Clinton in the War of Independence* (New York: Knopf, 1964), p. 97.

12. November 7, 1776, Burgoyne to Clinton, Gerald S. Brown, *The American Secretary: The Colonial Policy of Lord George Germain; 1775–1778* (Ann Arbor, Mich.: University of Michigan Press, 1963), pp. 88–89.

13. June 14, 1776, Chester, *Registers*, p. 422.

14. Pottinger, "John Burgoyne," p. 37.

15. Fitzmaurice, *Shelburne*, 1:250.

16. August 20, 1775, Burgoyne to Germain, Germain papers, Clements Library.

17. January 3, 1776, Burgoyne to the earl of Huntingdon, Historical Manuscripts Commission, *Report on the Manuscripts of the Late Reginald Rawdon Hastings, Esq., of the Manor House, Ashby de la Zouch*, 4 vols. (London: H. M. Stationery Office, 1928–47), 3:166. See also Burgoyne's suggestions for sending a cavalry regiment to America, proposals calculated to impress Germain with Burgoyne's expertise in such matters; January 4, 1776, Burgoyne to Germain, Germain papers, Clements Library, University of Michigan.

18. Mackesy, *America*, p. 62, concluded: "In high spirits he set out to sweep away the legacy of Dartmouth's timidity. If organization alone could have conquered, he would have succeeded," citing Historical Manuscripts Commission, *Report on the Manuscripts of the Earl of Carlisle* (London: H. M. Stationery Office, 1897), p. 362, and Historical Manuscripts Commission, *Hastings MSS.*, 4:166, 168.

19. George H. Guttridge, "Lord George Germain in Office, 1775–1782," *American Historical Review* 33:23–42.

20. Brown, *American Secretary*, p. 58, argued that those tensions which the appointments created tended to poison relationships between the officers and the secretary of state.

21. Peter O. Hutchinson, ed., *The Diary and Letters of Thomas Hutchinson*, 2 vols. (London: Sampson Low, 1883–86), 2:158.

22. May 22, 1777, Carleton to Germain, C.O. 42.36, ff. 271–78.

23. February 1, 1776, Germain wrote to Howe that Clinton would have gone to Canada had he not already departed for the south; P.R.O. 30.55.2, f. 117 (1–8).

24. Mackesy, *America*, p. 76.

25. March 8, 1776, Burrow to Legge, Historical Manuscripts Commission, *Dartmouth MSS.*, 2:599.

26. March 28, 1776, Germain to Burgoyne, C.O. 5.243, ff. 130–32.

27. Such orders were not unusual; Clinton was equipped with a dormant commission to supersede Howe upon the latter's death; April 25, 1776, Germain to Clinton, C.O. 5.243, f. 137.

28. March 28, 1776, Germain to Burgoyne C.O. 5.243, ff. 130–32.

29. March 28, 1776, Germain to Carleton, C.O. 5.253, f. 214.

30. Ibid. The copy has not been located. Reference to it may be found in Précis, C.O. 5.253, f. 213, and Précis [1776] C.O. 5.253, f. 33, which stated that Burgoyne was "furnished with a copy." [early 1776] "Measures taken for the relief of Quebec," Précis, C.O. 5.253, f. 213.

31. March 28, 1776, Germain to Burgoyne, C.O. 5.243, ff. 130–32.

32. Christopher Ward, *The War of the Revolution*, ed. John R. Alden, 2 vols. (New York: Macmillan. 1952), 1:138–39.

33. May 3, 1776, Germain to Howe, P.R.O. 30.55.2, f. 180; the second division, Brunswick, and Hessian artillery, plus 447 German recruits "For the British troops in Canada" sailed June 4. Précis [1776], C.O. 5.253, ff. 33–56, £5,000 in presents for Indians also sent, ibid. Among these was Major General Riedesel (Max Von Eelking, ed., *Memoirs and Letters and Journals of Major General Riedesel during His Residence in America*, 2 vols. [Albany, N.Y.: Munsell, 1868], 1:40–41), who would serve under Burgoyne the following year. Riedesel met Burgoyne on May 26, (ibid.), on board Burgoyne's ship, the *Blonde*.

34. The date of Burgoyne's arrival varies from source to source. May 6, according to "Intelligence from Quebec," dated June 10, 1776, Historical Manuscripts Commission *Dartmouth MSS.*,

2:420, seems too early. May 17, according to Sir John Irvine, in a letter dated June 10, 1776 to John H. Hutchinson, London, Historical Manuscripts Commission, *Twelfth Report, appendix, part IX, The Manuscripts of the Duke of Beaufort, K.G.* (London: H. M. Stationery Office, 1891), p. 286, seems more likely. Sir Francis Clerke, Burgoyne's aide-de-camp, arrived on May 29; see Clerke to Lord Polwarth, July 13, 1776, L 30.12.17.7, Bedford County Record Office. The whole embarkation had arrived by June 2, 1776, Précis [1776], C.O. 5.253, ff. 33–56.

35. July 13, 1776, Clerke to Lord Polwarth, Bedford County Record Office.

36. June 1, 1776, Burgoyne to Germain, Germain papers, Clements Library. Americans reacted to Burgoyne's arrival with dismay or anger. The presence of German troops raised tempers, and Rufus King, then a student at Harvard, was tempted to join the continental army to fight Burgoyne's "10,000 foreigners"; this even though King's father was a loyalist. Robert Ernst, *Rufus King: American Federalist* (Chapel Hill, N.C.: University of North Carolina Press, 1968), p. 19.

37. July 13, 1776, Clerke to Lord Polwarth, Bedford County Record Office.

38. Ibid. Carleton endorsed the plan: June 26, 1775; September 21, 1775; Précis [1776]. His purpose was not only to evacuate Quebec, but also: "if he succeeded, . . . that he could endeavour to take the Lakes as early as possible, and in his future progress contribute to the success of the Army under Genl. Howe. . . ." Précis [1776], C.O. 5.253, ff. 33–56. "High expectations" were held for the consequences of this "great arrangement." Communication with the Atlantic British army was expected to be opened, putting the American forces between two fires.

39. Carleton had 5,801 troops at Trois Rivières as of June 1; June 1, 1776, General Return, W.O. 17.1494. He reported on June 2 that reinforcements under Burgoyne and Fraser were "mostly arrived," but it was impossible to obtain exact returns at that time. June 2, 1776, Carleton to Germain, C.O. 5.253, f. 115; Précis [1776], C.O. 5.253, ff. 33–56.

40. July 13, 1776, Clerke to Lord Polwarth, Bedford County Record Office, in contrast to a Colonial Office account: Burgoyne's detachment, "being apprized of their march, were in readiness to receive them." Précis [1776].

41. July 13, 1776, Clerke to Lord Polwarth, Bedford County Record Office.

42. Ibid.

43. DeFonblanque, *Episodes*, p. 217.

44. July 13, 1776, Clerke to Lord Polwarth, Bedford County Record Office.

45. Ibid.; Clerke's letters offer another contrast to the annual summary of the Colonial Office. Clerke was obviously disappointed they escaped, but the Précis for 1776 said only that the Americans left "the King's Troops in the Full Possession of all Canada."

46. Clerke to Lord Polwarth, July 13, 1776, Bedford County Record Office.

47. William Digby, *The British Invasion from the North: The Campaign of Generals Carleton and Burgoyne from Canada 1776–1777 with the Journal of Lieutenant William Digby of the 53rd or Shropshire Regiment of Foot*, ed. James P. Baxter (Albany, N.Y.: Munsell, 1887), p. 108. Although Digby disliked Carleton, he praised his professional conduct: "I am positive every officer in the army, if called upon, would acquit him of acting imprudently in retiring from that place to winter in Canada, the season being so very severe and far advanced."

48. June 22, 1776, Burgoyne to Germain, Germain papers, Clements Library.

49. August 23, 1776, Germain to Burgoyne, Germain papers, Clements Library.

50. Ibid.

51. May 14, 1776, Carleton to Germain; June 21, 1776, Germain to Carleton, Alfred L. Burt, "The Quarrel between Germain and Carleton, an Inverted Story," *Canadian Historical Review* 11:202–22.

52. June 22, 1776, Lord North to the king, Fortescue, ed., *Correspondence*, 3:386.

53. June 22, 1776, the king to Lord North, ibid., p. 387.

54. Burt, "Quarrel," 11:202–22.

55. In fact, he relived Carleton on August 22; Burt, "Quarrel," pp. 206–9, civil appointments controversy, August 1776 to June 1777. For the military aspects of the quarrel, see ibid., pp. 210–14.

56. John Burgoyne, *The Substance of General Burgoyne's Speeches* (London: J. Almon, 1778) p. 2.

57. Even the Colonial Office account credited Carleton. But Riedesel complained: "this delay will lose us three weeks and materially impede our progress." June 22, 1776, Riedesel to Duke Ferdinand, Von Eelking, *Riedesel,* 1:45.

58. In September, Carleton received Germain's letter of June 21 criticizing his lack of plans for the future; September 28, 1776, Carleton to Germain, Canadian Archives, XII, 188, cited by Burt, "Quarrel," p. 210.

59. May 12, 1776, Howe to Germain, Historical Manuscripts Commission, *Stopford-Sackville MSS.,* 2:31–32.

60. Jane Clark, "The Command of the Canadian Army," *Canadian Historical Review* 10 (June, 1929):129–35, and Burt, "Quarrel," p. 213, discuss this matter; July 27, 1776, Germain to Knox, Historical Manuscripts Commission, *Report on the Manuscripts in Various Collections,* 8 vols. (London, Dublin and Hereford: H. M. Stationery Office, 1901–14), 6:123. Germain sent Howe duplicate instructions for Carleton in a letter of August 22 (Germain to Howe, C.O. 5.243, ff. 159–60). Howe did not receive this letter until November 28, after Carleton had already left for the Lakes (November 28, 1776, Howe to Germain, no. 3, House of Lords Record Office, copy).

61. August 22, 1776, Germain to Carleton, in John Burgoyne, *A State of the Expedition from Canada, as Laid before the House of Commons by Lieutenant General Burgoyne, and Verified by Evidence with a Collection of Authentic Documents and an Addition of Many Circumstances Which Were Prevented from Appearing before the House by the Prorogation of Parliament Written and Collected by Himself* (New York: Arno Press, 1969), appendix, pp. ii–iii. It is curious that Howe did not send Carleton word of Germain's new orders during the period November 1776 to May 1777.

62. Carleton now had 13,000 men. Additional Brunswick reinforcements arrived in September; Mackesy, *America,* p. 94.

63. Hutchinson, ed., *Diary,* 2:112.

64. See Ward, *Revolution,* 1:384–97, for an account of the Battle of Valcour Island. Carleton dismissed a party of Indians, who had come to volunteer, saying he wouldn't need them until the spring; Précis [1776], C.O. 5.253. f. 33.

65. Burt, "Quarrel," p. 211.

66. Ironically, that winter was "remarkably mild," December 7, 1776, Carleton to Barrington, W.O. 1.11, ff. 53–56.

67. October 23, 1776, Phillips to Burgoyne, DeFonblanque, *Episodes,* pp. 218–21.

68. October 15, 1776, C.O. 5.253, f. 55.

69. Carleton's withdrawal, wrote quartermaster Gabriel Christie, was "beyond all human comprehension," October 26, 1776, Christie to Germain, Historical Manuscripts Commission, *Stopford-Sackville MSS.,* 2:44–46.

70. November 9, 1776, Phillips to Carleton, C.O. 42.36, ff. 25–28.

71. October 23, 1776, Phillips to Burgoyne, DeFonblanque, *Episodes,* pp. 218–21.

72. November 7, 1776, Burgoyne to Clinton, Clinton papers, Clements Library. Burgoyne suggested the soldiers could have covered themselves in their "huts".

73. November 1, 1776, "Winterquarters for the British Troops, . . ." House of Lords Record Office, no. 8, Copy. "Rd. from Genl. Burgoyne."

74. Phillips believed Howe would occupy Crown Point after Carleton evacuated. But Howe had not even reached Peekskill. When Washington moved to New Jersey, Howe pursued him and abandoned the Hudson. Phillips to Burgoyne, n.d.

75. November 7, 1776, Burgoyne to Clinton, Clinton papers, Clements Library. It was generally known in London at this time that Burgoyne and Carleton were frequently in disagreement; Hutchinson, ed. *Diary,* 2:117.

76. November 7, 1776, Burgoyne to Clinton, Clinton papers, Clements Library. Burgoyne wished to lead three battalions, a corps of artillery, and a regiment of Indians and Canadians across

Lake Ontario to Oswego, thence to the Mohawk River as a diversion to the army in New York City, and a "yet more positive assistance to General Carleton." Sir John Johnston approved his scheme, as did Carleton but the governor had not taken sufficient ammunition with him to supply Burgoyne for a proposed diversion. Burgoyne also suggested that Carleton send a fleet into the lower part of Lake Champlain. This proposal was likewise rejected. Nor did Carleton heed Burgoyne's suggestion to attack Ticonderoga. That supply shortages were largely responsible for the failure of the 1776 expedition is the contention of R. Arthur Bowler, *Logistics and the Failure of the British Army in America, 1775–1783* (Princeton, N.J.: Princeton University Press, 1975), pp. 217–24.

77. October 21, 1776, Charles Douglas to the earl of Sandwich, in G. R. Barnes and J. H. Owen, eds., *The Private Papers of John, Earl of Sandwich, First Lord of the Admiralty, 1771–1782*, 4 vols. (London: Navy Records Society, 1932–38), 1:190.

78. November 7, 1776, Burgoyne to Clinton, Clinton papers, Clements Library.

79. Ibid.

10

Interlude in London

As he hastened into the capital city the day his ship docked at Spithead, Burgoyne may have become aware that he had lost some popularity in the view of his officer friends; Hans Stanley told the earl of Huntingdon that he was "very sorry to say, but not surprised to hear, that there is a very great clamour against Burgoyne, particularly in the army."[1] Moved by "the highest ambition and ardour to distinguish himself," Burgoyne was an object of envy to his enemies, who were believed also to resent his having been reinstated in the army in 1756 after selling out.[2] In Parliament, members complained about the British withdrawal from the lakes of New York,[3] and at court Burgoyne discovered that both he and Carleton were in disfavor.[4] One day after his return to London he obtained an interview with Lord George Germain, who declared that the operations were conducted "without sense or vigour."[5] Burgoyne quickly pointed out that he had been "strongly in opinion against" Carleton's decision to retreat.[6] Carleton received the burden of reproof,[7] particularly because he had given Burgoyne an intemperate letter for Germain in which he complained of the lack of boats and provisions for the advance into New York.[8]

During his interview with Germain on December 10, Burgoyne presented to him several other documents that Carleton had entrusted to his care, the most important of which was a "Memorandum . . . relative to the next campaign to be laid before the government."[9] To each of Carleton's requisitions Burgoyne attached his own observations, probably written in November while he was crossing the Atlantic.[10] Carleton also provided Burgoyne a separate memorandum, which was duly delivered, justifying the need for four thousand additional troops. Burgoyne appended his observation that only ten thousand rank-and-file soldiers were stationed in Canada, many of them "useless stuff."[11] He did not have much faith in the German mercenaries and also held a poor opinion of the Irish recruits and draftees. The "considerable number" of American prisoners recruited into Allan MacLean's Royal Highland émigrés worried Burgoyne, too, because so many had deserted in the last campaign; he expected large numbers to do so again. Burgoyne found the Royal Regiment of New York "not yet anything like soldiers," lacking commissioned officers and sergeants to train the privates. Because Burgoyne feared a repetition of Arnold's march to Quebec or Thompson's attack upon Trois Rivières, or possible "small incursions" into Canada, he agreed that three thousand soldiers had to remain in Canada, although "General Carleton may possibly think a thousand more" would also be needed to secure convoys and supplies, to keep Canada in "due subjugation" and "to enforce the Duty of Corvees which will be indespensibly necessary for the Supply of the Army." Burgoyne was confident that Canada would supply an adequate number of troops if the British army reduced the number of regulars posted in Canada.

Finally, Burgoyne attached a requisition for twenty-four gunboats, which Carleton had not included in his memorandum. Although William Phillips had suggested to Carleton the necessity for ordering gunboats, Carleton did not apparently think the matter sufficiently important to warrant a formal requisition. Burgoyne also advised the government to have built in England carriages of seasoned timber, needed to convoy the boats.

Burgoyne's memoranda are significant for several reasons, perhaps chiefly as examples of his capacity for organizing and improving the suggestions of others. The document also reveals Burgoyne's attitude toward Carleton.[12] In his summation he alluded very briefly to a delicate question: whether or not Carleton would remain in command of the British army in Canada.

> Upon the whole therefore when a moderate deduction of sick is added to the useless, the whole of the Canada Army as it now stands allowing for the recruits arrived in the Autumn, and I believe not all comprized in the return, will not exceed eight thousand men of such troops as I believe your Lordship would wish to risk the fate of an Offensive Campaign upon, or the Reputation of any General you may think proper to recommend to his Majesty.[13]

It seems reasonable to assume that Burgoyne knew Germain intended to replace Carleton for the 1777 campaign. He doubtless anticipated that he himself had as good an opportunity as anyone else to bid for it, if he played his cards right. Burgoyne was most likely informed of Germain's August 22 decision to remove Carleton as soon as he arrived in London in December 1776. Accordingly, Burgoyne set the tone of his memorandum to suit the prejudices of Germain.

Germain wished to inform George III of his conversation with Burgoyne before the general was granted a royal audience, but Burgoyne moved very quickly.[14] On the following day he obtained an interview with the king and remarked "that as the arrangements for the next campaign might possibly come under his royal contemplation before my return [from Bath] I humbly laid myself at his Majesty's feet for such active employment as he might think me worthy of."[15] Burgoyne impressed the monarch, who observed that he appeared to be "a more enterprizing Commander" than Carleton, who "may be too cold and not so active as might be wished."[16] Burgoyne's campaign for advancement seemed finally at an end. Two days after the interview the king informed Lord North that "Burgoyne may have the Corps to be sent from Canada,"[17] but postponed a final decision until the cabinet sat again. For once Burgoyne acted with discretion. A friend observed: "Mr. *Burgoyne*, since his return, I find, affects great sience, and only says, that *Carleton* intends to begin the next campaign as early as possible with the attack of *Ticonderoga*."[18] Since no official decision had yet been made, Burgoyne's silence was politically prudent.

Encouraged by his favorable reception at court, Burgoyne maintained a prominent role in public affairs during December 1777. He "harrangued the population" at Covent Garden on behalf of his aide-de-camp, Lord Petersham, who stood for election to Parliament *in absentia* for the Borough of Westminster on December 17.[19] He chatted with Lord Barrington at the war office, reviewing the matters which he had discussed with Germain and the king.[20] Burgoyne also gave Barrington a letter from Carleton and a list of troop returns. On Christmas Day he placed a bet of fifty guineas with Charles Fox at Brooks Club, wagering that he would return victorious from America the following December.[21] Burgoyne also found time to introduce the captain of his transatlantic ship, the *Isis,* to the king,[22] a privilege which bespoke the royal attitude toward Burgoyne. He left for Bath on the first day of the new year to take the waters prescribed by his physician,[23] but before departing he assured Germain, "should my attendence in town become necessary relatively [*sic*] to information upon the affairs of Canada, I shall be ready to obey your summons upon one day's notice."[24] He also asked the secretary of state to support his efforts to obtain the Canadian assignment, "a hope, my Lord, forwarded not only upon a just sense of the honour your Lordship's friendship must reflect upon me, but also upon a feeling that I deserve it, inasmuch as a solid respect & sincere personal attachment can constitute such a claim."[25] Burgoyne interrupted his residence in Somerset often during January and February. On January 8, "his Majesty took an airing on horseback in Hyde-park upwards of an hour, attended by Gen. Burgoyne," reported the *London Chronicle.*[26] Three days later, the press reported somewhat prematurely that Burgoyne had received a military assignment for North America, and that he would set out in the spring.[27] On January 14, Germain hinted to Howe that a major change in command was in the offing, that Carleton's withdrawal from Crown Point had been "a great mortification to me. . . . I trust, however, that my Expectations are likely to be gratified, when I presume the army will make more rapid Advances the next Campaign, and reach Albany sooner than you seem to expect."[28]

Burgoyne's ascendancy was obtained at Carleton's expense, as the governor of Canada knew.[29] Indeed, Germain consulted Burgoyne often concerning matters about which he should have questioned Carleton previously by post.[30] Germain had decided to equip the expedition for 1777 even before a commander had been officially appointed.[31] The colonial office conducted an exhaustive, if disorganized, study of all matters relating to Canada, at Germain's behest.[32] During the month of January Germain's under secretaries were presenting diverse reports to him. Early in February, the war office arranged for clothing,[33] naval transport[34] and horses[35] to be sent to Canada.

Burgoyne was not the only officer importuning Germain, who also had to contend with Howe's demands for another campaign in New York.[36] Having been in office little more than a year, the secretary seemed to become increasingly irritated by the frustrations of an unpopular and stubborn war. Exasperated by Howe's requests, furious with Carleton, still undecided about Burgoyne, Germain retired to his country estate at Drayton to nurse a cold.[37] Burgoyne, still lacking official confirmation of his appointment, returned to Bath to compose his thoughts.

Meanwhile, unknown to Germain and Burgoyne, General Henry Clinton set sail for London. Clinton, Howe's second in command, was a formidable competitor in any struggle for position. Germain commented irritably, "I am surprised at Clinton's coming home. Burgoyne will not be sorry to see that he is not the only General, second in command, who takes that liberty without the King's leave."[38] One month later, Clinton appeared more worthy in Germain's estimation when the secretary received news of the Rhode Island venture.[39] After the lapse of yet another month, Clinton's cause was further bolstered when Germain received a letter from Howe, who argued that he needed Burgoyne in New York and speculated that Clinton, who was senior to Burgoyne, might get the Canadian command.[40] After consideration, Germain decided to propose Clinton's appointment to the cabinet, which was scheduled to meet on February 25.[41] "I thoroughly approve of this" remarked the king, who was also having second thoughts about Burgoyne.[42]

Burgoyne, having perhaps heard rumors that Clinton would be recommended, presented for the consideration of the cabinet when it met on February 25 a detailed analysis of strategy that he had designed at Bath for the campaign of 1777.[43] In that document Burgoyne examined comprehensively the various routes an invasion force could take into New York, the value of diversionary expeditions, possibilities for forming junctions with other armies, the use of provincial and Indian auxiliary forces, problems of transport and supply, and other matters.[44] He also made clear his fear that Carleton might not cooperate with him if he were chosen to lead the army. At the same time he repeated recent criticism of the Canadian governor.[45] Clearly anticipating the appointment, Burgoyne suggested a solution to the supply problem that would develop when the political and military responsibilities for Quebec were divided between Carleton and himself: "Under these considerations," he wrote, "it is presumed that the general officer employed to proceed with the army will be held to be out of reach of any possible blame until he is clear of the province of Canada, and furnished with the proposed supplies."[46] Other sentences and phrases in the memorandum reveal that Burgoyne at the very least wished to believe he had already received the appointment. He referred to "my expedition," and at one point declared: "I should wish Lieutenant Colonel St. Leger" to command a diversionary force. The cabinet ministers were so impressed with the document that they sent to the king a request that Burgoyne "should again be employed in Canada."[47] George III had some reservations about certain details of Burgoyne's "Thoughts," but remarked that in general "The Out Lines [of the plan] are Founded on a proper Foundation."[48] He did not confirm the cabinet's request, nor did he indicate that he favored Clinton. Burgoyne had won the cabinet, if not the king; at least he forestalled a royal decision favorable to his rival.[49]

Meanwhile, Clinton arrived in London,[50] ostensibly to obtain relief from his assignment under Howe, for whom he had no respect.[51] He also wished to defend his direction of the failed expedition to South Carolina, which Germain had criticized.[52] Furthermore, he wished to assuage his disappointment of 1776, when the Canadian assignment went to Burgoyne.[53]

Clinton received a warm welcome upon his arrival in London, and his friends urged him to bid for the command of the 1777 expedition.[54] Much to everyone's surprise, Clinton refused to ask for it. Early in March Germain actually offered him the post, but Clinton refused it.[55] He said that "Burgoyne knew better what to do and how to do it."[56] As an alternative assignment, Germain suggested that Clinton accept one of the other responsibilities still held by Carleton, that of military governor of Canada.[57] Clinton again declined, out of deference for Carleton, for whom he had the greatest respect.[58] Clinton then astonished his friends by requesting to be retired.[59] Clinton's praise of Carleton could not have pleased Germain, who thereafter obtained for Clinton a knighthood to quiet him and sent him back to a secondary command.[60]

Burgoyne continued to act like a man who had already obtained the appointment. On March 2, he wrote to Pownall about naval operations in North America for 1777 implying that he had the assignment.[61] Nine days later, Thomas Hutchinson noted that Burgoyne was scheduled to depart for North America.[62] On March 18, the decision was finally made at a cabinet meeting. The ministry offered Burgoyne the independent command, and he accepted it.[63] Clinton became petulant and declared that Burgoyne had injured his sensibilities by accepting the offer. He was humiliated to see an officer junior to him "placed in the high Road to Glory."[68] To further add to his chagrin, the benighted Clinton was soon returned to New York under Howe.[65] Germain gave Burgoyne instructions for Carleton and for himself, and the general left London for Portsmouth on March 27.[66] A week later Burgoyne was still in Portsmouth, provoking the impatient Germain to exclaim, "I am sorry Burgoyne cannot avail himself of his fine wind. . . . I didn't know two winds were necessary . . . before they could put to sea."[67] An unnecessary outburst, for Burgoyne left for America and his fate on April 2.

Notes

1. December 18, 1776, Hans Stanley to the earl of Huntingdon, Historical Manuscripts Commission, *Hastings MSS.,* 3:188–89.

2. Ibid.

3. Many members of the House were dissatisfied with the retreat; Mackesy, *America,* p. 107.

4. December 13, 1776, the king to North, W. B. Donne, ed., *Correspondence of King George III with Lord North, 1768–1783* (London: J. Murray 1867), 2:44–45.

5. DeFonblanque, *Episodes,* p. 225, quoting Germain.

6. Burgoyne did not officially oppose Carleton's decision to retreat at Crown Point or Ticonderoga; Donne, ed., *Correspondence,* 2:45. In the Colonial Office's Précis for 1776 (inaccurately dated 1777), the following sentence is written in the margin: "Conversation with General Burgoyne after he arrived in England," C.O. 5.253, ff. 33–56. Burgoyne said he told Carleton that an expedition on the Mohawk would have been of "great advantage." all the Indians being "strongly attached to his Majesty." Burgoyne offered himself to conduct "this Enterprize" and "repeatedly urged" with others that such an expedition take place, and "at last prevailed" with Carleton. Carleton gave no reason why "it was not proceeded upon" but Burgoyne "has said he understood the General laid it aside because there were not provisions to spare for the Support of the Troops and Indians that were to be sent upon it."

7. North had defended Carleton to the king in November; "the great preparations Sir Guy has made perfectly well account for his delay"; [n.d.] North to the king, Fortescue, ed., *Correspondence,* 3:403; 1776, Carleton to Germain, C.O. 42.35, ff. 40–71–2.

8. In November, the king supported Carleton: he had given "Sufficient reasons for his not earlier attempting to pass the Lakes"; November 17, 1776, the king to North, Fortescue, ed., *Correspondence,* 3:403–4.

9. "Memorandum of General Carleton relative to the next campaign to be laid before government," [n.d.] Germain papers, Clements Library.

10. "Memorandum of Observations, relative to the Service in Canada, submitted to Lord George Germain," C.O. 42.36, ff. 11–24 and Germain papers, Clements Library. Carleton asked Burgoyne to write a memorandum incorporating Carleton's ideas for 1777, and present it to the ministry; October 22, 1776, Carleton to Burgoyne; October 22 letter also appears in *Parliamentary Register,* May 1779, 12:145–54.

11. George III commented later: "Burgoyne certainly greatly undervalues the German recruits," quoted by Nickerson, *Turning Point,* pp. 89–90.

12. "With all due deference to General Carleton: . . . upon the whole therefore I am persuaded the demands of Genl. Carleton: Though this requisition is not comprized in the memorandum given me by General Carleton." C.O. 42.36, ff. 11–24.

13. Ibid.

14. December 10, 1776, Germain to the king, Fortescue, ed., *Correspondence,* 3:405–6.

15. January 1, 1777, Burgoyne to Germain, C.O. 42.36, ff. 1–6. The interview was held on December 10; *London Chronicle* for December 12, 1776.

16. December 13, 1776, the king to North, Fortescue, ed., *Correspondence,* 3:406–7. Parliament recessed on this day and did not sit again until January 23; Cobbett, ed., *Parliamentary History,* 18:1456.

17. December 13, 1776, the king to North, Fortescue, ed., *Correspondence,* 3:405–6.

18. December 15, 1776, Claude Crespigny to Ralph Izard, Force, ed., *Archives,* fifth series, 3:1227.

19. December 19, 1776, *London Chronicle;* December 17, 1776, Walpole to Lady Ossory, Walpole, *Correspondence,* 32:336. Petersham, who won the election, was in North America.

20. December 17, 1776, Barrington to Germain, C.O. 5.168, ff. 605–8.

21. December 25, 1776, the Betts Book, Brooks Club, cited by Thomas G. Frothingham, *Washington: Commander in Chief* (Boston: Houghton Mifflin, 1930), p. 179, note 2.

22. December 26, 1777, *London Chronicle.*

23. January 1, 1777, Burgoyne to Germain, C.O. 42.36, ff. 1–6.

24. Ibid.

25. Ibid.

26. January 9, 1777, *London Chronicle.*

27. January 11, 1777, *London Chronicle.*

28. January 14, 1777, Germain to Howe, C.O. 5.243, ff. 176–80.

29. Sir Guy wrote bitterly to Shelburne: "The arrangements for this campaign have been made in England: even the disposition for posting the small corps that is to remain in the Province. It appears to be the attempt of a man who wishes to be thought a great military genius capable of commanding an army at 3000 miles distance; but his attempt here has succeeded so ill, that it exposes him to the ridicule of the subalterns of the army." January 13, 1777, Carleton to Shelburne, Fitzmaurice, *Shelburne,* 2:7, note 2.

30. January 20, 1777, Germain to Burgoyne (draft), C.O. 42.36, ff. 53–56; January 21, 1777, Burgoyne to Germain, C.O. 42.36, ff. 57–60.

31. See Clive Gee, "The British War Office in the Later Years of the American War of Independence," *Journal of Modern History* 26:123–26, who argues that Germain had organized supplies to fit the needs of Burgoyne's plan before the plan was officially released.

32. January 22, 1777, John Buddington, Office of Ordnance, to War Office, "for the information of Lord George Germain," C.O. 5.256, f. 120; January 29, 1777, Knox to Matthew Lewis, W.O. 1.682, f. 53.

33. February 3, 1777, Barrington to Germain, C.O. 5.256, f. 127; to reach the Saint Lawrence at the "earliest opportunity."

34. February 10, 1777, Buddington to Knox, C.O. 5.256, f. 128; 200 tons of shipping to go within ten days.

35. February 13, 1777, Barrington to Germain, C.O. 5.256, f. 117; 100 soldiers and sufficient horses for two regiments of light dragoon.

36. January 31, 1777, Germain to Eden, B.L., Add. MS. 34,413, ff. 147–48.

37. January 31, 1777, Germain to Eden: "I have had a . . . cold, which . . . I doctor by being in the Country at this season of the year, but I hope I shall not be prevented returning to Gov[ernmen]t so as to be at the next Levee."

38. December 31, 1776, Germain to Knox, Historical Manuscript Commission, *MSS. in Various Collections,* 6:128. Actually, Howe had given permission to Clinton for his leave of absence; Howe to Germain, cited by Brown, *American Secretary,* p. 101 and note 80. Burgoyne also received permission to leave.

39. January 22, 1777, Germain to the king, Fortescue, ed. *Correspondence,* 3:418.

40. December 31, 1776, Howe to Germain, Historical Manuscript Commission, *Stopford-Sackville MSS.,* 2:53–5.

41. February 24, 1777, Germain to the king, Fortescue, ed., *Correspondence,* 3:421. Germain said he would nominate Clinton at Howe's request.

42. February 24, 1777, the king to North, ibid., p. 421.

43. John Burgoyne, "Thoughts for Conducting the War on the Side of Canada," February 28, 1777, C.O. 42.36, ff. 37–52; C.O. 5.43, f. 36; manuscript copy dated February 25 presented to the cabinet on that date, Germain papers, Clements Library; Burgoyne, *State,* appendix, pp. iii–xii.

44. Burgoyne, "Thoughts," C.O. 42.36, ff. 37–52.

45. Ibid.

46. Ibid.

47. February 25, 1777, Cabinet Minute, Barnes and Owen, eds., *Sandwich Papers,* 1:285.

48. March 5, 1777, manuscript in the king's hand, Fortescue, ed., *Correspondence,* 3:443–45.

49. Germain continued to believe that Carleton must be removed; February 25, 1777, Germain to Eden, B.L. Add. MS. 34,413, f. 267.

50. December 19, 1777, Clinton to General Harvey, cited by Clark, "Command," p. 133.

51. Brown, *American Secretary*, p. 101.

52. Germain had published Clinton's defense of his conduct at South Carolina in the *Gazette*. Clinton had written about the ministry in strong language in the article, and publication of it was damaging to him.

53. Brown, *American Secretary*, p. 101.

54. Willcox, *Clinton*, p. 130; Clark, "Command," p. 133.

55. Brown contended that Clinton's arrival in a sour mood, which Germain changed by giving him a knighthood, was an "old story," since Clinton actually offered to resign; *American Secretary*, p. 101. But see Willcox, *Clinton*, pp. 134–35, on Clinton's diffidence.

56. Willcox, *Clinton*, pp. 134–35.

57. Clark, "Command," p. 135.

58. December 17, 1777, Clinton to Newcastle, Newcastle papers, cited by Clark, ibid. Clinton said he had had no objection to taking command of the army over *Burgoyne's* head, but that he was not allowed to do so. However, this thought was written a year later; Willcox, *Clinton*, pp. 135–36.

59. Willcox, *Clinton*, p. 136, note 5. Clark commented that this was bad psychology; Burgoyne practiced "high powered salesmanship." "Command," p. 133.

60. April 19, 1777, Germain to Howe, Willcox, *Clinton*, pp. 130–41.

61. March 2, 1777, Burgoyne to Pownall, Clinton papers, Clements Library.

62. March 11, 1777, Hutchinson, ed., *Diary*, 2:142.

63. March 18, 1777, Sandwich to the king, and March 18, 1777, Germain to the king, Fortescue, ed., *Correspondence*, 3:427.

64. Clinton's anger was momentary; he and Burgoyne resumed their cordial relationship in correspondence during and after the 1777 campaign, some of which is cited in subsequent chapters of this study. See also Willcox, *Clinton*, p. 135.

65. He arrived in New York City on July 5; Brown, *American Secretary*, p. 102.

66. March 26, 1777, Germain to Carleton, C.O. 42.36, ff. 101–16; March 26, 1777, Germain to Burgoyne, Burgoyne, *State*, p. 6; B.L., Add. MSS. 21,697, f. 158.

67. April 2, 1777, Germain to Knox, Historical Manuscripts Commission, *MSS. in Various Collections*, 6:129.

11

Strategy

If the ministry deliberated four months before making a decision about the appointment for North America, it devoted an even longer period of time to a consideration of strategy for the campaign. Burgoyne's thoughts were not the first professional suggestions for troop movements proposed during the year. On November 30, 1776, Sir William Howe sent to Germain a plan for the orderly conquest of the rebellious colonies, "to finish the War in one year."[1]

Howe's initial plan has been called an excellent one.[2] It provided, first, that an offensive army of 10,000 men seize Providence, Rhode Island, then penetrate through Massachusetts in order to reduce and hold Boston. Howe further saw need for a force of 2,000 additional soldiers, posted in Rhode Island, to safeguard that colony. A second offensive army of 10,000 soldiers, he thought, should proceed up the Hudson River from New York City to Albany, remaining there until the arrival of the Canadian army in September 1777. Sir William wished to quarter 5,000 soldiers on Manhattan to protect New York City. He intended to station another defensive army of 8,000 men in New Jersey to keep Washington in check by giving "a jealousy to Philadelphia."[3] When he had completed successfully the conquest of New York and Boston, Howe wanted to march into Pennsylvania and Virginia. The king's army might subdue South Carolina and Georgia during the winter of 1777–78, thus concluding the war.[4] Howe was anxious to surprise and awe the Americans, to weaken their morale by the magnitude of his operation.[5] Success depended upon the reduction of Boston and the junction of the two armies at Albany. Having "cut off and cut down" New England, he could then concentrate his forces in the southern colonies. But Howe said he required 15,000 reinforcements and ten ships of the line from Great Britain in order to execute the plan. Apparently aware that his request would be difficult to meet, Howe suggested that Germain purchase mercenary troops from Russia or Hanover.[6] He decided that he needed 35,000 men altogether, including in his estimate the requested reinforcements.[7] Germain did not approve Howe's advice. The secretary informed him early in 1777 that he could not possibly fill the "alarming" request for 15,000 men.[8] As an alternative proposal, Lord George offered to send about 8,000 Hessian mercenaries and British recruits. He approved the expedition to Rhode Island, but withheld his opinion concerning the rest of the plan until he received further information from Howe concerning "this momentous Affair." Germain was dismayed to receive Howe's ambitious proposal; he had expected the war to end altogether in 1776.[9]

Before Germain had an opportunity to send these comments to Howe, Sir William sent a second, and quite different, plan. He reported on December 20, 1776, that the inhabitants of Pennsylvania were "from the late Progress of the Army, disposed to Peace, in which sentiment they would be confirmed by our getting possession of Philadelphia."[10] The army in New York City should not go to Albany; instead, he wished it to act "defensively upon the lower part of Hudson's River, to cover Jersey on that side."[11] Realizing that his decision to move southward would affect the security of the army in Canada, Howe suggested that the force in New York City should "facilitate" in a limited way the progress of the northern expedition. But the fate of that army remained uncertain in his mind: "subsequent Operations of that Corps will depend on the State of things at the Time."[12] He desired to defer the proposed attack upon Boston until he had received reinforcement from Britain. Howe also wished to reduce the defensive armies in number to 2,000 for Rhode Island, 4,000 for New York City, and 3,000 for the Hudson River. Thus he should have 10,000 men available for the campaign in Pennsylvania and should not need a large number of reinforcements from Britain. He required 19,000 men altogether for the successful execution of his second plan.

Curiously, Howe sent his request before Germain replied to his first proposal. Sir William may have received unofficial advice that reinforcements could not be found in the numbers he required. Perhaps he wished on December 20 to substitute what he thought would be a more acceptable plan to a ministry he feared might not approve his request for such a horde of troops.[13] Certainly he was preoccupied with the problem of troop supply. Eight days later he suggested to Germain that volunteers could be drafted from regiments of dragoons stationed in Britain.[14] He proposed that Germain should send those new troops to him in North America. Shortly thereafter, Sir William lamented: "if the reinforcements are small, the Operations will be much curtailed."[15] "The King entirely approves" the second plan, replied Germain in March 1777. He noted that "the Reasons which have induced you to recommend this Change in your operations are solid and decisive."[16] But were they? It seems doubtful that a merely reported increase in loyalist sentiment at Philadelphia was a "solid and decisive" reason for substantially altering the first plan. Lord George probably approved the second proposal because it required fewer reinforcements. Germain wished Howe to include in his revised strategy a "warm Diversion" along the coast of Massachusetts so that the Americans would be compelled to maintain troops to defend that area. Sir William was expected to carry out the coastal diversion without the larger number of soldiers. Germain approved a plan that contained no provision for an offensive army to join with the Canadian force at Albany.

Before Germain's letter arrived in America, Howe sent a third plan to the secretary.[17] He again altered the proposed distribution of soldiers. Sir William suggested 11,000 men for the expedition to Pennsylvania; 3,500 for New York City; 1,200 for Staten Island; 2,400 for Rhode Island, and 3,000 provincials for use in the New York City area under command of Governor William Tryon. Howe believed that Tryon's force could assist the Canadian army if necessary, "upon Hudson's River, or . . . enter Connecticut as circumstances may point out." Howe also informed Lord George that he would take to the sea for his journey to Philadelphia, as he did not wish to waste time establishing communication posts overland. Thus he left the army in New York City "entirely without contact until Philadelphia had been taken. This change was highly significant."[18] Although at a later date Howe sent 7,000 men to General Clinton, who commanded the forces in New York City during Howe's absence, he did not instruct Sir Henry to assist the army in Canada. Nor was he able to send such an order after he sailed. Clearly Howe did not believe his third plan to be ideal. He complained that the hope of terminating the war in 1777 had "vanished." Yet he still believed that reinforcements would be sent.[19] He also feared that heavy snowfalls early in 1777 would delay the onset of the expedition. He still hoped to reduce Pennsylvania and New Jersey by the end of the campaign, but "this in some Measure must depend upon the Success of the Northern Army." Howe assumed that the army in Canada would proceed to Albany independently.

Germain received Howe's third plan on May 18.[20] Once again he informed Sir William that reinforcements were not available: "You will, however, be in some degree reconciled to your disappointment in not having your requisition complied with, when you recollect that there is but one Battalion of the Regiment of Artillery in Great Britain."[21] Germain assured Howe that many Americans were well disposed toward the crown. He hoped that "this Campaign will put an end to the unhappy Contest," although Howe had warned him to the contrary. Germain reported that "His Majesty does not hesitate to approve the Alterations which you propose," but then urged—for the first time in the entire correspondence—that Howe complete his reduction of Philadelphia "in time for you to cooperate with the Army ordered to proceed from Canada, and put itself under your Command."[22] This request is surprising, in view of Howe's statements that he expected to be delayed in Pennsylvania, and that he could not hope to finish the war in 1777. Perhaps Germain was no longer so confident that the northern army could penetrate into the wilderness of New York without support from New York City. He could not know that his letter would be delayed three months in transit. When Howe received it he was at sea, unable to comply with the secretary's request. Germain had ample time to clarify his instructions for Howe during the six-month period of correspondence. He should not have expected that Sir William could return to help Burgoyne so late in the year. Howe's judgment was equally defective. Familiar with geographical conditions in America, he must have expected that the army in Canada would encounter difficulties in northern New York. But Howe promised Burgoyne assistance only if Washington turned his force against the northern army. Had the American general proceeded to the Hudson, Howe still would have needed a considerable period of time to return to New York City, reduce the Hudson Highlands, then navigate the Hudson River through its narrowest passage in order to reach Burgoyne. His second and third plans were foolish, but Germain sanctioned them.

Lord George had formulated his own instructions for Burgoyne in a letter addressed to Sir Guy Carleton in March, 1777. He ordered Carleton "to detach Lieutenant General Burgoyne, or such officer that you should think most proper, with the remainder of the troops, and direct the officer so detached to proceed with all possible expedition to join General Howe, and to put himself under his command."[23] Germain also ordered Carleton, Burgoyne, and Lieutenant Colonel Barry St. Leger to write to Howe as soon as possible to inform him about plans for the junction so that Howe could instruct them. Since Germain knew that Howe would be detained in Philadelphia, he ordered the commanders of the northern expedition to act *as Exigencies may require* until they received instructions from Howe.[24] But in doing so, they must "never lose view of their intended Junction with Sir William Howe as their principal objects." Germain did not anticipate that Burgoyne would need reinforcement from the south. Burgoyne would proceed autonomously, he thought, using his own judgment until Howe instructed him. It seems reasonable to assume that Germain intended Howe and Burgoyne to conduct two independent expeditions which would join at a later date as the campaign's culminating act.

How did Germain's instructions to Burgoyne affect the thought and action of Sir William Howe? Several weeks later, a copy of Burgoyne's orders was sent to Howe.[25] Although Howe did not receive Germain's dispatch of May 18 approving his strategy until August, he did acknowledge on July 5 receipt of the duplicate instructions for Burgoyne. Furthermore, Germain's orders of March 26 at no point required Howe to assist Burgoyne. Consequently, Howe did not change any of his plans as a result of Germain's orders for Burgoyne.

Burgoyne formulated his own conception of the expedition.[26] His plan was not a "three-pronged" coordinated attack, terminating at Albany, in order to isolate New England from the other colonies. According to Burgoyne's design, one army would push toward Albany from Canada on the Hudson River; another force would proceed to the same destination on the Mohawk River. "These ideas," wrote the general, "are formed on the supposition that it will be the sole purpose of the Canada army to effect a junction with General Howe, or"—here Burgoyne hedged—"after cooperating so far as to get possession of Albany and open the communication to New York, to remain upon the Hudson's River, and thereby enable Howe to act with his whole force to the Southward."[27] Burgoyne's definition of the word "cooperating" is unclear. He knew Howe planned to move to the "southward." He did not insist that a junction with Howe's army was necessary for successful execution of the campaign, nor did he request the ministry to dispatch a supplementary expedition from New York City to assist his army. Most likely, Burgoyne desired a totally independent command in lieu of a junction with Howe. He knew well the perils which confronted an army in northern New York. In his memorandum, Burgoyne noted that transport and supply would be difficult; he recognized that his army would be unfamiliar with the terrain; he was aware of recently strengthened revolutionary forces in the lake region. He did not believe these problems were serious ones. In fact, Burgoyne's optimism led him to suggest an additional and quite independent goal for the Canadian expedition: "it may be highly worth consideration, whether the most important purpose to which the Canada army could be employed, supposing in possession of Ticonderoga, would not be to gain the Connecticut River."[28] Exuding confidence, Burgoyne hoped that operations on Lake Champlain might be completed with sufficient time to allow his naval commander to return to the Saint Lawrence "and reap laurels in the ocean."[29]

When he arrived at Montreal in May 1777, Burgoyne found awaiting him a letter from Howe to Carleton, in which Sir William warned that

Having but little expectation that I shall be able from the Want of sufficient Strength in this Army, to detach a Corps, in the Beginning of the Campaign, to act upon the Hudson's River, consistent with the operations already determined upon, the Force your Excellency may deem expedient to advance beyond your Frontiers after taking Ticonderoga, will I fear have little assistance from hence to facilitate their approach; and as I shall probably be in Pensilvania [sic] when that corps is ready to advance into this Province, it will not be in my Power to communicate with the officer commanding it so soon as I should wish; he must therefore pursue such Measures as may from circumstances be judged most conducive to the Advancement of His Majesty's Service consistent with your Excellency's Orders for his Conduct.[30]

Howe could not see the "further Progress" of the northern expedition "at this Distance of time" but the "Friends of Gouvernment in that Part of the Country will be found so numerous" that Burgoyne could reduce "the rebellious Parts" without difficulty. He did promise to order a detachment for the lower part of the Hudson River "sufficient to open Communications for shipping thro' the Highlands," but that was all. Burgoyne later claimed that he discredited the importance of this significant letter. He expected Howe to change his mind after receiving instructions from Germain concerning Burgoyne's expedition.[31] Yet Howe received dispatches written by Carleton and Burgoyne as late as July 1777, which contained nothing "more material than that the Artillery Stores . . . had not then arrived."[32] Had Burgoyne experienced apprehension upon reading Howe's letter to Carleton, he should have brought his fears to Howe's attention in the letters that he wrote to Sir William during May, June, and July. However, it seems clear that Burgoyne was most interested in personal glory and not at all interested in sharing it.

Unconcerned about Howe's change of plans, Burgoyne continued to propose an entirely independent expedition for Connecticut.[33] He asked Howe for additional latitude so that he might create a genuine diversion to Connecticut after taking Albany. One week later he complained to Germain that he felt restricted.[34] Early in August Burgoyne, filled with ambition and confidence, wrote once again to Howe.[35] It was not until after the disastrous battle of Bennington that Burgoyne for the first time expressed surprise that Howe would not come to his relief.

Howe had informed Burgoyne of his changed plan, and he also wrote Germain about it. He had encountered heavy winds during his voyage to Philadelphia. Because of further delays, he wrote to Germain in mid-August that he could not assist Burgoyne's army at all. In fact, his own progress "must be greatly impeded by the prevailing Disposition of the Inhabitants, who . . . seem to be . . . strongly in Enmity against us"[36] By that time, both expeditions were in difficulty, Lord Townshend expressed apprehension in London concerning their fate, and he had good reason to worry.[37] Not one of the three participants in the discussion of strategy for 1777 fully understood the implications of their plans. Howe's initial proposal was sound in its goals, but his reasons for abandoning the first plan were not compelling. If Howe blundered seriously when he proposed the second and third plans, Burgoyne was equally misguided. On balance, however, Germain was responsible for the planning disasters of 1777 and, ultimately, for the loss of the American colonies. It was his duty to coordinate strategy. Since he knew that he would be unable to fulfill Howe's requests for his first (and best) plan, the secretary ought to have designed an alternative proposal, accomplishing more limited goals with the more limited resources available. He could have eliminated the Rhode Island and New Jersey armies, then concentrated all available troops under Howe in New York City, then ordered both northern and southern armies to join at Albany. Speed was of the essence. The longer the British delayed, the greater was the opportunity for the American army to recruit additional personnel from the outlying areas. Burgoyne was overconfident, but he was following Germain's orders when he plunged unaided into the forests of New York. And although Germain ordered Burgoyne to place himself under Howe, Germain also allowed Howe to move south.

Notes

1. November 30, 1776, Howe to Germain, C.O. 5.93, ff. 304–5.

2. Alden, *American Revolution*, p. 113; Charles F. Adams, *Studies Military and Diplomatic, 1775–1865* (New York: Macmillan, 1911), p. 120.

3. Washington based his army near Trenton and Princeton during December, 1776. After battling Lord Cornwallis in those towns, he retired to winter quarters in Morristown until the spring of 1777.

4. November 30, 1776, Howe to Germain, C.O. 5.93, ff. 304–5.

5. Anderson, *Howe Brothers*, pp. 215–16. The writer has made use of Professor Anderson's interpretation of the Howes' strategy. He also accepts the findings of Professor Gruber, *Howe Brothers and the American Revolution.*

6. November 30, 1776, Howe to Germain, C.O. 5.93, ff. 305–6.

7. Ibid., f. 307.

8. January 14, 1777, Germain to Howe, C.O. 5.94, ff. 1–2; ibid., f. 3.

9. Anderson, *Howe Brothers*, p. 216.

10. December 20, 1776, Howe to Germain, C.O. 5.94, f. 20, and C.O. 5.253, f. 278, "Received February 23, 1777."

11. December 10, 1776, Howe to Germain, C.O. 5.94, f. 21.

12. Ibid., ff. 20–21.

13. Alden, *American Revolution* (1954), p. 113; Anderson, *Howe Brothers*, p. 219.

14. December 28, 1776, Howe to Germain, C.O. 5.94, f. 28.

15. January 20, 1777, Howe to Germain, C.O. 5.94, f. 101.

16. March 3, 1777, Germain to Howe, C.O. 5.94, f. 107. This letter was received May 8, 1777; Cobbett, ed., *Parliamentary History,* 20:685.

17. April 2, 1777, Howe to Germain, C.O. 5.94, ff. 143–47, "Received in London May 8."

18. Anderson, *Howe Brothers*, p. 223.

19. April 2, 1777, Howe to Germain, C.O. 5.94, ff. 143–47.

20. May 18, 1777, Germain to Howe, C.O. 5.94, ff. 169–70.

21. Ibid.

22. Ibid.

23. March 26, 1777, Germain to Carleton, Burgoyne, C.O. 42.36, ff. 101–16.

24. Italics added.

25. May 26, 1777, Germain to Carleton. For many years scholars assumed that the copy of Germain's letter for Carleton had been lost, but such was not the case, as shown in the following explanation: a "copy of this letter was sent to Sir William Howe in a letter from Mr. D'Oyay [D'Oyley] (which has not been entered) by the 'Somerset' man-of-war which arrived at New York the 24th day of May. Sir William Howe acknowledged receipt of it in his letter of July 5, no. 9"; March 26, 1777, Germain to Carleton, C.O. 42.36, ff. 101–16.

26. Burgoyne, "Thoughts," February 28, 1777, C.O. 42.36, ff. 37–52.

27. Ibid.

28. Ibid.

29. [n.d.] Burgoyne to John Pownall, cited by Willcox, *Clinton,* p. 146.

30. April 5, 1777, Howe to Carleton, C.O. 5.94, ff. 149–50. This letter was taken to Carleton by Sir John Johnson. Carleton carried the message to Montreal, which arrived before Burgoyne's departure; Howe to Germain, October 22, 1777, C.O. 5.253, ff. 352–53. Carleton gave the letter to Burgoyne; "Carleton's Evidence before the House," cited by Brown, *American Secretary,* p. 101. Copy sent to Germain enclosed in April 2, 1777, Howe to Germain, (enclosure #1). Reply: "I have the pleasure to acquaint you that his majesty entirely approves of your letter to Sir Guy Carleton," May 18, 1777, Germain to Howe, C.O. 5.94, ff. 169–70.

31. Burgoyne, *State,* pp. 22, 188–89.

32. July 7, 1777, Howe to Germain, C.O. 5.94, f. 262.

33. May 19, 1777, Burgoyne to Germain, in Burgoyne, *State,* appendix pp. xx–xxi. He would not disobey orders, however: "Rest assured . . . I shall *really* make no movement that can procrastinate the great object of my orders." Burgoyne's plans for Connecticut are significant because they indicate his overconfidence. See also May 19, 1777, Burgoyne to Harvey, ibid., pp. lvi–lviii.

34. July 11, 1777, Burgoyne to Germain, in Burgoyne, *State,* appendix, pp. xxxvi–xxxix.

35. August, 1777, Burgoyne to Howe, Anderson, *Howe Brothers,* p. 254.

36. August 30, 1777, Howe to Germain, C.O. 5.94, f. 311.

37. August, 1777, Lord Townshend, to John Beresford, in John Beresford, *The Correspondence of the Right Honourable John Beresford,* ed. William Beresford, 2 vols. (London: Woodfall and Kinder, 1854), pp. 15–16.

12

Preparing for War

The frigate *Apollo* departed from Portsmouth on April 2, 1777.[1] Its most distinguished passenger, now fifty-five years of age, embarked for the campaign that he expected would end the war and climax his career. The crossing was a swift one lasting only a month, but it was not pleasant, even for those times. "The seas were as high as ever remembered by any Sailor on board," wrote one of Burgoyne's officers.[2] For seven of the thirty-four days at sea, the ship could not move because of "rough Weather and contrary Wind." At length, on May 6, the *Apollo* entered the Saint Lawrence River, where the ice was melting in the warmth of the spring sun. The craft anchored at Quebec, and Burgoyne landed for a third time upon the North American continent.[3]

Although he had already written to Howe "upon the subject of the expedition and nature of the orders," he wrote again to Sir William from Quebec, protesting his lack of latitude. Burgoyne also presented Germain's fateful instructions to Sir Guy Carleton:

> . . . as the security and good government of Canada absolutely require your presence there, it is the King's determination to leave about 3,000 men under your command, for the defence and duties of that province, and to employ the remainder of your army upon two expeditions.[4]

When the governor read the orders he became enraged and sent a letter to Germain in which he deplored the secretary's lack of judgment.[5] Carleton continued to censure his superior in London throughout May and June. Finally, he declared that he could "no longer be of use to the King's service on this Continent," and asked leave to return to England in the autumn.[6] He would depart "with great satisfaction," though he hoped Germain would safeguard Quebec, "at least that the Dignity of the Crown may not appear beneath your Lordship's concern."[7]

Germain's directions made explicit the transfer of authority.[8] Carleton ordered his army to be ready to march under instructions "which will be given them by Lieutenant General Burgoyne to whom in the meantime they will make all reports."[9] He advised the quartermaster general and officers in charge of the hospital, the commissary, and the artillery likewise to "supply Lieutenant General Burgoyne."[10] Despite his rage at Germain, Carleton obeyed his orders to the letter, and did not refuse to act in an advisory capacity. He told Major General Phillips, Burgoyne's second in command "tho I have nothing further to do with them, I shall nevertheless go up to Montreal in order to be at hand to give every assistance in my power towards forwarding the King's service."[11] He also informed Germain that "[Burgoyne] shall have every assistance in my power, and most ardent wishes for the Prosperity of the King's Arms 'tis in no Man's power to slacken this."[12]

Whatever maneuverings Burgoyne had undertaken, the decision to replace Carleton was, in the last analysis, Germain's decision. Burgoyne wisely remained aloof from the recriminations, although he did not hesitate to add to the widespread praise and sympathy for Carleton that prevailed in Canada. Wrote one lieutenant: "I am positive every officer in the army . . . would acquit [Carleton] of acting imprudently."[13] Burgoyne confided to his friend Adjutant General Harvey that Carleton's conduct did him "infinite honour to his public and private character."[14] Burgoyne also remarked that his own brother could not have been more helpful than Carleton.[15] He even told Germain that "Carleton's zeal to give effect to [the King's] measures in my hands are equally manifest, exemplary, and satisfactory."[16] He must have recalled that a few months earlier he criticized Carleton in the presence of the king and of Germain, at a time when he himself had sought with alacrity the command of the Canadian expedition, and that he had expanded and "improved" the suggestions which Carleton had entrusted to Burgoyne for presentation at court. A few words in praise of Carleton cost little now that he had the command and perhaps they eased his conscience.

Satisfied that Carleton's wrath was reserved exclusively for the secretary of state, Burgoyne journeyed from Quebec to Montreal on May 14, where he met the British divisions of his force.[17] The army was twenty-five percent smaller than the 11,000-man force he had anticipated earlier in the year.[18] He found instead 6,740 British and German soldiers, 150 French-Canadians, and about 400 Indians, a total of 7,300 men.[19]

The Indians who joined the Burgoyne expedition did not appear all at once; they had to be coaxed. Representing the Iroquois and Algonquin nations, they lived and hunted in a large area which extended from Quebec to Lake Ontario and beyond.[20] Of the Iroquois, the Oneidas and Tuscaroras were influenced by American agents and refused to assist the British army.[21] The four other tribes of the Six Nations, however, followed the lead of Sir William Johnson's family, which had moved from New York to Canada, and supported Britain.[22] Preparations to obtain more Indian allies for the campaign were already underway when Burgoyne arrived in Canada, although Carleton's opinion of their value as allies was low.[23] "It is necessary to observe," he wrote Germain, "that there is always an uncertainty as to the force of the Indians, parties being continually leaving them and returning as their humor leads them.[24] If their native inclinations were not sufficient hindrance, Carleton declared, their loyalty was also questionable.[25] Sir Guy nevertheless promised to exert his best efforts to recruit further supplies of Indians. He blamed Germain for the loss of confidence in his leadership, which he said adversely affected the local population as well as the Indians. The combined efforts of Carleton, and several of his most experienced Indian recruiters provided Burgoyne with only about four hundred warriors.[26] However, Carleton, his Indian Superintendent Butler, and native Chief Joseph Brant were able to recruit over one thousand braves for St. Leger's use.[27] It is not known why these were not made available to Burgoyne, but Carleton had observed that "the difficulty is to prevent the number of them from being so great as to cause distress to his Majesty's service."[28] Perhaps the governor feared to release them to the principal expedition; if they caused disturbances during St. Leger's diversionary effort, the impact and the consequences could be less serious.

Few as they were, Burgoyne's warriors proved to be more of a hindrance than an asset. As for the Canadians, only 150 "awkward, ignorant, . . . and spiritless" French-Canadians appeared at Montreal.[29] Noting that thirty French-Canadians had deserted in one night, Burgoyne asked for 1,000 replacements and suggested that otherwise "the next return will be one general column of Non-effectives."[30] He imagined that recruitment "would be palatable to the Country if you thought proper to issue a proclamation limiting the time of their service." Burgoyne said that he also needed those reinforcements to drive his provision wagons. He hoped that later the French-Canadians would be able to bear arms.

Carleton was not surprised to learn about Canadian desertions, but he was critical of official naiveté, and by implication, Burgoyne's ignorance.[31] He recalled that he himself had cautiously suggested the use of only about three hundred Canadians, knowing that "a vast number" of inhabitants were engaged in the fisheries and fur trade, and thus could not be expected to join the army. When he made that estimate, still believing that he would lead the expedition himself, Carleton expected merely to train them, not to obtain military service in battle. "Ordering more would only tend to irritate their Disobedience, and our Difficulties," he observed.[32] Nonetheless, by the end of June 248 French-Canadians were on the way to Fort Saint John and Burgoyne's army, with 203 more following them.[33] Carleton also made arrangements to replace deserters with forty-four additional provincials.[34] He was not optimistic about their usefulness, and instructed his lieutenant governor to keep the Thirty-first Regiment of regulars in reserve; they would be needed should the French-Canadians again desert.[35] Altogether, about five hundred of them led by René Antoine de Boucherville and Captain Samuel Mackay embarked upon the expedition. Burgoyne now realized that they were "mere cyphers."

In his estimate of two thousand provincial auxiliaries, Burgoyne expected American as well as Canadian assistance.[36] Late in June, however, he wrote in dismay to Germain that the only Americans available were a small group of about one hundred New York loyalists, led by Lieutenant Colonel John Peters and Ebenezer Jessup.[37] Carleton had scheduled them to join Sir John Johnson and St. Leger, but, "being of a different part of the Country," they requested and received permission to join the Hudson River expedition. Another group of 100 arrived late in May from New York, where they had been trapped for some time. Thus of the 3,000 volunteers Burgoyne had expected, only 400 troublesome Indians, 500 unreliable French-Canadians, and 100 inexperienced Tories actually joined his expedition.

Burgoyne had also overestimated the number of regular troops he expected to command, although he was not so inaccurate in this instance. When Burgoyne, Carleton, and Germain prepared the original estimates, they decided to divide the northern army into two parts: the bulk of the troops for the expedition, and a smaller number for duty in Canada. They planned to leave 4,000 in Quebec, but Germain later discovered that he could spare only 1,600 fresh soldiers for Carleton.[38] To supply the remainder, he requested Sir Guy to detach infantry units from the Twenty-ninth, Thirty-first, and Thirty-fourth Regiments originally scheduled for Burgoyne.[39] These soldiers joined eleven companies of foot and MacLean's Regiment to bring Carleton's strength to 3,770.[40] But then further detachments were necessary for St. Leger. After deducting the regiments needed by Carleton and St. Leger, Burgoyne had only 6,700 British and German rank and file soldiers for his expedition.[41] When the Canadians, Indians, and Tories joined the regulars there were about 7,300 men all told at Burgoyne's disposal. Although the lieutenant general could not have foreseen that Germain would lack a full complement of fresh soldiers for Carleton, he did err seriously when he estimated so high a number of Canadians and Indians. His force was a formidable one; he would need the service of every available soldier for the arduous task ahead.

The regular British troops that Major Phillips presented to Burgoyne during a formal reception in Montreal were the backbone of the army. Regimental bands played as the seven corps of British infantrymen that constituted the battalion proper marched by.[42] These "regiments of the highest character" included some of the oldest and most distinguished companies in the British army.[43] They represented one half of Burgoyne's effective strength, about 3,724 men,[44] and were associated into three brigades.

Quebec was not the only Canadian town preparing for battle. The small riverside village of Trois Rivières, not far from Montreal, also surged with military activity in May, 1777. The Baron Friedrich von Riedesel, a German officer who commanded the left wing of Burgoyne's army, had managed to secure accommodation in the home of the local vicar.[45] Outside the house and throughout the village, Brunswick and Hessian soldiers, whose services the British government had purchased earlier in the war, drilled and marched.[46] Although the earl of Chatham, William Pitt, criticized the government for employing mercenaries, Burgoyne was glad to have them.

The British force also maintained a large artillery complement. Ranging from

24-pound cannon to 4.4-inch mortars, most of the 138 guns were left in July at Fort Saint John, Fort Ticonderoga, Fort George, and aboard the ships attached to the force. Thereafter, the army retained forty-two field pieces, ten of which composed a gun park for Major General Phillips.[47] The remainder were assigned to the battalions, two pieces attached to each regiment. Although these supplies were burdensome, Burgoyne believed that the "situation and resolution" of the Americans at Ticonderoga might "be such as to make artillery preparations requisite."[48] Two and one-half companies of British and Irish artillerymen manned the weapons, in cooperation with 150 infantrymen and seventy-eight Germans from the regiments of Hesse-Hanau.[49]

Burgoyne made use of the small naval flotilla used at Valcour Island to transport men and supplies. He was extremely pleased with the general appearance of his expedition.[50] The troops "could not have been more selected" to his satisfaction.[51] Nearly all of the soldiers were in "a state of health almost unprecedented," having weathered an unusually mild Canadian winter.[52] Burgoyne also had reason to be proud of his staff, which consisted of officers seasoned, talented, and distinguished. Thirty of them later became generals; four were already members of Parliament.

Morale in the army was high during May of 1777. Phillips went so far as to predict a total victory: "I will hope this year will prove the end of American troubles," he told Germain, "and that a peace, with every degree of submission on the part of the Rebel Colonies, and every proper consideration on the part of Great Britain may terminate the unhappy quarrel."[53] Burgoyne shared the high spirits of the troops. Lacking the great number of auxiliary soldiers originally planned, he also detected certain other shortages, but made light of them to Germain.[54] Five days after meeting his army Burgoyne exuded confidence in a letter to Lord Harvey: "I have reason to be exceedingly satisfied with all that has been done, and with most things that are doing: exertions have been made during the winter . . . in all departments, and preparations are very forward."[55] He realized that "extraordinary physical difficulties" lay ahead, that the forest hid Indians and scattered settlements of patriots, and that the land concourse to Albany ran through two hundred miles of dense underbrush. The twelve-mile gap between the lakes required transport for everything, including boats. But he did not wish to wait even for the arrival of reserve food supplies, which were expected shortly. He told Germain: "The hopes I expressed of being able to put the troops in motion without waiting the arrival of the fleets from England & Ireland are confirmed."[56]

As the spring thaw took place, Burgoyne continued to urge his troops, which were scattered all over Quebec and Montreal, to finish their preparations for departure. But the melting snow made roads muddy as segments of the army began to form on the banks of the Richelieu River.[57] Fatigued horses and defective wagons became mired in the wilderness paths.[58] "This difficulty will be removed," thought Burgoyne, "by exerting the service of the parishes as soon as the weather clears."[59] Meanwhile, he would employ "every means that water carriage admits" to drive the troops and stores toward Ticonderoga.[60] He did not think that clothing shortages would be a great problem either. When new uniforms did not arrive from England the soldiers cut their hats into caps and trimmed their coattails, using the material for patchwork.[61]

Toward the end of May, Burgoyne began to consider more seriously his transport and supply problems. He had neglected to obtain sufficient horses for the campaign and asked Carleton for eight hundred of the beasts "indispensably necessary" for the expedition.[62] Suggesting that Carleton rent them by the week, he proposed that one driver handle two horses. The horses, which had to be kept on "short call," could easily be transported to Crown Point, Burgoyne believed.[63] Carleton replied, perhaps with some irony, that "you should be the properest [sic] judge[,] having had frequent opportunities talking to the minister on the subject of these two expeditions."[64] Carleton also told Burgoyne that his idea was impractical, and that elaborate provision "could not be made by the ordinary methods of corvée, and that if proposed without compulsion to the country, the effect would be precarious, dilatory, and expensive."[65] One week later Phillips reminded Burgoyne of the perilous state of his transport system: "neither carriages nor horses will be had nearer than Albany . . . which must necessarily delay the operations of the campaign, after the reduction of Ticonderoga."[66] On June 6, Burgoyne read proposals presented by a local contractor for the procurement of one thousand horses to pull five hundred carts.[67] To save expense, Burgoyne reduced his estimates "much below what would be adequate to the service,"[68] choosing to "trust to the resources of the expedition for the rest."[69] Unfortunately, the contractors had not only neglected to supply horses, they also failed to produce carts in sufficient quantity.[70] Therefore, Burgoyne also suggested the need for five hundred wagons, which he noted "will barely cover fourteen days provision at a time."[71] Even then, transport of bateaux from Lake George to the Hudson and carriage of tents and baggage "will . . . remain unprovided for." Although he had considered supply problems as early as February 1777, Burgoyne implied that those problems were unforeseen difficulties when he wrote to Carleton in June.[72]

Carleton replied that Burgoyne's suggestions were "just and reasonable."[73] The carts were built. However, they displayed flaws in workmanship almost as soon as they were completed. Many of the conveyances, constructed of green, unseasoned timber, were to break down frequently during the course of the campaign. Fifteen hundred horses were sent on the basis proposed by the contractor. Burgoyne took credit for the idea and revealed to Germain his method of transporting them: "I am trying an experiment which I am confident will succeed of conveying the horses through the woods, swimming them over the small rivers, to meet the army at Ticonderoga."[74] The carts and horses, and the artillery as well, required considerable manpower to operate them, but the Canadians, who kept deserting, and the provincials, few in number, were unhelpful. Phillips observed early in June that "there has yet been no arrangement made for marching the field artillery by land."[75] Two weeks later, he virtually begged Carleton to send the Twenty-ninth regiment to Fort Saint John for extended garrison duty, otherwise "it will be impossible the service can go on."[76] Phillips also urged Carleton and Burgoyne to construct a chain of supply garrisons from Montreal to the lakes. Burgoyne had provided for such a scheme in his memorandum of the previous February, but apparently made no effort to put the idea into practice. Phillips hoped Carleton could deploy the Thirty-first regiment at Sorel, Fort Chambly, Saint John's, Isle aux Noix, and Point au Feu.[77] He urged Carleton to post still a third Canadian regular unit at Sorel to "enforce such orders, for the necessary Corvée required," and a fourth, MacLean's, to conduct similar policing of the French-Canadians at Fort Chambly."[78] Carleton agreed to all of these elaborate proposals and sent the necessary soldiers. Phillips promised to report Carleton's "marked goodness" to Burgoyne.[79]

The makeshift efforts to obtain wagons and horses, and men to move food, artillery, and personal baggage, were adequate for the moment. But the lack of planning and the muddled estimates prolonged the preparations for weeks. Forty-six days after his arrival in North America, Burgoyne sent Germain a description of his difficulties in which he bemoaned his situation.[80] Exasperated now, Burgoyne reported a thousand "difficulties and accidents" to Harvey.[81] Everyone who had helped him deserved praise and "ought to be justified [to] some acquaintances of yours and mine, who travel across a map very fast, and are very free in their comments, when others, who have ten times their knowledge and resources, do not answer their predictions and expectations." There were many factors tending to hinder the transport and supply of the army, but Burgoyne himself had anticipated all of them in February.

As Carleton had noted, the division of command in North America created problems. The governor said that Burgoyne was responsible "for the forwarding of the provisions which are to pass thro[ugh] this province for your Army after you shall be advanced, to which arrangements I shall give all the assistance in my power."[82] But he questioned Phillips's request to post soldiers at Point au Feu, the southeast garrison of Phillips's chain and a depot for provisions, artillery stores, and rafts for transporting the carts.[83] Phillips argued that although it was beyond the latitudinal limits of the province, "it is certainly within the Frontier which I have conceived to extend to Crown Point and Ticonderoga."[84] Carleton construed his orders from Germain strictly; he was told not to lead an army into New York, but to remain in his province. However, the governor relented: "I am fully persuaded of the ability of such a step, but I shall lay the blame if any be imputed to me for exceeding my orders, upon you."[85] Carleton also expressed doubt that he had any legal jurisdiction over French-Canadians accompanying Burgoyne past the border. Burgoyne wished Carleton to seize and court-martial those who deserted, but Sir Guy referred Burgoyne to the attorney general at Montreal for a legal opinion[86] and finally instructed Burgoyne to deal with the deserters himself.[87]

Further complications soon developed over the divided structure of command: the secretary at war, Lord Barrington, informed Burgoyne that all his brigadier generals ceased to hold valid commissions once they crossed the border from the Canadian to the American command. Burgoyne objected strenuously to that interpretation: "It would be superfluous [and] preposterous in me to state to your Lordship the impossibility of conducting an army in active service with a total vacancy of intermediate rank from a L[ieutenan]t General to a L[ieutenan]t Colonel."[88] Burgoyne resolved the new crisis by considering the order dormant, and by "not considering the geographical limits of Canada but that mine is the Army of Canada till it is the Army of Sir William Howe."[89] Carleton was not unaware of the difficulties involved. He was careful to send Germain copies of every order he issued on behalf of Burgoyne, so that

> your Lordship may be more particularly informed of all these matters and that you may see what great care has been taken, to avoid all those evils which might naturally follow to the publick from the chief commands being given to an inferior officer, while the King's commission of Commander in Chief is appointed by your Lordship to act as a subaltern office to the very command, and within its own limits."[90]

Carleton had successfully avoided getting into difficulties with Burgoyne while the general was within his province. If any part of the problem of transport derived from Germain's administrative decisions, the rest of it was due to Burgoyne's negligence and hurry. At least one historian has called the general's transport problem "the key to disaster."[91]

Burgoyne did not lack energy. While he neglected matters that in the long run proved to be very serious ones, he was attending to the immediate problems with dispatch. Four days after arriving in Montreal he sent scouts to examine "the State of the ground" at various points adjacent to the lake, which were found sufficient for temporary encampments. He appointed a corvée to repair the roads to Lake Champlain for his supply train. He ordered workmen to caulk the bateaux docked on the Richelieu, which Phillips directed with his usual dispatch.[92] He directed Captain Fraser to recruit more Indians. Although Burgoyne had wished to depart immediately without waiting for stores to arrive, he was still in Montreal when the man-of-war *Tartar* escorted victualing ships from New York City and Halifax to Quebec on May 27.[93] He continued to ask Carleton for direction on many details, but Sir Guy turned over more and more of the responsibility to Burgoyne.[94] The governor referred St. Leger and others to the general for orders, but cautioned Burgoyne against the establishment of extravagant staffs for officers.[95] On May 30, Carleton moved from Quebec to Montreal in anticipation of Burgoyne's embarkation for New York.[96]

Meanwhile the English troops continued to assemble at the base of the Richelieu River. After giving Burgoyne all of Germain's instructions for the expedition, Carleton wrote: "I also enclose for your private information, a copy of a letter, which I have received from General Sir William Howe, wishing you a happy and successful campaign."[97] On the evening of June 12, Burgoyne, Carleton, Riedesel and all the brigadier generals met at Phillips's quarters for a farewell dinner highlighted by generous courses of champagne and other wines.[98] A messenger from Quebec arrived at the dinner table to inform Riedesel that his wife and three children, who had journeyed from Europe across the Atlantic ocean, had arrived in Canada and would join the German baron shortly.[99] The messenger also reported that thirty-nine transport ships had arrived in Canada from Portsmouth, filled with money, clothing, dispatches, and eleven British army companies and 400 chasseurs from Hanau in addition to 100 recruits from Brunswick.[100] Burgoyne's plans were unchanged by the news: he would not wait for those men and supplies to arrive in Montreal.

On June 13 Burgoyne and Carleton moved to Isle aux Noix.[101] The latter bid farewell to Burgoyne shortly thereafter and returned to Montreal.[102] Contrary winds prevented Burgoyne's departure for two days.[103] On the seventeenth, however, he boarded the *Lady Maria,* his barge, and sailed from Isle aux Noix to Cumberland Point, a clearing near the River Bouquet on the west side of Lake Champlain, now known as Plattsburgh.[104] Poor winds forced Burgoyne to stay there for eight days.[105] Burgoyne wrote to Carleton, Harvey, and Germain concerning his progress up to that time.[106] He also prepared a remarkable collection of instructions and admonitions for his troops, the Indians, and the American people.

The army assembled in full at Cumberland Point by June 20.[107] Burgoyne, who had long held the admiration of his rank and file, began to read his standing orders for the day. His views had not changed greatly concerning the troops, and the orders revealed a commander who was still conscientious and good-humored.[108] He assured the ranks that a knowledge of the science of engineering was not necessary to find and supply "woodland resources." The general also reminded his men to fell trees "with their points outward." Advanced scouts should seek the protection of trees so that marksmen could not shoot at them. He urged frequent use of the bayonet.[109] Men half as strong as his own soldiers "and even cowards may be their match in fighting; but the onset of bayonets in the hands of the valiant is irresistible." Because he was personally courageous, Burgoyne wished to instill a similar disposition in his men, urging that "it will be our glory, and preservation to storm, when possible." He threatened stragglers and plunderers with reprisal by his Indians. Of his own force, the general demanded order, subordination, and obedience.

Burgoyne believed he knew his enemy after two campaigns in America. He still maintained that the patriots were "infinitely inferior to the King's troops in open space and hardy combat." However, experience had convinced him that the Americans were "well fitted by disposition, and practice for the strategems of [littoral] war." He cautioned that "neither the distance of camps, nor the interference of forests and rivers are to be looked upon as securities against their attempts." As drums beat, Burgoyne turned and boarded the *Lady Maria* with great pomp. The cannon of the ship boomed a signal and the march southward began.[110]

The next day Burgoyne met his Indian allies "in Congress."[111] St. Luc and Langlade assembled about four hundred warriors at a camp on the River Bouquet. Dressed in vermilion, black, and green warpaint, they presented a ghastly spectacle as they settled in the clearing to listen to the British general.[112] Addressing the native Americans through an interpreter, Burgoyne told them that he and his officers esteemed them as "brothers." He urged them to "go forth in the might and valour of your cause—strike at the disturbers of public order, peace and happiness, destroyers of commerce, parracides of the state."[113] But he urged them to carry out their task with restraint, and to fight by the rules "which I hereby proclaim for your invariable observation during the campaign."[114] Burgoyne prohibited bloodshed, and strictly forbade the taking of scalps from "the wounded or even dying." They could treat with less reserve "base, lurking assassins, incendiaries, rangers, and plunderers." Although they must retaliate against "any American Barbarities," the general emphasized that "the great essential reward, the worthy service of your alliance . . . will be examined and judged upon the test only of your steady and uniform adherence to my orders and counsels."[115] An old Iroquois chief, speaking for the tribes, replied that "they had sharpened their affections upon their hatchets," and were ready to serve their "great father."[116] Having completed his oration, Burgoyne allowed the warriors to be "regaled by liquor and other refreshments."[117] The Indians concluded the festivities with a war dance.[118]

Back at his field desk aboard the *Lady Maria*, Burgoyne penned a third speech, a "Proclamation to the American People," which was printed and distributed on June 24.[119] Addressing himself to the "temperate parts of the Public, and to the breasts of the suffering thousands in the Provinces," the general lamented the plight of the loyalists. The patriots had inflicted "Arbitrary imprisonment, confiscation of property, persecution and torture, unprecedented in the inquisitions of the Romish Church."[120] upon "the most quiet Subjects, without distinction of age or sex, for the sole crime . . . of allegiance to the Crown." Charging that the "profanation of Religion is added to the most profligate prostitution of common reason," Burgoyne warned that his troops were "in the full power of health, discipline, and Valour," and were "determined to strike when necessary." And they could strike far: "I have but to give stretch to the Indian forces under my direction," Burgoyne threatened, "and they amount to thousands, to overtake the hardened enemies of Great Britain, and America, wherever they may lurk."[121] Resistance would be punished; he would evoke the "vengeance of the state against wilful outcasts" through "devastation, famine, and every concomitant horror that a reluctant but indispensable prosecution of military duty must occasion." However, he had no great wish to deprecate the countryside and he promised not to disturb "the domestick, the industrious, the infirm, and even the timid inhabitants . . . provided they remain quietly at their houses."[122] Burgoyne encouraged countryside provincials to bring to him every sort of provision, for which they would be reimbursed in solid coin. He would assist loyal subjects to rescue their neighbors from patriot "Dungeons."[123]

The proclamations were widely distributed on both sides of the Atlantic.[124] They were not calculated deliberately to alienate readers, but Burgoyne wrote in so pompous a manner and in such insultingly specific detail that most Englishmen reacted with anger or laughter. An anonymous pamphleteer said the general "shone forth in all the tinsel splendour of enlightened absurdity."[125] "Old Hurlothrumbo," as Horace Walpole called him, "with consciousness of Christianity" could "reconcile the scalping knife with the Gospel."[126] Burgoyne became "General Swagger," his proclamation to the American people "a rhodomontade in which he almost promises to cross America in a hop, step, and a jump."[127] Edmund Burke confessed that he "couldn't understand the 'Burgoynese' dialect no less plain English."[128] The Irish philosopher rose to the occasion in Parliament, where he asked the members to imagine that a rebellion had taken place on Tower Hill, home of the royal menagerie:

> What would the keeper of His majesty's lions do? Would he fling open the dens of the wild beasts and address them thus? "My gentle lions—my humane bears—my tenderhearted hyenas—go forth! but I exhort you, as you are Christians and members of civilized society, take care not to hurt any man, woman, or child!"[129]

Tears of laughter were said to have rolled down the cheeks of the prime minister, who had approved the expedition.[130]

In America, James Thatcher, a surgeon in the Continental army, reported being "assailed by a proclamation of a very extraordinary nature."[131] The poet Francis Hopkinson delivered a withering counterblast to Burgoyne's speech.[132] Addressed to the "Most high, most mighty, most puissant and sublime General," Hopkinson's parody was read widely and heartily appreciated by the patriots. "We, the reptiles of America were struck with unusual trepidation and astonishment," when Burgoyne arrived in Quebec wrote Hopkinson. As his forces passed the lakes,

> The mountains shook before thee, and the trees of the forest bowed their lofty heads—the vast lakes of the North were chilled at thy presence, and the mighty cataracts stopped their tremendous career and were suspended in awe at thy approach.[133]

The prospects of the Americans were dreary until "like the sun in the horizon, your most gracious, sublime and irresistible proclamation opened the doors of mercy, and snatch'd us, as it were, from the jaws of annihilation."

Burgoyne was undisturbed by such disrespect. He was criticized more seriously by patriots in New York and Englishmen in London because he used Indians for the campaign.[134] In Parliament, the earl of Chatham condemned Burgoyne, claiming that the faces in the tapestry hanging in the House of Lords were frowning.[135] James Thatcher recorded the hostile reaction in America: "his manifesto excites universal indignation and contempt; instead of conciliating and increasing the number of his friends, serves only to exasperate and augment our means of resistence and opposition to his views."[136] A few came to the general's defense.[137] But the influence of Germain, who had urged Howe, Carleton and Burgoyne to use Indians, was reflected in the colonial office précis for 1776, which stated that "the assistance of the Indians & Canadians would be highly necessary . . . their tempers and dispositions [are] to be cultivated with particular attention."[138] Others noted that Montcalm and Wolfe engaged "savages" during the French and Indian War. Even American patriots accepted a few Stockbridge Indians in their ranks during the war. However, most people regarded the practice as despicable. Virtually useless as soldiers because unaccustomed to European notions of military discipline and doing battle, Burgoyne's Indians hindered his progress more than they hurt the patriot cause.

On June 21, Lieutenant Colonel Barry St. Leger left Montreal to begin his journey to Oswego, a small village on Lake Ontario.[139] His journey took him over a month.[140] As St. Leger's expedition got under way, Burgoyne seemed also ready to commence operations, his gunboats sailing to Crown Point in Lake Champlain.[141] But continual rains and contrary winds prevailed, and the gunboats returned.[142] Burgoyne sent a detachment of regimentals, light infantrymen, and Indians to reconnoiter Fort Ticonderoga and adjacent land, and also to distribute additional copies of his manifesto to the patriots. High winds and fog again delayed Burgoyne on the twenty-third.[143] On the afternoon of the following day, however, the gunboats sailed again, and although waves rolled very high, the oarsmen courageously forged ahead. Simon Fraser and the advanced corps went to Crown Point on the twenty-fifth, and Burgoyne ordered the army to prepare to leave for that destination, weather permitting.[144] The expedition was at last in motion; indeed, the flotilla was said to have resembled a miniature armada.[145]

Arriving at Crown Point the British discovered a small American garrison, which retreated quickly to Ticonderoga.[146] The German soldiers settled at Chimney Point, opposite Crown Point, where Burgoyne made camp.[147] He put his men to work, and they built a hospital, established magazines, and made cartridges.[148] They unloaded powder, balls, and paper from the magazine ship.[149] Burgoyne advised the men to be particularly attentive and take the greatest care of their musket cartridges, especially because it was so difficult to transport fresh supplies across the lake.[150] The soldiers lifted cannon, shell, and shot from the bateaux,[151] which were caulked with oakum at Chimney Point.[152] Workmen in the woods cleared paths through the dense underbrush, releasing mosquitos, "the swarming pests of summer," in great quantity.[153] These "noxious vermin" assailed the men continuously; the soldiers kindled large fires to disperse them.[154] By June 30, all the troops were assembled at Crown Point, "within sight of the enemy, where watch-boats were seen swarming about, but beyond the reach of our guns."[155] The advanced corps moved to Three Mile Point, so called because of its position north of Ticonderoga. Lieutenant William Digby observed in his recollection of the campaign that "we had a full view from our post of their work lines, etc. and their flag of Liberty displayed on the summit of the Fort."[156] While the advanced soldiers squinted through field glasses at the "very busy" Americans in Ticonderoga, the British gunboats anchored across the river from Three Mile Point.[157] Burgoyne decided to approach the fortress the next day, and issued general orders:

We are to contend for the King and the Constitution of Great Britain, to vindicate the Law and to relieve the Oppressed, a Cause in which His Majesty's Troops and those of the Princes his Allies, will feel equal Excitement. The Services required of this particular expedition are critical and conspicuous. During our progress occasions may occur, in which [neither] difficulty nor labour nor life are to be regarded. *This Army Must Not Retreat.*[158]

The campaign destined to change the course of the American Revolution had begun.

Notes

1. April 2, 1777, Germain to Knox, Historical Manuscripts Commission, *MSS. in Various Collections*, 6:129; Burgoyne, *State*, narrative, p. 2.

2. May 19, 1777, Clerke to Polwarth, Bedford County Record Office.

3. Ibid.; May 8, 1777, Riedesel to Brunswick, Von Eelking, *Riedesel*, 1:93–94; June 5, 1777, Riedesel to wife, Stone, *Journals*, pp. 66–67.

4. March 26, 1777, Germain to Carleton, C.O. 42.36, ff. 101–16.

5. May 22, 1777, Carleton to Germain, C.O. 42.36, ff. 271–78.

6. June 27, 1777, Carleton to Germain, C.O. 42.36, ff. 579–86.

7. Ibid. Carleton was not again permitted to take part actively in military affairs until after Germain resigned in 1782. Then Carleton was appointed commander in chief for North America, a post which he held briefly. Subsequently, as Lord Dorchester, he became governor of Canada; Eldon L. Jones, "Sir Guy Carleton and the Close of the American War of Independence," Ph.D. dissertation, Duke University, 1968.

8. July 1, 1777, Germain to Knox, Historical Manuscripts Commission, *MSS. in Various Collections*, 6:132.

9. May 10, 1777, Carleton's Orders, C.O. 42.36, ff. 365–68.

10. Ibid. On May 10, 1777, he surrendered the troops to Burgoyne, Von Eelking, *Riedesel*, 1:98.

11. May 12, 1777, Carleton to Phillips, C.O. 42.36, ff. 361–64.

12. May 20, 1777, Carleton to Germain, C.O. 42.36, ff. 187–212.

13. May 6, 1777, Digby, *Invasion*, p. 187. "The chivalric Carleton," wrote Riedesel, "so competent," was not to be allowed to follow up the advantages he had won; Von Eelking, *Riedesel*, 1:96.

14. May 19, 1977, Burgoyne to Harvey, *State*, appendix, pp. lvi–lviii. Suspicions had arisen in Canada immediately upon receipt of news that Burgoyne would replace Carleton to the effect that Burgoyne's visit to London "had not been solely to arrange his family affairs"; Burgoyne had a "peculiar talent for insinuating himself" into the good graces of London officials; Von Eelking, *Riedesel*, 1:96–97.

15. Burgoyne, *State*, narrative, p. 10.

16. May 14, 1777, Burgoyne to Germain, C.O. 42.36, ff. 179–86; Burgoyne, *State*, appendix, pp. xvii–xx

17. May 19, 1777, Burgoyne to Germain, C.O. 42.36, ff. 299–302; Burgoyne, *State*, appendix, pp. xx–xxi.

18. February 28, 1777, Burgoyne, "Thoughts," C.O. 42.36, ff. 37–52.

19. Germain thought the force sufficient for the purpose: "if that army is not able to defeat any force the rebels can oppose to it, we must give up the contest," he told Knox, July 27, 1777, Historical Manuscripts Commission, *MSS. in Various Collections*, 6:133–34.

20. James M. Hadden, *Hadden's Journal and Orderly Book*, ed. Horatio Rogers (Albany, N.Y., Munsell, 1884), pp. 14–15; Max Von Eelking, *German Allied Troops . . .* (Albany, N.Y., 1893), p. 91; Burgoyne, *State*, narrative, p. 10.

21. John R. Alden, *A History of the American Revolution* (New York: Knopf, 1969), p. 311.

22. Ibid.

23. Von Eelking, *Riedesel*, 1: 94–95.

24. June 26, 1777, Carleton to Germain, C.O. 42.36, ff. 343–8. See also March 31, 1777, report of Captain Samuel McKay, C.O. 42.36, ff. 249–53.

25. May 22, 1777, Carleton to Germain, C.O. 42.36, ff. 271–78.

26. Christopher Carleton, the governor's nephew, commanded one of the Indian regiments. It was said that he had two wives, one white and one Indian; Howard H. Peckham, *The War for Independence: A Military History* (Chicago: University of Chicago Press, 1958), p. 61.

27. May 18, 1777, Carleton to Butler, C.O. 42.36, ff. 393–96; June 15, 1777, Butler to Carleton, C.O. 42.36, ff. 619–24; June 26, 1777, Carleton to Germain, C.O. 42.36, ff. 343–48.

28. June 26, 1777, Carleton to Germain. Typical of Germain's naive assumptions about the Indians is a comment in his March 28, 1776 letter to Burgoyne, Germain papers, Clements Library: "of the good will and affection of the Indians there seems to be little doubt, if they are managed with attention and proper Persons are employed to negotiate with them."

29. May 14, 1777, Burgoyne to Germain, C.O. 42.36, ff. 179–86. Burgoyne reported 300 French-Canadians, but in *State*, narrative, p. 12, mentioned only 250.

30. May 26, 1777, Burgoyne to Carleton, C.O. 42.36, ff. 657–60.

31. May 29, 1777, Carleton to Burgoyne, C.O. 42.36, ff. 661–64.

32. Ibid. Again in June, Carleton warned that the service "could not be made by the ordinary methods of corvée, and that if proposed without compulsion to the country, the effect would be precarious, dilatory, and expensive," Burgoyne quoting Carleton in June 17, 1777, Burgoyne to Carleton, C.O. 42.36, ff. 433–36.

33. June 26, 1777, Carleton to Burgoyne, C.O. 42.36, ff. 519–22.

34. Ibid.

35. June 13, 1777, Carleton to Burgoyne, C.O. 42.36, ff. 481–84.

36. June 22, 1777, Burgoyne to Germain.

37. Burgoyne, *State*, narrative, pp. 10–17. Peter's regiment was entitled the "Queen's Loyal Rangers," W.O. 28.4, f. 103.

38. B.L. Add. MSS. 34,413, ff. 202, 207; C.O. 5.253, ff. 256–57; Historical Manuscripts Commission, *Stopford-Sackville MSS.*, 2:222.

39. March 26, 1777, Germain to Carleton, C.O. 42.36, ff. 101–16. Fifty men were detached from each regiment.

40. Burgoyne, *State*, pp. 10–17.

41. 3,016 Germans and 3,724 English; ibid., pp. 10–17; Hadden, *Journal*, pp. lix–lx. Two British units not mentioned in the figures cited above remained in England to recruit additional personnel; Hadden, *Journal*, p. lxx.

42. Burgoyne, *State*, pp. 10–17.

43. May 10, 1777, "Return," C.O. 42.36, ff. 365–68; Digby, *Invasion*, p. 196.

44. Each regiment was composed of ten infantry companies. A company contained fifty to sixty soldiers.

45. April 16, 1777, Riedesel to Baroness Riedesel, in *Baroness von Riedesel and the American Revolution: Journal and Correspondence of a Tour of Duty*, ed. Marvin L. Brown, Jr. (Chapel Hill, N.C.: University of North Carolina Press, 1965), p. 190,; sketch of Riedesel, Von Eelking, ed., *Riedesel*, 1:1–17.

46. [1776] Copy of Treaty with the Duke of Brunswick, C.O. 5.139, ff. 87–104. German regimental statistics may be examined in ff. 96–100.

47. May 12, 1777, Phillips to Germain, C.O. 42.36, ff. 975–98.

48. Burgoyne believed 4,500 soldiers defended Ticonderoga; ibid. Hudleston, *Burgoyne*, p. 121, criticized the general for including such a large artillery train. But Henry B. Carrington, *Battles of the American Revolution* (New York,: A.S. Barnes, 1888), p. 308, believed the artillery complement to be the lowest permitted by army regulations. Burgoyne put high value on those pieces that he had, and thought himself "under the necessity of waiting at Crown Point until the arrival of the ordnance ships from England." May 14, 1777, Burgoyne to Germain, C.O. 42.36, ff. 179–86. Burgoyne did encounter frequent delays during the course of his expedition. In many instances, the lack of speed was due in part to problems encountered while transporting the artillery.

49. Ray W. Pettingill, ed., *Letters from America 1776–1779* (Boston: Houghton Mifflin, 1924), p. xx; DeFonblanque, *Episodes*, appendix D, pp. 487–88.

50. Stone called it "an army which for thoroughness of discipline and completeness of appointment had never been excelled in America," William L. Stone, *The Campaign of Lieut. Gen. John Burgoyne and the Expedition of Lieut. Col. Barry St. Leger* (Albany, N.Y.: Munsell, 1877), pp. 9–10.

51. "A Journal of Carleton's and Burgoyne's Campaign," *Bulletin of the Fort Ticonderoga Museum* 11 (December 1964): 263. The original MS. is deposited in the library of the United States Military Academy, West Point, New York.

52. July, 1777, "Intelligence from America," Historical Manuscript Commission, *Dartmouth MSS.;* May 19, 1777, Burgoyne to Harvey, Burgoyne, *State*, appendix, pp. lvi–lviii. April 10, 1777, Riedesel to Duke Ferdinand of Brunswick, Von Eelking, ed., *Riedesel* 1:92–93.

53. May 12, 1777, Phillips to Germain, C.O. 42.36, ff. 295–98.

54. May 14, 1777, Burgoyne to Germain, C.O. 42.36, ff. 179–86.

55. May 19, 1777, Burgoyne to Harvey, *State*, appendix, pp. lvi–lviii.

56. May 19, 1777, Burgoyne to Germain, C.O. 42.36, ff. 299–302.

57. May 19, 1777, Clerke to Polwarth, Bedford County Record Office.

58. May 26, 1778, "Notes of General Burgoyne's Speech to the House of Commons," Historical Manuscripts Commission, *Stopford-Sackville MSS.*, 2:110–15.

59. Burgoyne, *State*, narrative, pp. 10–17; Hadden, *Journal*, p. 43.

60. Burgoyne, *State*, narrative, pp. 10–17.

61. May 6, 1777, Barrington to Germain, C.O. 5.256, f. 157: ". . . no part of the delay can be imputed to the War Office. . . . I do not believe that these delays arise from neglect of others." Mackesy, *America*, has suggested that the Navy Board and the Board of Admiralty did not cooperate; Précis of Supply Difficulties, C.O. 5.254, ff. 58–83. Supplies of uniforms had been sent

back to England "to secure them from the Rebels when Quebec was attacked." Précis [1776], C.O. 5.253, ff. 33–56.

62. May 26, 1777, Burgoyne to Carleton, C.O. 42.36, ff. 401–8.

63. Ibid.

64. May 28, 1777, Carleton to Burgoyne, C.O. 42.36, ff. 425–28.

65. June 7, 1777, Burgoyne quoting Carleton in Burgoyne to Carleton, C.O. 42.36, ff. 433–36. A corvée was a relay of French-Canadians used as carriers, until 1776 in the form of statute labor exacted of peasants.

66. June 4, 1777, Phillips to Burgoyne, *State,* appendix, pp. li–lii.

67. June 6, 1777, Jacob Jordan, "Proposals for furnishing Horses, Carriages, and Drivers," C.O. 42.36, ff. 437–40 and 441–44. On June 13, 1,500 horses were purchased in Canada for the army. They were to be sent overland to Crown Point; Von Eelking, *Riedesel,* 1:104.

68. June 7, 1777, Burgoyne to Carleton, C.O. 42.36, ff. 433–36. Riedesel's dragoons lacked horses for the duration of the campaign; Von Eelking, *Riedesel,* 1:101.

69. Burgoyne himself foresaw in February 1777 that Americans would take supplies with them as he pushed forward; Burgoyne, "Thoughts." C.O. 42.36, ff. 37–52.

70. By May 31, ships were so scarce that baggage had to be transported separately; troops that could not be crowded on board available ships had to march on land, parallel to the route of the ships, as far as Saint John's; Von Eelking, *Riedesel,* 1:100.

71. June 7, 1777, Burgoyne to Carleton, Burgoyne, *State,* appendix, pp. lv–lvi; Eldon L. Jones, "British Cavalry in the American War of Independence," Master's thesis, Duke University, 1965.

72. June 7, 1777, Burgoyne to Carleton, C.O. 42.36, ff. 433–36. Bowler, *Logistics,* 224–30, analyzes Burgoyne's supply problems and calls them the key to disaster for the 1777 expedition.

73. June 7, 1777, Carleton to Burgoyne, C.O. 42.36, ff. 445–48.

74. June 22, 1777, Burgoyne to Germain, C.O. 42.36, ff. 557–64.

75. June 4, 1777, Phillips to Burgoyne, *State,* appendix, pp. li–lii.

76. June 17, 1777, Phillips to Carleton, C.O. 42.36, ff. 493–96.

77. Ibid.

78. June 17, 1777, Phillips to Carleton (second letter), C.O. 42.36, ff. 497–500.

79. June 18, 1777, Carleton to Phillips, C.O. 42.36, ff. 501–4; June 26, 1777, Carleton to Burgoyne, C.O. 42.36, ff. 519–22.

80. June 22, 1777, Burgoyne to Germain, C.O. 42.36, ff. 557–64.

81. June 22, 1777, Burgoyne to Harvey, Burgoyne, *State,* appendix, pp. lviii–lx.

82. May 28, 1777, Carleton to Burgoyne, C.O. 42.36, ff. 425–28.

83. June 18, 1777, Carleton to Phillips, C.O. 42.36, ff. 501–4.

84. June 19, 1777, Phillips to Carleton, C.O. 42.36, ff. 509–14.

85. June 26, 1777, Carleton to Phillips, C.O. 42.36, ff. 515–18.

86. May 26, 1777, Burgoyne to Carleton, C.O. 42.36, ff. 657–60.

87. June 15, 1777, Burgoyne to Carleton, C.O. 42.36, ff. 485–88; June 17, 1777, Carleton to Burgoyne, C.O. 42.36, ff. 489–92.

88. July 11, 1777, Burgoyne to Germain, private, C.O. 42.36, ff. 719–30.

89. Ibid. Burgoyne wrote angrily to Harvey on June 22: "Had Lord Barrington condescended to have communicated his intentions to me in London, I think I could have convinced him of the impropriety" of the ruling on commissions; Burgoyne, *State,* appendix, pp. lviii–lx.

90. June 26, 1777, Carleton to Germain, C.O. 42.36, ff. 343–48. Later in the campaign Burgoyne encountered further difficulties because of the division of command.

91. Nickerson, *Turning Point,* p. 176, censured both Carleton and Burgoyne for the transport problem. He believed that Carleton could have prepared a surplus of horses, carts, drivers, Indians, and French-Canadians during the previous winter. DeFonblanque thought so, too, *Episodes,* p. 234; the only explanation for the inadequate preparation was their belief that wherever communications broke between lakes and rivers, corvées would work; thus they did not order

horses quickly. Yet Burgoyne had said, "Due exertions were used in the course of the winter" to insure adequate transportation. See also Bowler, *Logistics*, pp. 224–30.

92. May 26, 1777, Burgoyne to Carleton, C.O. 42.36, ff. 401–8. The main supplies to construct ships and boats, as well as other war material, had to come from England, as army contractors were recipients of government patronage and ministers were jealous of colonial encroachments on this privilege; DeFonblanque, *Episodes*, p. 231 and note 1; Norman Baker, *Government and Contractors: The British Treasury and War Supplies 1775–1783*, University of London Historical Studies, vol. 30 (London: Athlone Press, 1971), contains much new and valuable information on the subject.

93. May 27, 1777, Carleton to Germain, C.O. 42.36, ff. 287–90.

94. May 28, 1777, Carleton to Burgoyne, C.O. 42.36, ff. 425–58.

95. Ibid.

96. May 30, 1777, Williams, "Diary," C.O. 42.36, f. 739.

97. June 10, 1777, Carleton to Burgoyne, C.O. 42.36, ff. 449–52. This copy may have been Howe's letter of April 5 to Carleton, which Burgoyne ignored because he believed Howe would change his plans after receiving Burgoyne's dispatch; Nickerson, *Turning Point*, p. 190; June 11–12, Williams, "Diary," f. 740; June 13, 1777, Riedesel to his wife, *Letters and Journals Relating to the War of the American Revolution, and the Capture of the German Troops at Saratoga*, trans. W. L. Stone (Albany, N.Y.,: Munsell, 1867), pp. 78–80.

98. June 13, 1777, Riedesel to his wife, Von Eelking, *Riedesel*, 1:103.

99. Ibid.

100. Ibid.

101. June 13–14, 1777, Williams, "Diary," f. 740.

102. Ibid.; Von Eelking, *Riedesel*, 1:104.

103. June 16–17, 1777, Williams, "Diary," f. 741; "Canada, 1777," C.O. 5.253, ff. 335–36.

104. June 17, 1777, Williams, "Diary," f. 741; June 26, 1777, Carleton to Germain; Burgoyne, *State*, narrative, p. 7.

105. June 18, 1777, Williams, "Diary," f. 741.

106. Ibid.; June 22, 1777, Burgoyne to Germain C.O. 42.36, ff. 557–64, and June 22, 1777, Burgoyne to Harvey Burgoyne, *State*, appendix, p. xxxii.

107. June 26, 1777, Carleton to Germain, C.O. 42.36, ff. 343–48.

108. June 20, 1777, "Standing Orders," Burgoyne, *Orderly Book*, p. 2.

109. Americans hated the bayonet just as the British hated the patriots' sniping. British troops were at their best in close order volley, rather than as marksmen; Mackesy, *America*, p. 78.

110. Von Eelking, *Riedesel*, 1:106.

111. June 21, 1777, "Substance of the Speech of Lieut[enant] General Burgoyne to the Indians in Congress at the Camp upon the River Bouquet, June 21st 1777 and of their Answer," C.O. 42.36, ff. 571–74.

112. Burgoyne, *State*, narrative, p. 10.

113. June 21, 1777, Burgoyne, "Speech . . . to the Indians," C.O. 42.36, ff. 571–74.

114. The Indians reportedly greeted Burgoyne's remarks with cries of "Etow! Etow!" Thomas Anburey, *Travels Through the Interior Parts of America in a Series of Letters*, 2 vols. (London: W. Lane, 1789), 1:286.

115. June 21, 1777, Burgoyne, "Speech . . . to the Indians," C.O. 42.36, ff. 571–74.

116. DeFonblanque, *Episodes*, p. 243; the chief pledged obedience to Burgoyne.

117. Roger Lamb, *Memoir of His Own Life*, 2 vols. (Dublin: J. Jones, 1811), 1:169.

118. Ibid.

119. June 24, 1777, "Camp at the River Bouquet. By John Burgoyne, Esq.; etc. etc. Lieut. General of his Majesty's forces in America, Colonel of the Queen's Regiment of Light Dragoons, Governor of Fort-William in North-Britain, one of the Representatives of the Commons of Great-Britain, in Parliament and commanding an Army and Fleet in an Expedition from Canada, etc. etc. etc." [Printed] C.O. 42.36, ff. 569–70.

120. Ibid.

121. Ibid.

122. Ibid.

123. June 22, 1777, Burgoyne to Germain, copy enclosed, C.O. 42.36, ff. 557–64. This second proclamation is printed in *London Chronicle*, June 29, 1777, copy in B.L. Add. MS. 5,847, f. 378*; Digby, *Invasion*, pp. 189–92; *Proceedings of the Massachusetts Historical Society*, for 1871–73, first series (Boston: Massachusetts Historical Society, 1873) 12:89–90.

124. Even in Germany. See H. E. to William Eden, September 6, 1777, B.L. Add. MS. 34, 414, ff. 138–39.

125. Hudleston, *Burgoyne*, p. 148.

126. September 23, 1777, Mason to Walpole, *Correspondence*, 28:332.

127. Hudleston, *Burgoyne*, p. 147.

128. Sir George O. Trevelyan, *George the Third and Charles Fox*, 2 vols. (New York: Longmans, Green, 1909–14), 1:212.

129. Ibid.

130. Ibid.

131. July 1, 1777, Thacher, *Military Journal*, p. 81: "From the pompous manner in which he has arranged his titles, we are led to suppose that he considers them as more than a match for all the military force which we can bring against him."

132. Hudleston, *Burgoyne*, pp. 148–52.

133. Ibid.

134. Burgoyne later defended his action: The Indians "spread terror without barbarity . . . treated . . . Americans . . . with European humanity." Burgoyne, *State*, narrative, pp. 10–17.

135. See DeFonblanque, *Episodes*, p. 244, note 1; p. 243, note 2.

136. Thacher, *Military Journal*, p. 94.

137. Lamb, *Memoir*, p. 172.

138. Précis [1776], C.O. 5.253, f. 34.

139. Alden, *A History*, p. 311.

140. June 26, 1777, Carleton to Germain, C.O. 42.36, ff. 343–48. A company of Canadians joined the Royal Regiment of New York and a detachment of the Thirty-fourth Regiment; 100 Hanau chasseurs were en route to join Burgoyne.

141. June 22, 1777, Williams, "Diary," ff. 743–44.

142. June 22, 1777, Burgoyne to Germain, C.O. 42.36 ff. 557–64; Von Eelking, *Riedesel*, 1:108.

143. June 23, 1777, Williams, "Diary," f. 744; Von Eelking, *Riedesel*, 1:108.

144. June 25, 1777, Burgoyne, *Orderly Book*, p. 8.

145. Hadden, *Journal*, p. 54; Roger Lamb, *An Original and Authentic Journal of Occurrences during the Late American War to the Year 1783* (Dublin: Wilkinson and Courtney, 1809), p. 134; "one of the finest sights in the world," July 5, 1777, Clerke to Polwarth, Bedford County Record Office.

146. Burgoyne, *State*, narrative, pp. 10–17.

147. June 26, 1777, Burgoyne, *Orderly Book*, pp. 8–9; June 26, 1777, Williams, "Diary," f. 745.

148. June 28, 1777, Burgoyne, Orderly Book, pp. 11–13; Burgoyne, *State*, narrative, pp. 10–17.

149. Ibid.

150. Ibid.

151. June 28, 1777, Williams, "Diary," f. 746.

152. June 29, 1777, Burgoyne, *Orderly Book*, pp. 13–16.

153. Lamb, *Memoir*, p. 168.

154. Ibid.

155. Ibid.

156. Digby, *Invasion*, p. 201.

157. June 30, 1777, Digby, *Invasion*, p. 201.

158. June 30, 1777, Burgoyne, *Orderly Book*, pp. 16–20.

13

The Campaign Opened

Ticonderoga contained few soldiers during the spring and summer of 1777. Most of the force there in October 1776, dispersed after Carleton retreated from Crown Point. Six months later, an American inspector reported that the garrison was poorly clothed, underfed, and undermanned.[1] In June General Philip Schuyler, then commander of the American troops in the northern department of the Continental army, ordered Major General Arthur St. Clair to Ticonderoga.[2] Schuyler sent him only twenty-five hundred regulars; nine hundred provincials arrived later. St. Clair had to distribute this meager army throughout posts at Forts Ticonderoga, Independence, Anne, Edward, and Albany.[3]

The Americans in northern New York were aware that the British army would advance against them. Indeed, Burgoyne himself was mortified to discover that the whole design of the campaign had been published in Montreal before the expedition left Canada.[4] "My own caution has been such that not a man of my own family has been left into the secret," he wrote to Lord Harvey, whom he requested to ask "my friend D'Oyley" whether anyone in the ministry might have let out the plans. Burgoyne considered the leak "of no great consequence here, except as far as regards St. Leger's expedition; but such a trick may be of most prejudicial consequence in other cases."

Schuyler advised St. Clair to concentrate all his men in Fort Independence and hold out as long as possible. If Burgoyne attacked Ticonderoga, then St. Clair should evacuate all his men.[5] St. Clair was not hopeful; five days later, he wrote to Schuyler: "I cannot help repeating to you the disagreeable position we are in, nor can I see the least prospect of our being able to defend the post, unless the militia come in. . . . What can be expected from troops ill armed . . . and unaccoutred?"[6] St. Clair could not look to General George Washington for assistance. The commander in chief remained with his own army of seven thousand men in winter quarters at Morristown. He did not know whether he would move toward the Hudson or into the southern colonies because Howe had not yet made clear his intentions. If Sir William did pass the highlands, he had only to contend with General Israel Putnam's nominal force posted there. In that case, Washington probably would have to move to St. Clair's defense.

General Philip Schuyler, by John Trumbull. Reproduced by permission of the Yale University Art Gallery.

Nor was Washington certain of Burgoyne's plans. He hoped the northern British army would not attack Ticonderoga. If it did, however, Washington believed Burgoyne would conduct only a feint at Ticonderoga.[7] Congress, which acted on advance reports of the British plan, empowered the American commander in chief

> to write to the eastern States, from whence the troops to be employed at Ticonderoga are expected, and to request them in the name of Congress to adopt and pursue every means, particularly those recommended by Congress in their Resolutions of the 14 of this month for compleating and forwarding the regiments which he has already ordered for that service, it being the opinion of Congress that a delay in this matter will be attended with the loss of that important pass.[8]

Washington did request Major General William Heath and the Massachusetts legislature to send troops to him early in May.[9] However, Major General Horatio Gates advised him that reports of an invasion from Canada were groundless.[10] Washington asked General Israel Putnam to hold four regiments ready at Peekskill to join Schuyler should Ticonderoga be attacked, but he was primarily concerned about Howe in New York.[11] Of Burgoyne's threat, Washington wrote to Schuyler: "I cannot conceive that it will be in the power of the Enemy to carry it into execution; . . . the garrison of Ticonderoga is Sufficient to hold it against any attack."[12] Of one thing he was fairly certain: "A Man of Gen[era]l Burgoyne's Spirit and Enterprise would never have returned from England, merely to execute a plan from which no great Credit or Honour was to be derived."[13]

If the Americans were puzzled about British plans, Burgoyne was misinformed about the strength of Ticonderoga. "I understand that they have laboured hard to strengthen Ticonderoga, and threaten a vigorous resistance there," he wrote to Germain in May,[14] and his belief was seemingly confirmed by a combination of intelligence from different spies.[15] Burgoyne was convinced, as he told Howe, that a siege was necessary, and that he should not attack until all his artillery was available.[16] However, Burgoyne could move his force closer, and he did so on July 1. Certain that St. Clair waited for him in great force, Burgoyne forged ahead undaunted.[17]

Early on the morning of July 2, smoke was observed in the American camp.[18] Perceiving that it arose in the area of Lake George, Burgoyne sent out his Indian scouts.[19] They discovered a considerable number of St. Clair's soldiers marching along a road that circled the right of the British camp. Burgoyne surmised that an evacuation was taking place from Mount Hope and immediately ordered Phillips to lead part of Fraser's advanced corps to seize any abandoned works and drive the Americans from posts wherever they could.[20] He also dispatched Captain Fraser, with his marksmen and Indians, to form a circuit near Mount Hope to divert the Americans from the main force heading for the hill, and to intercept the retreating detachment.[21] In the ensuing skirmish only one British officer died, a lieutenant of the Thirty-third; one artillery lieutenant was wounded.[22] None of the Americans was captured by the British. In the evening, Phillips and the right wing took Mount Hope, located about one thousand yards from the fort, and the key to the portage; Burgoyne now controlled Lake George.[23]

Burgoyne's Indians became drunk that evening and wandered toward the American lines. They wounded a British lieutenant who tried to save them from their own folly, an incident that prompted Burgoyne to issue strict orders forbidding the sale of liquor to the warriors.[24] Neither camp slept well that night, for the Americans continued a sporadic and unnerving fire while the British beat drums to terrorize the soldiers in the fort. The next morning Burgoyne strengthened the force on Mount Hope and completed the British line from the westernmost environs of Ticonderoga to Three Mile Point. On the eastern shore of Lake Champlain, General Riedesel and the German advanced corps began to encircle Fort Independence.[25] The Americans watched these activities with trepidation. Burgoyne's intent soon became clear. Mount Defiance was discovered to be both unoccupied and accessible.[26] Providing an excellent view of Ticonderoga one thousand five hundred yards to the northwest, it also gave clear sight of Independence, one thousand four hundred yards northeast, and from its top the British could observe all American preparations and even count troop numbers.

The plan was flawless. With artillery installed on the top of Mount Defiance, Burgoyne could prevent the Americans from escaping by water to the south or across Lake George. Riedesel's Germans were to block the only remaining route to safety, the bridge between Independence and Hubbardton to the East.[27] Laboring all day under the intense summer sun, engineers and woodsmen constructed a road for the artillery on July 4. The artillery was installed the same day.[28] Burgoyne's grand scheme was foiled by two factors, however, and the general was denied the easy and total victory he had counted on. First, the secrecy demanded to insure such a victory was violated when some of the Indians built a fire on Mount Defiance during the night of July 4, thus betraying the British presence there. St. Clair, realizing that his position was untenable, began to evacuate both Independence and Ticonderoga on the night of July 5.

All might still have gone well for Burgoyne had Riedesel's men remained where they had been stationed. But Riedesel, who later maintained that darkness had necessitated the move, withdrew his men to their camp, allowing St. Clair's principal force to slip undetected across the bridge. To cover their retreat, the American soldiers "kept a constant fire of great guns the whole night, and, . . . [amid] clouds of smoke they evacuated the garrison."[29] Great fires were also built at Independence and powder kegs arranged so that they blew up every half hour.[30] One British observer surmised that the garrison was being destroyed.[31] Others feared that the Americans were trying to lure them into a trap.

At dawn the morning of July 6 Burgoyne learned, doubtless to his dismay, the real purpose of the patriot fires. He immediately sent part of his forces after the fleeing Americans. With the other part he marched on Fort Independence. "Where a goat can go, a man can go," declared Phillips, whom Burgoyne selected to be major, "and where a man can go he can drag a gun."[32] The British forces had no difficulty penetrating Fort Independence. A footbridge of small crafts remained intact despite hurried attempts by American soldiers to burn it; furthermore, the few patriot soldiers guarding the entrance to Fort Independence were said to have fallen asleep after excessive drinking.[33]

The pursuit to Skenesborough was a bloody affair.[34] Fraser, who led the British troops, accomplished seventeen miles by marching all day and half the night of July 6. Fraser's force encountered the fleeing Americans on July 7. Extremely fierce fighting ensued along the line when, at the critical moment, Riedesel arrived with two companies of chasseurs and eighty grenadiers and light infrantrymen.[35] "His judgment immediately pointed to him the course to take," wrote Burgoyne.[36] The Americans retreated and the battle ceased. Although Burgoyne reserved most of his praise for Fraser, Riedesel seems to have contributed to the British victory in a decisive way. Although the Americans were not totally routed during the three-hour battle, they did suffer a substantial defeat.[37] Many patriots fell to the ground, mortally wounded. Of those who escaped death, many Americans suffered injuries or fled into the wilderness; Hale and others became prisoners of war.[38] Of Fraser's and Riedesel's 850 men, 36 were dead and 147 wounded. Acland and Balcarres suffered injuries.[39] While the British soldiers plundered greedily among the fallen, the heavens poured forth torrential rains, cooling the recently hot fields of battle.[40] Then the "wolves came down in numbers from the mountains to devour the dead, and even some that were in a kind of manner buried, they tore out of the earth."[41]

The ensuing battle of Hubbardton was one of the most sanguinary small contests of the Revolutionary War. British soldiers discovered that forest combat was not easy; Sergeant Lamb observed, "in fighting in the woods the battalion maneuvering and excellency of exercise were found of little value: to prime, load fire and charge with the bayonet expeditiously were the chief points worthy of attention."[42] Lieutenant James Hadden commented that the British troops "certainly discovered that neither were they invincible or the rebels all poltroons."[43]

While the battle raged at Hubbardton, Burgoyne, leaving a regiment each at Independence and Ticonderoga, boarded ships to pursue the American fleet. The American surgeon traveling in the fleet wrote:

The night was moon-lit and pleasant. The sun burst forth in the morning with uncommon lustre, the day was fine, the water's surface serene and unruffled. The shore on each side exhibited a variegated view of huge rocks, caverns, and clefts, and the whole was bounded by a thick and impenetrable wilderness . . . a scene . . . enchantingly sublime.[44]

While the drum and fife corps played a favorite tune, the Americans discovered several dozen bottles of choice wines among their stores, and "we cheered our hearts with the nectareous [sic] contents."[45] At three o'clock in the afternoon the American fleet reached Skenesborough harbor. As Thacher recorded, "Here we were unsuspicious of danger, but behold! Burgoyne himself was at our heels. In less than two hours we were struck with surprise and consternation by a discharge of cannon from the enemy's fleet."[46] Late in the afternoon of the sixth, Burgoyne's secretary observed that "The General came from Ticon[deroga], on board the Royal George, and litterally [sic] had but time to drink one Glass of Wine after Dinner before clearing Ship, and that, as Toastmaster, I made a Bumper to the Success of the Evening."[47]

Burgoyne's force obtained great quantities of provisions at Ticonderoga and Skenesborough, including ninety-three pieces of iron ordnance ranging from thirty-two-pound cannon to petards.[48] They also found over three thousand rounds of shot and shells, and thirty-eight barrels of powder.[49] From the vessels at Skenesborough, Burgoyne's men took fourteen pieces of iron ordnance, destroying the remaining items. The British soldiers took one ship containing an unknown quantity of powder, blew up another laden with explosives, and confiscated over one hundred pieces of artillery.[50] Even more valuable, Burgoyne obtained thousands of barrels of flour, pork, beef, salt, rum, and biscuits.[51]

The pursuit by sea had been a success for Burgoyne, a blow to the Americans. Seeking to crush the patriots, Burgoyne also attempted to capture the American soldiers who had landed at Skenesborough. He dispatched the Ninth, Twentieth, and Twenty-first Regiments, along with some Indians and Canadians to that town, where the patriots were posted in a stockaded fort.[52] The general ordered the regiments to climb the mountains in back of the fort. The American officers attempted to rally their men to battle, but "in the utmost panic they were seen to fly in every direction for personal safety."[53] The Americans' "precipitate flight rendered this maneuver ineffectual," wrote Burgoyne. It also rendered capture impossible, for most of the American soldiers moved south to Fort Anne, a small picket post eight miles below Skenesborough. The Americans were soon routed from Fort Anne, but not before they set it afire.[54] Because Burgoyne was able to occupy the sawmill and blockhouse, he claimed the skirmish a victory, which it was not.[55] From that point the patriots retreated safely to Fort Edward, taking with them one of Burgoyne's captains and a British surgeon.[56]

Shortly thereafter, in a final push, a detachment of Burgoyne's Sixty-second

Regiment stationed at Ticonderoga began to move bateaux, provision vessels, and gunboats into Lake George.[57] Burgoyne established his headquarters at the home of Colonel Skene.[58] Though the loyalist's sawmills and iron works had been destroyed, his manor house, barns and the town fort remained in good repair; it is reported that Burgoyne was able to acquire the services of Skene's servants and household staff.[59] Safely entrenched in the port village, Burgoyne decided to discontinue the pursuit for a time.[60] The nature of the country required him to construct roads; furthermore, he had to wait for provisions and transport equipment to reach his camp.

The British general now held posts along the Richelieu River from Sorel to Saint John; along Lake Champlain from Isle aux Noix and Crown Point to Ticonderoga and Independence; on South Bay and Wood Creek from Skenesborough to Fort Anne; and soon controlled Lake George from the portage at the north to the fort on the south. He had destroyed the American fleet. He commanded the road from Ticonderoga to Castleton to Skenesborough, and soon gained possession of the dirt path from Fort George to Fort Anne. The lake country, the key area of communication between Carleton's force in Canada and lower New York, was at last recovered for the crown—a substantial and swift accomplishment. Burgoyne was now seventy miles from Albany. "These rapid successes," Burgoyne told his troops on July 10, "after exciting a proper sense of what we owe to God, entitle the Troops in General to the warmest praise; and in particular, distinction is due to Brigadier General *Fraser*."[61] He declared the following Sunday a day of rejoicing, scheduled Divine Services for the morning, and ordered a *feu de joie* at sunset.

Burgoyne was much pleased with his success; he boasted of his victory despite "Remote situations of the troops, currents, winds, roads," and other adversities, and reported to Germain that the success at Ticonderoga was followed by equally fortunate victories.[62] Flushed with success, Burgoyne was convinced that the Americans had no man of military science because the patriots had "expended great treasure and the unwearied labour of more than a year to fortify [Ticonderoga], upon the supposition that we should only attack them on the point where they were best prepared to resist."[63] Echoing his commander's sentiments, Burgoyne's secretary boasted to Lord Polwarth that "The Enemy that prided themselves in the Woods, were taught to know that even there the british Bayonet will ever make its Way."[64] Skene joined the chorus of praise, telling Dartmouth that "as an officer and a civilian, [Burgoyne's] plans are . . . well formed, as executed, and with great oeconomy [sic]"[65] Burgoyne dispatched one of his aides to Canada, whence the officer sailed to England to convey the news of the July conquests.[66]

Burgoyne's early victories delighted London. The king was reported to have rushed into Queen Charlotte's boudoir, exclaiming: "I have beat them! I have beat all the Americans!"[67] Germain was equally impressed, and told General Irwin that "Burgoyne is fortunate and deserves it. His account of his success is not exaggerated, and we have reason to hope his progress will be rapid."[68] The secretary informed Burgoyne that his victory achieved benefits "so many, so important, and so obvious" that the wisdom of appointing him

> was immediately seen and universally applauded, and I must take the liberty of acquainting you, that had your progress been less rapid, or if it had been possible for your conduct in any instance to have been different from what it has been, you would have disappointed the well-grounded expectations of the Public.[69]

Germain reported the king's high opinion of Burgoyne, and went on to say:

> nor will you, who appears to take delight in doing justice to the merit of those who have the happiness of serving under you, be less pleased to be assured, that the behaviour of Major Generals Riedesel, Phillips, Brigadier General Fraser, & of the other officers . . . has been honoured with His Majesty's highest approbation.[70]

With his usual wit and irreverence, Walpole quipped, "I hear Burgoyne has kicked Ticonderoga into one of the Lakes—I don't know which, I am no geographer."[71] Germain published Burgoyne's accounts in the *Gazette,* and the general's fame became widespread; only Walpole found fault:

> I heard to-day at Richmond that Julius Caesar Burgonius's Commentaries are to be published in an extraordinary Gazette of three-and-twenty pages in folio tomorrow—a counterpart to the *Iliad* in a nutshell![72]

Burgoyne had anticipated that his success might prompt such a general outburst of admiration for him. Earlier in the year he had written to Lady Charlotte's nephew, now the twelfth earl of Derby, and asked him to make known to the government that he would not accept the Order of the Bath should it be offered to him.[73] Derby learned that the ministry was considering such a step and wrote Germain of Burgoyne's attitude.[74] Derby hinted that another favor would be acceptable instead. Before the secretary received that letter, he sent Derby word that "The King speaks of Burgoyne as an officer of distinguished merit, and immediately declared he would honor him with the vacant Red Ribbon; I trust he will hereafter receive more substantial marks of favour."[75] Derby was obliged to inform Germain that "from whim, caprice, or some other motive, he has, I know, a strong objection to the honour."[76] What bothered Burgoyne? It is possible that the officer, who had a low opinion of Carleton and who had been downgrading Sir Guy's military expertise, might have been protesting the fact that Carleton had been given the Red Ribbon for his work during the siege of Quebec. Whatever the reason, Lord Germain was not pleased to learn of Burgoyne's decision, and complained to Derby that "it is difficult to reward the services of a general officer who is employed upon the staff, who has a regiment of dragoons, and a government." Derby informed Burgoyne that he had succeeded in "putting by this ribbon," but he hoped he had not given Burgoyne the impression he had "pressed the thing too warmly."[77] Walpole believed Burgoyne declined to accept it because the king had neglected to bestow it upon him in 1762 after the Portuguese campaign,[78] but as DeFonblanque observed, Burgoyne's rank disqualified him for it at that time.[79] Wedderburn offered a more shrewd analysis of Burgoyne's rejection:

> Burgoyne is much in the right to have left a Caveat ag[ains]t the reward intended him. He did not propose to lose a Province or to suffer a Republic and he supposed he should have no occasion for the reward he had seen bestowed on such services.[80]

Whatever the reason for his unwonted modesty, Burgoyne was pleased to learn that the ministry had promoted him by brevet to the rank of lieutenant general on August 29.[81]

Notes

1. April 1, 1777, Worthington C. Ford, et al., eds., *The Journals of Continental Congress, 1774–1789*, 34 vols. (Washington, D.C.: United States Government Printing Office, 1904–37), 7:217.

2. Don Gerlach, *Philip Schuyler and the American Revolution in New York, 1733–1777* (Lincoln, Nebr.: University of Nebraska Press, 1964), provides information about Schuyler's activities during 1777, pp. 292–311.

3. Officers Nathan Hale, Pierce Long, and Seth Warner arrived with the reinforcements. American Colonel Richard Varick provided a detailed picture of Ticonderoga's weaknesses in a letter of June 13, 1777, to General Philip Schuyler, Schuyler manuscripts, New York Public Library.

4. May 19, 1777, Burgoyne to Harvey, *State*, appendix, pp. lvi–lviii.

5. Paul Allen, *A History of the American Republic* (Baltimore, Md.: F. Betts 1822), p. 27.

6. June 25, 1777, St. Clair to Schuyler, Arthur St. Clair, *The St. Clair Papers. The Life and Public Services of Arthur St. Clair with his Correspondence*, ed. William H. Smith, 2 vols. (Cincinnati: Robert Clarke, 1882), 1:407. The Board of War told St. Clair Burgoyne would move troops to Howe by sea, that the attack on Ticonderoga was just a feint; ibid.

7. July 2, 1777, George Washington to the president of Congress, *The Writings of George Washington from the Original Manuscripts, 1745–1799*, ed. John C. Fitzpatrick, 39 vols. (Washington, D.C.: United States Government Printing Office, 1931–44), 8:328–31.

8. May 3, 1777, Washington to the Massachusetts Legislature, Fitzpatrick, ed. *Writings*, 8:10; Resolve of April 29, 1777, Ford, ed., *Journals of the Continental Congress*.

9. May 2, 1777, Washington to Heath, Fitzpatrick, ed., *Writings*, 8:3.

10. June 7, 1777, Washington to Major General John Sullivan, ibid., 8:198. Schuyler thought the invasion would take place via the Mohawk.

11. June 20, 1777, Washington to the president of Congress, Fitzpatrick, ed., *Writings*, 8:271–72.

12. June 20, 1777, Washington to Schuyler, ibid., 8:273–74.

13. July 2, 1777, Washington to Schuyler, ibid., pp. 332–33.

14. May 14, 1777, Burgoyne to Germain, C.O. 42.36, ff. 179–86. Indian scouts surveyed Ticonderoga, Fort George, Fort Anne, Fort Edward, and Skenesborough during February; "report of Captain Mackay," March 31, 1777, C.O. 42.36, ff. 249–53.

15. May 19, 1777, Burgoyne to Germain, C.O. 42.36, ff. 299–302; Burgoyne to Harvey, Burgoyne, *State*, appendix, p. xxxii.

16. July 2, 1777, Burgoyne to Howe, C.O. 5.94, f. 286, and Germain papers, Clements Library.

17. Hadden, *Journal*, p. 82; July 1, 1777, "Journal of the late principal proceedings of the Army," Burgoyne, *State*, appendix, pp. xxv–xxxvi. July 1, 1777, Burgoyne to Germain, C.O. 42.36, ff. 685–708; "Journal of the Brunswick Corps in American under General Von Riedesel," in Peckham, ed., *Sources of American Independence*, 1:275–85, covers the period July 1–12, 1777.

18. Burgoyne, *State*, appendix, p. xxviii.

19. July 2, 1777, Thacher, *Military Journal*, p. 82.

20. July 5, 1777, Clerke to Polwarth, Bedford County Record Office.

21. Von Eelking, *Riedesel*, 1:112.

22. Burgoyne, *State*, appendix, pp. xxv–xxxvi. Of Captain Fraser's rangers, one Indian officer was killed, three Indian infantrymen and one English infantryman were wounded; July 2, 1777, "The List of Killed and Wounded," C.O. 42.36, f. 709.

23. Hadden, *Journal*, p. 83.

24. Hadden, *Journal*, p. 83; July 3, 1777, Burgoyne, *Orderly Book*, pp. 24–26.

25. July 3, 1777, Burgoyne, *Orderly Book*, pp. 24–26; July 5, 1777, Clerke to Polwarth, Bedford County Record Office.

26. Burgoyne, *State*, appendix, pp. xxv–xxxvi. Digby, *Invasion*, p. 203.

27. July 4, 1777, Burgoyne, *Orderly Book*, pp. 26–27.

28. Ibid.; July 5, 1777, Clerke to Polwarth, Bedford County Record Office.

29. July 5, 1777, Digby, *Invasion*, p. 205.

30. Ibid.

31. Ibid.

32. Burgoyne, *State*, appendix, pp. xxviii–xxix.

33. Lamb, *Memoir*, p. 173, which, as Stone observed, *Campaign*, p. 18, note 2, may indicate the American retreat was not as panic-stricken and disorderly as some observers reported.

34. Digby, *Invasion*, p. 209.

35. Von Eelking, *Riedesel*, 1:115.

36. July 7, 1777, Burgoyne, *State*, appendix, pp. xxxii–xxxiv.

37. July 7, 1777, Digby, *Invasion*, p. 210; Lamb, *Memoir*, pp. 174–75.

38. July 7, 1777, Burgoyne, *State*, appendix, pp. xxxii–xxxiv, Burgoyne, *Orderly Book*, p. 33; Hadden, *Journal*, p. 88, put the estimate of captured at seventy; Digby, *Invasion*, p. 215, discussed Hale's judgment. Stone, *Campaign*, p. 22, note 1, reported that Burgoyne testified that Hale did not communicate with him treasonably, as charged.

39. "Our friend Lord Balcarres behaved gallantly on the 7th Instant, and had many Escapes, no less than five Balls went through his Cloathes." July 17, 1777, Clerke to Polwarth, Bedford County Record Office; July 7, 1777, "List of Killed and Wounded," C.O. 42.36, f. 709, listed no prisoners and no missing soldiers. Howard W. Peckham, ed., *The Toll of Independence: Engagements and Battle Casualties of the American Revolution* (Chicago: University of Chicago Press, 1974), p. 37, estimated 200 British casualties after Hubbardton.

40. July 7, 1777, Digby, *Invasion*, p. 216.

41. Digby, *Invasion*, p. 246.

42. Lamb, *Memoir*, p. 174.

43. Hadden, *Journal*.

44. July 6, 1777, Thacher, *Military Journal*, p. 83.

45. Ibid.

46. Ibid., p. 84.

47. July 17, 1777, Clerke to Polwarth, Bedford County Record Office.

48. July 6, 1777, "Return of the Ordnance, Shot & Shells taken at Ticonderoga and Skenesborough," C.O. 42.36, ff. 711–14.

49. Ibid.

50. July 6, 1777, "Return of Ordnance taken and destroy'd in the five arm'd Vessels at Skenesborough," C.O. 42.36, ff. 711–14.

51. July 6, 1777, "Return of the different Provisions taken at Ticonderoga and Fort Independence," C.O. 42.36, ff. 715–18.

52. July 6, 1777, Burgoyne, *State,* appendix, pp. xxx–xxxii; Burgoyne, *Orderly Book,* pp. 32–33; Hadden, *Journal,* p. 85.

53. July 6, 1777, Thacher, *Military Journal,* p. 84.

54. July 8, 1777, Burgoyne, *State,* appendix, pp. xxiv–xxxv.

55. July 2–8, 1777, "List of the Killed and Wounded . . ." C.O. 42.36, f. 709.

56. July 8, 1777, Burgoyne, *State,* appendix, pp. xxiv–xxxv. Digby likewise claimed victory for Britain and "great losses" for America, p. 221; Von Eelking, *Riedesel,* 1:118, said: "The English after a long fight at Fort Anne were forced to retreat." Stone, *Campaign,* p. 27, maintained that Americans reoccupied Fort Anne on the thirteenth. Lamb, *Journal,* said he stayed there seven days, always fearing an American attack which did not come; p. 27.

57. Burgoyne, *State,* pp. xxv–xxxvi.

58. July 8, 1777, Burgoyne, *Orderly Book,* pp. 30–31.

59. Doris B. Morton, *Philip Skene of Skenesboro* (Granville, N.Y.: The Grastorf Press, 1959), pp. 53–55.

60. Burgoyne, *State,* narrative, p. 17.

61. July 10, 1777, Burgoyne, *Orderly Book,* pp. 32–36; Digby, *Invasion,* p. 226; Von Eelking, ed., *Riedesel,* 1:119; John Burgoyne, *Supplement to A State of the Expedition from Canada . . .* (London: J. Robson, 1778), p. 15.

62. July 11, 1777, Burgoyne to Germain, C.O. 5.236, ff. 112–13.

63. July 11, 1777, Burgoyne to Harvey, DeFonblanque, *Episodes,* pp. 247–48.

64. July 17, 1777, Clerke to Polwarth, Bedford County Record Office.

65. July 15, 1777, Skene to Dartmouth, Skenesborough, Historical Manuscripts Commission, *Dartmouth MSS.,* 2:440–41.

66. Digby, *Invasion,* p. 222; July 11, 1777, Burgoyne to Germain, C.O. 5.236, ff. 112–13.

67. August 22, 1777, Horace Walpole, *Journals of the Reign of King George the Third, 1771–1783* ed. D. Doran, 2 vols. (London: R. Bentley, 1859), 2:131; Benjamin F. Stevens, ed., *Facsimiles of Manuscripts in European Archives Relating to America 1773–1783,* 25 vols. (London: Malby and Sons, 1889–98), vol. 16, no. 1573.

68. August 23, 1777, Germain to Irwin, Historical Manuscripts Commission, *Stopford-Sackville MSS.,* 1:138–39.

69. Germain told the king Burgoyne's "short Letter is most satisfactory," August 22, 1777, Germain to the king; Fortescue, ed., *Correspondence,* 3:469.

70. Ibid.

71. Hudleston, *Burgoyne,* p. 157.

72. August 24, 1777, Walpole to Lady Ossory, Walpole, *Correspondence,* 32:376; "General Burgoyne has . . . been compared in several papers to Caesar, and others" reported the *Public Advertiser;* ibid., note 34.

73. 1777, Burgoyne to Derby, mentioned in Derby to Burgoyne, DeFonblanque, *Episodes,* 250–52.

74. August 31, 1777, Derby to Germain, Historical Manuscripts Commission, *Stopford-Sackville MSS.,* 2:75.

75. August 29, 1777, Germain to Derby, DeFonblanque, *Episodes,* p. 248.

76. September 2, 1777, Derby to Germain, ibid., pp. 248–49.

77. September 17, 1777, Derby to Burgoyne, DeFonblanque, *Episodes,* pp. 250–52.

78. Steuart, ed., *Last Journals of Walpole,* 2:42.

79. DeFonblanque, *Episodes*, p. 253.

80. September 6, 1777, Wedderburn to Eden, Stevens, ed., *Facsimiles*, 22:82.

81. August 29, 1777, "List of Officers serving in America who were promoted by brevet," W.O. 4.274, f. 12; *Army List* for 1777, p. iii.

14

From Ticonderoga to Bennington

While he marked time at Skenesborough during July 1777, consolidating his forces and probably frolicking with his mistress, Burgoyne had to choose one of two routes to transport his troops south to Fort Edward and the Hudson River, which he had to approach in order to fulfill his instructions to reach Albany. As a first option, he could return to Ticonderoga, send his army through the portage, then sail up to Lake George. From the base of that lake, the troops would travel but ten miles by road to Fort Edward. It was, as Burgoyne himself had observed in England before the campaign had begun, "the most expeditious and commodious route."[1] However, the general now believed that such a passage would entail "considerable difficulties," that the narrower parts of the river would be impassable, that the artillery, provisions and other material would have to be transported by land, and finally, that his force would face American-held Fort William Henry at the base of Lake George[2]—all of which would, in his opinion, considerably delay his progress. He feared even more that "a retrograde motion" by his troops north to Ticonderoga would make a "harmful impression . . . upon the minds of both enemies and friends."[3]

Consequently, for the reasons that he expressed to Carleton or for reasons of his own, Burgoyne decided not to take this relatively convenient passage.[4] Instead, on July 10 he elected to continue moving south of Skenesborough by land, a sixteen-mile trip through the wilderness. The difficulties he encountered were far greater than the problems he would have faced during a passage of Lake George. Over six hundred wagons containing the army's heavy artillery, provisions, baggage, and other supplies required adequate roads and bridges on which to travel. About fifty teams of oxen collected in the countryside added to the bulk of his army and also required good transport facilities.[5] Schuyler quickly took advantage of Burgoyne's vulnerability and instructed his men to block the forest path from Fort Anne to Fort Edward with rocks, trees, and any other means they could devise.[6] His woodsmen placed layers of intertwined timber across the road in such a way that Burgoyne's engineers had great difficulty removing them.[7] Moreover, the Americans destroyed forty bridges that British carpenters had to rebuild.[8] At one point Burgoyne's men constructed a two-mile causeway of logs to replace one of the destroyed spans. Schuyler's men also diverted streams and obstructed Wood Creek, a tributary of South Bay that ran parallel to the land route for a few miles. The invading army lost time and energy clearing the creek so that bateaux and provision vessels could reach the army at Fort Edward. In London several months earlier, as he planned his route of invasion, Burgoyne had already suspected that these difficulties might occur.[9] The report his secretary sent to Lord Polwarth in England virtually repeated the general's "Thoughts for Conducting the War on the Side of Canada" that he had written the previous February. "The whole of our Movem[en]ts," wrote Clerke, "are among Woody Mountains & Rocks, concieve [*sic*] then the Labour of clearing Roads & Communications & bringing up Artillery.[10] Although his men worked diligently, they were "attended with incredible toil" and made slow progress. The army traveled only twenty miles in as many days, reaching Fort Edward on July 29.[11]

Aware that officials in London might question his judgment, Burgoyne prepared justifications for his decision in letters to Germain and Harvey.[12] His secretary also tried to forestall censure by admitting to Polwarth that the road clearing would be "a work of time for us, tho I am clear the great good Health & Spirit of the Army will overcome all these Difficulties; at the same time however we must beg you not to travel too fast by Map in England, it is not proper Justice to us."[13] After the arduous passage was completed, Burgoyne told Carleton that he then meant "to abandon entirely the communication by Skenesborough and perhaps [I] should not have made use of it at all had not the pursuit from Ticonderoga necessarily thrown me so forward."[14] Nevertheless, Burgoyne saw himself "Much more forward in point of time" because he interpreted the American evacuation of Fort George as a direct consequence of his land march: "seeing me master of one communication they did not think it worthwhile to destroy the other."[15] Burgoyne further justified his land route to Carleton by suggesting that he gave "great jealousy to Connecticut and New England, and thereby prevented the junction of the militia from that quarter." "The issue had justified my perseverance," he concluded somewhat prematurely, when the Sixty-second Regiment at Ticonderoga took Fort Edward on July 30.[16] Burgoyne did not realize that his proximity to Connecticut and the rest of New England was precipitating the very junction of American troops that he claimed to have inhibited.

Burgoyne's choice of route was a foolish one. Historians surprised by his rash haste have developed a theory that the general chose the land route in order to please Colonel Philip Skene, who wished Burgoyne's men to construct permanent roads linking his village of Skenesborough with the rest of upper New York.[17] Although Skene was ambitious to become a local land baron,[18] there is no reason to believe that Burgoyne was influenced by whatever inducements the colonel may have offered.[19] In fact, it was simply Burgoyne's desire to pursue glory as quickly as possible that was responsible for his failure of judgment. He, too, was tempted to travel too fast by map.

American patriots had not only escaped from the path of the British army, they successfully exerted all their energy to delay Burgoyne. The British general, during seven weeks of enforced delay in the vicinity of Skenesborough in order to collect supplies and build roads, had directed his attention almost exclusively to the affairs of his own army. Burgoyne erred further in overestimating the strength of forts Edward, Miller, and Hardy, each of which his army had to confront on the march to Albany. He was aware that American forces were thought to be skilled in the art of entrenching themselves in redoubts such as Fort Edward, whose field works he might have to demolish. He also knew that he might need big guns to reply to attacks from across the Hudson River. Consequently, Burgoyne felt obligated to haul with his army a large collection of artillery originally intended for besieging Ticonderoga but now possibly of value in new circumstances.[20] The army dragged fifty-two pieces to Fort Edward; forty-two of them were brought even further south.[21] At least one British soldier thought the heavy artillery burdensome.[22] Grumbling developed in the ranks because of the chronic deficiency in horses and carts to draw the guns. Burgoyne admitted that transportation efforts without sufficient horses and carts had been "extremely laborious in this sultry weather. . . . Heavy work of the same sort [grows] upon me every hour."[23] The fifty teams of oxen taken from the countryside were useful, he declared, "but their resources together were found far inadequate to the purposes of feeding the army, and forming a magazine at the same time."[24] Through exceedingly heavy rains the regular British troops and those French-Canadians who finally agreed to join the expedition moved the artillery and provisions. Only about 500 of the 1,400 horses that Burgoyne anticipated were delivered; the work was arduous as well as slow.

The different ethnic and regional elements within the army—English, French-Canadian, American loyalist, Indian, and German—created further difficulties for Burgoyne. He found it necessary to forbid recriminations between the British and Germans, "who had previously lived in peace."[25] He censured all of them for lading the expedition with excess baggage, "much more . . . than they can possibly be supplied with means of conveying when they quit the Lakes and Rivers."[26] Burgoyne himself carried thirty cartloads of personal effects,[27] but he admonished Riedesel's Germans to return excess baggage, and repeated the warning several times.[28]

After Ticonderoga, several hundred armed provincials joined the loyalist forces of Jessup and Peters.[29] Skene, however, had flattered Burgoyne when he assured him that "large numbers of the yeomanry" would flock to his army if he encouraged their support.[30] Hoping to strengthen his provincial force, obtain additional provision, and pacify the neighboring areas, Burgoyne sent Skene into the countryside with instructions to give "further encouragement to those who have complied with the terms of my late manifesto."[31] He empowered Skene to issue receipts for livestock obtained, to administer oaths of allegiance to the crown, and to grant certificates of protection to loyal inhabitants.[32] Skene was directed to make known "locations upon which the persons and properties of the disobedient may yet be spared," and to assure those who did not sign the oath of allegiance that they would not be molested—providing they did not violate the manifesto.[33] Burgoyne commanded the inhabitants to send representatives to Castleton on July 15, where they would meet Skene. "This fail not to obey under punishment of execution," he threatened. Skene soon reported that loyal inhabitants were hurrying in large numbers to pledge loyalty to the king.[34]

Meanwhile, the patriot committees of correspondence, which had earlier ridiculed Burgoyne's manifesto, worked to counteract his efforts at persuasion.[35] Moreover, the efforts of Burgoyne and Skene to pacify the countryside alarmed the governor of New York, who wrote to his legislature:

> The Grants are in a very delicate situation. Skene is courting them with golden offers. He has already gained many, and many more are compelled to submission. . . . At present it is of infinite importance to get as many of these people as possible to move their families and effects, particularly their teams and provisions, from the immediate vicinity of Burgoyne's army.[36]

To further thwart Burgoyne, Schuyler issued his own manifesto in which he declared to be traitors all those who "should in any way assist, give comfort to, or hold correspondence with, or take protection from the enemy."[37] He ordered all the provincial militia companies addressed by Burgoyne to march to his army on the Hudson without delay.[38]

Schuyler's strategy was more effective than Burgoyne's in the long run, although many loyalists continued to move to the British camp during July.[39] About four hundred Tories went to Castleton to take the oath of allegiance, although the majority were not in earnest but merely wished to discover who the real loyalists were in their communities. Burgoyne reported optimistically to Germain that "those who escape bring their cattle to my camp and swear allegiance to the King; Many take arms & the Corps already established afford a fair prospect of strength & utility to the cause of Government."[40] Local inhabitants brought sheep to the camp and offered them for sale.[41] So many dwellers approached the base at Fort Edward for various reasons that Skene's duties became too extensive to be executed by one person.[42] Accordingly, Burgoyne appointed assistants.[43] Unfortunately for Burgoyne, prospects of loyal assistance were not so fair as to justify so much attention and administrative labor. Many loyalists entered his camp destitute and on the verge of starvation. To refuse them food would be "without equal in humanity," he wrote.[44] But Burgoyne had not been able to forage successfully and had barely enough provision for his own troops. He dismissed Schuyler's attempts to drive cattle from Burgoyne's path as an act of desperation or folly: "the only purpose it can answer is to retard me for a time; which it certainly does; it cannot finally impede me."[45] Burgoyne hoped eventually to obtain provision both for his army and for the local inhabitants who had sought his protection. In the long term, however, the opposition of the patriots more than counterbalanced the support of loyalists. Finally, the murder of Jane McCrea by some of Burgoyne's Indian allies almost totally destroyed the good will which the general and Skene had attempted to create in the Hudson Valley.

Early in July Burgoyne had complained to Germain about the conduct of his Indians. If left unwatched, they would commit "enormities too horrid to think of," he wrote.[46] Although the Indians were not kept under stringent discipline, they did not do any extensive plundering until the midpoint of the month.[47] Then on July 20 Charles Langlade finally arrived with the Ottawa nation, which had a reputation for bloodthirstiness.[48] Decorated with the feathers of birds and the skins of wild beasts, they gathered to confer with Burgoyne, who warned them to scalp none but the dead.[49] But the Ottawas, whom Carleton and Burgoyne knew to be more warlike than the other nations, failed to follow instructions. Three days after their arrival, Burgoyne announced that "great enormities [had] been committed at different times upon the People of the Country," and that all of his Indians were to remain in their transport ships until they completed the voyage from Skenesborough to Fort Anne.[50] On July 27, the Ottawas arrived at Fort Edward.[51] That evening, several of them brought two scalps to the base, one of an officer, the other of the eighteen-year-old Jane McCrea, who has since become a legend. The circumstances of that outrage soon passed into a folklore that has persisted for two centuries.[52] The incident provided Major General Horatio Gates with a splendid opportunity to match Burgoyne's propaganda. In a widely circulated letter to the British commander, Gates revealed the temper of local inhabitants as well as his own feelings about Burgoyne:

> That the savages of America should in their warfare mangle and scalp the unhappy prisoners is neither new nor extraordinary; but that the famous lieutenant-general Burgoyne, in whom the fine gentleman is united with the soldier and the scholar, should hire the savages of America to scalp Europeans and the descendants of Europeans, nay more that he should pay a price for every scalp so barbarously taken, is more than will be believed in England until the authenticated facts shall in every gazette convince mankind of the truth of this horrid tale.[53]

Burgoyne read Gates's letter for what it was and replied with dignity. He denied premeditation and he also denied that he had offered bounties for scalps. It was true that Burgoyne had threatened "the horrors of retaliation" against what he called American barbarity toward German and provincial prisoners of war. Nevertheless, Burgoyne denied Gates's allegations with great fervor. "I would not be conscious of the acts you pretend to impute to me for the whole continent of America," he wrote, "though the wealth of worlds were in its bowels and a paradise upon its surface."[54] Conceding that the guilty

Indian ought to have suffered an ignominious death, although punishment "by our laws and principles of justice would have been perhaps unprecedented," he also shrewdly attacked Gates's rather lurid literary descriptions when he wrote: "Respecting Miss McCrea; her fall wanted not the tragic display you have laboured to give it, to make it as sincerely abhorred and lamented by me, as it can possibly be by the tenderest of her friends."[55] An eyewitness in the expedition reported that, in general, Burgoyne had been able to control the Indians; "indeed," he wrote, "it was very remarkable how he restrained their ferocity during the short time they were with our army, and in order to do this the more effectually, he took to his aid a favourite priest of them who had more control over the passions of the Indians than all their chiefs put together."[56] Nevertheless, the murder caused a sensation. Patriots in the Hudson Valley were outraged when they learned of the atrocity, vengeful when Burgoyne's clemency to the offending Indian became known.[57] The tragedy apparently inspired some inhabitants to volunteer for service in the American army, and even British soldiers realized how detrimental to their cause was the presence of Indians. "The terror excited by the Indians," wrote Sergeant Lamb, "instead of disposing the inhabitants to court British protection, had a contrary effect."[58]

The Indians continued to trouble the general, who decided to dispatch a British officer to accompany each party of Indians and take notes of their plundering and other activities.[59] La Corne St. Luc and the Indians were not pleased by that decision. Burgoyne became convinced that "a cordial reconciliation with the Indians was only to be effected by a renunciation of all my former prohibitions and indulgence in blood and rapine."[60] But this he would not do, and when the warriors threatened to desert, Burgoyne told St. Luc that he would rather lose "every Indian, than connive at their enormities." Many of them left on August 5. The next day Burgoyne wrote to Howe that he had taken measures "to keep up their Terror and avoid their Cruelty," and he believed that he had "in a great measure Succeeded. They attack very bravely; they Scalp the Dead only; and spare the Inhabitants."[61] Nevertheless, he admitted to Howe that "there is reason to believe that the Deserters from the 53d Regiment have been scalped by the Savages."[62] Curiously, Burgoyne did not refer to the McCrea massacre at all, although he admitted having some difficulty managing the representatives of seventeen nations who accompanied his expedition.

Burgoyne had not only to discipline marauding Indians, control bickering Germans, and care for impoverished loyalists; his own British troops soon caused him concern. Burgoyne assured his soldiers that their faithful attachment to the cause of the king gave him no apprehension that desertion would spread, but "to prevent the Straggling from the Camp for the purpose of marauding, drunkenness, or other Disorders, leading to Desertion," he warned, "it is positively ordered that a Report of absent men be sent to Head Quarters within *one hour* after each roll-calling, in order that parties of Savages may be immediately sent in pursuit, who have orders to Scalp all Deserters."[63]

But it was not Indians alone who punished deserters. One deserter, a soldier in Riedesel's regiment, was apprehended by the regular army and shot to death by order of court-martial.

As the days passed, the beleaguered commander had to divide his attention between the continuing problems within the army and the administrative difficulties arising from the divided command structure of the British forces in North America. Burgoyne had left 950 men at Ticonderoga, 200 on Diamond Island in Lake George, and another 200 at Crown Point in Lake Champlain. He assumed that eventually Carleton would garrison Ticonderoga with his own soldiers so that Burgoyne could proceed to Albany at full strength.[64] When Carleton did not send forces from the Canadian army to protect Ticonderoga, Burgoyne wrote anxiously to him, pointing out that his communications would become weaker as he proceeded, that detachments of soldiers for various purposes would further weaken his force, and that replacement forces were absolutely necessary if he were to accomplish his mission.[65] Burgoyne wanted Carleton to release soldiers to relieve the Sixty-second Regiment at Ticonderoga, and he also wanted men and gunboats to permanently secure Fort George when Burgoyne completed his advance to Fort Edward.[66] He argued that Ticonderoga could be considered within the borders of Carleton's jurisdiction and noted that Germain had already instructed Carleton to give Burgoyne every possible assistance. Carleton replied that such an arrangement would be contrary to his orders, which prohibited him from acting beyond the borders of Canada.[67] Burgoyne wrote again to the governor and stressed even more urgently his need for immediate reinforcement. Carleton, he hoped, would appreciate that his situation was difficult and that enemy interruption of his communication lines and bases would force him to ruin or retreat.[68] Burgoyne warned that such losses when combined with the ordinary drains upon his army would reduce his effectiveness against the American force. Carleton finally agreed to send seven regiments, but he justified his departure from Germain's orders by citing Barrington's instructions to give Burgoyne every possible assistance.[69] Ultimately, the secretary of state approved Carleton's decision, calling it a wise one.[70]

While he halted at Skenesborough and Fort Edward, Burgoyne wrote at length and frequently to Carleton and Germain, but he painted circumstances quite differently for each. To Carleton he complained of poor transport facilities, lack of horses and forage, excess baggage, and troop losses. Reporting a more optimistic interpretation of events to Germain, he announced on July 11 that the army was "in the fullest Powers of Health and Spirit." "Upon the whole of my situation, my Lord," he declared exultantly, "I am confident of fulfilling the object of my orders. The instruments I have to employ are so good that my merit will be small should I appear to have any."[71] Burgoyne was so pleased with his success thus far that he believed he could accomplish much more. If only he were permitted to march on his left rather than on his right, he told Germain, he was confident that he could subdue "before winter the provinces where the rebellion originated."[72] However, Burgoyne lamented, Germain had ordered him to join Howe at Albany before making other plans. The general bemoaned the lack of flexibility in his orders. "Your Lordship will pardon me if I a little lament that my orders do not give me the latitude I ventured to propose in my original project for the Campaign, to make a real effort instead of a feint upon New England."[73] Nonetheless, Burgoyne realized that Albany rather than New England was his immediate target.

Surprisingly, Burgoyne did not discuss Howe's decision to move to Philadelphia rather than Albany. Howe had written to Carleton in May concerning his new plan, and Burgoyne read that letter while he was in Montreal. However, he concealed it from his troops and did not refer to any of it in his military dispatches. He did not even reply to Howe until July 2, and when he did, Burgoyne made no reference to Sir William's new strategy. Nor did he indicate that he would need any support from Howe. He merely recounted the events of his campaign to that date and assured Howe that he would "implicitly follow the ideas I communicated to your Excellency in my letters from Plymouth and Quebec."[74] Sir William received the report with satisfaction and told Germain on July 16 that "General Burgoyne will meet with little interruption otherwise than the difficulties he must encounter in transporting stores."[75] In fact, Howe was sufficiently pleased with Burgoyne's self-confidence that he felt free to move even his reserve force in New York to Pennsylvania if Washington decided to turn south. Howe believed that

> the strength of Gen[era]l Burgoyne's Army is such as to leave me no room to dread the Event, but if Mr. Washington's Intention should be only to *retard* the approach of General Burgoyne to Albany, he may soon find himself exposed to an Attack from this Quarter and from General Burgoyne at the same time, from both which, I flatter myself, he would find it difficult to escape.[76]

If Washington did turn south, Howe planned to approach Philadelphia by land rather than by sea so that he would be in a better position to trap the American commander.

Howe wrote to Burgoyne on July 17, acknowledging receipt of the general's letters of April, from Plymouth, May, from Quebec and Montreal, and July, from Ticonderoga.[77] Once again, he reminded Burgoyne that he soon would leave for Philadelphia, where he expected to confront Washington. If Washington turned instead toward the northern expedition, "and you can keep him at bay, be assured I shall soon be after him to relieve you."[78] Howe assumed that Burgoyne would easily subdue, beat back, or evade Washington and reach Albany safely. Thereafter, "the movements of the enemy will guide yours; but my wishes are, that the enemy be drove out of [New York] before any operation takes place in Connecticut."[79] He betrayed no fear that Burgoyne might need help but promised only that Clinton would act from New York City "as occurrences [may] direct . . . success be ever with you."[80]

Burgoyne, however, became anxious for news from Howe, whose letters of July 17 did not arrive until August 3. When he arrived at Fort Edward on July 29, he mentioned to Carleton that he had no news of Howe.[81] On the following day, Howe's reply of July 17 had still not arrived, and Burgoyne for the first time began to express apprehension concerning Howe's activities. He told Germain:

> I have spared no pains to open a correspondence with Sir William Howe. I have employed the most enterprizing [*sic*] characters and offered very promising rewards, but of ten messengers sent at different times and by different routes not one is returned to me, and *I am in total ignorance of the situation or intentions of that General.*[82]

Burgoyne later used that letter as evidence to argue that he had done all he could to keep in touch with Howe, and that as late as August 20, 1777, he was unaware of Howe's change of plans for the campaign. One scholar has concluded that Burgoyne's letter of August 20 was just that—the first step of an argument based upon evidence that he developed in order to vindicate his conduct should the expedition fail.[83] Indian troubles, transport problems, and desertion had lowered the morale of his army and delayed the progress of the expedition. Moreover, the patriots were massing on the Hudson for a confrontation with the British army. Burgoyne may have seized upon the ambiguity of the strategy of 1777 to ensure his exculpation from possible blame in the future.

Although Burgoyne distorted the facts, there were elements of truth in his version. Howe's letter of July 17 did not arrive until August 3. Burgoyne had taken pains to correspond with him, and, as of July 30, he said that he was in complete ignorance of Howe's situation. But it cannot be denied that Burgoyne was well informed concerning Sir William's move to Philadelphia. Clinton told Burgoyne in July, possibly in August, that "Howe is gone to the Chesapeak bay with the greatest part of the Army. I hear he is landed but am not certain[.] I am left to command here with too small a force to make any effectual diversion in your favour. I shall try something at any rate. It may be of use to you. I owe to you I think Sir W.'s move just at this time the worst he could take."[84] Burgoyne's fabrication was precautionary rather than desperate. He had not yet encountered the bulk of the American army in battle, and his record was not yet marred by defeat.

Howe's letter finally arrived on August 3, and three days later Burgoyne replied to it. He hoped that communication problems would soon decrease, and declared that he would follow carefully the instructions in Howe's letter. He assured Howe that he had "the fullest satisfaction in the alacrity" of his own army, and he defended the choice of his second route southward, despite laborious rebuilding, "which puts me well forward." Having just formed a plan to secure fresh provision at Bennington, Burgoyne confidently announced that he expected to reach Saratoga on August 23. He did not request assistance from

New York, nor did he ask Howe where he was going, nor did he refer to the Philadelphia expedition at all. Apparently Burgoyne wanted to have his cake and eat it, too: he wanted the glory of reaching Saratoga all to himself, so he led Howe to believe that he did not need him; at the same time, in case he should fail, Burgoyne wanted it to appear that he had failed because of Howe's absence.

During the course of the campaign Germain had begun to worry about the strategy he had so carelessly approved. In mid-May he urged Howe to complete his Philadelphia excursion in time to meet Burgoyne at Albany.[85] However, Germain concealed his approval of the new objective for some time; he must have been aware of the contradictions inherent in approving both of the plans—if he could put the blame on his staff officials, so much the better for his own reputation. Even Germain's under secretary, D'Oyley, was unaware of the revised plan for Howe, or else he did not wish to let former governor Thomas Hutchinson know it, for on July 30—the very day Burgoyne proclaimed his ignorance of Howe's movements—D'Oyley assured Hutchinson that Howe was not going to Philadelphia; "I suppose he is gone with a great part of the army & fleet to New England," he wrote. Germain himself seemed to be confused about Howe's ultimate destination, for on August 17 he told Knox that "Col[onel] Olgivie has been here. . . . He hopes Sir W[illia]m Howe is going to Boston, and not to the southward, but everything is kept a profound secret."[86] Since Howe was at sea, he could not write to Germain, a fact that the agitated secretary had not absorbed as late as August 22. He complained bitterly to Knox: "I hoped our letters would have given us some reason why the campaign began so late, but we are to remain in ignorance."[87] Two weeks later, Knox finally obtained more definite news and told Thomas Hutchinson that "Howe certainly intended to go to Philadelphia when he left New York."[88] Howe also sent the secretary Burgoyne's letter of his progress to Ticonderoga. Germain decided to send the dispatch to the *Gazette* for publication, which the king approved, for he praised Burgoyne's conduct.[89] On August 22, Germain sent all of Howe's letters to the king, and planned to attach the following comment:

> The Private Letter Confirms the opinion Lord George always had of the Generals pursuing his intended operations to the Southward. Your Majesty will be pleas'd to remark, that no reason is assigned for the Campaign opening so late.[90]

The secretary did not send that note to the king until December 9, after the news of Saratoga had arrived. Germain's excuse was that he had neglected to enclose it, but it is possible that he did not want the king to know how fully he had permitted Howe to abandon Burgoyne.[91]

Germain continued to put the best interpretation on events.[92] He displayed additional anxiety concerning Burgoyne in a letter to General Sir John Irwin, then commander in chief of the British army in Ireland, which he wrote one day after his "lost" dispatch to the king: "I confess I feared that Washington would have marched all his forces towards Albany, and attempted to demolish the army from Canada."[93] But when Germain learned that Washington had gone to Morristown after sending only three thousand soldiers to Albany, he said, "If that is all he does he will not distress Burgoyne." Then, in a letter to the king, Germain remarked that Burgoyne's progress "is as rapid as could be Expected, and the difficulties he has surmounted do him great honour."[94] Having given Howe permission for his diversion, Germain attempted to persuade the king that he was ignorant of Sir William's movements. The secretary complained in a secret letter to the king that he had sent ten messengers to New York "and not one had then return'd."[95] The secretary of state was now misrepresenting events even more seriously than had Burgoyne. Informed opinion in England, both public and private, had exposed the folly of Germain's strategy, and the pressure exerted on the secretary inspired him to deception and a hunt for a scapegoat. Howe's cause was lost. Germain did not tell him so, while continuing to correspond with him. The secretary was able to continue justifying Burgoyne for the moment. Wrote Germain to Knox: "I am sorry the Canada army will be disappointed in the junction they expect with Sir William Howe, but the more honour for Burgoyne if he does the Business without any assistance from New York."[96]

If the strategy puzzled London, the American commanders were even more surprised. Washington could not bring himself to believe that Philadelphia was Howe's object:

> Whatever were his intentions . . . he certainly ought in good policy to endeavour to Cooperate with General Burgoyne. I am so fully of opinion that this will be his plan that I have advanced the Army thus far to support our party at Peekskill, should the Enemy move up the River.[97]

Several weeks later, Washington's mind was unchanged. He continued to express to Gates his disbelief: "Gen[era]l Howe's, in a manner, abandoning Gen[era]l Burgoyne, is so unaccountable a matter, that till I am fully assured it is so, I cannot help casting my Eyes continually behind me."[98] Whatever Burgoyne knew of Howe's strategy, and it appears that he understood it fully, he concealed any apprehension from Germain. "Nothing has happened" he wrote "since I had the honour to write last to change my sentiments of the Campaign."[99]

While Washington was pondering the mysteries of British strategy, Burgoyne made his customary annual request for leave. He asked Germain to grant him a leave of absence as soon as he had completed his assignment for his "health & satisfaction."[100] Learning that Carleton had resigned his post and was about to leave Canada, Burgoyne presumed to imagine that the government might appoint him to replace Sir Guy as governor of Canada. "[My] experience of his Majesty's grace toward me," he declared, "makes many surmizes in my own favour probable." Having proposed the idea, Burgoyne proceeded to decline the offer, "as I am conscious I am not adapted either by talent or constitution to do due service in the Province of Canada." Since Burgoyne also refused a knighthood during 1777, it may be speculated that he wished to avoid any special honors until the campaign was assured of a successful conclusion. New appointments might be embarrassing if they were awarded for services not yet fully rendered, and Albany was still far in the distance.[101] Burgoyne asked Germain to decline the offer on his behalf and to submit the name of Brigadier William Phillips for consideration in place of his own.[102]

With the roads constructed and the bridges repaired by July 24, Burgoyne was able to move the bulk of his army the fifteen miles from Skenesborough to Fort Anne in two days,[103] despite the fact that the bateaux had to be moved one at a time.[104] On the twenty-eighth the army moved to a height of land beyond Fort Edward.[105] Burgoyne took possession of the post and established headquarters nearby at a red house that American soldiers had evacuated a few days earlier.[106] The Canadians, Indians, and provincials were employed continuously, transporting the bateaux back and forth between Ticonderoga, Skenesborough, and Fort Edward.[107] The fragile transport system worried Burgoyne, who ordered his troops not to overload the carts with regimental baggage because of "the slightness of the carts and the [necessity for the] preservation of the horses."[108]

On Lake George, several weeks of intense activity were drawing to a close. In mid-July Burgoyne had sent Phillips to Ticonderoga.[109] The brigadier supervised the passage of ships from Lake Champlain through the portage to Lake George.[110] On the seventeenth Burgoyne received the first faint reports that the American troops had evacuated Fort George.[111] By the twenty-fourth, heavy cannon were moved down the lake on transport vessels.[112] Five days later a great embarkation under Phillips's direction arrived at Fort George.[113] On the same day, the road from Fort George to Fort Edward passed into British control.[114] Burgoyne put his men to work moving the bateaux, artillery, and other materials necessary for proceeding from Phillips's post at Fort George over the road to Fort Edward.[115] During the first week in August, the general moved further south to Fort Miller, and there prepared to cross the Hudson for the final stage of his journey to Albany.

Burgoyne had lost a month—July 9 to August 9—because of the enormous difficulties encountered while moving the army's equipment.[116] From July 30 until August 15, Burgoyne reported, "every possible measure was employed to bring forward bateaux, provisions, and ammunition, from Fort George to . . . Hudson's River, a distance of eighteen miles . . . the delay was not imputable to neglect, but to the natural accidents attending so long and intricate a combination of land and water carriage."[117] Now another delay ensued because of a lack of food, which was becoming a critical problem. Burgoyne remarked that a general in America must spend twenty hours pondering how to feed his army for every single hour he devoted to battle. In order to secure the necessary stores, Burgoyne engaged in a diversion that led to disastrous consequences.

Notes

1. February 28, 1777, Burgoyne, "Thoughts," C.O. 42.36, ff. 37–52.
2. July 29, 1777, Burgoyne to Carleton, *State*, pp. lxxv–lxxvi; C.O. 42.36, ff. 237–48.
3. July 29, 1777, Burgoyne to Carleton, DeFonblanque, *Episodes*, pp. 267–68; July 30, 1777, Burgoyne to Germain, ibid., pp. 268–70; Burgoyne, *State*, narrative, p. 17.
4. For discussions of Burgoyne's motivation here, see Nickerson, *Turning Point*, pp. 163–64.
5. August 20, 1777, Burgoyne to Germain, *State*, appendix, pp. xxxix–xliv.
6. July 12, 1777, Thacher, *Journal*, p. 85.
7. "The Rebels are exerting every nerve to make the very bad Roads between this & Fort Edward much worse, by felling timber, breaking up bridges." July 17, 1777, Clerke to Polwarth; July 13, 1777, Burgoyne, *Orderly Book*, pp. 39–40; July 30, 1777, Burgoyne to Germain, C.O. 42.36, ff. 771–76.
8. July 30, 1777, Burgoyne to Germain, C.O. 42,36, ff. 771–76.
9. February 28, 1777, Burgoyne, "Thoughts," C.O. 42.36, ff. 37–52.
10. July 5, 1777, Clerke to Polwarth, Bedford County Record Office.
11. Burgoyne, *State*, pp. 18–19.
12. July 11, 1777, Burgoyne to Germain, C.O. 42.36, ff. 719–30; June 22, 1777, and July 11, 1777, Burgoyne to Harvey, *State*, appendix, p. lviii–lxii.
13. July 5, 1777, Clerke to Polwarth, Bedford County Record Office.
14. July 29, 1777, Burgoyne to Carleton, DeFonblanque, *Episodes*, pp. 267–68.
15. Ibid.
16. July 30, 1777, Burgoyne to Germain, C.O. 42.36, ff. 771–76.
17. Morton, *Skene;* Nickerson, *Turning Point*, pp. 166–67; Nickerson contended that Skene would have become wealthy after the war if roads connected his land to the Hudson.
18. Skene had 25,000 acres of land by a patent granted to him on March 31, 1765; Irving Mark, *Agrarian Conflicts in Colonial New York 1711–1775* (New York: Columbia University Press, 1940), p. 2, note 10.
19. Stone, *Campaign*, p. 28, note 1, maintained that Burgoyne would not have accepted a bribe.
20. Burgoyne, *State*, narrative, pp. 12–13. In his "Reflections," the general anticipated battering down field works after taking Ticonderoga.
21. For an analysis that supports Burgoyne's decision to bring a large artillery supply with him, see Theodore Ropp, *War in the Modern World* (Durham, N.C.: Duke University Press, 1959), pp. 77–78, and p. 77, note 19.
22. Digby, *Invasion*, p. 247.
23. July 5, 1777, Burgoyne to Germain, DeFonblanque, *Episodes*, p. 246, note 1.
24. August 20, 1777, Burgoyne to Germain, *State*, appendix, p. xl.
25. July 16, 1777, Burgoyne, *Orderly Book*, pp. 44–46.
26. July 12, 1777, Burgoyne, *Orderly Book*, pp. 37–39.
27. Ibid.
28. July 18, 1777, Burgoyne to Riedesel, DeFonblanque, *Episodes*, pp. 265–66; July 29, 1777, Burgoyne to Carleton, ibid., 267–68.
29. July 11, 1777, Burgoyne to Germain, C.O. 42.36, ff. 719–30; July 11, 1777, Burgoyne to Harvey, *State*, appendix, pp. lx–lxii.
30. Quoted by Stone, *Campaign*, p. 29.
31. July 10, 1777, "Instructions for Colonel Skene," P.R.O. Treasury 1.605, ff. 85, 81a, 86.
32. July 12, 1777, Burgoyne, *Orderly Book*, pp. 37–39.

33. July 15, 1777, Burgoyne to Skene, Treasury 1.605, f. 85b; he wanted a report of grain, stock available, "and Mills to Grind it in."

34. July 15, 1777, Skene to Dartmouth, Historical Manuscripts Commission, *Dartmouth MSS.*, 2:1895.

35. July 11, 1777, Burgoyne to Germain, C.O. 42.36, ff. 719–30.

36. July, 1777, Governor Morris to New York Legislature, Morton, *Skene*, p. 56.

37. Carrington, *Battles*, p. 318.

38. Ibid.

39. July 30, 1777, Digby, *Invasion*, p. 243.

40. July 30, 1777, Burgoyne to Germain, C.O. 42.36, ff. 771–76.

41. August 2, 1777, Burgoyne, *Orderly Book*, p. 63.

42. August 6, 1777, ibid., pp. 65–66.

43. Ibid.

44. July 30, 1777, Burgoyne to Germain, C.O. 42.36, ff. 771–76.

45. Ibid.

46. July 11, 1777, Burgoyne to Germain, C.O. 42.36, ff. 719–30.

47. July 15, 1777, Skene to Dartmouth, Historical Manuscripts Commission, *Dartmouth MSS.*, 2:1895.

48. July 20, 1777, Digby, *Invasion*, pp. 228–29.

49. Ibid.; Burgoyne announced the forthcoming congress in orders of July 17, 1777; Burgoyne, *Orderly Book*, pp. 44–46.

50. July 23, 1777, Burgoyne, *Orderly Book*, pp. 47–48.

51. Lamb, *Memoir*, pp. 177–78.

52. Digby, *Invasion*, p. 235 and p. 235, note 175; September 3, 1777, Burgoyne to Gates, Gates papers, New-York Historical Society; Thacher, *Military Journal*, p. 95. A summary of the McCrea literature appears in R. Don Higginbotham, *The War of American Independence: Military Attitudes, Policies, and Practice 1763–1789* (New York: Macmillan, 1971), p. 201, note 33.

53. September 2, 1777, Gates to Burgoyne, Gates papers; Thacher, *Military Journal*, p. 95.

54. Ibid., p. 279.

55. September 3, 1777, Burgoyne to Gates, Gates papers.

56. Lamb, *Journal*.

57. Thacher wrote: "In the hands of the barbarians under his command . . . [Burgoyne] . . . murdered [Miss McCrea] in a manner extremely shocking to the feelings of humanity." *Military Journal*, p. 95.

58. In a deposition sent to Philip Schuyler, an American spy reported from Skenesborough "that he heard the Regular officers say, that they would let the Indians at Random to Sweep the Grants, which they thought could be done in Three days . . . that he saw the Indians Cutt both the Hands of three Prisoners lately taken, and afterwards Hang'd two up by the Heels on a Tree and Roasted them," thereafter eating the flesh of those they roasted; July 29, 1777, John Williams to Philip Schuyler, Schuyler papers, New York Public Library.

59. Carrington, *Battles*, p. 327.

60. [August 1777] Burgoyne to Germain, ibid.

61. August 6, 1777, Burgoyne to Howe, House of Lords Record Office; C.O. 5.94, ff. 352–53.

62. August 6, 1777, Burgoyne, *Orderly Book*, pp. 65–66; additional atrocities were disclosed on August 13, 1777, Dr. John Bartlett to Philip Schuyler, Schuyler papers, New York Public Library.

63. Ibid.

64. July 2, 1777, Burgoyne to Howe, C.O. 5.94, f. 286.

65. July 11, 1777, Burgoyne to Carleton, DeFonblanque, *Episodes*, p. 261.

66. July 29, 1777, Burgoyne to Carleton, ibid., pp. 261–62.

67. (July 1777), Carleton to Burgoyne, ibid., p. 261.

68. July 29, 1777, Burgoyne to Carleton, Burgoyne, *State*, appendix, pp. lxxv–lxxvi.

69. July 31, 1777, Carleton to Barrington, W.O. 1.11, ff. 101–4.

70. September 15, 1777, Germain to Burgoyne, C.O. 5.243, f. 232.

71. July 11, 1777, Burgoyne to Germain, C.O. 42.36, ff. 719–30.

72. July 11, 1777, Burgoyne to Germain, private letter, Burgoyne, *State*, appendix, pp. xxxvi–xxxix.

73. Ibid.

74. July 2, 1777, Burgoyne to Howe, C.O. 5.94, f. 286.

75. July 16, 1777, Howe to Germain, C.O. 5.94, f. 290.

76. Ibid.

77. July 17, 1777, Howe to Burgoyne, Burgoyne, *State*, appendix, p. lxix.

78. July 17, 1777, Howe to Burgoyne, Burgoyne, *State*, appendix, p. lxix.

79. Ibid.

80. Ibid.

81. July 29, 1777, Burgoyne to Carleton, DeFonblanque, *Episodes*, pp. 267–68.

82. July 30, 1777, Burgoyne to Germain, private letter, ibid., p. 270.

83. Alden, *American Revolution*, p. 143.

84. [July–August, 1777] Clinton to Burgoyne, Clinton papers, Clements Library; reproduced in William M. Dabney, *After Saratoga: The Story of the Convention Army,* University of New Mexico Publications in History, no. 6 (Albuquerque, N.M.: University of New Mexico Press, 1954), frontispiece.

85. May 18, 1777, Germain to Howe, C.O. 5.94, f. 169; August 15, 1777, Robert Auchmuty to the earl of Hardwicke, B.L. Add. MS. 35,614, ff. 30–31.

86. August 17, 1777, Germain to William Knox, Historical Manuscripts Commission, *MSS. in Various Collections,* 6:135–36.

87. August 22, 1777, Germain to Knox, ibid., pp. 136–37.

88. September 1, 1777, Hutchinson, ed., *Diary,* 1:158.

89. September 25, 1777, Germain to Knox, Historical Manuscripts Commission, *MSS. in Various Collections,* 6:139.

90. August 22, 1777, Germain to the king, Fortescue, ed., *Correspondence,* 3:469.

91. December 9, 1777, Germain to the king, ibid., p. 507.

92. August 23, 1777, Germain to General Irwin, Historical Manuscripts Commission, *Stopford-Sackville MSS.,* 1:138–39.

93. Ibid.

94. September 25, 1777, Germain to the king, Fortescue, ed., *Correspondence,* 3:480.

95. Ibid.

96. September 29, 1777, Germain to Knox, Historical Manuscripts Commission, *MSS. in Various Collections,* 96:139.

97. July 19, 1777, Washington to Heath, Fitzpatrick, ed., *Writings,* 3:439.

98. July 30, 1777, Washington to Gates, ibid., p. 499.

99. July 30, 1777, Burgoyne to Germain, C.O. 42.36, ff. 771–76.

100. Ibid.

101. Ibid.

102. The post was eventually offered to General Frederick Haldimand, who accepted it; August 29, 1777, Germain to Knox, Historical Manuscripts Commission, *MSS. in Various Collections,* 6:137.

103. July 23, 1777, Burgoyne, *Orderly Book,* pp. 47–48; July 24, 1777, Digby, *Invasion,* p. 233.

104. Digby, ibid.

105. July 29, 1777, Burgoyne, *Orderly Book,* pp. 58–59; July 29, 1777, Burgoyne, *State,* narrative, p. 18.

106. Ibid.; August 12, 1777, Captain Pearson to ?, Historical Manuscripts Commission, *Dartmouth MSS.,* 2:442.

107. July 26 and 29, Burgoyne, *Orderly Book,* pp. 55–59.

108. July 29, 1777, Burgoyne, ibid., pp. 58–59.

109. July 15, 1777, Skene to Dartmouth, Historical Manuscripts Commission, *Dartmouth MSS.*, 2:440–41.

110. July 12, 1777, Williams, "Journal," C.O. 42.36, ff. 731–32.

111. July 17, 1777, Clerke to Polwarth, Bedford County Record Office.

112. July 24, 1777, Digby, *Invasion*, p. 233.

113. July 29, 1777, Burgoyne, *State*, narrative, p. 18.

114. July 29, 1777, Digby, *Invasion*, p. 240.

115. July 29, 1777, Burgoyne, *State*, narrative, p. 18.

116. August 20, 1777, Burgoyne to Germain, Burgoyne, *State*, appendix, pp. xxxix–xl.

117. Ibid.

15

The First Defeat

After fifteen days of exertion, Burgoyne wrote to Germain, he had managed to extend his line of supply from Montreal to Fort Miller. But he could not yet risk further penetration toward Albany until he had improved his transport system and food supply.[1] The general spent all his time supervising the clearing of roads and the movement of his army, and did not give much thought to purely tactical matters. Late in July, Baron von Riedesel reminded Burgoyne that his dragoons still lacked horses, a complaint the German officer had repeated to him since the beginning of the campaign.[2] Riedesel advised Burgoyne to organize a detachment of Tories and dragoons and send them into the countryside near Castleton to obtain oxen, draft horses, and especially saddle horses.[3] After some hesitation Burgoyne approved the plan, but he did not take action. Two weeks later, the supply problem became acute: "[t]he alternative, therefore, was short: either to relinquish the favourable opportunity of advancing upon the enemy, or to attempt other resources of supply."[4] Burgoyne's disinclination to retreat forced him to the second alternative. The British knew that supplies of cattle for the American army passed from Manchester to Arlington and other parts of the Hampshire Grants, to Bennington, and thence to the main army on the Hudson.[5] Philip Skene, the Tory colonel, urged Burgoyne to send a detachment to Manchester where an abundant store of supplies lay virtually unguarded.[6] Skene assured Burgoyne that loyalists in the Grants would help him confiscate supplies.[7] Burgoyne accepted the colonel's proposal and asked Riedesel to revise his earlier suggestions concerning a foraging expedition. Burgoyne needed 300 horses, but wanted more. He already had acquired draft oxen. If the foraging expedition were successful, detachments guarding magazines at Ticonderoga and elsewhere could be brought back to the main force, allowing the entire army to act "with energy and dispatch."[8]

Burgoyne also wanted the detachment to engage in political activity. They must "try the affections of the country" and "disconcert the councils of the enemy." They should hold "the most respectable people" as hostages, and imprison "all persons acting in committee, or any officers acting under the direction of Congress, whether civil or military."[9] In addition, the general ordered his force to levy taxes in kind whenever they could. Furthermore, since he wished to create confusion concerning his strategy, Burgoyne hoped the detachment would give the impression that it was the advanced guard of a much larger army, which the Americans would presumably believe was en route to Boston to crush the center of rebellion and end the war.[10] Finally, the general hoped the detachment would obtain recruits.[11] These grandiose plans and objectives required careful implementation, but Burgoyne seemed unworried.

The instructions included a detailed route of march for the force, which was expected to move from Batten Kill on the eastern bank of the Hudson to Arlington, where they were to remain until Captain Sherwood and the provincials arrived. They were then expected to push on to Manchester and secure the pass through the mountains from Manchester to Rockingham by dispatching the Indians to Otter Creek. If the Indians found Rockingham safe, the party would march to that town and take it. Remaining at Rockingham until the purpose of the expedition was fulfilled, the detachment was then expected finally to descend via the Connecticut River to Brattleboro and quickly return on the Great Road to Albany.[12] The troops were urged to leave behind tents and baggage, to refrain from plundering, and to avoid any considerable risks.

Burgoyne instructed Riedesel to deliver those orders to Lieutenant Colonel Friedrich Baum, whom the general considered qualified to lead the expedition. However, the German officer's unfamiliarity with the English language ought perhaps to have caused Burgoyne to think twice before entrusting to him the complicated and sophisticated task the detachment was to undertake.[13] True, Colonel Philip Skene was instructed to advise Baum concerning the operations of the detachment "upon all matters of intelligence, negotiation with the inhabitants, roads, and other means depending upon a knowledge of the country, for carrying his instructions into execution."[14] As Riedesel later remarked, much was expected of Skene because of his "supposed knowledge of the Country and influence amongst the inhabitants."[15]

Baum had under his command the whole left wing of Burgoyne's army: about 650 men, including 200 Brunswick dragoons, 100 Hesse-Hanau artillerymen and grenadiers, 50 British marksmen, and 300 Tories, Canadians, and Indians.[16] Burgoyne believed that the German soldiers employed in that diversion were "of the best I had of that nation."[17] Two small three-pound cannon were attached to the force."[18] Baum was instructed to attack or withdraw according to his own judgment, "always bearing in mind that your corps is too valuable to . . . be hazarded."[19]

The reaction of Burgoyne's staff was mixed. Kingston feared that the isolated expedition would be vulnerable to American opposition, as patriotic feeling was stronger in Manchester than in Castleton—the area originally recommended by Riedesel.[20] Fraser disliked the Germans, who were in his opinion sluggish soldiers, but thought the plan might do.[21] Kingston urged Fraser to make known his views to Burgoyne, but both officers remained silent.[22]

Riedesel believed that the plan would be executed too late and that the force was too small.[23] He wrote to the duke of Brunswick that he barely recognized his own suggestions.[24] He discussed those opinions privately with Burgoyne, not wishing to break openly with the general.[25] Although Burgoyne knew that Colonel Seth Warner and his militia were posted at Manchester, he believed it highly probable that the patriots would retreat upon the arrival of his detachment.[26]

Burgoyne was not aware, however, of recent American activity in New Hampshire.[27] The Vermont Committee of Safety had warned its counterpart in New Hampshire on July 15 that Burgoyne's expedition might invade the Green Mountain countryside unless New Hampshire sent help. The appeal was received three days later at Exeter, where the General Court of New Hampshire was in session. That assembly replied on July 19 that New Hampshire would send a brigade of three battalions for two months' service under the command of John Stark.[28] Stark demanded a wide latitude of command, and in fact threatened not to serve unless his request was granted.[29] Accordingly, the legislators authorized him to cooperate with provincial militia, or with the Continental army, or to act "separately, as it shall appear expedient to you for the protection of the people or the annoyance of the enemy."[30] Reluctantly, Stark accepted the responsibility.

Within a week, over fourteen hundred men responded to the legislature's appeal.[31] Such enthusiasm was surprising, for morale in New England had ebbed after Burgoyne's success at Ticonderoga.[32] Perhaps the proximity of the British army and the appeal of Stark as a military leader accounted for the widespread cooperation. Stark quickly gathered equipment and supplies for his expedition. He marched to Charleston, New Hampshire, on July 30, as Burgoyne settled into Fort Edward.[33] One week later, Stark arrived at Manchester and met Seth Warner, who had brought with him a regiment of 200 rangers and the New Hampshire militia. Stark discovered that Schuyler, who previously wanted to organize a flank attack against Burgoyne's rear guard at Ticonderoga, now decided to deploy as many soldiers as possible at Stillwater, a point on the western shore of the Hudson twenty miles south of Fort Edward.[34] Indeed, the New Hampshire militia was packed and ready to march. Stark was displeased with the American commander's new plan.[35] Colonel Benjamin Lincoln, sent to reason with Stark, observed that Stark seemed "exceedingly soured . . . and is determined not to join the Continental army until the Congress gives him rank therein.[36] Differences between the two men disappeared, however, when Stark and Lincoln agreed to cooperate in attacking Burgoyne's army.[37]

On August 8, Stark moved from Manchester twenty miles south to Bennington, then a tiny hamlet of six log cabins. The New Hampshire battalion pitched camp there on the next day and waited for Lincoln to appear. With new recruits arriving daily, Stark soon commanded between 1,000 and 1,300 New

Hampshire and Vermont troops. Pondering his future movements, Stark did not know and could not consider the fact that Burgoyne's foraging expedition was at that moment moving toward the supplies that he guarded.[38]

On the same day, August 9, Baum departed from Fort Edward.[39] He marched seven miles south to Fort Miller, where General Fraser handed over command of the advance corps to him.[40] He was obliged to halt on the next day, however, because the Canadians and Indians intended for him had gone to Stillwater.[41] About one hundred of Breymann's soldiers took their place. At the same time, Baum received instructions from Burgoyne to move toward Bennington rather than Manchester, "Intelligence being received that the Rebels had a Considerable Magazine" at the new destination.[42] The report, which included information concerning extensive supplies of poorly guarded food and horses, was supplied by Skene.[43] On August 11, Baum marched from Fort Miller to Batten Kill opposite Saratoga, but was again halted by a violent storm.[44] A day later, he marched the force for twelve hours.[45] Now sixteen miles east of the Hudson in the Hampshire Grants, about eighty of Baum's advance guard of loyalists and Indians encountered and defeated a small party of about forty patriots who had been guarding cattle.[46] Presently, a second party of fifteen Americans appeared, shot at Baum's guard, and departed.[47] Baum took eight prisoners and obtained 1,000 bushels of wheat and some carts, but he did not find horses.[48] More significantly, he reported to Burgoyne that his men had encountered American soldiers in the area.[49] Baum told the general that there were considerably more than 300 patriots at Bennington, and that he would be "particularly careful, on my approach at that place, to be fully informed of their strength and situation, and take the precautions necessary to fulfill both the orders and instructions of your Excellency."[50] Burgoyne replied that the "accounts you have sent me are very satisfactory."[51] Urging Baum to continue the search for horses, and to send the cattle and carts back to camp as soon as possible, Burgoyne cautioned the German officer:

> should you find the enemy too strongly posted at Bennington, and maintaining such a countenance as would make a coup de main too hazardous, I wish you to take such a post as you can maintain 'till you hear further from me upon your report, and other circumstances, and I will either support you in force or withdraw you.[52]

When the small party of Americans returned to Bennington they informed Stark that Burgoyne's army was marching toward him. The New Hampshire officer sent Colonel Gregg and 200 of his advance guard to take post at a mill on Owl Creek, a small waterway that passed near the Bennington road.[53] Early on the morning of August 14 Baum was leading his troops from Cambridge along that path when suddenly the Americans in the mill fired a volley and retreated down the road.[54] Baum ordered his men to pursue the patriots who were crossing a bridge over Little White Creek, a tributary of Owl Creek. As

Baum advanced, several volunteers from Gregg's force offered to remain behind to burn the bridge, which they did.[55] Burgoyne's detachment was delayed
about an hour and the 200 patriot soldiers escaped.[56] After the bridge was
repaired, Baum posted thirty provincials there and continued to march for
about five miles. Soon he approached Stark's camp, four miles west of Bennington. One of the captured Americans informed him that Stark expected
large reinforcements from the Continental army and intended to attack him "as
soon as the Reinforcements had joined them."[57] Accordingly, Baum moved
back about a mile and encamped.[58] He wrote another letter to Burgoyne,
reporting that between 1,500 and 1,800 soldiers were posted at Bennington,
"but are supposed to leave at our approach."[59] Nevertheless, he asked for a
reinforcement in a report which Riedesel observed was written

> in such high spirits that the General was induced to believe, that he asked for
> a Reinforcement, more to enable him to attack the Enemy than from any
> apprehension of his Corps being in Danger of being Attacked.[60]

Baum did not hint that he was in serious danger.[61]

That second letter arrived in Burgoyne's camp early on the morning of the
fifteenth.[62] Since Baum had given no reason for alarm, Burgoyne did not
arise.[63] He gave instructions to Sir Francis Clerke to select Colonel Heinrich
Breymann to lead the reinforcements, which were being sent "in consequence
of the good news . . . received from Lieutenant Colonel Baum."[64] Breymann
also received at eight o'clock in the morning Burgoyne's written orders to
depart one hour later with 642 men, including a company of chasseurs, a
battalion of grenadiers and light infantry, Major Barner's battalion, and a rifle
company.[65] Breymann's progress was exceptionally slow. The carts were unreliable, the roads and hills became muddy from a relentless rainfall, and Breymann's guide lost his way.[66] An exhaustive search for the guide was conducted
in vain, and "all these differences delayed us much."[67] Breymann contributed
to the deadly pace by stopping his troops frequently to redress ranks. He
accomplished less than one-half mile per hour, less than eight miles for the
day.[68] Breymann sent a messenger to alert Baum that he was on the way.[69]

During that same rain-drenched August 15, Baum devoted himself to de-
ploying troops, constructing entrenchments, dividing the force into detachments, and personally commanding the dragoons, his largest single unit, which
he posted on a steep hill west of the Walloomsac River. His force constructed
breastworks of fallen timber and covered the entire fortification with earth.
Baum placed the Canadians on either side of the Bennington Road, which led
to a bridge over the Walloomsac River one-half mile southeast of the main
encampment. He then stationed elements of Fraser's corps and a few Germans
on a nearby hill. A number of loyalists assisted the operation. Indians held a
plateau beyond the main deployment. Several hundred yards to the southwest

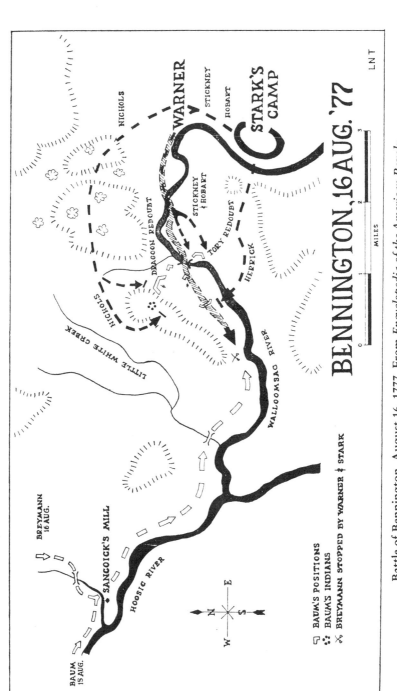

Battle of Bennington, August 16, 1777. From *Encyclopedia of the American Revolution*, by Mark Boatner III. Reprinted by permission of the David McKay Company.

of the bridge, 150 loyalists began to construct breastworks of fence rails.[70] Baum's deployment was a bad one: he had scattered his men over a wide area and posted himself at the top of an accessible hill.[71]

At dawn on August 16, rain was still falling. Baum left his detachments dispersed over a mile, as he had posted them the previous day. He took that risk with confidence, considering the American troops nothing more than "uncouth militia."[72] The weather cleared at noon and, probably anticipating that Breymann would soon arrive, Baum chose to fight. His adversary, now commanding about two thousand continentals, militia, volunteers, and a few Indians, was almost twice as powerful, but Baum said he was encouraged by the success of his first attack. Stark also prepared for battle. He instructed Colonels Nicholas and Hendrick to lead two units in a wide circular movement to surround Baum's position to the north and to the south.[73] One unit was ordered to assault dragoons on the northern side of the hill and hold their attention while the second unit attacked German infantrymen and loyalists south of the hill. Stark would not begin the principal assault until the flanking detachments had reached their respective destinations. All told, Stark deployed about 1,150 soldiers to begin the attack.[74] At about nine o'clock a number of Americans disguised themselves as loyalists and infiltrated the British lines.[75] Baum observed the swelled ranks of the loyalists. Skene had previously assured the colonel that the new volunteers could be trusted, but Baum sent scouts to reconnoiter the positions of these newcomers.[76] When the scouts informed Baum that he was surrounded by Americans, it was too late.

The Bennington expedition was a signal victory for the Americans, a disaster for Burgoyne. Patriot casualties were not heavy. Perhaps thirty were killed, fifty more wounded.[77] Burgoyne's detachment was not so fortunate. One hundred sixty-two of Breymann's 642 men lost their lives, and all of his horses were killed.[78] The commanders of Baum's detached posts and nine of his soldiers returned to camp, but Baum himself and the rest of his detachment were dead or imprisoned.[79] All told, the Americans held 700 of Burgoyne's men.[80] They also captured four brass cannon, trophies of victory.[81]

When he reported the disaster to Germain on August 20, Burgoyne attempted to defend his decision to send troops to Bennington. Putting the best interpretation upon his strategy, and neglecting to inform Germain that his staff disapproved the idea, Burgoyne insisted that "in hazarding this expedition, I had the soundest principles of military reasoning on my side, viz. that the advantages to be expected from success were, in a great degree, superior to the evils that could attend miscarriage."[82] Although Baum was "well qualified" to lead the detachment, Burgoyne implied that the colonel had disobeyed his orders, which were "positive to keep the regular corps posted while the light troops felt their way, and not to incur the danger of being surrounded, or having a retreat cut off."[83] Burgoyne declared that Baum showed great personal courage and was defeated by superior numbers, but he also said, "My defence only compels me to say that my cautions were not observed, nor the reinforcements advanced with the alacrity I had the right to expect."[84] Burgoyne called

Baum's soldiers brave men but said they failed "partly [due] to delusion in respect to the enemy, and partly to surprise and consequent confusion."[85] Likewise, the general praised Breymann's courage and gallantry but criticized his lethargic pace; had he "marched at the rate of two miles an hour any given twelve hours out of the two and thirty, success would probably have ensued." Skene did not escape Burgoyne's censure: "A provincial gentleman of confidence, who had been set with the detachment, as knowing the country and the character of the inhabitants, [he] was so incautious as to leave at liberty such as took the oath of allegiance."[86]

Burgoyne argued that bad weather, poor roads, tired horses, and the "profligacy" of the supposed loyalists contributed to the disaster. He admitted that no cattle were secured, but he minimized the casualties sustained. The Americans, he maintained wrongly, "have small cause of exultation[;] their loss in killed and wounded being more than double to ours, by the confession of their prisoners and deserters, and of many inhabitants who were witnesses to the burial of their dead."[87] The area abounded in the "most active and most rebellious race of the continent, and hangs like a gathering storm upon my left," wrote Burgoyne in disclosing to Germain the real state of affairs in the Hampshire Grants:

> The great bulk of the country is undoubtedly with the Congress, in principle and zeal, and their measures are executed with a secrecy and dispatch that are not to be equalled. Wherever the King's forces point, militia, to the amount of three or four thousand assemble in twenty four hours; they bring with them their subsistence, etc., and, the alarm over, they return to their farms.[88]

At last Burgoyne began to entertain real doubts about his future progress. Although he told Germain that the failure at Bennington would have little effect upon the strength or the spirit of the army, he found prospects "far less prosperous" than before. He doubted the "sincerity or the resolution of the professing loyalists." Only half of his four hundred Tories were dependable, the rest being "trimmers, merely actuated by intent." On the other hand, the patriots with "indefatigable and certain" industry kept moving cattle and corn from his path, so that portable magazines were necessary to obtain supplies.

The worried general reported dangers to the north and south of his army: "from the hour I pass the Hudson's River and proceed towards Albany, all safety of communication ceases. I must expect a large body of the enemy, from my left, will take post behind me."[89] To leave Ticonderoga weakened would be a dangerous experiment, yet he could not permit his garrison to remain there because he needed those soldiers for his depleted force.

Problems to the south were even more pressing. In a private dispatch sent to Germain, Burgoyne complained that he had still not been able to open a communication with Howe, that his messengers had been hanged.[90] He also attempted to explain his previous silence concerning the lack of support from

New York City: "When I wrote more confidently, I little forsaw that I was to be left to pursue my way through such a tract of country, and hosts of foes, without any co-operation from New-York."[91] Although Burgoyne had not requested assistance from the south at any time during his correspondence of May, June, and July, he complained bitterly that "No operation, my Lord, has yet been undertaken in my favour; the Highlands have not yet even been threatened."[92] Indeed, Sir Henry Clinton, who commanded the New York forces in Howe's absence, had written to Burgoyne on August 10 that in his "present starved condition," he could not do anything to help Burgoyne, but would try something toward the close of the year.[93] Consequently, Burgoyne noted, Washington's commander at Peekskill, General Israel Putnam, was free to send two brigades to Gates, whose army, "superior to mine in troops of the Congress, and as many militia as he pleases," waited for him at the junction of the Mohawk and Hudson Rivers. Thus the British general found himself trapped.

Burgoyne interpreted his instructions rigidly when he attempted to defend a decision not to retreat:

> Had I a latitude in my orders, I should think it my duty to wait in this position, or perhaps as far back as Fort Edward . . . till some event happened to assist my movement forward; but my orders being positive, to "force a junction with Sir William Howe," I apprehend I am not at liberty to remain inactive longer than shall be necessary.[94]

Burgoyne misquoted his orders "to force his way to Albany,"[95] for as he himself knew, the two armies were expected to move to Albany and Philadelphia independently, joining only after both campaigns had ended. Nor was Burgoyne or any field officer expected to plunge into a dangerous situation; he himself had just censured Baum for incaution. Baum's orders were specifically designed, warning him not to risk losing his army. Burgoyne's instructions were more loosely worded, but common sense dictated prudence. Nevertheless, Burgoyne would "think no more of a retreat." He was determined to push to Albany: "I yet do not despair."[96]

Howe was now in the Chesapeake at Head of Elk. He wrote to Germain on August 30: "As I have not heard from General Burgoyne since my last Advices. . . . I cannot presume to say what Credit is to be given to the Success of the Rebels in that Quarter as mentioned in the enclosed Newspapers."[97] Howe chose to believe that the reports were much exaggerated. He also reminded Germain that the king had approved alteration of his plan. The reminder was necessary if Germain was to receive Howe's next ominous bit of news without becoming enraged: "My progress," said Sir William, "must be greatly impeded by the prevailing Disposition of the Inhabitants, who . . . seem to be . . . strongly in Enmity against us."[98] Howe hinted that perhaps he could not help Burgoyne at all.

In general, Howe's reaction to Burgoyne's defeat at Bennington was mild.[99]

Others were not so optimistic. "General Burgoyne has had but bad sport in the woods," chuckled his enemy Horace Walpole.[100] Among his own soldiers, Burgoyne found grave discontent. Lieutenant Digby regretted that "British were not sent" in place of the Germans and Indians.[101] Skene was blamed by all, and in an address to the army, Burgoyne denounced the

> credulity of those who managed the department of intelligence and who suffered great numbers of the rebel soldiers to pass and repass, and perhaps count the numbers of the detachment and upon an ill-founded confidence induced Lieut.-Col. Baume to advance too far to have a secure retreat.[102]

There was a grain of truth in Burgoyne's summary statement that the expedition to Bennington "failed of Success through the chances of War."[103] No one could have known that Stark was moving to Bennington at the precise moment that Baum was approaching the same objective.

The patriots recognized and publicized the magnitude of their victory. Thacher said that the British general "must feel the clipping of another wing."[104] Stark called the battle "the hottest I ever saw in my life," and swore that only the coming of night kept him from total victory: "Our men behaved with the greatest spirit and bravery imaginable. Had they been Alexanders or Charleses of Sweden they could not have behaved better."[105] Gates told Stark that "the whole country resounds with the fame of your victory,"[106] triumphantly exclaimed that the "boasting stile" of Burgoyne was at last reduced: the general began "in some degree to think and talk like other men."[107] Stark received the thanks of the New Hampshire General Court, promotion to brigadier general, and a new uniform, which prompted James Hadden to remark that "either the General was *Stark* naked or the Congress stark mad."[108] Hadden struck an isolated, almost desperate, note of humor; Burgoyne's army was in critical danger.

Notes

1. August 20, 1777, Burgoyne to Germain, C.O. 5.236, ff. 123–31.

2. Burgoyne, *State,* narrative, p. 18.

3. Ibid.

4. August 20, 1777, Burgoyne to Germain, Burgoyne, *State,* appendix, p. xli. An occasional party of "country People" brought in sheep for sale, as on August 2 (Burgoyne, *Orderly Book,* p. 63), but not frequently enough.

5. August 20, 1777, Burgoyne to Germain, Burgoyne, *State,* appendix, p. xli.

6. Ibid.

7. For a description of conditions in the Hampshire Grants and the Hudson Valley, see Mark, *Agrarian Conflicts,* pp. 164–94.

8. August 20, 1777, Burgoyne to Germain, Burgoyne, *State,* appendix, p. xli.

9. [August, 1777], "Instructions for Lieutenant-Colonel Baume," in Burgoyne, *State,* appendix, pp. lxiii–lxviii.

10. Ibid., and [August, 1777] Burgoyne to Skene, Burgoyne, *State,* appendix, p. lxxi. Boston was indeed filled with stories of imminent invasion; Forbes, *Revere,* p. 333.

11. [August, 1777] "Instructions," Burgoyne, *State,* pp. lxiii–lxviii, and Hadden, *Journal,* pp. 111–17.

12. Burgoyne, *State,* pp. lxiii–lxviii.

13. Von Eelking, *Riedesel,* 1:127, 133. Burgoyne later said that he was obliged to designate the left wing for service in the Hampshire Grants, despite Baum's ignorance of the language and the slowness of the German troops. Military etiquette, said Burgoyne, required the left wing of the army to undertake assignments in the region which it flanked. He could also have attempted to justify his decision to use Baum by citing the presence of the interpreter, Skene, with the detachment. "Colonel Skene will be with you as much as possible," Burgoyne assured Baum, "in order to assist you with his advice, to help you distinguish the good subjects from the bad, to procure you the best intelligence of the enemy; and to choose those people who are to bring me the accounts of your progress and success. . . ." (August 10, 1777, Kingston to Skene, T. 1.605, f. 86a; August 10, 1777, Burgoyne to Skene and August 11, 1777, Burgoyne, *Orderly Book,* p. 70.)

14. [August, 1777] Burgoyne to Skene, Burgoyne, *State,* appendix, pp. lxxi–lxxii.

15. August 28, 1777, Riedesel to Germain HLRO, #43.

16. Lamb, *Memoir,* p. 151; Von Eelking, *German Allied Troops,* pp. 130–31.

17. Burgoyne, *State,* p. 19.

18. Ibid.

19. [August, 1777] "Instructions," Burgoyne, *State,* appendix, pp. lxiii–lxviii.

20. Both Phillips and Fraser were "entierement contre cette expedition," according to a report entitled "Affair at Bennington," anon. September 4, 1777, Montreal, Historical Manuscripts Commission, *Stopford-Sackville MSS.,* 2:75–77.

21. Ibid.

22. Ibid.

23. Von Eelking, *German Allied Troops,* pp. 130–31.

24. Ibid.

25. Ibid.

26. [August, 1777] "Instructions," Burgoyne, *State,* appendix, pp. lxiii–lxviii.

27. None of the accounts indicate that Burgoyne knew of Stark's expedition until August 16.

28. Frank W. Coburn, *The Centennial History of the Battle of Bennington* (Boston: G. E. Littlefield, 1877), pp. 22–23.

29. Herbert D. Foster and Thomas D. Streeter, "Stark's Independent Command at Bennington," *Proceedings of the New York Historical Association* 5 (1905):29–96.

30. Ibid.

31. Ibid.

32. Coburn, *Centennial,* p. 31.

33. Ibid., p. 30.

34. Foster and Streeter, "Bennington," p. 36.

35. For further details of Lincoln, see John Cavanagh, "General Benjamin Lincoln in the War of the American Revolution," 1775–81 (doctoral dissertation, Duke University, 1968).

36. August, 1777, Lincoln to Schuyler, Continental Congress papers, Schuyler letters, 153, 2:237; Stark told Lincoln to "mind his own affairs."

37. August, 1777, Schuyler to unknown correspondent; Schuyler had called the disagreement a "source of new distress to us," quoted by Claude H. Van Tyne, *The War of Independence: American Phase 1775–77,* (Boston: Houghton Mifflin, 1929), p. 405.

38. Ibid.

39. August 9, 1777, "Relation of the Expedition to Bennington," enclosed in August 28, 1777, Riedesel to Germain, House of Lords Record Office, no. 44.

40. The Americans had evacuated Fort Miller a few days earlier; Digby, *Invasion,* p. 244.

41. August 10, 1777, Riedesel, "Relation," in August 28, 1777, Riedesel to Germain, House of Lords Record Office MSS.

42. Ibid.

43. Ibid., September 4, 1777, "Affair at Bennington," Historical Manuscripts Commission, *Stopford-Sackville MSS.*, 2:75–77.

44. August 11, 1777, Digby, *Invasion*, p. 248; August 11, 1777, Riedesel, "Relation," in August 28, 1777, Riedesel to Germain, House of Lords Record Office MSS.

45. August 13, 1777, Baum to Burgoyne, *State*, appendix, pp. lxix–lxx.

46. August 12, 1777, Riedesel, "Relation," in August 28, 1777, Riedesel to Germain, House of Lords Record Office MSS.

47. August 13, 1777, Baum to Burgoyne, *State*, appendix, pp. lxix–lxx.

48. August 12, 1777, Riedesel, "Relation," H.L.R.O.; Von Eelking, *German Allied Troops*, p. 31; Digby, *Invasion*, p. 248.

49. August 13, 1777, Baum to Burgoyne, *State*, appendix, pp. lxix–lxx.

50. Ibid.

51. August 14, 1777, Burgoyne to Baum, Gates papers. The paragraph was rewritten by Burgoyne for the printed version, although the meaning is unchanged; Burgoyne, *State*, appendix, pp. lxx–lxxi.

52. Ibid.

53. Henry B. Dawson, *Battles of the United States*, 2 vols. (New York: Johnson, Fry, 1858), 1:260.

54. Ibid.

55. August 14, 1777, Thacher, *Military Journal*, pp. 92–93.

56. August 14, 1777, Baum to Burgoyne, Burgoyne, *State*, appendix, pp. lxx–lxxi; August 14, 1777, Riedesel, "Relation," H.L.R.O.

57. August 14, 1777, Riedesel, "Relation," H.L.R.O.

58. Coburn, *Centennial*, pp. 39–42.

59. August 14, 1777, Baum to Burgoyne, Burgoyne, *State*, appendix, pp. lxx–lxxi.

60. August 14, 1777, Riedesel, "Relation," H.L.R.O.

61. August 14, 1777, Baum to Burgoyne, Burgoyne, *State*, appendix, pp. lxx–lxxi.

62. August 14, 1777, Riedesel, "Relation," H.L.R.O.

63. Riedesel was upset by the news; Von Eelking, *Riedesel*, 1:127, 130.

64. August 15, 1777, Burgoyne to Baum.

65. August 15, 1777, Breymann's "Account of an affair which happened near Walloon Creek, August 16th, 1777," enclosed in August 28, 1777, Riedesel to Germain, House of Lords Record Office, no. 43.

66. "Each guns and Ammunition cart was obliged to be dragged up the Hills, one after another," ibid.; Von Eelking, *Riedesel*, 1:130.

67. Breymann, "Account," H.L.R.O., #43. The guide was replaced.

68. August 13, 1777, Breymann, "Account," H.L.R.O., #43.

69. August 15–16, 1777, ibid.

70. Dawson, *Battles*, 1:260.

71. August 16, 1777, Digby, *Invasion*, p. 250.

72. Ibid.

73. August 16, 1777, Thacher, *Military Journal*, p. 251.

74. Ibid.

75. Riedesel, "Relation" H.L.R.O.; Von Eelking, *Riedesel*, 1:130; Pettingill, ed., *Letters*, pp. 88–89.

76. August 16, 1777, Riedesel, "Relation" H.L.R.O.; Von Eelking, *Riedesel*, 1:130.

77. William Heath, *Memoirs of Major-General William Heath*, ed. William Abbatt, (New York: Sidney Charles, 1901), p. 135, said only twenty-five were killed; Peckham, ed., *Toll of Independence*, p. 38.

78. August 22, 1777, Stark to Gates, Historical Manuscripts Commission, *Report on American Manuscripts in the Royal Institution of Great Britain* [Carleton papers], 4 vols. (London: H. M. Stationery Office, 1904–09), 1:143; Gates papers, New-York Historical Society.

79. Baum died on August 19. Von Eelking, *Riedesel*, 2:130–32; Breymann, "Account," H.L.R.O.; Pettingill, ed., *Letters*, p. 97.

80. Heath, *Memoirs*, p. 135; Burgoyne estimated only 400 men were captured, August 20, 1777, Burgoyne to Germain; Thacher, *Military Journal*, p. 94, believed 934 were captured. Peckham, ed., *Toll of Independence*, p. 38, listed 696 of the British captured and "perhaps 200 killed."

81. These cannon were retaken by British troops at Detroit on August 16, 1812; they were recovered again by the American Army at Niagara; Stone, *Campaign*, p. 35, note 1.

82. August 20, 1777, Burgoyne to Germain, private letter, Burgoyne, *State*, appendix, p. xliv.

83. Ibid. Skene blamed the dead Baum for failure; August 20, 1777, Skene to Dartmouth, Historical Manuscripts Commission, *Dartmouth MSS*, 2:443.

84. Quoted by DeFonblanque, *Episodes*, p. 272.

85. Ibid.

86. August 20, 1777, Burgoyne to Germain, Burgoyne, *State*, appendix, p. xlii. George B. Upham, "Burgoyne's Great Mistake," *New England Quarterly*, 3:657–80.

87. August 20, 1777, Burgoyne to Germain, Burgoyne, *State*, appendix, p. xliii.

88. August 20, 1777, Burgoyne to Germain, private letter, Burgoyne, *State*, p. xlvi. "I expect . . . your Lordship will in your goodness be my advocate to the King, and to the world, in vindication of the plan. . . ." added Burgoyne.

89. Ibid.

90. Ibid. Burgoyne neglected to mention that he had received Howe's letter of July 17 on August 6. He had sent Coronet James Grant to Clinton, but Grant was forced to return; August 10, 1777, Digby, *Invasion*, pp. 246–47. He received another communication from home on September 1. Fraser recorded in his Account Book a fee of £5.16.8 paid "to a person who conducted a messenger from Sir William Howe. . . ." Treasury 1.605, f. 86. A further £3.10.0 paid "to a person sent with dispatches to Sir William Howe," ibid., f. 88. September 2, 1777.

91. Ibid. August 20, 1777. Burgoyne to Germain, private letter, Burgoyne, *State*, p. xlviii.

92. Ibid., p. xlvii.

93. August 10, 1977, Clinton to Burgoyne, B.L. Add. MS. 34,414, f. 251, "Abstract of Correspondence."

94. August 20, 1777, Burgoyne to Germain, private letter, Burgoyne, *State*, appendix, p. xlvii.

95. See Burgoyne's instructions in March 26, 1777, Germain to Carleton, C.O. 42.36, ff. 101–16.

96. As Burgoyne said later in his own defense, what would the government, the army, and the country have said if he had retreated? William Cobbett, ed., *Parliamentary History*, 19:1189.

97. August 30, 1777, Howe to Germain, C.O. 5.94, f. 313, received October 28, 1777.

98. August 30, 1777, Howe to Germain, separate, C.O. 5.94, f. 311.

99. Pio Knox was an exception. He said Burgoyne "highly merits the command His Majesty had been pleased to confer upon him. . . ." Knox to Barrington, September 20, 1777, W.O. 1.11, ff. 357–60. Knox had formed a hospital at Ticonderoga and stayed there until September 9, when illness forced him to retire.

100. September 29, 1777, Walpole to Lady Ossory, Walpole, *Correspondence*, 32:382.

101. August 17, 1777, Digby, *Invasion*, p. 250.

102. August, 1777, Burgoyne, *Orderly Book*.

103. August 17, 1777, ibid., pp. 76–77.

104. Thacher, *Military Journal*, p. 94.

105. August 22, 1777, Stark to Gates, Gates papers, New-York Historical Society.

106. August 19, 1777, Gates to Stark, Gates papers, New-York Historical Society.

107. September 3, 1777, Gates to president of Congress, Gates papers, New-York Historical Society.

108. Hadden, *Journal*, p. 131. Gates shortly thereafter copied Burgoyne by issuing a proclamation to counteract the British general's "sanguinary manifesto," September 2, 1777, Thacher, *Military Journal*, p. 94.

16

Freeman's Farm

We have frequent dinees [*sic*], and constantly musick; for my part, & I know it is your opinion, this campaigning is a favourite [particle] of life: and none but stupid Mortals can dislike, a lively Camp good Weather, good Claret, good Musick and the Enemy near. I may venture to say all this, for a little fusillade during dinner does not decompose the Nerves of even our Ladies.[1]

These comments might have been written by Burgoyne himself; not surprisingly, they were the thoughts of his aide-de-camp and secretary, Sir Francis Clerke. Revealing a glimpse of the less strenuous moments during the campaign, Clerke also described accurately the English manner of warfare in the eighteenth century. Good claret and good music were essential elements of the life that Burgoyne had known in England; indeed, they accompanied British and European commanders whereever they went. Marching through the wilderness of the new world, however, Burgoyne and his army encountered the suspicion and censure of Yankees and Yorkers who could hardly reconcile the luxuries of London with the stark realities of a pioneer society at war. In their view, the purpose of warfare was to kill the enemy and win the battle, whether he stood in line, hid in trees, or crouched behind cannon. Rather than a gentleman's game, fought for honor and by the rules, war was a deadly competition, the inevitable consequence of that political dispute which self-interest and common sense had told them was worthy of their lives.

Burgoyne pushed ahead. He was determined to "put an Elbow fast" on the west bank of the Hudson, so that he could march to Albany.[2] Having finally obtained thirty days' provisions, the general was ready to cross the river on September 14.[3] His men had already received instruction in the art of raft making; those vehicles were more suitable than bateaux for the shallow waters at Fort Miller.[4] Now Burgoyne's carpenters and woodsmen used their newly acquired skills to shape a bridge of rafts across the Hudson near Fish Kill, opposite Saratoga.[5] As the troops marched over to the west bank, Burgoyne broke the last link in his communication with Canada and the lakes.[6] He was intrepid, posting his men defiantly "on the Heights and in the plains of Saratoga."[7] The expedition was still plagued by enormous mismanagement of

General Horatio Gates, by Charles Willson Peale. Reproduced by permission of Independence National Historical Park, Philadelphia.

baggage and transport carts,[8] morale was at a low point, and soldiers had been deserting for ten days "for the pitiful consideration of potatoes or forage."[9] The local population was hostile, and the New England militia were massing before the British army.[10] Burgoyne could not expect help from the north or south. Undaunted, he sought out "the countenance of General Gates."[11]

Gates and Burgoyne were alike in some respects.[12] Both were born Englishmen. Both could boast distinguished, or at least prominent sponsors at their christenings.[13] Gates and Burgoyne were socially ambitious, married above their social class, and desired military careers from an early age. And yet Gates's circumstances were in many ways quite different from those of Burgoyne. The family of the latter officer were quite closely connected to a line of baronets, while Gates's people were primarily servants of the rich. Then, Burgoyne advanced partly by an exertion of personal charm and sheer persistence, while Gates achieved promotion more often upon the basis of ability. Like Burgoyne, he turned his attention from military affairs to politics after 1763, although he was unsuccessful in that endeavor. Gates left London for Virginia, where he bought a farm and cultivated a friendship with George Washington. Entering the Continental army in 1775, Gates served so efficiently that he was commissioned a major general. Two years later, by means fair and foul, he managed to replace Schuyler as commander in chief of the northern department of the American army in New York.[14]

Despite some similarity in the experiences of the two men, substantial difference was to determine the success of one, the defeat of the other. Gates's real training in warfare took place in America, which he knew well. Burgoyne, unable to discard his lifelong military experience in Europe, did not learn much about American fighting methods or the American soldier. The two men did share a ruthless ambition; Gates's desire to acquire power regardless of the method used did not endear him to his colleagues nor members of Congress. His contentious grumbling contrasted with Burgoyne's smooth charm. Nonetheless, Gates assumed control of the northern army on August 19, 1777, and Schuyler greeted him with the same courtesy with which Carleton had surprised Burgoyne. If Gates was not as gracious in accepting it as was Burgoyne, Schuyler's superior organization must have pleased him.

In fact, Schuyler handed over an experienced army of about six thousand men to Gates. In late August and early September, that force was made stronger by the arrival of several distinguished officers. Brigadier General Benedict Arnold, a formidable fighter flushed with his victory against St. Leger at Fort Stanwix, returned to the army of the Hudson. Washington sent Colonel Daniel Morgan and his superb riflemen. Benjamin Lincoln and Seth Warner aided Gates in the Hampshire Grants. Learning that Burgoyne had crossed the Hudson, Gates moved his army cautiously from Stillwater to Bemis Heights, several miles north, and encamped near the river.[15] His large Continental army was augmented daily by the arrival of militia from the countryside. The terrain of uneven pine forests and swampy ravines was ideal for a defensive operation.

It was Gates's task to stop Burgoyne's progress and to destroy his army. Confident that Burgoyne would attack, Gates ordered Thaddeus Kosciusko to design fortifications, and then he posted his troops. Near the Hudson on a height of land, Gates ordered Brigadier Generals John Glover, John Nixon, and John Paterson to act in concert as his right wing. In the center, Brigadier General Ebenezer Learned commanded the continental brigade and militia

Benedict Arnold, engraving by I. Fielding from a drawing by Du Simitiere. Reproduced by permission of the New-York Historical Society.

from New York and Massachusetts. To the west near the Neilson house, Arnold directed Morgan's riflemen and Lieutenant Colonel Henry Dearborn's light infantry, the advanced guard of his left wing.[16] Arnold also commanded six militia regiments from New York, New Hampshire, and Connecticut.[17] Here Gates waited with his troops for the advance of the royal army.[18]

Burgoyne's troops filed across the bridge on September 14, and one day later moved to "a good position," or so thought Burgoyne, three miles south of

Saratoga.[19] There the army stayed on the sixteenth while detachments surveyed the country, repaired bridges, and helped float the provisions and heavy artillery down the Hudson.[20] On the seventeenth, the army marched three miles further and made camp.[21] They had traveled only six miles in four days, but Burgoyne did not know Gates's position, and he acted with caution. He tried to send scouts into the forest to locate the American headquarters, but they were turned back by the pickets of Gates's advanced guard.[22] On the eighteenth, thirty of Burgoyne's scouts were killed in a potato field.[23] The patriots had again checked Burgoyne's reconnaissance, but they also had provoked the British army. Wrote one officer concerning the slain: "They might without difficulty have been surrounded and taken prisoners, but the Americans could not resist the opportunity of shedding blood."[24] Another large party of Americans obstructed a group of workmen who were repairing bridges.[25] These incidents created tensions that were released the next day when Burgoyne determined to attack Gates. In order to reach Albany, he was obliged to strike first. Although Burgoyne could not yet see the American camp, or know their position or numbers, he marched southward on the nineteenth until he found them.[26]

On the morning of September 19, Burgoyne prepared for battle. He detached six companies from the Forty-seventh Regiment to guard the bateaux docked in the river and posted the regiment of Hesse-Hanau infantry to guard the baggage.[27] Then he divided the rest of his army into three mobile columns.

Burgoyne's plan of attack was hardly ideal, since two of the three columns became isolated as soon as they plunged into the forest. Furthermore, he had sent his strongest column into the woods to the furthest point west, while Riedesel's weaker unit was exposed on the Great Road.[28] Rather than order his whole force to assault the American army frontally, Burgoyne apparently wished to smash through or to march around Gates's force.[29] Either alternative was risky. Although circumstances might have favored a frontal attack, the British general had no opportunity to execute such a plan.

In the American headquarters, Gates and Arnold disagreed at first about appropriate strategy. Gates, who had been informed of Burgoyne's advance, wished to attract the general to his camp. However, Arnold urged Gates to send troops to fight the battle in the forest.[30] He argued that American marksmen were better fighters among the trees, where they need not fear the British bayonets and artillery. If they fought the battle near their headquarters, the effectiveness of their effort would be diminished and Burgoyne's heavy guns might destroy them.[31] Gates eventually agreed with Arnold, and sent out Morgan's advanced guard.[32]

At about three o'clock in the afternoon, both armies fell into line to begin a general action in the clearing adjacent to Freeman's Farm.[33] Having tasted the preliminaries of battle, American and British troops were ready to "conquer or die."[34] The astonishing roar and blaze that ensued could be heard as far as the Hudson River, where Riedesel and Phillips remained with Burgoyne's left

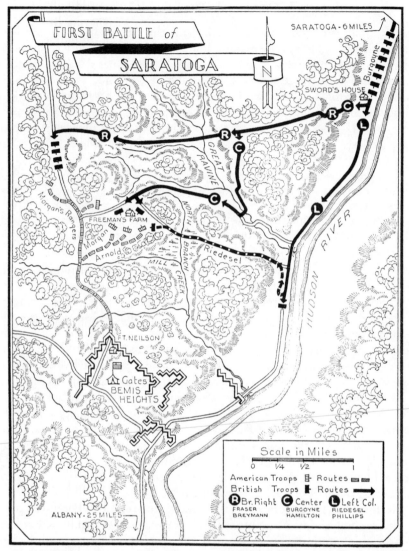

First Battle of Saratoga, September 19, 1777. From *Rag, Tag, and Bobtail: The Story of the Continental Army, 1775–1783* by Lynn Montross. Reprinted by permission of Harper and Row.

wing.[35] Phillips hastened through a difficult part of the woods and arrived at the battlefield.[36] Shortly thereafter, Phillips's aide-de-camp, Captain Green, was shot through the arm by one of Morgan's riflemen as the aide was delivering a message to Burgoyne.[37] "The mistake, it was said, was occasioned by having his saddle furnished with rich lace, and was supposed by the marksmen to be the British commander."[38] The British soldiers, believing Burgoyne had been killed,[39] increased their fire furiously, but soon Burgoyne appeared "everywhere,"[40] behaving

> with great personal bravery. He shunned no danger; his presence and conduct animated the troops, for they greatly loved the General. He delivered his orders with precision and coolness, and in the heat, danger, and fury of the fight, maintained the true characteristics of the soldier serenity, fortitude, and undaunted intrepidity.[41]

Whatever else had been said of Burgoyne, his courage in battle was fast becoming universally acknowledged.[42]

Although the British general withstood Arnold's attempt to cut through his center and right wings, and despite the fact that Phillips had saved the Sixty-second from annihilation, the situation was grave. Fraser's strong column was out of action, Burgoyne's men were exhausted, and Arnold continued to receive reinforcement. Furthermore, Riedesel had yet to arrive. Although at two o'clock a scout informed the German officer that action was imminent, Riedesel did not receive specific orders to join Burgoyne. It was not until five o'clock that one of Riedesel's aides returned with instructions from Burgoyne.[43] The general wanted Riedesel to leave a detachment of his column by the river and lead the rest of his men to Freeman's Farm to join the main force.[44] Accordingly, the German moved the rest of his soldiers as quickly as he could toward the battlefield, leaving behind the Forty-seventh, Specht's Regiment, and part of the Regiment of Rhetz.

Meanwhile the fight continued; the three central regiments continued to hold forth, standing amidst heaps of the dead.[45] Lieutenant William Digby recorded that "such an explosion of fire I never had any idea of before, and the heavy artillery joining in concert like great peals of thunder, assisted by the echoes of the woods, almost deafened us with the noise.[46] The lines pushed back and forth across the field, the Americans capturing momentarily Burgoyne's artillery, then, because they lacked linstocks to load the guns or horses to drag them away, relinquishing them again to the British.[47] The patriots continued with great obstinacy, and eventually achieved an advantage.[48] To Burgoyne's dismay, the British soldiers used their bayonets repeatedly but without effect,[49] and when they tried their guns, their "impetuosity and uncertain aim" ruined accuracy.[50] The battle was "raging at its fiercest" when Riedesel finally arrived,[51] sending his advance at once to the rescue: "With drums beating and his men shouting 'Hurrah!' he attacked the enemy on the double-quick."[52]

Riedesel arrived none too soon, for the British line had thinned to one-half its former strength.[53] Burgoyne's pickets were almost continuously firing and skirmishing,[54] and soliders became so fatigued that some of them—including officers—slept while exposed to the enemy's fire.[55]

The tide finally turned to Burgoyne's advantage. The British general seemed even more favored by Gates's apparent decision to withdraw Arnold, whom he replaced with Ebenezer Learned.[56] Learned, who was not familiar with the lines of battle, marched his men toward Fraser, who still held fast to the height

Burgoyne's Encampment after the First Battle of Freeman's Farm, engraver unknown. Reproduced by permission of the Manuscript Department, William R. Perkins Library, Duke University.

on the west.[57] The American line now lacked unity and Burgoyne had an opportunity to break through if he employed Riedesel's fresh troops.[58] However, dusk was closing in, and the general ordered a halt to the advance after several British soldiers mistakenly fired at Germans.[59] Burgoyne's order was poorly received by the rank and file, who complained loudly as he retired from the field. Fraser and Riedesel told Burgoyne "he did not know how to avail himself of his advantages," although Fraser had contributed little to the British effort during the battle and was hardly in a position to criticize anyone. Soon the American army "gave ground on all Sides and left us completely Masters of the Field of Battle."[60]

Eyewitnesses to the conflict described the carnage on both sides as prodigious.[61] An American surgeon declared that "few actions have been characterized by more obstinacy in attack or defense."[62] Baroness von Riedesel wrote, "I saw the whole battle myself, and knowing that my husband was taking part in it, I was filled with fear and anguish and shivered whenever a shot was fired, as nothing escaped my ears."[63] Lady Harriet Acland was exposed "to great fatigue, and inexpressible anxiety" for her husband, who stood in front throughout the action.[64] According to Burgoyne, the Americans lost 500 men, with 1,500 more wounded.[65] The American surgeon James Thacher's much lower and more widely accepted estimates were: 64 patriots killed, 217 wounded, 38 missing.[66] Burgoyne himself lost about 600 soldiers, over 10 percent of his force.[67] The British general nevertheless claimed a victory, as did Riedesel, although the latter noted that the victory was a technical one.[68] Thacher acknowledged that Burgoyne claimed victory, but added: "They were the assailants—they held their ground during the day, and at the close retired without being pursued."[69] One day after the battle, Burgoyne was willing to interpret the results more realistically: he conceded that "no fruits, honor excepted, were attained by the preceeding Victory."[70] Americans were well aware that Burgoyne's triumph was Pyrrhic, as Thacher observed:

> The advantages obtained over the enemy on this occasion excites the greatest exultation and rejoicing throughout our army and country. It is indeed a remarkable fact, which must animate the heart of every friend to the cause of America, that our troops, so little accustomed to encounter the prowess of European veterans, and the peculiar warfare of the savages, should face these enemies with such undaunted courage and intrepidity.[71]

During the night the half-frozen soldiers slept on their firearms. Their loyalty to Burgoyne remained constant despite the perilous situation of the expedition. One of them recalled that "we were all in good spirits and ready to obey with cheerfulness any orders the general might issue before morning dawned."[72]

On September 20, Burgoyne discovered that Gates's men were laboring with redoubled energy to strengthen their left wing; their right was already secure.[73] The general's first response was to order his army to march within cannon shot of the American force, but he reconsidered and decided to dig in.[74] He ordered the erection of strong redoubts to protect his magazines. Extending his left wing to the Hudson to cover the river battery and hospital, Burgoyne continued fortifying his camp and watching the enemy, whose numbers increased daily.[75] A pale ray of hope greeted the beleaguered general on September 21, when a letter arrived from Sir Henry Clinton.[76] When Howe left for Philadelphia he told Clinton that he need not point out the utility of a diversion to favor Burgoyne.[77] Although Clinton declared that he had not heard from Howe for six weeks and had no orders to cooperate with Burgoyne,[78] he did send a message to the general in cypher on September 12, offering to mount a small diversion in the Hudson Highlands in favor of the northern army. Nine days later, Burgoyne pondered the contents of that dispatch, in which Clinton assured the general, "You know my good will and are not ignorant of my poverty. If you think 2,000 men can assist you effectually, I will make a push at Montgomery in about ten days."[79] Burgoyne instantly sent an affirmative reply by messenger.[80] He painted a dark and accurate picture of his circumstances for the New York commander. He had only 5,000 men.[81] On the other hand, the American force was 12,000 strong and only one mile distant, with 4,000 more troops hovering about. Therefore, wrote Burgoyne, "an attack, or the Menace of an Attack upon Montgomery, must be of great Use, as it will draw away a part of this Force, and I will follow them close. Do it, my dear Friend, directly."[82]

Burgoyne had no doubt that he could continue south, but he feared that he could not survive the winter at Albany without provisions and communication. Requesting more assistance than Clinton had offered, Burgoyne hoped Sir Henry could open a line of communication from Montgomery to Albany and thereafter obtain supplies of food from New York City. He also considered the possibility of a retreat, although he was aware that a substantial American force gathered near Lake Champlain cut off entirely his communication with Canada.[83] Had he not expected a cooperating army from Albany, wrote Burgoyne, he "would not have given up his Communication with Ticonderoga." Hinting that Howe was responsible for his dilemma, Burgoyne told Clinton to open a communication to Albany or else order Burgoyne to retreat, "conveying in the plainest and most Positive meaning how he should act for the good of his Majesty."[84] If Clinton ordered a retreat, Burgoyne declared that he ought not to stay at Freeman's Farm longer than October 12. If, on the other hand, Clinton thought it advisable to go to Albany, then Burgoyne could wait there until October 16. However, rations were short, and the winter ice would soon be forming in the Hudson. If Burgoyne did not receive a reply by the twelfth, he would retire. At last permitting himself to become fully aware of the urgency of his situation, Burgoyne requested a reply in triplicate.[85] He himself sent six additional copies of his own dispatch.[86]

Burgoyne was caught in the contradictions inherent in the strategic design of the campaign. Having requested and obtained an independent command, he had previously expected to reach Albany without the assistance of the New York army. Now he needed that help, and he attempted to put some of the responsibility for his own overconfident calculations upon Howe, or in his absence, on Clinton. He asked to be directed, but Clinton was not inclined to make decisions for himself, let alone for other officers. Nor was he obliged to instruct Burgoyne. He replied that he had received no instructions from Howe relative to the northern army.[87] Sir Henry was unacquainted even with Howe's intention concerning its operation, except for his wish that they should go to Albany. As for himself,

Sir H. Clinton cannot presume to give any Orders to General Burgoyne. General Burgoyne could not suppose that Sir H. Clinton had an idea of penetrating to Albany with the small force he mentioned in his last Letter. What he offered in that Letter he has now undertaken; cannot by any means promise himself Success, but hopes it will be at any rate serviceable to General Burgoyne.[88]

Clinton declared that he was surprised to learn that Burgoyne was in distress. He had neither heard nor suspected Burgoyne's real condition, which filled his mind "with the most anxious reflections." Although Clinton feared that any help he could offer would be too late, he had received reinforcements numbering about three thousand from England late in September,[89] which enabled him to maintain the security of New York City and Rhode Island while he created the planned diversion in the highlands. However, he could not bring himself to advise Burgoyne, nor would he push as far north as Albany.

Meanwhile Burgoyne waited for Clinton's reply and watched the activities of his troops. The Indians and the French-Canadians, greatly dissatisfied and discouraged, deserted day after day.[90] The warriors, who were the eyes and ears of his army, were joined by loyalists who scented the shift of fortune.[91] The morale of his soldiers at last began to decline seriously as conditions of life in the camp became almost inhuman. Sergeant Lamb observed that "the bodies of the slain, thrown together into one receptacle, were scarcely covered with the clay and the only tribute of respect to fallen officers was, to bury them by themselves, without throwing them into the common grave."[92] Heavy rains exposed the bodies of the dead.[93]

To add to his misfortunes, Burgoyne received on September 28 alarming news from the north. Brigadier General Benjamin Lincoln had crossed the mountains of the Hampshire Grants with one thousand five hundred militiamen, marched to Skenesborough, and attacked Burgoyne's rear guard on the eighteenth.[94] Lincoln detached Captain Brown and five hundred soldiers to Lake George while two other detachments moved toward Forts Ticonderoga, Independence, Anne, and Edward. Brown captured Fort George and threatened Mount Defiance and Mount Hope.[95] Brigadier Henry Powell at Ticonderoga and Captain Thomas Aubrey at Diamond Island on Lake Champlain were in grave danger, but they pushed the patriots back. Although Burgoyne's soldiers still held Ticonderoga, Lake George was now in American possession.[96]

The army threatened from the rear, the camp at Freeman's Farm sunk in gloom, no word from Clinton—these were problems enough for Burgoyne. But the general must also turn his attention once again to the activities of the large American army waiting one mile south of his force, an army he already had tried to crush without success. The first battle of Saratoga brought little comfort to the victor.

Notes

1. September 10, 1777, Clerke to Polwarth, Bedford County Record Office. For a contrasting explication of American revolutionary ideology in terms of benevolence, disinterestedness and virtue, see Charles Royster, *A Revolutionary People at War: The Continental Army and American Character, 1775–1783* (Chapel Hill, N.C.: University of North Carolina Press, 1979), pp. 3–24.

2. Ward, *Revolution*, 2:504, noted that Burgoyne had a choice of marching either on the east bank or the west. He chose the latter route, though Gates was certain to block it, because Albany was located on the west side of the Hudson.

3. September 13, 1777, Burgoyne, *Orderly Book,* pp. 101–5; Thacher, *Military Journal,* p. 96; Lamb, *Memoir,* p. 190.

4. August 13, 1777, Burgoyne, *Orderly Book,* pp. 76–77.

5. September 13, 1777, ibid., pp. 101–5; Neilson, *Campaign,* p. 131.

6. September 13, 1777, Burgoyne, *State,* narrative, p. 22.

7. September 14, 1777, Burgoyne, "Account," in October 20, 1777, Burgoyne to Germain, House of Lords Record Office, no. 51.

8. September 14, 1777, Burgoyne, *Orderly Book,* pp. 105–6.

9. September 18, 1777, ibid., pp. 113–14.

10. Jane Clark, "Responsibility for the Failure of the Burgoyne Campaign," *American Historical Review* 35 (April 1930): 542–49.

11. "Gates," *DAB;* Samuel Patterson, *Horatio Gates: Defender of American Liberties* (New York: Columbia University Press, 1941); Paul D. Nelson, *General Horatio Gates* (Baton Rouge, La.: Louisiana State University Press, 1976). Nelson's study of Gates is the most recent and most reliable account.

12. Nelson, *Gates,* pp. 2–6.

13. Horace Wapole was Gates's godfather. Like Lord Bingley, Walpole was thought to be the natural father of his godson.

14. Paul D. Nelson, "Legacy of Controversy: Gates, Schuyler and Arnold at Saratoga, 1777," *Military Affairs* 37:41–46.

15. Henry Dearborn, *The Revolutionary Journals of Henry Dearborn,* ed. Lloyd A. Brown and Howard H. Peckham (Chicago: Caxton Club, 1939), p. 104.

16. Willard M. Wallace, *Traitorous Hero: The Life and Fortunes of Benedict Arnold* (New York: Harper, 1954), p. 146; September 11, 1777, H. B. Livingston to Philip Schuyler, September 12, 1777, Richard Varick to Schuyler, September 13, 1777, Varick to Schuyler, September 16, 1777, Varick to Schuyler, September 16, 1777, H. B. Livingston to Schuyler, Schuyler papers, New York Public Library.

17. Ward, *Revolution,* 2:506; George A. Billias, *General John Glover and his Marblehead Mariners* (New York: Holt, 1960), p. 139. The brigades of Glover, Nixon, and Patterson did not participate in this battle; ibid., p. 141.

18. The patriots had intelligence that informed them with precision of the movements of Burgoyne's army; September 13, 1777, Thacher, *Military Journal,* p. 96.

19. September 15, 1777, Burgoyne, "Account,"; H.L.R.O. #51; Neilson, *Campaign,* p. 132; Lamb, *Memoir,* p. 190.

20. September 17, 1777, Burgoyne, *Orderly Book,* p. 112; Lamb, *Memoir,* p. 190; Neilson, *Campaign,* p. 132.

21. September 17, 1777, Burgoyne, "Account," H.L.R.O., #51.

22. Neilson believed that Gates had sent Arnold to attack Burgoyne, but that Arnold could not get through the dense brush; *Campaign,* p. 132.

23. Dearborn, *Journal,* p. 105.

24. September 18, 1777, Lamb, *Memoir;* Stone, *Campaign,* p. 43.

25. *Orderly Book,* pp. 113–14; Burgoyne, "Account," H.L.R.O, #51; Lamb, *Memoir,* p. 190.

26. September 19, 1777, Burgoyne, *State,* appendix, p., lxxxv

27. September 19, 1777, Burgoyne, *State,* appendix, p. lxxxv; Burgoyne, "Account," H.L.R.O. #51.

28. Nickerson, *Turning Point,* p. 306.

29. Neilson, *Campaign,* p. 134, believed Riedesel was intended to lead a frontal assault while the other columns executed a turning motion.

30. Wallace, *Arnold,* pp. 147–48; Ward, *Revolution,* 2:508.

31. See also Paul D. Nelson, "The Gates-Arnold Quarrel, September 1777," *The New-York Historical Society Quarterly* 55:235–52.

32. September 19, 1777, Neilson, *Campaign,* p. 136.

33. Ibid., p. 141.

34. September 19, 1777, Thacher, *Military Journal*, pp. 97–98.

35. Ibid.; Neilson, *Campaign*, p. 142.

36. Burgoyne, "Account" H.L.R.O., #51; Lamb, *Memoir*, pp. 190–91.

37. Lamb, *Memoir*, pp. 198–99; Neilson, *Campaign*, p. 143.

38. September 19, 1777, Thacher, *Military Journal*, p. 97.

39. Lamb, *Memoir*, pp. 198–99.

40. Digby, *Invasion*, p. 274.

41. Lamb, *Memoir*, p. 160; Hadden, *Journal*, pp. 161–6.

42. Digby, *Invasion*, p. 274, note 197, and p. 289.

43. September 19, 1777, Von Eelking, *Riedesel*, 1:149.

44. Ibid.

45. The Twentieth, Twenty-First, and Sixty-second Regiments fought over four hours without intermission; Burgoyne, "Account."

46. Digby, *Invasion*, p. 273.

47. Linstocks were match-holders.

48. Burgoyne, "Account," H.L.R.O. #51.

49. September 19, 1777, Thacher, *Military Journal*, p. 97 and appendix, note 1, p. 357; Neilson, *Campaign*, p. 152.

50. September 20, 1777, Burgoyne, *Orderly Book,* p. 116.

51. Stone believed Riedesel's arrival saved Burgoyne from "total rout"; *Campaign*, p. 47.

52. September 19, 1777, Von Eelking, *Riedesel*, 1:149.

53. Lamb, *Memoir*, p. 160.

54. Burgoyne, "Account," H.L.R.O., #51.

55. Ibid.

56. Wallace, *Arnold*, p. 148, citing Wilkinson's unreliable testimony (James Wilkinson, *Memoirs of my Own Times*, 3 vols. [Philadelphia: Abraham Small, 1816], 1:245–46). Whether Arnold was actually on the field of battle remains a matter of dispute. See Wallace, ibid., pp. 326–32; Ward, *Revolution*, 2:941–42. These scholars agree with Riedesel (Von Eelking, 1:150) that Arnold was indeed on the field of battle.

57. Wallace, *Arnold*, p. 148.

58. Stone, *Campaign*, p. 48, reported that Breymann and Fraser were planning to follow up their advantage before Burgoyne declared the battle at an end.

59. Ibid.

60. Burgoyne, "Account," H.L.R.O., #51.

61. September 20, 1777, Thacher, *Military Journal*, p. 97.

62. September 19, 1777, ibid., appendix, note I, p. 357.

63. September 19, 1777, Baroness Riedesel to ?, in M. E. Brown, ed., *Journals*, p. 48.

64. September 19, 1777, Thacher, *Military Journal*, appendix, p. 359.

65. Burgoyne, "Account," H.L.R.O., #51.

66. Thacher, *Military Journal*, pp. 97–99; Alden, *A History*, p. 323. Peckham ed. *Toll of Independence*, p. 41, reported 316 American casualties.

67. September 27, 1777, Burgoyne to Clinton, C.O. 5.94, ff. 361–62. Hadden, *Journal*, p. 165, recorded that only 800 of Burgoyne's 5,500 men were continually engaged. The Sixty-second declined from 350 to 60 men; the Twentieth and Twenty-first lost 60 men each; 250 were killed, wounded, or missing from the rest. Peckham, ed., *Toll of Independence*, p. 41, listed 556 British casualties.

68. Von Eelking, 1:149–50; Lamb, *Memoir*, p. 194; Burgoyne, "Account," H.L.R.O., #51.

69. Thacher, *Military Journal*, p. 99.

70. September 27, 1777, Burgoyne to Clinton; the battle was of "no material advantage"; Burgoyne, "Account," H.L.R.O., #51.

71. October 4, 1777, Thacher, *Military Journal*, p. 100.

72. Hudleston, *Burgoyne*, pp. 188–89.

73. Burgoyne, "Account," H.L.R.O., #51.

74. Burgoyne, *Orderly Book*, p. 114.

75. September 1777, Burgoyne to Germain, Hudleston, *Burgoyne*, p. 189.

76. Burgoyne, *State*, appendix, p. lxxxviii.

77. July 30, 1777, Howe to Clinton, Clinton papers, Clements Library.

78. September 17, 1777, Clinton to Harvey, Rockingham, *Memoirs*, cited by DeFonblanque, *Episodes*, p. 280, note 1.

79. September 12, 1777, Clinton to Burgoyne, C.O. 5.94, f. 357. Clinton papers, Clements Library. A copy of this letter in the Revolutionary War Collection, Perkins Library, Duke University, is dated September 10.

80. September 21, 1777, Burgoyne to Clinton, Clinton papers, Clements Library, and "Conversation with Captain Campbell," attached to C.O. 5.94, ff. 357–58; "Copy of an Enclosure received from Lieut.-Gen. Sir H. Clinton . . . ."

81. September 21, 1777, Burgoyne to Clinton, Clinton papers, Clements Library.

82. September 21, 1777, Burgoyne to Clinton, Clinton papers, Clements Library.

83. September 28, 1777, Burgoyne to Clinton, duplicate dispatch, C.O. 5.253, ff. 357–58; delivered by Campbell.

84. Paraphrase of Campbell's message, September 21, 1777, Clinton to Burgoyne; see below, p. 351, note 87.

85. September 28, 1777, Burgoyne to Clinton, C.O. 5.253, ff. 357–58.

86. The six messages were sent on the following dates:

September 22, 1777, verbal communication by an officer in disguise; Burgoyne, *State*, appendix, p. lxxxviii.

September 23, 1777, verbal communication by a messenger in disguise; ibid.

September 23, 1777, letter, C.O. 5.94, f. 355; C.O. 5.253, ff. 356–57, "General Précis for 1777–1778," House of Lords Record Office, no. 6.

September 24, 1777, letter, C.O. 5.94, f. 715. Received September 29; B. M. Add. MS. 34, 414, f. 251, "Abstract of Correspondence, Lt.-Gen. John Burgoyne—Lt.-General Henry Clinton."

September 27, 1777, letter confirming Campbell's arrival at Freeman's Farm, carried by Captain Thomas Scott of the 24th Regiment; "Captain Scott's Journal," entry for May 16, 1778, DeFonblanque, *Episodes*, pp. 287–90. Received October 9, 1777, C.O. 5.94, ff. 361–62; C.O. 5.523, f. 359, "General Précis." B. M. Add. MS. 34, 414, f. 251b, and House of Lords Record Office no. 9.

September 28, 1777, letter, C.O. 5.253, f. 357, "General Précis," and House of Lords Record Office, no. 7. Received October 4, C.O. 5.253, f. 358, and B. M. Add. MS. 34, 414, f. 251, "Abstract." An "exact duplicate" of the September 27 message; carried by Campbell.

One of these messages, enclosed in a silver bullet, fell into the hands of patriot Governor George Clinton; DeFonblanque, *Episodes*, p. 287.

87. September 21, 1777, Clinton to Burgoyne, "Answer by Captain Campbell," C.O. 5.94, f. 358; also [n.d.] same to the same, C.O. 5.253, f. 358, "General Précis"; October 4, 1777, "the following Answer by Captain Campbell . . ." attached to September 28, 1777, Burgoyne to Clinton, House of Lord Record Office, no. 7. Received October 5, 1777; Clinton, "Historical Detail," Willcox, *Clinton*, p. 74. October 6, 1777, same to the same, B. L. Add. MS. 34, 414, f. 251b. October 10, 1777, Campbell and Scott were redispatched with Clinton's answer; B. L. Add. MSS. 34, 414, f. 251b.

88. September 21, 1777, Clinton to Burgoyne, C.O. 5.94, f. 358.

89. September 24, 1777, Ward, *Revolution*, 514. Only 1,700 of these troops were fit for duty; "Abstract of Précis for 1777–1778," Germain papers, Clements Library.

90. September 19 to October 4, 1777, Thacher, *Military Journal*, pp. 100–10.

91. September 21, 1777, Lamb, *Memoir*, p. 194.

92. Ibid., p. 192.

93. September, 1777, Digby, *Invasion*, p. 281.

94. September 28, 1777, Burgoyne, *Orderly Book*, p. 122.

95. September 24, 1777, Thacher, *Military Journal*, p. 99.

96. September 28 and October 1, 1777, Burgoyne, *Orderly Book,* pp. 122, 124–25, and pp. 10–11, note 1.

17

Catastrophe

During the last week of September and the first of October the leaves on the trees in the Hudson Valley shed the summer's green hues and turned crisp orange and red. The scene of the recent battle was far from arcadian, however, for Gates was exerting new pressure upon Burgoyne's now shaken army. Brigadier General John Glover, who had shown talent for warfare during the campaigns on Long Island, suggested that Gates send raiding parties toward the British army to increase the tension in Burgoyne's camp.[1] Gates saw the value of the plan, and on September 28 Glover's parties attacked their enemy in force. About two hundred of the patriots killed three British soldiers, wounded others, and departed unscathed with booty.[2] These raids, continuing for several days, prevented Burgoyne from reconnoitering Gates's force, which the general had been attempting to do since September 21.[3] In addition to Glover's military smoke screen, Burgoyne's scouts had to contend with the intricacy of the ground and other obstacles.[4] The autumnal mists of the valley hindered these efforts, too, although attempts were rescheduled again and again, providing the fog lifted.[5]

Burgoyne's scouting parties failed as dismally as had the foraging raids. On October 3, the general was forced to cut rations for his troops, an event they accepted with surprising cheerfulness.[6] Assuming that Clinton's expedition was under way, Burgoyne put up a brave front and told his soldiers that "other powerful Armies are actually in cooperation with these Troops."[7] But morale continued to decline, and Gates's force daily made its presence known. Lamb recollected that he "could distinctly hear the Americans felling and cutting trees and they had a piece of ordnance which they used to fire as a morning gun, so near to us that the wadding from it struck against our works."[8]

Caught in the wilderness, Burgoyne sustained his courage and called Generals Riedesel, Fraser, and Philips to a war council to discuss the future of their enterprise.[9] If Clinton refused to direct the general, perhaps these officers could endorse his plan to break through Gates's army. He proposed to leave eight hundred soldiers by the Hudson to guard bateaux and supplies while he marched the rest toward the left wing of Gates's force. If he could flank it, and get past the American rear guard, his army could then free itself of the enormous force blocking its progress. However, Generals Riedesel, Fraser, and Philips objected to the plan. As one historian has observed, Burgoyne's officers were losing confidence in his judgment, and indeed the staff's objections were reasonable ones.[10] They observed that the American position was not accurately known, that even though 800 men were posted by the Hudson, they would not be sufficient to guard the British supplies located there. Moreover, the American army could destroy the bridge across the river and block an escape route for Burgoyne's army. On the fifth, Burgoyne held a second council[11] during which Riedesel suggested that the army retreat to Batten Kill, reopen the communication with Lake George, and wait for Clinton to complete his expedition.[12] General Simon Fraser endorsed the plan, but Burgoyne rejected it.[13] His orders were positive to force a junction, said Burgoyne, and he was determined to do so, regardless of the peril involved. He objected that a retreat to Canada would be difficult and that he was reluctant to allow Gates's strong army the freedom to pursue Howe, should he retreat.[14] He wrote to Germain after the expedition ended:

> This consideration operated forcibly to determine me to abide Events as long as Possible, and I reasoned thus, the Expedition I commanded was evidently meant at first to be *hazarded* Circumstances might require it should be *devoted* [sacrificed]; a critical Junction of Mr. Gates's force with Mr. Washington might possibly decide the fate of the War; the failure of my Junction with Sir Harry Clinton, or the loss of my retreat to Canada would only be a Partial Misfortune.[15]

Burgoyne doubtless recalled the abuse he and others had heaped upon Carleton the previous year for allowing an American force to move against Howe. However, the man's immense pride and perhaps his gambling instinct may have weighed even more heavily in his decision to go forward. He knew that Gates's army outnumbered his force three to one, and he was also aware that St. Leger's expedition had failed. But he would not retreat until he had made one last attempt to break through or march around the patriot army.[16]

Burgoyne got his way; the officers attending the council of war deferred to his decision, if not to his judgment, as expressed in a second plan that he submitted to them. He proposed to march the balance of his troops toward Gates "to gather forage, and ascertain definitely the position of the enemy, and whether it would be adviseable to attack him."[17] The reconnaissance in force, Burgoyne hoped, would discover the weak points in Gates's defenses and determine whether the height of land near the American left wing, which Fraser held during the first battle, could be seized and used as an artillery base to besiege the patriot army. He proposed a force of 1,500 regulars and auxiliaries to conduct the bold attack upon Gates. However, if American troops appeared to have an overwhelming superiority of strength, Burgoyne would agree to retreat as far north as Batten Kill.[18]

General Daniel Morgan, by Charles Willson Peale. Reproduced by permission of Independence National Historical Park, Philadelphia.

In the American headquarters high spirits prevailed. Many of the messages that Burgoyne had sent to Clinton had been intercepted there, and it was known that he needed assistance.[19] Gates's staff considered Burgoyne's position precarious.[20] The American commander wrote with confidence to George Clinton: "Perhaps Burgoyne's despair may dictate to him to risque [sic] all upon one throw; he is an old gamester, and in his time has seen all chances. I will endeavour to be ready to prevent his good fortune, and if possible, secure my own."[21]

On October 7, the British general acted. He had only five days remaining to his self-imposed deadline for evacuation. Although he knew Clinton had begun to push through the highlands, Burgoyne was not aware that Sir Henry had taken Fort Montgomery on the sixth. However, he decided that it was advisable to play his last card. At about eleven o'clock in the morning, he set the reconnaissance in motion. During the conflict that ensued, a shot ripped through Burgoyne's hat and another tore his waistcoat as he urged Fraser to send the light brigade and the Twenty-fourth Regiment to fill gaps created by American fire.[22]

An American surgeon called the fight "The hardest fought battle, and the most honorable to our army since the commencement of hostilities . . . they fought like heroes."[23] Patriot losses were remarkably low, only 30 killed and 100 wounded of the 4,000 engaged.[24] Burgoyne lost 600, and the British army was understandably depressed.[25] Burgoyne's aide-de-camp, Sir Francis Clerke, who possessed in the general's opinion "every quality that can create esteem," had been mortally wounded and captured. Clerke's last hours were spent in the American headquarters, where Gates harangued him about the causes of the war. Major Acland was also imprisoned in Gates's camp. His wife was permitted to join him after Burgoyne sent a letter to Gates requesting a safe passage for her. Baroness von Riedesel's husband was unscathed, but she could not resist complaining: "We had gained an advantage over the enemy, but the sad, disheartened faces I saw indicated quite the contrary."[26] General Fraser lingered into the next day. He had a last request, which Burgoyne received sympathetically: "If General Burgoyne would permit it," Baroness von Riedesel recorded, "he should like to be buried at six o'clock in the evening, on the top of a mountain, in a redoubt which had been built there."[27] When the courageous Fraser, whom an American called "one of the most valuable officers in the British service," died during the morning of the eighth.[28] Burgoyne granted his last wish and arranged a ceremony for sunset. Chaplain Brudenell, accompanied by Burgoyne, Phillips, and Riedesel, led the procession.[29] The service was "unusually solemn and awesome" because Gates had not been informed of the event, and a cannonade was directed at the hilltop where the service took place.[30] As bullets flew over the head of the baroness and as the chaplain was covered with dust, darkness closed in. Burgoyne recorded that the ceremony "will remain to the last of life on the mind of every man who was present."[31]

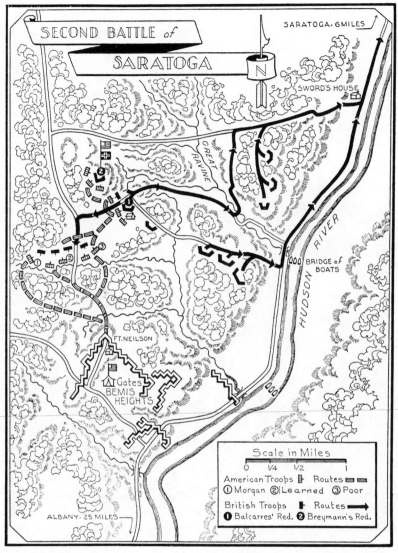

Second Battle of Saratoga, October 7, 1777. From *Rag, Tag, and Bobtail: The Story of the Continental Army, 1775–1783* by Lynn Montross. Reprinted by permission of Harper and Row.

The game was up, and every moment lost made a retreat less and less probable. Burgoyne's implementation of Fraser's last request, the baroness said, "caused an unnecessary delay and served to increase the army's misfortune."[32] But the general still could not bring himself to believe that all was lost. During October 8 he reorganized his lines and changed his front in order to "force the Americans to form a new disposition." He declared that "the Army continued offering Battle to the Enemy in their new Position the whole day of the 8th."[33]

Burial of General Fraser. Reproduced by permission of the National Army Museum, London.

However, Burgoyne received intelligence later in the day that Gates had sent a column to turn his right wing, which had been weakened the previous day. At nine o'clock in the evening Burgoyne reluctantly ordered his men to retreat toward Saratoga, Riedesel commanding the "vanguard" and Phillips the rear. After stopping the night to rest, the army resumed its march on the morning of the ninth, and within an hour the British troops spotted a reconnaissance party of 200 Americans nearby who "could have easily been taken prisoners by our troops, if General Burgoyne had not lost his head," or so believed the baroness. Indeed, from the account the noblewoman reconstructed thirty years after the campaign, it would appear that Burgoyne had finally lost his spirit. When

Riedesel came to a halt only half an hour from Saratoga, the baroness took issue with Phillips: "I asked General Phillips, who came up to me, why we did not continue our retreat while there was yet time, as my husband had promised to cover our retreat and bring the army through." Phillips replied: "If only you were our commanding general! He thinks himself too tired and wants to spend the night here and give us supper."[34]

Burgoyne himself declared later in the month that an enormous quantity of luggage and a heavy rain occasioned delays that prevented the army from reaching Saratoga until the night of the ninth.[35] But he also admitted that the artillery and parts of the force did not reach Saratoga until the tenth because the fords of the Fishkill could not be negotiated.[36] Among those who remained, the baroness recollected, were Burgoyne and his mistress, who stayed at the home of General Schuyler, and "In fact, Burgoyne liked having a jolly time and spending half the nights in singing and drinking, and amusing himself with the wife of a commissary, who was his mistress, and who, as well as he, loved champagne."[37] Since the British officers and soldiers who kept diaries of the campaign at no time mentioned the existence of Burgoyne's mistress, it cannot be said with authority that such a woman did in fact accompany the general.[38] The baroness disliked Burgoyne, possibly because her husband held a lesser post, and possibly because he was British and she was German. Her testimony cannot entirely be credited. In marked contrast to the frolics reported by the baroness, Sergeant Roger Lamb of the Fifty-third Regiment wrote:

> General Burgoyne's dilemma was at this time calamitous, and even desperate. Forsaken by the Indian and Provincial auxiliaries, and reduced in force by continued disaster and losses to about 3500 effective men, of whom but 2000 were British, he was disabled from retreating, and could entertain fourfold in number, and possessing every advantage over him.[39]

Rain continued to pour forth in abundance during the day as the army waited patiently in the chilly woodlands. The Indians deserted at every setback.[40] On the morning of the tenth, Burgoyne ordered Schuyler's house burned and the retreat was continued.[41] After another short march, the troops halted again. "The greatest misery at this time prevailed in the army," the baroness declared.[42] Finally the bedraggled force reached Saratoga, causing a detachment of 600 of Gates's troops to cross to the east bank of the Hudson where an American regiment stood posted to block Burgoyne from retreat.[43] The general decided to send artificers to repair bridges and roads so that he could evacuate to Fort Edward. Captain Fraser started to lead the Forty-seventh Regiment, his marksmen, and Mackay's provincials out of the camp when he discovered American soldiers in great force on the heights of the Fishkill, making a disposition to fight.[44] Fraser was recalled, and the provincials repairing the first bridge fled after a slight attack. The patriots meanwhile continued to fire upon the supply ships docked by the west bank of the Hudson. Several bateaux were lost and a few British soldiers were killed and wounded during the day of October 10. The next morning, Burgoyne ordered the provisions to be carried from the bateaux to camp, which his soldiers did under fire and with difficulty. From all sides Burgoyne's army received injury, for Gates's army had surrounded him. On October 12, Gates replied to Burgoyne's request of safe passage for Lady Acland, and could not resist the opportunity to boast of his conquest. To his credit, he ascribed the victory to the "Fortune of War" rather than to the directions that he had issued from headquarters. Gates also discussed the incendiary activities of the British army:

> The Cruelties which mark the Retreat of your Army, in burning the Gentlemen's and Farmer's Houses, as they pass along, is almost, among civilized Nations, without a precedent, they should not endeavour to ruine those they could not conquer, this Conduct betrays more of the vindictive Malice of a Monk, than the Generosity of a Soldier.[45]

Others in the American army agreed with Gates. The surgeon James Thacher reported "it is a fact, both wanton and disgraceful, that on their retreat they committed the most wanton devastations, burning and destroying almost every house within their reach; the elegant and valuable country seat of General Schuyler, near Saratoga, did not escape their fury.[46] Schuyler assured Burgoyne later that he would have done the same thing in similar circumstances.[47]

On October 12, Burgoyne called Riedesel, Phillips, and Hamilton to a council of war.[48] He reported that Gates now had fourteen thousand men at his command threatening to attack, and that a second army of possibly one thousand four hundred was posted between Fort Edward and Fort George to block his escape.[49] The patriots controlled a bridge over the Hudson, but Burgoyne could not construct another one for his army because the bateaux had been destroyed. Consequently, he proposed a retreat to Fort Edward, and thence around the western side of Fort George. "This last passage was never made but by Indians or very small Bodies of Men," Burgoyne warned. Furthermore, if the army chose that route, it would have to repair bridges while under fire from American troops on the opposite side of the ravine. One bridge alone would take fifteen hours to reconstruct, during which time the patriots posted east of the Hudson could cross to Fort Edward and block Burgoyne's escape, while Gates followed in the rear. Burgoyne abandoned the plan when he at last received news from spies and deserters that Clinton had seized Fort Montgomery in the Hudson Highlands. He also informed his council that provisions could last until the twentieth.

Burgoyne then asked the council to consider five possible courses of action. The army could wait where it was, either for an attack from Gates or the chance of favorable events. Alternatively, Burgoyne could take the initiative and attack Gates. Or the army could retreat, repairing the bridges for the artillery in order to force the passage of the ford. As a fourth possibility, they could leave all the artillery and luggage, and if they could not pass the ford using musketry, they might try the circuit west of Lake George. His fifth alternative was to "march rapidly for Albany. . . . In case the enemy by extending to their left leave their rear open."

Quite rightly, the council decided that it would be unadvisable to attack Gates and that a retreat involving the repair of bridges was impracticable. Burgoyne thought the fifth proposal worthy of consideration, as did Phillips and Hamilton, but "the position of the Enemy yet gives no open for it." Accordingly, the council endorsed the fourth suggestion as the only solution, provided that six days' provision was available and that the march was conducted in secrecy. However, scouts sent out to observe the position of Gates's lines reported "that the Enemy's position on our right was such, and they had so many small parties out, that it would be impossible to move without our march being immediately Discovered."[50] The night march was abandoned, and with it went Burgoyne's last opportunity to escape. As Riedesel observed:

Every hour the position of the Army grew more critical, and the prospect of salvation grew less and less. There was no place of safety for the baggage, and the ground was covered with dead horses that had either been killed by the enemy's bullets or by exhaustion, as there had been no forage for several days. . . . Even for the wounded, no spot could be found which could afford them a safe shelter—not even, indeed, for so long a time as might suffice for a surgeon to bind up their ghastly wounds. The whole camp was now a scene of constant fighting. The soldier could not lay down his arms day or night, except to exchange his gun for the spade when new entrenchments were thrown up. The sick and wounded would drag themselves along into a quiet corner of the woods and lie down to die on the damp ground. Not even here were they longer safe, since every little while a ball would come crashing down among the trees.

On the thirteenth Burgoyne called another council, this time including all the general officers, field officers, and captains.[51] Burgoyne announced that Gates had now firmly entrenched soldiers at Fort Edward, but he bravely volunteered to "undertake at their head any enterprize of Difficulty or hazard, that should appear to them within the Compass of their Strength or Spirit." Burgoyne admitted publicly for the first time the possibility of a capitulation, which "had been in the contemplation of some, perhaps of all, who knew the real Situation of things." Because the decision was of such importance to "National and personal honour," Burgoyne wished the whole assembly to vote upon it and it was resolved that "the present Situation justifies a Capitulation upon honourable terms."[52] Burgoyne then drew up a paper that provided the foundations for such a treaty, and the council unanimously endorsed it.[53] He also dispatched a letter to Gates in which he requested a meeting. Gates replied that Burgoyne could send a representative to him at ten o'clock on the morning of the fourteenth.[54] Adjutant General Kingston delivered Burgoyne's answer, a message filled with the pride of a defeated man who knew that his personal courage was greater than that of his opponent. "After having fought you twice," Burgoyne said, he waited "some days in his present Position determined to try a third conflict—against any force you could bring to attack him."[55] Because he perceived Gates's superior numbers and disposition, however, Burgoyne felt compelled by compassion to establish "principles and precedents of State, and of War, to spare the lives of brave men upon honourable terms." If Gates agreed to negotiate, Burgoyne proposed a cessation of arms.

Gates read the dispatch, took a packet of documents from his pocket, and handed Kingston his own terms for Burgoyne's surrender.[56] The truce continued until sunset, when Gates received Burgoyne's reply. By the next morning Burgoyne's bargaining position was finally reinforced, for Sir Henry Clinton's dispatch of October 8 arrived in British headquarters on the fifteenth. Clinton's message was at least a cause for some hope and at most it gave Burgoyne leverage in his negotiation with Gates:

Nous y voilà and nothing now between us but Gates. I sincerely hope this little Success may facilitate your Operation. In answer to your Letter of the 20th of September by Captain Campbell I shall only say I cannot presume to order or even advise, for reasons obvious. I heartily wish you success.[57]

Although he refused, even in that dire emergency, to direct Burgoyne, Clinton affected the circumstances of Burgoyne's army in other ways. Forging through the highlands, he had captured Fort Clinton and Fort Montgomery. Burgoyne now hardened the terms he sent to Gates, who also knew that Clinton was hovering below his army.[58]

Burgoyne insisted that the treaty should be called a convention rather than a surrender—the word surrender was unacceptable to him. Among the thirteen articles Burgoyne sent to Gates was a provision allowing the British troops "to march out of their Camp with the honors of War."[59] He also demanded that Gates allow British officers to order the soldiers to pile their guns. Furthermore, he wanted the entire army to receive a free passage to England, in return for which he promised that they would not serve again in North America during the war. Burgoyne also wanted to release persons belonging to the Canadian establishment, whom he wished dispatched immediately to the southernmost British post on Lake George. The rest of the army, he declared, would "march to Massachusetts Bay by the Easiest, most expeditious & convenient Route; and to be quartered in, near, or as convenient as possible to Boston, that the March of the Troops may not be delayed, when Transports arrive to receive them." During and after the march, Burgoyne wrote, "the Officers are not, as far as Circumstances will admit, to be separated from their Men"; they were to be admitted on parole and to be permitted to wear their sidearms while in Massachusetts. "These Articles are to be mutually Signed &

Exchanged tomorrow morning at nine o'clock," Burgoyne concluded, "and the Troops under Lieut[enant] Gen[era]l Burgoyne are to march out of their entrenchments at three o'clock in the afternoon." The proposals were sent to Gates on the sixteenth, and to Burgoyne's surprise, he accepted them without reservation. Gates had intercepted a copy of Clinton's exuberant letter of October 8 and did not wish to risk losing a captive army. Even though New York's Governor George Clinton told Gates that Sir Henry Clinton was by no means confident of a junction, the American commander wanted to complete his victory without further risk.[60]

In the British camp, Burgoyne responded to Gates's unwonted friendliness with caution. A loyalist had recently delivered further intelligence from southern New York indicating that Clinton had not only seized two forts in the Hudson highlands, but that he had also ordered Major General John Vaughan to burn "the beautiful village of Kingston," which he did.[61] However, Clinton had insufficient troops to sustain such grandiose activities. Furthermore, Howe demanded additional detachments from New York for his Philadelphia campaign; and accordingly, Sir Henry Clinton withdrew his troops from the once tranquil Dutch town and returned to headquarters in New York City.[62] Although Burgoyne did not know that Clinton had withdrawn his forces, he did know that he had moved as far north as Kingston, and the report gave pause to the British commander. He was unable, however, to persuade his war council to revoke their approval of Gates's preliminary articles, which they had accepted on October 15.[63] There was a general atmosphere of hopelessness prevailing in the British headquarters which, it was said, extended even to Baron von Riedesel, who began to drink heavily.[64] Burgoyne's optimism could not move his staff, and they voted fourteen to eight that they could not honorably withdraw from the treaty.[65] The general, weary and crestfallen, finally capitulated.[66] Early on the morning of the seventeenth, Burgoyne prepared to address his staff. He "entered into a detail of his manner of acting since he had the honour of commanding the army; but he was too full to speak," observed Lieutenant Digby:

> About 10 o'clock, we marched out, according to treaty, with drums beating & the honours of war, but the drums seemed to have lost their former inspiriting sounds, and though we beat the Grenadiers march, which not long before was so animating, yet then it seemed by its last feeble effort, as if almost ashamed to be heard on such an occasion. . . . Thus was Burgoyne's Army sacrificed to either the absurd opinions of a blundering ministerial power [Germain]; the stupid inaction of a general [Howe], who, from his lethargic disposition, neglected every step he might have taken to assist their operations, or lastly, perhaps, his own misconduct in penetrating so far as to be unable to return.[67]

Burgoyne went to the head of the American army, where he met Gates. The British commander bowed to his adversary and said, "General, the caprice of war has made me your prisoner."[68] To which Gates replied, "You will always find me ready to testify that it was not brought about through any fault of your Excellency."[69] Riedesel and Phillips accompanied Burgoyne to Gates's headquarters, where a dinner was prepared and toasts were drunk. When Gates raised his glass to salute George III, Burgoyne, undaunted, toasted George Washington.[70] The ironically festive board groaned with rum and hard cider as Burgoyne spoke highly of the patriots and their ability to fight. When Burgoyne presented his sword to Gates, the latter gallantly returned it. Gates now could afford such pleasantries, for he had beaten his foe and apparently achieved some personal satisfaction. He wrote to his wife:

> The voice of fame, ere this reaches you, will tell how greatly fortunate we have been in this department. Burgoyne and his whole army have laid down their arms, and surrendered themselves to me and my Yankees. Thanks to the Giver of all victory for this triumphant success. . . . Major General Phillips, who wrote me that saucy note last year from St. John's, is now my prisoner, with Lord Petersham, Major Acland, son of Sir Thomas, and his lady, daughter of Lord Ilchester, sister to the famous Lady Susan, and about a dozen members of Parliament, Scotch lords, etc.[71]

Late on the evening of the seventeenth, and during the next day, the captured army began its long march to Boston. Gates had granted generous terms, and the American soldiers did not display the disdain of the victor for the vanquished that occasionally occurs in war. Baroness von Riedesel recorded: "In the passage through the American camp, I observed with great satisfaction, that no one cast at us scornful glances. On the contrary, they all greeted me, even showing compassion on their countenances at seeing a mother with her little children in such a situation."[72] She was guided to the American headquarters, the baroness related, where she encountered Gates along with

> Generals Burgoyne and Phillips, who were on an extremely friendly footing with him. Burgoyne said to me, "You may now dismiss all your apprehensions, for your sufferings are at an end." I answered him that I should certainly be acting very wrongly to have any more anxiety, when our chief had none, and especially when I saw him on such a friendly footing with General Gates.[73]

At Albany General Philip Schuyler received the army with such graciousness that Burgoyne was moved to exclaim: "Is it to me, who have done you so much injury, that you show so much kindness!" Schuyler is said to have replied, "Such is the fate of war; let us not talk about it any more."[74] Schuyler's wife was equally kind, and invited Burgoyne to stay at her home while he was in Albany.

Burgoyne obtained from Gates the best terms he could possibly get, including his own passage on parole to England, and a promise to release his troops as well. Riedesel remarked that he had not previously known a defeated army to have saved so much honor, and Burgoyne boastingly told Germain on October 20 that he virtually "dictated" the terms.[75]

Within two weeks, almost all of the British forces in New York north of Manhattan were either captured or driven out. The Ticonderoga garrison fled; Clinton's superb highland campaign became meaningless. Sir Henry returned to New York City, the only major post besides Philadelphia still in British possession. American forces had accomplished a signal victory. Burgoyne's failure, despite his efforts to minimize it, was a catastrophe for the British war effort.

Notes

1. Neilson, *Campaign*, p. 157.
2. Billias, *Glover*, p. 142.
3. September 21–29, 1777, Burgoyne, *Orderly Book*, pp. 114–23. They often used their energy building roads and marking trees.
4. September 21, 1777, Lamb, *Memoir*, p. 195; October 5, Burgoyne, *Orderly Book*, p. 127.
5. Ibid.
6. October 3, 1777, Burgoyne, "Account" H.L.R.O., #51; Burgoyne, *State*, appendix, p. lxxxviii troop response, DeFonblanque, *Episodes*, p. 291.
7. October 3, 1777, Burgoyne, *Orderly Book*, pp. 125–26.
8. Lamb, *Memoir*. Seven deserters from Burgoyne's army were scalped by American Indians; British Indians were in pursuit of the rest; September 30, 1777, Burgoyne, *Orderly Book*, pp. 123–24. The Board of Regulation discharged thirty of Peter's Loyal Rangers between August 22 and October 1. Eighty were missing since September 19; October 1, 1777, "Return, Queen's Loyal Rangers"; W. O. 28.4, f. 103. Canadians and Indians were deserting; October 4, Thacher, *Military Journal*, p. 100.
9. October 4, 1777, Neilson, *Campaign*, p. 161.
10. Mackesy, *America*, p. 141, note 1.
11. Neilson, *Campaign*, p. 161.
12. Mackesy p. 141, further concluded that Riedesel at no time during the campaign really supported Burgoyne's ideas; von Eelking, *Riedesel*, 1:238; Edward J. Lowell, *The Hessians and other German Auxiliaries of Great Britain in the Revolutionary War* (New York: Harper, 1884), pp. 136–37; Von Eelking, *German Allied Troops*, p. 135; Baroness Riedesel, *Journal*, pp. 174, 176.
13. Von Eelking, 1:238.
14. Burgoyne, *State*, appendix, p. lxxxix. He was 200 miles from Montreal, only 45 from Albany.
15. October 20, 1777, Burgoyne to Germain, H.L.R.O., #51.
16. Both Fraser and Riedesel believed a retreat to Ticonderoga was both feasible and honorable, although Phillips remained silent; "Burgoyne's Account before Parliament."
17. Quoted by Stone, *Campaign*, p. 56.
18. Von Eelking, vol. 1, pp. 161–62.
19. October 1, 1777, Thacher, *Military Journal*, p. 99.
20. Ibid.
21. October 4, 1777, Gates to Clinton, Hudleston, *Burgoyne*, p. 185.
22. Ibid., pp. 103–4. Professor Don Higginbotham maintained that it was Daniel Morgan who ordered Murphy to shoot; Don Higginbotham, *Daniel Morgan: Revolutionary Rifleman* (Chapel Hill, N.C.: University of North Carolina, 1961), pp. 73–74.

23. Thacher, *Military Journal*, p. 101.

24. Ibid., p. 102. Peckham, ed., *Toll of Independence*, p. 42, concurred in these estimates.

25. Peckham, ed., *Toll of Independence*, p. 42.

26. Brown, ed., *Journal*, p. 52. The baroness was also disturbed because a house which Burgoyne had ordered constructed for her had been burned.

27. Ibid., p. 52.

28. Thacher, *Military Journal*, p. 122.

29. Thacher, *Military Journal*, appendix, note 1, p. 358; Brown, ed., *Journal*, p. 53.

30. Thacher, *Military Journal*, appendix, note 2, p. 364.

31. Burgoyne, "Account," H.L.R.O., #51.

32. Brown, ed., *Journal*, p. 53.

33. Burgoyne, "Account," H.L.R.O., #51.

34. Brown, ed., *Journal*, p. 55.

35. Burgoyne, "Account," H.L.R.O., #51.

36. Ibid.

37. Brown, ed., *Journal*, pp. 55–56.

38. Louise H. Tharp, *The Baroness and the General* (Boston: Little, Brown, 1962), uses the story, without convincing documentation.

39. Lamb, *Memoir*, p. 201.

40. Brown, ed., *Journal*, p. 55.

41. Ibid.

42. Ibid.

43. Burgoyne, "Account," H.L.R.O., #51. The soldiers slept in rain-drenched clothes; Lamb, *Memoir*, p. 201.

44. Ibid.

45. October 12, 1777, Gates to Burgoyne, Gates papers, New-York Historical Society.

46. Thacher, *Military Journal*, p. 103.

47. Von Eelking, *Riedesel*, vol. 1.

48. October 12, 1777, "Minutes of a Council of War held on the heights of Saratoga," House of Lords Record Office no. 60, enclosure no. 9 in October 20, 1777, Burgoyne to Germain, H.L.R.O., #51.

49. Gates actually had over twenty-one thousand infantrymen; October 16, 1777, "Return of the Army," Gates papers, New-York Historical Society, published in full in Charles H. Lesser, ed., *The Sinews of Independence: Monthly Strength Reports of the Continental Army* (Chicago: University of Chicago Press, 1976), p. 50.

50. Ibid.

51. October 13, 1777, "Minutes and Proceedings of a Council of War . . . ," House of Lords Record Office, no. 60.

52. Ibid.

53. Von Eelking, *Riedesel*, 1:181–82.

54. October 13, 1777, Gates to Burgoyne, House of Lords Record Office, No. 52.

55. Ibid.

56. October 14, 1777, "Major Gen[era]l Gates's Proposal," House of Lords Record Office, no. 54 and Ford, ed., *Journals*, 9:857–58.

57. October 8, 1777, Clinton to Burgoyne, House of Lords Record Office, no. 49.

58. Von Eelking, *Riedesel*, 1:196–97.

59. October 16, 1777, "Articles of Convention between Lieut[enant] General Burgoyne and Major General Gates," P.R.O. 30.55.6, f. 705, pp. 1–4; copy, miscellaneous papers, Clements Library.

60. Nelson, *Gates*, pp. 138–39.

61. November 2, 1777, intelligence received in Baltimore for William Smith, B.L. Add. MS. 34,414, f. 302.

62. Clinton, "Historical Detail," 1:94, cited by Dabney, *After Saratoga: The Story of the Convention Army* (Albuquerque: University of New Mexico, 1954), p. 12, note 22; Alden, *American Revolution*, pp. 148–49.

63. October 15, 1777, "Minutes and Proceedings of a Council of War."

64. Nickerson, *Turning Point*, p. 395.

65. Ibid.

66. October 16, 1777, "Terms of Convention," Justin Winsor, ed., *Narrative and Critical History of America*, 8 vols. (Boston: Houghton Mifflin, 1887–89), 4:317.

67. Digby, *Invasion*, pp. 321–22.

68. Von Eelking, *Riedesel*, 1:190, note 1.

69. Ibid.

70. Ibid.

71. October 17, 1777, Gates to wife. Gates papers, New-York Historical Society.

72. Thacher, *Military Journal*, p. 370, note 2.

73. Ibid.

74. Brown, ed., *Journal*, p. 65. See also Don R. Gerlach, "After Saratoga: The General, His Lady, and 'Gentleman Johnny' Burgoyne," *New York History* 52:5–30.

75. October 20, 1777, Burgoyne to Germain, House of Lords Record Office, #51.

18

A Defeated General in Boston

After Burgoyne signed the Articles of Capitulation, he remained in Albany for about ten days. His period of residence at the home of General Schuyler was not entirely pleasant, however much the relief from offensive military operations may have eased the mind of the captured officer. During a moment of quiet Burgoyne wrote to his nieces in England, informing them that he was exhausted "to that degree with business that I can scarce hold my pen."[1] Filled with anxiety concerning his army, which had been in "the jaws of famine," Burgoyne had not slept for sixteen nights. He admitted that he was exhausted in mind and body. The American soldiers had shot him through the waistcoat and had killed his closest advisors. Still, he had yet another war to look forward to—a conflict with ministers in London, who "will always lay the blame upon the employed who miscarries." "In all these complicated anxieties, believe me, my dear girls, my heart has a large space filled with you, and I will bring it home, when God shall so permit, as replete with affection as when I left you." Burgoyne wrote another letter while he was at Albany. He was so concerned that all his explanations be made known in London, he told Lord Derby, that he requested Derby to publish a copy of a dispatch he had written to Germain, should the secretary of state "mangle or curtail any part of it in their Gazette."[2] Burgoyne also sent to Lord North extracts of private letters, so that North would be able to defend him against the "attacks that necessarily follow unsuccessful events." Burgoyne believed that the ministry would shift the focus of investigation from the planning of strategy to the execution of instructions, thereby exonerating Germain but implicating Burgoyne.

General Gates arrived at the home of Schuyler to offer Burgoyne safe passage to England in an American ship, but the British officer refused to accept.[3] He decided not to leave until American authorities released all his troops. Burgoyne, surprised by the conduct of his captors, wrote a long letter to General Howe, speculating about the motivations of the Americans: "The treatment of the officers and troops in general is of so extraordinary a nature in point of generosity that I must suppose it proceeds from some other motive than mere kindness of disposition."[4] Indeed, the patriots had received the British army honorably and charitably. They greeted with compassion rather than derision the arrival of the baroness von Riedesel, her children, and all of the British troops. The British were unable to accept such hospitality with equanimity.[5]

Meanwhile, British and American officers began to prepare for the task of transporting the captive army to Boston. According to the terms of capitulation, the American army was required to escort the British force on the two-hundred-mile journey from Albany to Boston, where Burgoyne and his army would remain until they were officially released and returned to England. While the evacuation took place, American patriots near Albany watched in amazement as the British took with them their pets, including foxes, racoons, deer, and a bear on a chain.[6] The records do not indicate how well the animals endured the trek, but the troops marched through Indian trails and wagon paths in great misery.[7] Moreover, freezing temperatures, the lack of suitable shelter, and the scarcity of warm clothing contributed to their hardships and caused two men and one horse to die during the journey.[8] Not a British voice was raised against Burgoyne during that ordeal, if one of his officers can be believed, although the German troops criticized the commander for being inexcusably merry.[9] The Germans also reported that the Americans developed considerable animosity toward their prisoners, especially the Germans.[10] Burgoyne himself departed for Boston at the conclusion of his ten-day visit with Schuyler.[11]

The inhabitants of Boston, long-suffering in the midst of war, were less inclined to offer hospitality than the residents of Albany had been. As soon as it received word of the defeat at Saratoga, the Massachusetts Legislature prepared a joint resolution to obtain suitable housing for the officers and barracks for the rank and file.[12] The legislators reached decisions on November 7, when they ordered the troops to occupy barracks on Winter Hill and Prospect Hill, about two miles northwest of the town of Cambridge, in the area today called Somerville.[13] Colonel David Henley of the American army guarded the rank and file with the assistance of about 1,200 patriot soldiers.[14] Americans had constructed the barracks during the siege of Boston and the structures had not been maintained or repaired since 1775. The men disliked their quarters, where "wind, rain and snow swept through them; they have no windows, only holes."[15] According to Sergeant Lamb, it was not unusual to find 30 or 40 soldiers crowded together indiscriminately in "a small, miserable, open hut."[16] At first the troops had to make do with short rations, little wood for their fires, and less straw for beds. At night, many soldiers sat up in the cold to shake off the snow that had drifted on them through openings in the walls.[17] Amidst abysmal conditions, 773 soldiers deserted between October 17, 1777, and April 1, 1778.[18] Riedesel and Phillips took roll call four times a day, and paraded the troops twice a week.[19]

The legislature also moved to find a house for Burgoyne's use. At first, Burgoyne, Riedesel, and Phillips had to take temporary lodgings at great cost in the Blue Anchor, an inn located a short distance from Harvard Square.[20] It was there that Burgoyne met Major General William Heath, an ambitious

Roxbury farmer who had been assigned general supervision of the captured army while it stayed in Massachusetts. Heath, a bluff, good-natured man, had anticipated his new assignment with mixed emotions; he confided to his diary that his instructions to negotiate with Burgoyne opened "a new, important, and delicate field" for him.[21] Heath controlled the local military department, supervising supplies, guards, and other matters.[22] Burgoyne and Heath got along well during their first encounter, although later innumerable tensions beset them and hindered negotiations. Burgoyne first requested to tour Boston, and Heath permitted him to do so. American spectators thronged the streets, but there were no incidents until Burgoyne and Heath arrived at Province House. Burgoyne turned to his officers and declared: "There is the former residence of the Governor," to which an onlooker replied loudly, *"and on the other side is the riding school,"* referring to Old South Meeting House, where Burgoyne had stabled horses in 1775.[23] The inhabitants had long memories, but Burgoyne made no reply. In fact, he soon observed to Heath his astonishment "at the civility of your people, for, were you walking the streets of London in my situation, you would not escape insult."[24]

Burgoyne continued to give priority to the question of housing. Although Heath assured the general that ultimately he would be quartered in one of the best houses of Cambridge, Burgoyne continued formally to protest against the conditions he had to endure.[25] On November 11 he told Heath that if it pleased the Americans to make his accommodations even worse, "I persuade myself I shall continue to persevere as becomes me."[26] Burgoyne examined various proposals for housing, all of which he found inconvenient. Finally, he delivered a broadside to General Gates, to whom he conveyed his feelings after "being amused with promises of Quarters for eight days . . . still in a dirty small miserable Tavern."[27] Burgoyne said that the lack of common hospitality was so offensive that it constituted a violation of the Anglo-American agreement of the previous October. "The public faith is broke," he declared, thus perhaps unwittingly preparing an opportunity for further difficulties between the British and the Americans.[28] If Britain could substantiate the charge, it would become an important weapon for bargaining, for the British wished ideally to reclaim all captured troops without having to exchange Americans or provide indemnities. Heath and Gates understood that fact, for Heath was careful to deny at all times that the convention had been broken.[29] Gates also understood that the Americans could benefit if the British could be shown to have violated the convention, thus releasing all parties from obligations. Gates sent Burgoyne's complaint to Congress, which planned to use it to advantage at a later time.[30]

Heath did attempt to make known Burgoyne's difficulties, writing to the Massachusetts legislature during November, privately admitting that "the honour of the state is in danger[,] the public faith responsible" for Burgoyne's "disgraceful" situation.[31] At length the problem was resolved and Burgoyne occupied a house "without a Table, Chair, or any one Article of Furniture," which cost him £150 sterling for occupancy through April 1778.[32] He was required to pay the full rental in advance, without a partial refund if he left earlier. Completed in 1763, the house, afterward called "the Bishop's Palace," was an elaborate structure and it is not surprising, therefore, that Burgoyne finally settled for it even though it was unfurnished.[33]

The problem of obtaining barracks for the troops remained a difficult one to resolve however. Both officers and privates were packed into inferior quarters. Burgoyne complained to Heath that such accommodations "would be held unfit for Gentlemen in their situation in any part of the World. I have seen many jails preferable," he added.[34] By mid-November, in fact, cases of prisoner maltreatment were being reviewed by an American court of inquiry, which also looked into the inadequacy of the barracks. Burgoyne insisted upon examining personally those Americans who were charged with neglecting British prisoners of war during the trial.[35] It was observed that the general "more than once proved himself a great pleader—has even caused the entire court to shed tears"; Burgoyne's impact was probably the result of his forceful, personal style.[36] His facts were at least partly correct, for Colonel Henley had mistreated officers and soldiers in their crowded quarters. Simmering discontent in the barracks eventually led to Henley's court-martial for murder, and Burgoyne again testified personally against him. If Burgoyne had known that the barracks had just been used as an "innoculating hospital" for smallpox, he surely would have been even more outraged.[37]

At first conciliatory toward his captors, Burgoyne became increasingly irritable as the weeks of confinement bore down upon him. His complaints to Heath about winter clothing, housing conditions, American attempts to obtain defectors from his ranks, and other matters increased in frequency and length.[38]

The feuds that developed from these problems were forgotten temporarily when Burgoyne learned in November that ships from Lord Howe's fleet were arriving at the coast of Rhode Island to take his soldiers back to England.[39] Although the German troops were to be sent home, Howe wanted the English troops to go to Philadelphia to reinforce his brother's army. Since the Americans had not complied with exchange agreements in the past, Howe maintained, the British were under no obligation to do so either.[40] Although Howe's plan was not officially known in the American camp, both Washington and Congress suspected that the British commanders fully anticipated using the convention troops again as soon as they could do so. Consequently, Congress became determined to create obstacles to the release of British troops. Thus the legislators seized immediately upon Burgoyne's unfortunate phrase "the public faith is broke" as sufficient reason for a congressional inquiry into the activities of the convention army. Henry Laurens sent Gates a long letter on November 23, revealing the questions that members of Congress asked concerning Burgoyne's troops.[41] If the British general claimed that faith was broken, asked congressmen, what had he done to comply with the agreement? What had become of the regimental colors, military chests, and cartouche boxes, they asked? Where were the muskets, bayonets, and other weapons? Gates replied on December 3 that Burgoyne had told him that the regimental colors were in Canada; that the whereabouts of the military chest, which contained cash, was unknown; that cartouches had been sold for drams of beer or rum on the road to Boston; ammunition had been confiscated and bayonets had been pilfered by Americans.[42] The report was hardly satisfactory to Congress, which continued to create obstacles for Burgoyne.

Burgoyne received a letter from General Washington, who refused to become involved officially in the question of violations of the convention. Washington encouraged him to write personally to Congress but he had no intention of permitting the British general to ship troops to Howe.[43] Congress, stating specifically that transportation of the troops southward to Providence would be a violation of the terms of the charter, refused to grant Burgoyne permission to do so, and the general on January 4 so informed the fleet at Rhode Island.[44] Burgoyne soon realized, as he wrote to Lord Howe and others, that Congress was determined "to impede the Embarkation of the Troops as long as possible."[45] When Heath warned that either the whole convention army would be released or else none would go, Burgoyne became convinced that Heath and his superiors were creating new problems in order to block Burgoyne's own departure, that they hoped to hold him as a hostage. These new requirements he said, were "exorbitant in every degree."

Meanwhile Heath received another Burgoyne outburst and he was "not a little surprized at Some Expressions in it."[46] Did his generous offer for transportation merit the "epithets which you are pleased to bestow on me," Heath asked? "I have ever aimed to treat you with Politeness, & the plighted faith and Honour of my country require me to pay strict attention to the Convention." Exasperated with Burgoyne's angry, persistent demands, Heath managed nevertheless to exercise restraint. He assured Burgoyne that British transports would be permitted to enter Boston harbor. However, Heath finally lost his temper in mid-January 1778, when he replied to Burgoyne:

> If Cambridge and Boston abound with ill designing Men, I hope I shall be able to distinguish my Enemies; but I can scarcely believe that one who is frequently bestowing invectives either on my Country, its Laws, Officers, or Inhabitants (I need not say myself) can be a Friend, and I wish you, Sir, carefully to avoid such expressions in your letters unless you mean to give offence.[47]

The next day Heath regained his composure and apologized for his outburst.[48] Shortly thereafter, Burgoyne received a bill for £37,494—the long awaited cost of provisioning the British army.[49] He also received a bill for additional commissary charges of £13,175 6s. 11d., payable at 5 percent interest.[50] Fifty thousand pounds sterling was a considerable sum to pay, and Burgoyne did not settle the account promptly.

Meanwhile, the general became involved in an extended investigation of the activities of Colonel Henley, the American officer who supervised the convention troops. Burgoyne had sent several complaints to Heath concerning the lack of law and order in the surrounding community; in fact, he asked the American general, as "guardian and servant" of the people, to investigate such charges.[51] Burgoyne also complained that Heath's officers were insulting and frequently provocative during squabbles in the barracks and surrounding areas. The bad language used by American officers incited Burgoyne's men to "the most bloody purposes," he claimed.[52] Finally, Burgoyne accused Colonel Henley of murder.[53] Heath replied that his men had not been guilty of misconduct, that British officers had in fact been abusive and were to be confined to guard ships.[54] However, Heath did arrest Henley and ordered a court of inquiry to determine his innocence or guilt.[55] Burgoyne objected to the public inquiry, and claimed that a court-martial was in order because Henley committed "unprovoked, unmanly, wanton severity, of wilful, deliberate, malicious bloodshed, in three several instances." It was a matter for trial, rather than an "inadequate, dilitory & nugatory" inquiry.[56] Heath was unimpressed and proceeded to call a court of inquiry for January 13,[57] despite a protest from Burgoyne which the court refused to hear.[58]

Four days later, Heath changed his mind and agreed upon the basis of new evidence to submit the Henley case to court-martial, with the charge of murder.[59] Brigadier General John Glover presided at the trial, which lasted from mid-January to February 1778. Burgoyne appeared as a hostile witness, warning the officers in charge against "evasion, subterfuge and lawcraft" when interpreting testimony.[60] Henley, said Burgoyne, was clearly guilty of "independency, scurrility and impiety." The court then called witnesses who testified on behalf of Henley. Finally, Burgoyne presented to the court a remarkably melodramatic summation of his case against Henley:

I stand in this circle, at best an unpopular, with the Sanguine enemies of Britain perhaps an obnoxious character. This situation, though disagreeable, does not make me miserable. I wrap myself in the integrity of my intention and can look round with a smile. . . . To the multitude who only regard me with the transient anger that political opinions and the occurrences of the time occasion, I retain not a thought of resentment, because I know the disposition and hour will come, when steadfastness of principle, that favourite characteristic in America, will recommend me amongst my worst enemies: as Christian, I trust they will forgive me; in spite of prejudice I know they will respect me.[61]

The judge advocate, Lieutenant Colonel Tudor, thanked Burgoyne for his "Attic language" but remained unimpressed. Invoking the memory of Jane McCrea, whose murderer Burgoyne had refused to execute, Tudor argued persuasively in favor of Henley. According to Burgoyne's construction of events, Henley had called British Sergeant Reeves "a great rascal."[62] Reeves denied the charge, but said that he soon hoped to carry arms for Sir William Howe. Henley thereupon lost his temper, insulted Reeves and Great Britain, and lunged at the sergeant with a firelock and fixed bayonet, wounding slightly the British officer. He also pushed his sword into the side of Corporal Hadley. The court, however, did not consider this evidence convincing, nor did other interested parties. Henley was ultimately acquitted of the charge of murder.

Burgoyne presented to Heath other grievances while the trial was taking place. He accused the American army of attempting to entice his troops to join the patriot cause. Heath challenged Burgoyne to provide evidence of such subterfuge. If he could do so, Heath promised to bring to trial any officer who had tried to persuade British soldiers to commit treason. Burgoyne remained silent.[63] He did, however, accuse the American army of a lack of civility, which Heath denied: "I will venture to say as much generosity & Hospitality may be found in my Country as in any, and I will add more than in some others, if we may judge from the treatment of the unfortunate."[64] Nevertheless, continued Burgoyne, Heath's propagandists, who were trying to undermine the morale of their captives, were contaminating the very air with lies.[65] As evidence, Burgoyne submitted documents to prove that Heath's men were indeed swaying British soldiers from their allegiance. Finally, Burgoyne came "to the last paragraph of your Letter in which you recapitulate and sum up all Abuses, Riots, Rescues, Insults, etc. that you are informed have been committed by these Troops, and you conclude with a suspicion of Highway robbery."[66] Burgoyne denied most of the accusations, although he admitted his troops were sometimes guilty of "Levities, Indiscretions, faults of Omission, of neglect & of Liquor"—all of which had been atoned by the "beatings, imprisonments and death received at the hands of your people."[67]

There is no doubt that Burgoyne, his officers, and possibly his troops were indulging themselves in entertainments and other activities that prisoners of war usually did not have an opportunity to enjoy. For instance, Burgoyne and Phillips organized a formal dance and invited ladies in Cambridge and Boston to attend. Although all of the committees of the revolutionary government issued orders prohibiting patriots from attending, two of General Schuyler's daughters did appear at the ball.[68] Burgoyne, perhaps recalling his elaborate festival at The Oaks in 1774, provided a race course, beer, billiards, fowling, cockfighting and tenpins for the entertainment of his staff.[69] His rank and file also appear to have enjoyed themselves in Cambridge, for Mercy Otis Warren called them "an idle and dissipated army," who "corrupted the students of Harvard College."[70] Consequently, it is difficult to accept all of Burgoyne's testimony concerning the hardships he and his army encountered in captivity. True, American officers instructed Burgoyne and his staff to cease playing billiards at "unseasonable hours" in a house located in Cambridge, but the general's lot was not an unhappy one.

Burgoyne did complain to Howe that his health had "suffered considerably by my residence in this Climate and is likely to do more so.—but that representation had no avail in one application I made for Embarkation at Rhode Island as matters of favor and it would be vain to try it a second time."[71] During January and February he informed Lord Howe and General Pigot of his further suffering, and he told the latter that "the value of life has been for some time over with me, and whether I resign it with my Country by climate or by Arms I am indifferent—to the last of it I shall retain due value for distinguished and amiable characters.[72] Perhaps Burgoyne was more wearied by endless argument with Heath than anything else for he admitted, "it can be [as] painful to me as it is troublesome to you to find matter of complaint the continual subject of our Correspondence."[73] The transport ships safely secured at Cape Cod, Heath again asked Burgoyne to present a detailed list of all noncommissioned officers, a requirement that had to be met before soldiers could be paroled and returned to England.[74] Burgoyne declined to do so, reviving instead the subject of poor provisioning. Heath in turn created a new issue by demanding to inspect all of Burgoyne's outgoing correspondence. Burgoyne had no choice but to comply with the request. When Heath read Burgoyne's recent dispatch to Howe, in which he called Heath's order to pay for all provisions in sterling a violation of the convention and objected to Heath's demand for a list of non-commissioned officers, he was incensed.[75] Heath particularly objected to the absence of any reference to an optional plan for payment in kind rather than in sterling.[76] He also disliked Burgoyne's comments concerning the list, and pointed out that Burgoyne himself, arguing that Britain did not recognize the government that had created those ranks, had treated indiscriminately officers and privates whom he had captured at Ticonderoga. A further problem developed, however, which eclipsed these other considerations.

It will be recalled that the Continental Congress had long watched the activities of the captive troops and despite a crowded agenda had in fact begun to investigate purported infractions of the convention. As early as November 5, Washington expressed disappointment with developments.[77] Thereafter Congress, suspecting the perfidy of Howe, devised a number of methods for postponing the embarkation. Congress then seized upon Burgoyne's statement that the public faith was broken and used it as an excuse to pass a resolution on January 8 suspending the departure of the troops unless the British government ratified the convention.[78]

One month later, Heath received copies of the congressional decision and supplied one set of resolutions to Burgoyne, who read them slowly and with considerable anger.[79] Congress condemned Burgoyne's refusal to deliver munitions, his refusal to submit descriptive lists of officers and privates, his statement that the "convention was broke," and his willingness to "avail himself of such pretended breach of the Convention, in order to disengage himself and the army under him of the obligations they are under to these United States, and that the security which these States have had of his personal honor is hereby destroyed."[80] Consequently, Congress resolved to prevent the departure of Burgoyne and his troops until "a distinct and explicit ratification of the Convention of Saratoga shall be properly notified by the Court of Great Britain to Congress." But that was not all: a detailed report of the deliberations of the congressional committee that prepared the resolutions accompanied the official documents. Burgoyne's motivations were condemned even more explicitly in this document. Concerning the charge that the convention was broken, the committee remarked: "he cannot be considered of so light a character as to have acted in a Serious Matter of State upon a sudden impression."[81] The committee also declared unreasonable Burgoyne's charge of bad faith, which he based upon the shortage of high-quality housing in Boston. For those reasons and others the committee recommended strongly that Congress pass the resolutions, which it did.[82]

Burgoyne immediately wrote a lengthy reply to Henry Laurens, president of Congress, in which he answered item by item all of the charges contained in the resolves.[83] Heath also permitted Burgoyne to inform Lord Howe of the congressional decision.[84] Sir William Howe had already received a copy of Burgoyne's letter to Heath regarding the resolves on February 5, and he wrote immediately to Washington.[85] Among other things, General Howe told the Virginian that he was providing rations for American prisoners of war in his army and that Congress had made allegations against the British forces which were too "illiberal to deserve a serious answer." Although Howe told Burgoyne that his letter would induce Washington to release him immediately,[86] Washington informed Heath he suspected Burgoyne would consider himself "at liberty to make use of any means to effect an escape."[87]

Writing again to Henry Laurens on February 11, Burgoyne confessed that he was in a dilemma concerning his obligations as a prisoner of war. If Congress rejected his arguments, he could either sacrifice his life or accept a passport to England, "should the Congress think proper to grant it as a matter of Indulgence."[88] Although in ordinary circumstances loyalty to king and country required Burgoyne to sacrifice his life, Burgoyne said, he thought that a request for release based upon personal concerns would not endanger British national interests. As Riedesel was said to have remarked, Burgoyne was glad to remain with his troops only as long as departure seemed imminent.[89] In the event, Burgoyne made application for release:

> My Health, to which the climate of America was always averse, has lately declined by more than ordinary Degrees. The Symptoms of a complaint I have been subject to before, to which the Bath waters have been found the only Remedy are daily increasing; and it is the opinion of my physicians as well as my own that my Life under God depends in great measure upon the Resource.[90]

Burgoyne also argued that he had to settle with the British treasury complicated accounts which, if he left unresolved before his death, would embarrass relatives and friends. Finally, Burgoyne had to defend his character in

England against "all the aspersions & erroneous interpretations that the malevolent, prejudiced or misinformed may choose to cast upon it."

Appealing to justice and humanity, Burgoyne asked Congress to permit him as well as the officers of his staff and their families and servants to go to Rhode Island or New York or any other approved route. In conclusion, he made a significant pledge, one that would haunt him later:

> I am willing to give a further parole that should the suspension of Embarkation be by . . . any means prolonged behind the time apprehended I will return to America upon Demand of the Congress, & due notice given, redeliver my person into their power, and abide the Common fate of my brethren in this Army.

Such a reckless promise perhaps seemed wise to Burgoyne, who needed to make as many concessions as possible in the face of prolonged confinement.

In due course, Congress resolved on March 3, "that Lieutenant General Burgoyne on account of his ill state of Health have leave to embark for England by Rhode Island or any more expeditious Route with the officers of his Family and his Servants, that General Heath furnish the necessary passports, accepting parole from Lieut[enant] General Burgoyne."[91] The news was "joyous to the General," as Heath noted. Horatio Gates graciously sent a formal farewell letter to Burgoyne from his headquarters at Albany:

> Your Case I feel as I ever shall that of the unfortunate Brave: if Courage, Perseverence and a Faithful attachment to your Prince could have prevailed, I might have been your prisoner. The Chance of War has determined otherwise. The Congress now send the passports you desire, and I am happy to acquaint you that the Major and Lady Harriet Acland are in New York, and may possibly be in England as soon as, or very soon after, You.[92]

Washington also wrote to Burgoyne from his headquarters in Pennsylvania and paid tribute to his captured adversary. Washington was delighted that Congress had relieved him of the obligation to intervene on behalf of the general. On March 7, Burgoyne learned that his transports were ready, and he began to make preparations.[93] He requested Heath's permission to depart on March 8, but Heath replied that he would conform strictly to the wishes of Congress.[94] Heath noted that there were large quantities of flour aboard the transports that he would gladly receive as payment for debts still outstanding.[95] Burgoyne asked the commander of the *Juno* to send the flour to Heath, and he also presented the officer with a turkey, a gift inspired, perhaps, by the general's improved spirits at his imminent departure.[96] Colonel Dalrymple duly acknowledged the gift and shipped 1900 barrels of flour to Heath.[97]

There remained several unsettled matters, including ammunition cartridges that Burgoyne had neglected to surrender to the American army, and which Heath had tried to obtain since January 2.[98] Now American officials demanded the immediate return of all such cartridges.[99] Consequently, Lord Howe sent the ships back to Rhode Island pending further decisions of Heath and the Assembly.[100] On March 17 the Massachusetts legislature issued a general warrant to search Burgoyne's barracks for what assemblymen believed was a considerable quantity of firearms.[101] Although the legislature had instructed couriers to keep the warrant a "profound secret" until Burgoyne was confronted with it, searchers found no firearms; only ten rusty fusees were reported.[102] Burgoyne volunteered to surrender thirty additional cartridges, which his men would no longer need. After the search he told Heath: "I have been lately too much habituated to Extraordinary Events to feel surprize or agitation on any, and in the present Instance I sincerely assure you I find myself much more inclined to smile than to take umbradge [sic]."[103] By March 27, as Burgoyne became impatient to leave, Heath had still not completed the accounting, and the two officers held a conference concerning the debts. Burgoyne reminded Heath that Congress instructed him to depart without delay, and called Heath's demand for a financial settlement in the face of American refusal to submit a bill "a strange species of persecution."[104] Furthermore, his health was worsening. He suffered "an attack of gout" in his stomach on March 29, and he was convinced that each new delay endangered his life. Two days later Heath presented Burgoyne with final Articles of Agreement, which included detailed accountings of all costs alleged and accepted by Burgoyne.[105] The general agreed to pay immediately £30,263 for items chargeable to Heath, and an additional £8,252 7s. 6d. to the Glover account, which included expenses incurred during the march from Albany to Boston during November 1777. Burgoyne reported to Howe that he had paid £38,000 to the Americans, and that the paymaster would furnish the balance to total £100,000. Finally, Burgoyne signed the articles of agreement on April 10, making official a parole written eight days earlier.

The matter of exchange, mentioned in the parole, was an important one. If Burgoyne could obtain regular exchange, he would be released from the parole. Consequently, he informed General Howe that Charles Lee or even a major general or a colonel might be acceptable in exchange for himself, a lieutenant general.[106] Charles Lee, in fact, asked Henry Laurens on April 17 to exchange one or more officers for Burgoyne, since Burgoyne was of no further value to Britain. Perhaps because he cautioned that General Washington could not do without his own services, Lee's plan was rejected.[107] During 1778 and 1779, the British government attempted without success to return Burgoyne to Congress but the general was finally exchanged in 1781.[108]

On April 15 Burgoyne sailed for England, just six months after the ordeal of captivity had begun. Despite difficulties with Heath concerning equipment, arms, provisions, court-martials, entertainments, debts, violations of the convention, and other matters, Burgoyne had held his own.[109] Having obtained good terms for surrender, given the circumstances, Burgoyne managed to get himself released. He was unable to do as much for his troops, whom he had defended consistently and honorably during his stay in Boston. The convention army soon moved to Virginia, where they remained in considerable misery until the war was over. The future was not a great deal brighter for the general, who had now to face a hostile nation and ministry.[110]

Notes

1. October 1777, Burgoyne to his nieces, Hudleston, *Burgoyne,* pp. 245–46.

2. October 20, 1777, Burgoyne to Colonel Richard Phillipson, accession no. 2257, Manuscripts Department, University of Virginia Library, Charlottesville. The letter is printed in Barnes and Owen, eds. *Sandwich Papers,* 1:306–9.

3. October 17, 1777, Burgoyne to Gates, Historical Manuscripts Commission, *Report on American Manuscripts in the Royal Institution of Great Britain,* 4 vols. (London, 1904–7), 1:142.

4. October 20, 1777, Burgoyne to Howe, ibid., 1:141.

5. October 20, 1777, Friederike C. von Riedesel, Brown, ed., *Journal,* p. 66.

6. William Matthews and Dixon Wecter, *Our Soldiers Speak* (Boston: Little, Brown, 1943), pp. 49, 51; Ray W. Pettingill, "To Saratoga and Back," *New England Quarterly,* 10 (1937), p. 787.

7. Von Eelking, *Riedesel,* 1:215.

8. Ibid.

9. Ibid.

10. Ibid.

11. October 25, 1777, Burgoyne to Howe, Historical Manuscripts Commission, *Report on American MSS.,* 1:143–44.

12. October 23, 1777, *Boston Gazette;* Massachusetts Legislature, *House Journal,* Court Records, 38:145, cited by Samuel D. Batchelder, *Burgoyne and his Officers in Cambridge, 1777–1778,* (Cambridge, Mass.: Cambridge Historical Society, 1926), p. 20.

13. William Heath, *The Heath Papers: Collections of the Massachusetts Historical Society,* fifth series, (Boston: Massachusetts Historical Society, 1878), contains some of Washington's correspondence with Heath for 1777–78, esp. pp. 65–82.

14. December 18, 1777, Batchelder, "Cambridge," p. 18.

15. Hudleston, *Burgoyne,* p. 251.

16. November 14, 1777, Burgoyne to Gates, Heath, MSS., Massachusetts Historical Society, vol. 7, f. 37.

17. Lamb, *Memoirs.*

18. Von Eelking, *German Allied Troops,* p. 144; Hadden, *Journal,* p. 327; Von Eelking, *Riedesel,* 2:23.

19. Von Eelking, ed., *Riedesel,* 2:1–42, for daily routine of the captured troops in Cambridge, Massachusetts.

20. Batchelder, "Burgoyne and his Officers," p. 20.

21. Heath, *Memoirs,* p. 124.

22. October 25, 1777, Heath to Hancock, Hudleston, *Burgoyne,* p. 251.

23. November 8, 1777, Heath, *Memoirs,* p. 126.

24. Ibid.

25. Heath to Burgoyne, November 11, 1777, B. L. Add. MS. 38,343, f. 138, C.O. 5.179, ff. 7–9.

26. Burgoyne to Heath, November 11, 1777, Gates papers, New-York Historical Society; B. L. Add. MS. 38,343, f. 140.

27. November 14, 1777, Burgoyne to Gates, Heath papers, Massachusetts Historical Society, vol. 7, f. 37.

28. November 14, 1777, Burgoyne to Gates, Hudleston, *Burgoyne,* p. 256, citing March, 1778, *Journal of Congress.*

29. November 11, 1777, Heath to Burgoyne, B. L. Add. MS. 38.343, f. 140.

30. November 14, 1777, Burgoyne to Gates, Heath papers, Massachusetts Historical Society, vol. 7, f. 37.

31. November 7, 1777, Heath to Colonel Chase, Heath papers, Massachusetts Historical Society, vol. 7, f. 27; November, 1777, Heath to unidentified correspondent, Hudleston, *Burgoyne,* p. 257.

32. November 14, 1777, Burgoyne to Gates, Heath papers, Massachusetts Historical Society, vol. 7, f. 37.

33. The structure was rehabilitated in 1924 to become the residence of the master of Adams House in Harvard University; Batchelder, "Cambridge," p. 30 and Pottinger, "John Burgoyne," p. 32.

34. November 10, 1777, Burgoyne to Heath, C.O. 5.179, ff. 5–6; B. L. Add. MS. 38,343, ff. 136–37.

35. November 16, 1777, "Court of Enquiry held on Colonel Henley for Maltreating Prisoners," Batchelder, "Cambridge," pp. 34–35.

36. January 13, 1778, Cleve to Schlozer, Batchelder, "Cambridge," p. 34, note 4.

37. April 8, 1777, Massachusetts Archives 213/170 file, November, cited by Batchelder, "Cambridge," p. 33.

38. November 18, 1777, Burgoyne to Heath, C.O. 5.179, ff. 25–26 and B. L. Add. MS. 38,343, f. 148; same to same, November [19?] 1777, C.O.5.179, ff. 27–28 and B. L. Add. MS. 38,343, ff. 149–50.

39. November 5, 1777, Tatum, ed., *Serle,* p. 263.

40. November 16, 1777, Howe to Burgoyne, Jane Clark, "The Convention Troops and the Perfidy of Sir William Howe," *American Historical Review* 37:721–23.

41. November 23, 1777, Henry Laurens to Gates, Laurens papers, South Carolina Historical Society.

42. December 3, 1777, Gates to Laurens, Gates papers, New-York Historical Society.

43. December 20, 1777, Washington to Burgoyne, C.O. 5.179, ff. 65–66.

44. January 4, 1778, Burgoyne to Pigot, C.O. 5.179, ff. 345–46 and P.R.O. 30.55.7, f. 839, pp. 1–2.

45. January 4, 1778, message from Burgoyne, P.R.O. 30.55.7, f. 839, pp. 3–4.

46. January 5, 1778, Heath to Burgoyne, C.O. 5.179, ff. 79–80 and P.R.O. 30.55.7, f. 841, pp. 1–2; Heath, *Memoirs,* pp. 135–36.

47. January 15, 1778, Heath to Burgoyne, B. L. Add. MS. 38,343, f. 164.

48. January 16, 1778, Heath to Burgoyne, B. L. Add. MS. 38,343, f. 165, and C.O. 5.179, ff. 143–44.

49. January 17, 1778, Clarke to Burgoyne, P.R.O. 30.55.8, f. 883.

50. January 17, 1778, Burgoyne to Heath, C.O. 5.179, ff. 145–46, and B. L. Add. MS. 38,343, f. 166.

51. January 9, 1778, Burgoyne to Heath, C.O. 5.179, ff. 104–05.

52. Ibid.

53. Ibid.

54. January 10, 1778, Heath to Burgoyne, C.O. 5.179, nos. 107–8, 110; Heath, *Memoirs,* pp. 139–41.

55. Heath, *Memoirs,* pp. 139–41.

56. January 12, 1778, Burgoyne to Heath, C.O. 5.179, f. 126; B. L. Add. MS. 38,343, ff. 154–55.

57. January 10, 1778, General Orders, Heath, *Memoirs,* p. 141; January 13, 1778, Heath to Burgoyne, B. L. Add. MS. 38,343, f. 156, C.O. 5.179, ff. 119–20.

58. January 14, 1778, Robert Kingston, B. L. Add. MS. 38,343, ff. 159–60 and C.O. 5.179, ff. 129–30.

59. January 18, 1778, Parole, Headquarters, B. L. Add. MS. 38,343, f. 167 and C.O. 5.179, ff. 147–48.

60. Hudleston, *Burgoyne*, p. 274.

61. February 27, 1778, Heath, *Memoirs*, p. 143. Burgoyne's antics during the Henley trial may have inspired George Bernard Shaw to write his fictionalized drama *The Devil's Disciple: A Melodrama. Being the First of Three Plays for Puritans* (London: Grant Richards, 1901).

62. January 9, 1778, Burgoyne to Heath, C.O. 5.179, ff. 104–5; Heath, *Memoirs*, pp. 138–39. The Reverend Samuel Cooper described Burgoyne's participation in the trial: "he exhibited himself, Iam Mercurio quam Marte. I could have pity'd him, had it not been for the cruelty with which he invaded us." June 1, 1778, Cooper to Benjamin Franklin, American Philosophical Society. The author thanks Dr. John Buchanan for bringing this manuscript to his attention.

63. January 10, 1778, Heath to Burgoyne, C.O. 5.179, f. 110.

64. January 13, 1778, Heath to Burgoyne, C.O. 5.179, ff. 119–20.

65. January 13, 1778, Burgoyne to Heath, C.O. 5.179, ff. 121–24 and B. L. Add. MS. 38,343, ff. 157–58.

66. Ibid.

67. Ibid.

68. Hudleston, *Burgoyne*, p. 288.

69. Ibid.

70. Ibid.

71. January 18, 1778, Burgoyne to William Howe, P.R.O. 30.55.8, f. 887; C.O. 5.179, ff. 353–54.

72. January 26, 1778, Burgoyne to Richard Howe, C.O. 5.179, ff. 367–68; January 26, 1778, Burgoyne to Pigot, C.O. 5.179, ff. 369–70.

73. January 15, 1778, Burgoyne to Heath, C.O. 5.179, ff. 139–40 and P.R.O. 30.55.8, f. 873, pp. 1–2.

74. January 14, 1778, Heath to Burgoyne, B. L. Add. MS. 38,343, f. 161 and C.O. 5.179, ff. 133–34.

75. January 18, 1778, Burgoyne to William Howe, P.R.O. 3.55.8, f. 887; C.O. 5.179, ff. 353–54.

76. January 19, 1778, Heath to Burgoyne, C.O. 5.179, ff. 151–52 and B. L. Add. MS. 38,343, f. 169.

77. November 5, 1777, Washington to Heath, Fitzpatrick, ed., *Writings*, 10:10.

78. January 2, 1778, Witherspoon Speech, Edmund C. Burnett, ed., *Letters of Members of the Continental Congress*, 8 vols. (Washington, D.C.: The Carnegie Institution of Washington, 1921–36), 3:5–9; January 8, 1778, Congressional Resolution, Ford, ed., *Journals of the Continental Congress*, 10:34–35.

79. February 4, 1778, Heath to Burgoyne, C.O. 5.179, ff. 173–74.

80. January 8, 1778, "Resolves of the Congress," C.O. 5.179, ff. 175–86; Ford, ed., *Journals*, 10:34–35.

81. January 8, 1778, "Resolves of the Congress," C.O. 5.179, ff. 175–86.

82. Hudleston, *Burgoyne*, pp. 257–58, 260.

83. February 11, 1778, Burgoyne to Henry Laurens, C.O. 5.179, ff. 187–94; and P.R.O. 30.55.8, f. 933, pp. 1–9.

84. February 4, 1778, Burgoyne to Heath, C.O. 5.179, ff. 207–08.

85. February 5, 1778, William Howe to Washington, P.R.O. 30.55.8, f. 929, pp. 1–4, and C.O. 5.179, ff. 357–60.

86. February 5, 1778, William Howe to Burgoyne, P.R.O. 30.55.8, f. 928.

87. January 22, 1778, Washington to Heath, Hudleston, *Burgoyne*, p. 279 and note.

88. February 11, 1778, Burgoyne to Henry Laurens, C.O. 5.179, ff. 203–4, P.R.O. 30.55.8, f. 937, pp. 1–4. Burgoyne also wrote to Washington on the subject.

89. Von Eelking, *Riedesel,* 2:15–16.

90. February 11, 1778, Burgoyne to Laurens, C.O. 5.179, ff. 203–4, P.R.O. 30.55.8, f. 937, pp. 1–4.

91. March 3, 1778, "In Congress," B. L. Add. MS. 38,343, f. 190.

92. March 5, 1778, Gates to Burgoyne, Hudleston, *Burgoyne,* pp. 330–31.

93. March 4, 1778, Dalrymple to Burgoyne, C.O. 5.179, ff. 373–74; Heath, *Memoirs,* p. 145.

94. March, 8, 1778, Burgoyne to Heath, B. L. Add. MS. 38,343, f. 176. March 8, 1778, Heath to Burgoyne, C.O. 5.179, ff. 229–30.

95. March 9, 1778, Heath to Burgoyne, C.O. 5.179, ff. 235–36.

96. March 9, 1778, Burgoyne to Dalrymple, C.O. 5.179, ff. 375–76.

97. March 15, 1778, Dalrymple to Burgoyne, C.O. 5.179, ff. 377–78.

98. March 16, 1778, Heath to Burgoyne, C.O. 5.179, ff. 237–38; March 16, 1778, Heath to Burgoyne, C.O. 5.179, ff. 238–39.

99. Ibid.

100. March 16, 1778, Richard Howe to Burgoyne, C.O. 5.179, ff. 281–82.

101. March 17, 1778, Warrant to Search the Barracks, C.O. 5.179, ff. 239–40; March 17, 1778, Heath to Keith, B. L. Add. MS. 38.343, ff. 181–82; March 18, 1778, Heath to Burgoyne, B. L. Add. MS. 38,343, f. 184, C.O. 5.179, ff. 246–47.

102. March 17, 1778, Heath to Keith; also C.O. 5.179, f. 241.

103. March 18, 1778, Burgoyne to Heath, B. L. Add. MS. 38,343, f. 185 and C.O. 5.179, ff. 247–48.

104. March 27, 1778, Burgoyne to Heath, C.O. 5.179, ff. 280–81.

105. April 2, 1778, C.O. 5.179, ff. 295–96; Return of Provisions, B. L. Add. MS. 38,343, f. 204.

106. April 9, 1778, Burgoyne to Howe, W.O. 34.110, f. 191.

107. April 17, 1778, Charles Lee to Henry Laurens, *Lee Papers,* 2:389–90.

108. See below, chapter 19.

109. Burgoyne's physical condition was not good; he was suffering from recurrence of stomach gout. See April 9, 1778, Burgoyne to Clinton, Clinton papers, Clements Library.

110. Detailed criticism of Burgoyne had been circulating in London since news of his defeat had arrived; January 12, 1778, Hans Stanley to A. S. Hammond, accession no. 4390, Manuscripts Department, University of Virginia Library, Charlottesville.

19

Recriminations

After yet another uneventful journey, his last Atlantic crossing, Burgoyne landed at Portsmouth in mid-May 1778,[1] and shortly thereafter appeared in London.[2] His arrival was anticipated, for William Howe alerted Germain late in April that Burgoyne had been released.[3] Burgoyne conferred with the secretary of state for two hours, during which time Germain informed him that he could not have an audience with the king until he had appeared at a parliamentary inquiry and court-martial.[4] Immediately after the interview, Germain advised the king to ask Jeffrey, Lord Amherst, the commander in chief, whether Burgoyne could be placed under arrest.[5] Amherst proceeded to locate suitable precedents, and he established guidelines for a court of inquiry. He referred to Viscount Barrington, secretary at war, and the names of General Thomas Gage, General Jeffrey Amherst, the earl of Loudoun, and General Robert Moncton, whom the king had nominated to serve on the board of inquiry.[6] He also instructed Lord Suffolk, secretary of state, to issue a warrant for Burgoyne's arrest.[7] Suffolk forwarded the warrant to the war office.[8] However, Barrington refused to dispatch the order since he did not have in his possession the papers pertinent to the expedition, nor did he comprehend all of the complexities of the investigation that the cabinet wanted to have conducted. Consequently, Barrington requested Amherst to present only a draft of the warrant before the cabinet for consideration.[9] Amherst agreed to do so, and the cabinet approved the draft.[10] Thus, by May 1778 the government appeared to be determined to arrest Burgoyne for court-martial and parliamentary investigation.

Meanwhile, Burgoyne encountered difficulty concerning his right, or lack thereof, to sit in the commons. The general, settled once again into his town house in Mayfair, told Germain that he intended to return to Parliament before appearing at the court of inquiry,[11] and he did so, much to the amusement of Horace Walpole:

> The event of yesterday was the apparition of General Burgoyne in the House of Commons. It was literally so in the strict sense of the term; for as spectres, you know, cannot speak unless they are spoken to, and as nobody adjured it in the name of the Father, Son and Holy to say what it was, it stalked out

again, and did not disburthen its mind. I suppose the assembly was a little terrified, for there is no learning certainly whether the weapon it seemed to have by its side was a sword or a cutlass. *Phantasmato* critics are divided whether a ghost that leaves its prison-house is entitled to seem to wear either.[12]

Indeed, there was considerable speculation whether Burgoyne ought to have been seated in the house, for the general's status as a prisoner of war was still unclear.

On May 20, in an attempt to clarify the issue, Barrington sent to Charles Gould, judge advocate general of the Army, a draft of a warrant authorizing an inquiry.[13] Upon receipt of the notice, Gould immediately wrote to Burgoyne, informing him of the purpose of the inquiry.[14] Gould also called the committee members into session for May 22.[15] The judge advocate asked Burgoyne whether he had been given parole previous to his departure from America.[16] The general replied that he had never been considered a prisoner of war:

I hold myself a free man in every circumstance except that I am restricted by the Convention of Saratoga, not to serve in America during the War; with this further Parole on my leaving America that should the embarkation of the convention troops be by any means prolonged beyond the time apprehended I will return to America upon demand, and due notice given by Congress and will redeliver myself into the power of Congress unless regularly ex-changed.[17]

Burgoyne's reply prodded the committee to ask the king whether the inquiry should proceed, considering the circumstances which Burgoyne brought to their attention. The committee declared that if the inquiry continued while Burgoyne remained on parole, it could tend, however remotely, "to restrain, or affect his Person," and it could also affect the well-being of Burgoyne's troops in America.[18] The king informed Gould, who in turn notified Burgoyne, that he found it expedient to postpone the inquiry, "though unwillingly," until a more suitable time, and he therefore discharged the officers from further proceedings.[19] Thus, because Burgoyne was returned to England "by the permission of Congress"—which the British government did not recognize as a legal entity—he could not receive a hearing. The king's summons was therefore quashed. Gould's frequent consultation with Germain in his office is sufficient evidence of the secretary of state's influence upon the course of events. It was Germain who wished to dissolve the investigation.[20]

The ministry had won the first round. Burgoyne's friends, however, were victorious in their attempts to keep him in the House of Commons. Although Alexander Wedderburn, the solicitor general, objected that Burgoyne was a prisoner on parole and therefore had no right to attend Parliament, others defended the general, and the house voted against Wedderburn's ruling.[21] Burgoyne was still discontent, however, because the king had dissolved the board of inquiry. He continued to demand the right to answer all questions concerning his conduct.[22] On May 26, it appeared that he had a second opportunity. Charles Vyner moved that the house resolve itself into a committee of the whole in order to consider the terms of the Saratoga convention. John Wilkes quickly seconded the motion, which Charles Fox amended so that all transactions of the expedition might properly be considered within the purview of the committee. The motion passed.

During the course of the ensuing debate, Burgoyne spoke at great length concerning virtually all the controversies surrounding his conduct of the army, a speech that he thought sufficiently significant to have published.[23] Burgoyne defended his decision to use Indians for the expedition, and he denied that he regulated them improperly: despite every effort on his part to restrain them, the Indians continued to plunder, and accidents occurred, most notably the murder of Jane McCrea. However, he was not responsible for such unfortunate occurrences, and in fact La Corne St. Luc continually opposed his attempts to discipline the Indians. St. Luc was certainly not Burgoyne's friend. However, the general wished him to testify at the bar of the house. Burgoyne himself wrote the "Indian Proclamation," which, he said, gained him respect and acknowledgment, not scorn.

Burgoyne denied charges that he wantonly burned the countryside. He recalled only one order to destroy colonial property, General Schuyler's house in Saratoga, valued at ten thousand pounds. Burgoyne contended that he had to burn it for strategic reasons. Schuyler himself acknowledged the correctness of Burgoyne's decision, although other Americans were not so easily convinced, especially after the expedition ended. Burgoyne had prepared a report concerning the convention troops, but it was so voluminous that three of Germain's clerks had not yet digested it. He expected to present it to the public shortly, since he felt obliged to make known his unjust treatment by Congress. It was true that large numbers of his army deserted during his confinement in Boston, but those were honorable desertions. From five hundred to six hundred soldiers left his force, in obedience to the general's order to join Howe or Clinton, Burgoyne maintained.

Burgoyne defended the strategy of the expedition. He had no objection to the plan for 1777 as it was originally proposed. But the later plan was not his; the clause permitting the commander latitude had been erased. Germain knew that such was the case, but he refused to present to the House the orders in their changed and "garbled" state, because they would have been proof that the elimination of latitude confined the plan to one object: "the *forcing* a passage to Albany."[24] In the final form, therefore, the orders could only be understood "as positive, peremptory, and indispensable." Burgoyne denied that a "saving clause" existed, as some critics maintained. "Saving to whom?" the general asked. He argued that the order to act "as exigencies may require" had to be interpreted within the context of other instructions. Suppose, he said, his exigency was such that he had to abandon communication and risk retreat.

What would have been said of him? Was such a decision a vigorous exertion to force his way to Albany? Were not the American troops inferior? Were not thousands of loyalists and Henry Clinton waiting to help him? He would have been condemned for inactivity and cowardice; he would have lost the campaign ignominiously. If the order to act as exigencies required were interpreted another way, such that he was forced to follow the spirit and the letter of the order, he would have been required to contest each inch of ground and would have miscarried. Then he would be disgraced for rashness. Such an interpretation was equally unacceptable; no minister would have intended that; it would have been "the equivocation of a fiend." The saving clause as understood by Burgoyne, Howe, and everyone who read it at the time it was penned was interpreted "as referring solely to exigencies after the arrival of my army at Albany." Thus, charges that Burgoyne did not avail himself of the saving clause were meaningless.

Burgoyne dismissed other accusations, including the "malevolent story" that Phillips and Fraser urged him not to cross the Hudson. Both officers were very loyal, he declared, and thought Burgoyne's decision to cross the Hudson "a glorious danger." Branding the story an "abominable falsehood," he disputed other charges of mismanagement as well. Denying that his baggage train was "a merit of Eastern pomp," Burgoyne stated that Phillips was consulted in the matter of the artillery, which he said never delayed the progress of the army.

Finally, Burgoyne exclaimed, he returned to England to discover ministerial machinations which "almost unhinged" his faculties. Some of the papers presented to the House of Commons were "deficient and superfluous," the general maintained, while others were misleading. Germain released Burgoyne's letter of December 1776, filled with professions of respect for the secretary of state. Some people interpreted statements in that letter as attempts by Burgoyne to displace Carleton for the 1777 expedition, but, the general declared, that question had been resolved in August 1776. Why did Germain not release other letters, in which Burgoyne described Carleton as a "gallant friend," he asked. Obviously the ministry sought to discredit him in every imaginable way; now, Burgoyne concluded, he was barred from the king's presence and denied an investigation. Burgoyne formally demanded a hearing: "Give me inquiry; I put the interests that hang most emphatically upon the heartstrings of men, my fortune, my honour, my head, I had almost said my salvation, upon the test."[25]

Burgoyne's speech was well received. A member moved for inquiry, which Burgoyne rather dramatically seconded himself. However, Germain and several of his colleagues again tried to forestall such an investigation, at which point Temple Luttrell attacked the secretary of state in a bitter, personal diatribe:

> General Burgoyne was a gallant officer, whose only crime had been that he was too zealous. . . . Had he on the contrary *receded from his colours,*

disobeyed the commands of his superiors, and hid himself from danger, such conduct would have given him pretensions to the patronage of the First Lord of the Treasury, and the honours and emoluments of the American Secretaryship.[26]

In response, Germain demanded a duel, and both men were immediately placed in the custody of the sergeant at arms until their tempers subsided.[27]

Two days later, Burgoyne spoke in support of David Hartley's motion not to prorogue Parliament.[28] During the course of his speech, Burgoyne attacked the government:

That I think myself a persecuted man I avow; that I am a marked victim to bear the sins that do not belong to me I apprehend; but this is not the first time that I have dared the frowns of power for parliamentary conduct, and whatever further vengeance may be in store for me I hope I shall endure it as becomes me. I am aware that in far better times officers have been stripped of their preferment for resisting the possessors of that bench. They cannot take from me a humble competence; they cannot deprive me of a qualification to sit here; they cannot, I trust they cannot strip me of the confidence of my constituents who placed me here; they cannot, I am sure they cannot, strip me of principle and spirit to do my duty here.[29]

There was some truth in Burgoyne's charge of persecution, for the committee of inquiry did not meet, and Parliament was prorogued as scheduled. On June 5, the fullness of Germain's plan became evident. The secretary at war sent to Burgoyne a letter that Amherst had ghostwritten and that the cabinet had approved:[30]

The King, judging your presence material to the Troops detained Prisoners in New England under the Convention of Saratoga, and finding in a letter of yours to Sir William Howe dated 9th April 1778 "that you trust a short time at Bath will enable you to return to America," His Majesty is pleased to order that you shall repair to Boston as soon as you have [tried] the Bath Waters in the manner you propose.[31]

Such an order by a government to a general was virtually unprecedented in English history. Burgoyne replied to the letter two weeks later while he was staying at Knowsley.[32] He disputed Barrington's reference to his letter to Howe in which he expressed a desire to return to the service—or, as Barrington interpreted it, to "return to America." Burgoyne explained that he had written the letter to Howe "in the fulness of zeal" and although he retained the appearance of health, "much care is still wanting to restore me to my former state." Furthermore, Burgoyne doubted the captured army in America would benefit from the return of a disgraced officer. He could not understand why the troops would believe their return imminent because someone had advised the king "of so harsh an act as sending an infirm, calumnated, unheard complainant across the Atlantic merely to inspect the embarkation." But Burgoyne's weightiest argument, he believed, concerned the vindication of his honor. Until he had been given the opportunity to a fair trial, the general would consider an order to return to America "the severest sentence of exile ever imposed." In conclusion, he offered to resign all his commissions.

Barrington read the letter, drafted a reply, and consulted Amherst,[33] who urged Barrington to assure Burgoyne "as early a Trial as the circumstances of your Situation will admit of." However, Amherst warned that Burgoyne clearly disobeyed the king's order of June 5, and therefore the trial ought to be a court-martial for "neglect of duty & disobedience of Orders." Amherst doubted that Burgoyne seriously intended to resign before such a trial, and he advised Barrington to ask the general whether he really wished to

> *lay before the King* your resignation of the Queen's Reg[imen]t of L[igh]t Dragoons; of the Gove[r]nm[en]t of Fort W[illia]m; and of your appointment to the American Staff—I shall therefore not do it unless in answer to this Letter you shall acquaint me that such is your intention and desire.[34]

Burgoyne withheld his resignation. The king continued until June 27 to press for Burgoyne's return. Thereafter, he agreed to suspend the order temporarily and Burgoyne had ample time to prepare a justification of his conduct.[35]

During the rest of 1778 and throughout 1779, Burgoyne began to assemble material which he published in 1780 in book form as *A State of the Expedition from Canada.* He also continued to write at great length to his colleagues in government and his speeches did not diminish either in volume or verbosity. Burgoyne repeatedly urged Parliament and Congress to ratify and execute the provisions of the Saratoga convention so that his troops could return to England.[36] Addressing his constituents at Preston upon that subject and distributing two parliamentary speeches that he had published in June, Burgoyne clung to the hope that the ministry would appoint a committee to vindicate his conduct.

Burgoyne retained certain loyalties to the king and to his colleagues at court but he was becoming increasingly discontent. He had flirted with the opposition for brief periods during a long career in Parliament; he could join forces permanently with them if the ministry continued to persecute him. In September 1778 the general wrote to John Lee, a prominent lawyer and formerly solicitor general in the Rockingham administration. Burgoyne praised highly the merits of the marquis of Rockingham, who led one faction of parliamentary opposition, and he also expressed a desire to speak with Rockingham at his home in Wentworth, where Lee customarily consulted with the leader. Four days later Lee replied to Burgoyne.[37] He assured the general that he could safely visit Wentworth without fearing that his journey would be misinterpreted as a tender of political connection.[38] It is not known whether Burgoyne visited the marquis, or what conversation took place during such a meeting. However, Burgoyne continued to cultivate friendships with opposition politicians, including Charles Fox, who wrote sympathetically to Burgoyne during November 1778. "Despondency is never right," counseled Fox. Appealing to Burgoyne's ego, Fox attempted to revive the general's ambition:

> I have always thought it a miserable accusation against Cato and Brutus that they attempted to save the republic when it was too late. If it is not now too late, and I will not allow myself to think it is, I feel as sure as I can be of anything there is but one possible road to safety, and one I think there is.[39]

Fox urged Burgoyne to unite with the opposition in order to bring down the ministry. He believed that the political power that they would obtain ought to derive from the consent of the people rather than from the generosity of the king. They should unite with one common principle: "a real love for a free constitution." Burgoyne considered this advice carefully and ultimately he acted upon it.

Parliament reconvened on November 26, 1778.[40] After the king's speech and preliminary condemnations of the ministry by John Wilkes, Burgoyne launched upon an extensive and scathing denunciation of the ministers responsible for the conduct of the war.[41] Germain replied that Burgoyne had no cause for complaint; he would not be sent to American until his health improved, although "he seemed to be in perfect health."[42] Burgoyne spoke the next day, and ignored the question of his health by focusing his attack upon the decision to return him to America. That decision was a clear example of designed oppression, he felt:

> The order was in his Majesty's name, but understanding that a noble Lord [Amherst] whose virtues and abilities he held in the highest veneration and esteem, had lately been appointed to the post of commander in chief[,] he was much surprised that the order instead of coming directly from the office of the secretary at war, had not come through what he deemed the only proper channel, that of his Lordship.[43]

Burgoyne asked Amherst why the order was sent in such manner, and whether it reflected cabinet approval. Amherst, declaring that the order was sent to him by the king "or by his directions, as coming from himself," said it was his duty to transmit it to Barrington. Disclaiming responsibility for decisions concerning overseas military matters, Amherst concluded that "the affair was entirely out of his cognizance, further than to obey the King's orders." Turning to the subject of his proposed resignation, Burgoyne declared that "his fixed purpose was, in case the above conditional order had been made positive, to lay at his Majesty's feet his commissions, requesting only to retain that of lieutenant general, to enable him to fulfill his parole, or to make him answerable to a court martial." Burgoyne interpreted the second order, which he received on June

27, as merely a reaffirmation of an earlier directive. He replied to it "no further than to *acknowledge* its receipt; and should it now be made peremptory, he knew how he *ought* and *would* act, be the consequences what they might." The general again requested a hearing.

Germain "barely acknowledged" and quickly forgot about Burgoyne's reply to the order, which the general described as a cabinet transaction. Burgoyne said he was glad to learn that Germain, "on his own account, was ignorant of the answer; because if he had not it would have been a good ground, on which to impeach his veracity," and that "it would have been mean, disgraceful, and pitiful; and would have betrayed a shameful spirit of revenge in him, to be instrumental in removing a man out of the way who he knew *taxed* him with *injustice;* and between whom and his Lordship there was a *long account* to be settled before the public." Germain insisted that the orders for Burgoyne's return to America had not been his own, but had come from the cabinet, or perhaps ultimately from the king. Fox questioned the constitutionality of such an order, if indeed the king had acted without advice of council. Germain replied that he presumed the king had been advised, but not having been present at the meeting, he pleaded ignorance. Since the measure was the responsibility of the war department, Germain said he "heard no more" of it "till carried into execution . . . that in whatever manner the order originated, he was equally exempt from any censure."[44]

Shortly after Germain's summation of his defense, the Howe brothers urged the house to open an investigation, and Burgoyne proposed that the government order all of the officers of the convention troops to appear and testify in the house.[45] On February 15, 1779, Parliament met again, and the opposition resumed the assault upon ministerial policy. Barré and Burke condemned Germain for the defeat at Saratoga. In the face of continued administrative procrastination, Fox declared on March 3, "[the] Ministers have hitherto evaded everything which might lead to proofs of their guilt or innocence."[46] Three weeks later, Sir William Howe moved formally to consider the conduct of the war, and his motion carried without a division.[47] Burgoyne immediately informed Germain that he wanted "every word" of the intermediate correspondence from May 14 to October 20, 1777, delivered to the House of Commons.[48] Nevertheless, when on April 27 Howe again called for inquiry, the government supplied only some of the relevant documents.[49] Witnesses were not called, Germain refused to speak, and on the following day, in the words of Lord Pembroke, "the ministry mustered all their forces, & crushed it."[50]

On April 29, Burgoyne spoke in favor of a motion to call Cornwallis and other witnesses to Howe's campaign, and North complained to the king that Burgoyne was very long-winded in "mixing all his business with Howe."[51] Although Fox and the opposition favored the proposal, North was able to muster the support of Germain, Jenkinson, and others to defeat it. The king declared that he was glad that the House defeated the motion, although he was surprised Germain wanted the entire investigation quashed.[52] The government was not able to block Parliament's decision to appoint a select committee to investigate Howe. Sir William produced all his dispatches, proving that Germain had approved Howe's letter to Carleton on April 5 saying that he would not take responsibility for meeting or assisting Burgoyne.[53] Howe also presented Germain's letter approving in the king's name the expedition to Philadelphia and later revisions of that plan. Howe then challenged Germain to produce any dispatch ordering him to assist Burgoyne. None was forthcoming.[54] Burgoyne rose to charge ministers with the object of using him as a scapegoat to deflect attention from their own mistakes; he also accused them of "leaving officers unprotected" but at the same time "laying snares to effect their ruin." He denied that he had drawn his own instructions himself and continued to condemn Germain for not presenting the appropriate correspondence.[55]

Germain finally protested openly against Burgoyne's charges and denied that he had ever insinuated that Burgoyne was responsible for the failure of the expedition.[56] However, a few days later Rigby, a tool of the ministry, attacked Burgoyne in most acrimonious terms, charging him with the sacrifice of an army "while he himself was enjoying the luxuries of London." Burgoyne rose to condemn "the most abominable falsehoods circulated against him." He also disclosed that the government refused to permit him active service when, in 1778, he requested an opportunity to campaign against the French. Their statement that he was by that time a prisoner of war did not satisfy him. Finally on May 10 Barré moved for an investigation of the Burgoyne expedition, and it was approved without a division, despite the objections of North and Germain. Chancellor Thurlow had already taken steps to obtain evidence from under secretary of state Knox concerning the motives for the expedition, the events of the campaign, and the reason for its failure. When Knox presented him with the Colonial Office précis for 1777, Thurlow exclaimed:

"Why, this is the very thing I wanted, and you have done it already; pray, do the Ministers know of this?"

"Yes, Sir, they have all had copies of it."

"Then by God, they have never read it, for there is not one of them knows a tittle of the matter."[57]

Several days later Thurlow returned with a list of questions and comments concerning Burgoyne's expedition. He was particularly interested to know why Burgoyne employed Hessians at Bennington, and when Knox replied that Howe had done so at Trenton on the basis of military etiquette, Thurlow replied: "So, because one damn'd blockhead did a foolish thing the other blockhead must follow his example."[58]

Unaware that Thurlow and others had prepared evidence to discredit him, the general defended his conduct in a lengthy speech which he delivered on May 10, 1779. Recapitulating the events of the expedition, Burgoyne used ministerial dispatches and other letters for documentary evidence. He also called witnesses, including all the chief officers of the North American command. Although Phillips and Riedesel were still under arrest and Fraser was dead, he managed to persuade a number of other officers to testify, all of whom spoke well of his courage in battle. The general managed to create a highly favorable impression of his conduct, but Rigby, Jenkinson, and others began to clamor for prorogation, which the king (and others, angered by the spectacle of yet another inquiry) supported. Burgoyne and Thomas Townshend bitterly objected, but Parliament rose on July 3 and consequently the committee of inquiry was unable to prepare a report.[59]

General John Burgoyne, engraving by Ritchie. Reproduced by permission of the William L. Clements Library, University of Michigan.

Burgoyne's case remained unresolved.[60] However, Edmund Burke urged him to publish a vindication of his conduct in order to acquaint the public with his defense. When Burke offered to read a draft of his finished work, the general journeyed to Beaconsfield, where he revised the manuscript.[61] However, Burgoyne had yet to confront a second attempt to spirit him out of the country. On September 4, Amherst asked Jenkinson for a copy of Burgoyne's letter to Barrington of June 5, 1778, and three weeks later he sent Jenkinson a proposed draft of a new letter to Burgoyne, who was to be informed that "your not returning to America, and joining the Troops[62] . . . is considered as a neglect of duty and disobedience of Orders transmitted to you by the Secretary at War in his Letter of the 5th of June 1778."[63] At last the government had forced his hand, and on October 9 Burgoyne had to choose either to return to America or to resign all his appointments. He chose the latter alternative, for reasons he expressed to Jenkinson in a statement later revised and published as a letter to his constituents.[64] Rather than neglect of duty, Burgoyne explained, he had remained in England to vindicate his honor from barbarous attacks. He noted that the conditional order of June 5 left to Burgoyne's own judgment a decision to return to America; consequently, he could not understand the charge of disobedience. Nor did he comprehend how the British government could legally order a British subject into captivity without trial. "On pretence of Military Obedience," he concluded, "I am ordered to the only part of the World where I can do no Military Service . . . . An Enemy's Prison is not the King's Garrison nor is anything to be done or suffered there any part of an Officer's duty." Burgoyne said he could interpret the letter only as a dismissal. He requested either a trial, restoration to active duty, or acceptance of his resignation.

On the same day, Burgoyne wrote to Germain and repeated the arguments which he had previously stated.[65] He demanded the justice and generosity due from all governments to those who served them. If he received a peremptory order to return to America, Burgoyne wrote, he would resign all of his commissions except that of lieutenant general. In a burst of passionate anger, he attacked the secretary personally: *"There are many accounts to settle between your Lordship and me before the tribunals of the world; I give you this notice of one particularly intended:* I am persuaded you will not willingly conspire to remove a man who thinks you have injured him; you will not willingly decline to face an inquiry into your duty to the State." Burgoyne sent a similar letter to Jenkinson on October 10,[66] and two days later Jenkinson sent Amherst a draft of his reply. "It may perhaps be supposed" he wrote, "that Gen[eral] Burgoyne by the words *early Trial* does not mean an immediate trial, and to take him at his Word & accept his Resignation because he cannot have an immediate trial is more than he intended & is therefore using him ill."[67] Amherst told the king that acceptance of the resignation would be "severe useage."[68] However, George III thought otherwise:

The whole tenour of Lieut[enant]-Gen[eral] Burgoyne's conduct since his return from America has been so very contrary to military obedience, that I am very far from clear what lenient measures He has left me room to employ without a total subversion of all Military Discipline . . . . [The Secretary at War's Letter] must be looked upon as waste paper if no mark of rigour attends so Attorney like an Epistle as the Answer the Lieut[enant] Gen[eral] has sent to it.[69]

The king declared that he had no further opinion until Amherst informed him what the cabinet thought after perusing "the very indecent Answer which has been sent to the Secretary at War when writing by my command." The cabinet's reaction was predictable, and on October 15 Jenkinson told Burgoyne that "His Majesty considers your Letter to me as a Proof of your Determination to persevere in not obeying His Orders. . . . And for this Reason His Majesty is pleased to Accept your Resignation."[70] After two days of stunned silence, Burgoyne acknowledged receipt of the letter, retorting "that I was refused a Court Martial on that Disobedience, for my perseverance in which, you tell me, my Resignation is accepted."[71] Claiming again the right to a court-martial, he argued "that if I am not subject to a Trial for Breach of Orders, it implies that I am not subject to the Orders themselves." He cited others who were given further appointments although their circumstances were similar to Burgoyne's. Jenkinson replied noncommittally on October 22, saying that he took the first opportunity to present Burgoyne's reply to the king.[72] On the same day, Colonel Harcourt took command of Burgoyne's regiment of dragoons.[73]

The general sought escape, attending a farce and dinner with Richard Sheridan.[74] Word of his ultimate humiliation spread rapidly although Burgoyne received sympathy from Frederick, Lord Cavendish, who told Countess Spencer that Burgoyne's case had "some reasoning in it."[75] He sent his recently concluded correspondence with government to Rockingham, claiming pathetically that he had followed the impulse of honor.[76] On November 9, he sent a letter to his constituents announcing his resignation, and explaining the reasons for it.[77] An anonymous pamphleteer replied to the "Letter," censuring the general, who was "not exactly fitted to parliamentary debate."[78] Praising his bravery and honor, the writer said that Burgoyne was also imprudent, "and most an enemy to yourself." Here was a critic who understood the general. Burgoyne, he said, pretended to find in his orders *as positive a direction as any Cabinet ever framed,* maintaining that such orders compelled him to rashness and imprudence. Another "Letter" to Burgoyne written late in 1779 by "an Englishman," was less kindly.[79] The author condemned the general for mistakes in judgment during the course of the campaign and ridiculed his negotiation after defeat with leaders of a revolution.

Horace Walpole joined the chorus of ridicule when Burgoyne's letter to his constituents appeared in print. He told Lady Ossory that Dr. Johnson was expected to answer Burgoyne, "and they say the words are to be so long that the reply must be printed in a pamphlet as large as an atlas, but in an Elzevir type, or the first sentence would fill twenty pages in octavo."[80] Two days later Walpole told Mason that Burgoyne "flatters himself that everybody will forget their own sorrows to be occupied with his. I will allow Lord Gower and Lord Weymouth to be mightily touched for him, but beg to be excused myself. I cannot forget how ready he was to be a great favourite."[81]

The resignation left Burgoyne in "contented poverty," or so he recalled at a later date, although he was forced to borrow money from Nathaniel Day, formerly his commissary in Canada during the 1777 expedition. He also had ample time to work on his book, published in 1780 as *A State of the Expedition from Canada*. The volume, however shaped to Burgoyne's advantage, is a valuable historical document, for the general included much original material, especially the bulk of the correspondence for the 1777 expedition. Burgoyne was apparently unaware that some of the letters he published did not strengthen his defense. Burgoyne also wrote another play, *The Lord of the Manor*, the plot of which he took from Marmontel's *Silvain*. It was written, he said, "to relax a mind which has been engaged in more intense application." William Jackson of Exeter, an artist of great reputation, composed the music, all of which was original. In the preface, Burgoyne declared that his object was to make comic opera familiar on the English stage. One historian called it an improvement on *The Beggar's Opera* in that the music was original, although the Lord Chamberlain did not like all of it; he censored those portions that ridiculed the British army. Burgoyne's characters had fanciful, humorous names: Captain Trepan, Sergeant Crimp, Corporal Snap, and Moll Flagon. One passage, a critic observed, may have been intended as a tribute to Lady Charlotte:

> Encompassed in an angel's frame,
>   As angel's virtues lay,
> Too soon did heaven assert its claim
>   To call its own away.[82]

In 1780 Burgoyne also devoted much time to strengthening his friendships among opposition members of Parliament, and the Gordon Riots of that year gave Burgoyne an opportunity to be of assistance to Burke. When a mob threatened to destroy Burke's home, the opposition leader hurriedly removed his papers while a contingent of soldiers guarded the building and ultimately saved it from destruction. The following day, when Burke removed his books and furniture, Burgoyne invited him and his wife to stay temporarily at his home in Hertford Street.[83]

The year was a turbulent one in politics, for the king decided to hold new elections. Although John Fenton ran in opposition to Burgoyne for the seat at Preston, Fenton was defeated and lost an appeal to Parliament.[84]

Burgoyne's status as a prisoner on parole was finally resolved in 1781. Although the British government never ratified the convention of Saratoga, Congress passed a resolution on April 3, 1781, ordering Burgoyne and other officers who were absent on parole to return to America. In July, Burgoyne learned of that decision, which was apparently provoked by British treatment of Henry Laurens in the Tower of London.[85] Burgoyne realized that the North ministry would be only too happy to return him to America. He appealed for advice to the duchess of Choiseul and to Burke, who advised Burgoyne to ask the American army for either an immediate exchange or for his discharge.[86] John Lee and Charles Fox also favored that plan, and Burgoyne accepted their judgment.[87] Burke then wrote on Burgoyne's behalf to Benjamin Franklin, formerly a friend and correspondent, who addressed Burke as a philosopher and friend of mankind.[88] In his reply, which was delayed six months in transit, Franklin declared that Congress did not intend to persecute Burgoyne and that Franklin had already been designated a negotiator to exchange Laurens for the British general. However, Burke realized that such a procedure would require approval of the ministry, which he distrusted.[89] Franklin's plan was not implemented.

In November, Sir Henry Clinton inquired about the exchange of both Lord Cornwallis and Burgoyne in a letter to Jenkinson, who replied that he had given Germain control of that task. Burgoyne and Burke realized that they could expect no satisfaction from the secretary, who, Burke feared, would give Cornwallis priority, since the news from Yorktown had just arrived in London. Consequently, Burke visited Henry Laurens in the Tower because he was convinced that the officers there were mistreating their prisoner, and on December 3 told the House of Commons that he intended to bring the case of Laurens to public attention. Although the ministry challenged Burke to prove his contention, at the same time they announced that the exchange for Burgoyne was being negotiated.[90]

Still distrustful, Burke continued to explore new strategies. On December 17, he presented to the Commons a petition written by Laurens, who claimed mistreatment. Burke cited the cases of both Laurens and Burgoyne as justification for designing a new bill to regulate more carefully procedures of exchange.[91] He also discussed his correspondence with Franklin, and in conclusion demanded that the government exchange Laurens for Burgoyne. However, the ministry ignored Burke's request and decided to exchange Burgoyne for the less well-known General William Moultrie and 1,047 officers and soldiers. It was a humiliation for Burgoyne, who had expected to be exchanged for a prominent American officer.[92] On January 14, 1782, American Major Abraham Skinner wrote from Elizabeth, New Jersey, to propose formally to British officer Joshua Loring the exchange of Burgoyne.[93] General Henry Clinton directed Loring to ratify the proposal and on February 9, Loring did so.[94]

It was Germain's last move, for the colonial secretary finally retired on February 11, 1782, rewarded by a grateful government and seated in the House of Lords as Viscount Sackville. Less than a month later, on March 27, 1782, the North ministry collapsed and the king appointed Lord Rockingham prime minister.

Notes

1. May 12–19, 1777, *London Chronicle.* It is possible that Charles Fox intercepted Burgoyne at Hounslow, hoping to persuade him to join the parliamentary opposition; DeFonblanque, *Episodes*, p. 351, note 2.

2. Hutchinson, ed., *Diary*, 2:205; May 15, 1778, Burgoyne to Germain, Germain papers, Clements Library.

3. April 19, 1778, Howe to Germain, P.R.O. 30.55.10, f. 1108, pp. 1–4.

4. May 13, 1778, Germain to the king, Fortescue, ed., *Correspondence*, 4:141; letter of Burgoyne to the king enclosed.

5. May 14, 1778, Amherst to the king, ibid., 4:142.

6. May 14, 1778, Amherst to Barrington, W.O. 1.616, ff. 69–72.

7. May 14, 1778, Amherst to Suffolk, W.O. 34.226b, f. 39.

8. May 15, 1778, Barrington to Amherst, W.O. 1.616, ff. 65–68.

9. Ibid.

10. May 15, 1778, Amherst to Barrington, W.O. 1.616, ff. 73–76; May 16, 1778, same to same, W.O. 1.616, ff. 89–92.

11. May 18, 1778, Burgoyne to Germain, Historical Manuscripts Commission, *Stopford-Sackville MSS.*, 2:110.

12. May 19, 1778, Walpole to Lady Ossory, Walpole, *Correspondence*, 33:12–13.

13. May 20, 1778, Barrington to Gould, B.L. Add. MS. 38,343, ff. 119–20.

14. May 21, 1778, Gould to Burgoyne, W.O. 81.13.

15. May 21, 1778, Gould to Loudoun, W.O. 81.13, f. 190.

16. May 22, 1778, Burgoyne to Gould, W.O. 70.11, ff. 35–36.

17. Ibid.

18. May 23, 1778, Loudoun, Moncton, Gage, Amherst and Morris to the king, W.O. 30.1–4, f. 74.

19. May 23, 1778, Gould to Burgoyne, W.O. 81.13, ff. 193–94; *Annual Register*, 1778, 21:196*.

20. May 26, 1778, Gould to Knox, C.O. 5.168, ff. 163–66.

21. May 28, 1778, "Note, reflecting the Second debate," Burgoyne, *Substance.*

22. May 22, 1778, Burgoyne to Speaker of the House of Commons, DeFonblanque, *Episodes*, p. 352, note 1.

23. Burgoyne, *Substance.* See also Cobbett, *Parliamentary History*, 19:1178–95.

24. Burgoyne, *Substance*, p. 22.

25. Burgoyne, *Substance*, p. 22. See also May 26, 1778, "Notes on General Burgoyne's Speech to the House of Commons," Historical Manuscripts Commission, *Stopford-Sackville MSS.*, 2:110–15.

26. DeFonblanque, *Episodes*, p. 354.

27. Ibid., note 1.

28. Ibid., p. 356.

29. May 28, 1778, Burgoyne, *Substance*, pp. 34–42; Cobbett, *Parliamentary History*, 19:1210–14, 1216–17, 1274.

30. June 4, 1778, Barrington to Amherst, W.O. 34.226A, f. 177; June 5, 1778, Barrington to Amherst, W.O. 34.226B, f. 177.

31. June 5, 1778, Barrington to Burgoyne, W.O. 34.110, f. 192.

32. June 22, 1778, Burgoyne to Barrington, W.O. 1.1001, ff. 7–12.

33. June 26, 1778, Amherst to Barrington, W.O. 1.1001, ff. 15–18, and B.L. Add. MS. 38,210, f. 65.

34. June 26, 1778, Barrington to Burgoyne, including marginal revisions, B.L. Add. MS. 38,210, f. 64; June 27, 1778, Barrington to Burgoyne, B.L. Add. MS. 38,210, f. 68, amendations, clause B, B.L. Add. MS. 38,210, f. 63 and clause C, f. 66. The quotation is taken from June 27,

1778, Barrington to Burgoyne, B.L. Add. MS. 38,210, f. 68. The italicized words are crossed out of the final draft.

35. July 8, 1778, Amherst to Barrington, W.O. 1.616, ff. 105–8. Amherst sent Barrington's letter to Burgoyne, which had been written on June 27, to the king, along with Burgoyne's noncommittal reply on the twenty-ninth (Burgoyne to Barrington, W.O. 1.1001, ff. 21–24), "on which the King did not give any particular commands. . . ." The ministry decided to retain Burgoyne on the North American staff for the moment; November 14, 1778, Barrington to Germain, C.O. 5.168, ff. 303–6.

36. In September, 1778, Clinton still in America, reproached Congress for a breach of good faith concerning the convention; Congress replied that "Congress makes no answer to insolent letters," ibid., p. 320, note 1.

37. September 14, 1778, Burgoyne to John Lee, noted in Lee's letter of the eighteenth, printed in DeFonblanque, *Episodes*, pp. 363–65.

38. September 18, 1778, John Lee to Burgoyne, ibid., pp. 363–65.

39. November 2, 1778, Fox to Burgoyne, DeFonblanque, *Episodes*, pp. 367–71, quotation, p. 369.

40. November 26, 1778, *Parliamentary Register*, 11:29.

41. November 26, 1778, Burgoyne's speech, ibid., 11:48–50.

42. November 26, 1778, Germain's reply, ibid., 11:49–50.

43. November 26, 1778, Burgoyne's reply, ibid., 11:70–75.

44. November 27, 1778, Germain's reply, ibid., 11:77–80.

45. December 14, 1778, ibid., pp. 158, 169.

46. Ibid., p. 169.

47. February 15, 1779, ibid., 241–42. Howe also called for witnesses, and although North voted against that motion, it passed 77 to 66; ibid., 684. March 29, 1779, North to the king, Fortescue, ed., *Correspondence*, 4:314–16.

48. March 31, 1779, Burgoyne to Thomas Dagredy, C.O. 5.182, ff. 115–18.

49. April 27, 1779, Pembroke to Coxe, Sidney C. Herbert, ed. [Lord Pembroke], *Henry, Elizabeth and George, 1734–80: Letters and Diaries of Henry, Tenth Earl of Pembroke, and his aide* (London, Cape, 1939), 176.

50. Ibid.

51. April 30, 1779, North to the king, Fortescue, ed., *Correspondence*, 4:330–32.

52. April 30, 1779, the king to North, ibid., 4:332–33.

53. "Howe's Narrative before a Select Committee," C.O. 5.94, f. 299.

54. Ibid.

55. DeFonblanque, *Episodes*, p. 373.

56. Cobbett, ed., *Parliamentary History*, 20:714–15, 801–2.

57. May 8, 1779, *MSS. in Various Collections*, 6:270.

58. Ibid., p. 271.

59. Cobbett, *Parliamentary History*, 20:737, 748, 766–67, 769, 780–803, 866, 931; June 15, 1779, North to the king, Fortescue, ed., *Correspondence*, 4:357; May 10, 1779, the king to North, ibid., p. 338.

60. The earl of Pembroke, however, was convinced that "the Howe inquiry has perfectly cleared Burgoyne also," July 9, 1779, Pembroke to Lord Herbert, Herbert, ed. *Henry, Elizabeth and George*, 204. For a detailed analysis of the Howe inquiry, see Ira D. Gruber, *The Howe Brothers and the American Revolution*, pp. 337–50.

61. August 31, 1779, Burgoyne to Burke, Sheffield MSS., Sheffield City Libraries; September 1, 1779, Burke to Burgoyne, Burke, *Correspondence*, 4:127–28.

62. September 4, 1779, Amherst to Jenkinson, W.O. 1.616, ff. 477–80.

63. September 23, 1779, Amherst to Jenkinson, W.O. 1.1001, ff. 27–30; September 23, 1779, Jenkinson to Burgoyne, W.O. 34.118, f. 17.

64. October 9, 1779, Burgoyne to Jenkinson, B.L. Add. MS. 38,212, f. 144; W.O. 1.1001, f. 25, pp. 1–8.

65. "The severity of the treatment shown me is so incompatible with the natural benignity and

justice of the King that I should have been convinced, had other information been wanting, either that it proceeded entirely from His Majesty's counsellors, who are pursuing my ruin as a political measure, or that the Royal Ear has been atrociously prejudiced and abused." October 9, 1779, Burgoyne to Germain, DeFonblanque, *Episodes*, pp. 383–86, quotation, pp. 383–84.

66. October 10, 1779, Burgoyne to Jenkinson, W.O. 1.1001, ff. 41–44.

67. October 12, 1779, Jenkinson to Amherst, W.O. 34.119, ff. 705–6; Jenkinson acknowledged that there might be errors in the draft, and requested corrections.

68. October 12, 1779, Amherst to the king, Fortescue, ed., *Correspondence*, 4:456.

69. October 12, 1779, the king to Amherst, ibid., 4:456–57.

70. October 15, 1779, Jenkinson to Burgoyne, W.O. 4.108, ff. 33–36. (Enclosed were commissions of March 23, 1776, W.O. 1.1001, ff. 63–66, 219–52. Also enclosed were proposed clauses for letter, W.O. 1.1001, ff. 67–68, clause B and ff. 70–72, clause C.)

71. October 17, 1779, Burgoyne to Jenkinson, B.L. Add. MS. 38,212, f. 175.

72. October 22, 1779, Jenkinson to Burgoyne, ibid., f. 184.

73. October 22, 1779, *London Public Advertiser*.

74. October 25, 1779, Sheridan to Richard Fitzpatrick, B.L. Add. MS. 47,582, ff. 177–78.

75. October 18, 1779, Frederick, Lord Cavendish to Countess Spencer, Spencer MSS., Althorp, Northamptonshire.

76. November 5, 1779, Burgoyne to Rockingham, cited by John Brooke, "John Burgoyne," in Namier and Brooke, eds., *Commons*. 2:141–45.

77. John Burgoyne, *A Letter from Lieutenant-General Burgoyne to his Constituents, upon his Late Resignation* (Manchester: Manchester Mercury, November 23, 1779).

78. [Anon.] *A Reply to Lieutenant General Burgoyne's Letter to his Constituents* (London: J. Wilkie, 1779), 46 pp.

79. ["An Englishman"] *A Letter to Lieut. Gen. Burgoyne, on his Letter to his Constituents* (London: n.p. 1779).

80. November 14,1779, Walpole to Lady Ossory, *Correspondence*, 33:136.

81. November 16, 1779, Walpole to Mason, *Correspondence*, 28:475.

82. Burgoyne, *Dramatic and Poetical Works*, 1:123–235, for the complete text of the play.

83. June 13, 1780, Burke to Richard Shakleton, Burke, *Correspondence*, 4:245.

84. Clemesha, *Preston*, p. 207.

85. Cone, *Burke*, p. 332.

86. August 2, 1781, Burgoyne to Burke, Sheffield City Libraries.

87. Ibid.

88. August 1, 1781, Burke to Franklin, Cone, *Burke*, p. 332.

89. Burke said Burgoyne always behaved "with the Temper which becomes a great Military Character that loves nothing so much in the profession as the means it so frequently permits of generosity and humanity. . . ."

90. December 3, 1781, Charles Jenkinson to Henry Clinton, *Report on American Manuscripts*, 2:358. Burgoyne frequently solicited Clinton's assistance with respect to exchange. See for example April 9, 1778 Burgoyne to Clinton and February 12, 1779, same to same, both in Clinton papers, Clements Library.

91. December 17, 1781, Cobbett, ed., *Parliamentary History*, 22:862–64 December 20, 1781; David D. Wallace, *Life of Henry Laurens* (New York: Putnam, 1915), pp. 363–84.

92. April 2, 1782, Richard B. Sheridan to Charles Sheridan, William Fraser Rae, *Sheridan: A Biography*, 2 vols. (London: R. Bentley, 1896), 1:382; Historical Manuscripts Commission, April, 1782, William Eden to [Lord Carlisle] Historical Manuscripts Commission, *Carlisle MSS.*, pp. 618–20.

93. January 14, 1782, Skinner to Loring, Historical Manuscripts Commission, *Reports on American MSS.*, 2:382.

94. January 21, 1782, Clinton to Loring, Historical Manuscripts Commission, *Report on American MSS.*, 2:384; see also ibid., 2:397; February, 1782, "Proposal for Exchange of General Burgoyne for an American Prisoner of War," C.O. 5.104, f. 267.

20

Ireland

The tumultuous political and military events that led to the loss of America, the fall of the North ministry, and his own retirement continued to affect the life of General Burgoyne. Shortly after the king reluctantly permitted the marquis of Rockingham to form a new government, the general received welcome news. The earl of Carlisle and Lieutenant General Sir John Irwin were vacating their posts as lord lieutenant of Ireland and commander in chief of the British army in Ireland. Rockingham had selected the duke of Portland to replace Carlisle, and he removed Irwin to make room for Burgoyne.[1] Burgoyne also became a privy councillor of Ireland, colonel of the Fourth Regiment of Foot in Ireland, the King's Own, and he obtained a sinecure as muster master general for the Foreign Forces in Canada.[2] As the general later confided to Lord Sydney, the king had "restored me conspicuously to my profession."[3] Indeed, the post of commander in chief was of some importance because Britain's war with the American colonies caused economic dislocation and political unrest in Ireland. The new commander in chief, although an advocate of imperial reform in India, scarcely understood the Irish more than he had the Americans. In fact, Burgoyne's primary concern upon arrival was not a new constitution for Ireland or army problems, but rather the status of his financial accounts.

Burgoyne nevertheless responded ebulliently to his return to public life. He appeared in Dublin on May 16, and quickly settled into "the hurry of business" at his official quarters in the Royal Hospital, Kilmainham. He was commander of 15,000 soldiers, and he undertook to master the details of his work, if not to comprehend the complexities of life in Ireland. His army was expected to be available for immediate emergency service anywhere in the British world, and indeed many regiments had already seen action in North America during the revolution.[4]

Although he was now associated with the opposition in British government, Burgoyne had no desire to embark upon ambitious programs to improve the quality of civil or military life in Ireland. As commander in chief, it was his task to prepare reports for the lord lieutenant concerning staff requirements and to recommend augmentations or reductions in the size of the army rank and file. Additionally, he conducted a voluminous correspondence in which he recommended promotions, transfers or exchanges of officers, wrote letters of reference based upon his observation of the discipline and "general fitness" of various soldiers, supervised the composition and structure of regiments, arbitrated disputes between civilians and army personnel, executed the terms of the Mutiny Act, advised the commander in chief of the British army in London, and made arrangements for military parades and other functions. During the first week of June 1782, the general and the earl of Charlemont made arrangements for the royal troops to fire volleys for the king's birthday at Dublin Castle, home of the lord lieutenant; almost simultaneously, Burgoyne attempted to arbitrate a conflict that had arisen between a British regiment posted in Galway and the residents of that town. Burgoyne and Portland attended a grand reception that Belfast staged in honor of their arrival. The townspeople of Belfast, if their superiors are to be believed, wished to have credit of "outdoing the lads of Leinster" in the military review which they planned. Burgoyne also devoted attention to other matters, including unfinished business concerning his troops in the United States.[5]

Although his appointment began April 16, and although he took up his duties on May 16, Burgoyne did not officially become commander in chief until June 7, on which day the Rockingham ministry also officially assumed the powers of office. On July 1, the exhausted Lord Rockingham died and the king was delighted to replace him with the earl of Shelburne, whom George III had favored with his confidence throughout the Rockingham ministry. Four days after the death of Rockingham, Burgoyne learned from Portland that his new-found career was in jeopardy. The earl of Shelburne was not politically or personally close to Portland; moreover, the lord lieutenant of Ireland usually resigned when the ministry that appointed him lost favor; finally, the commander in chief and the lord lieutenant worked so closely that when Portland resigned, it was thought that Burgoyne would quickly follow him back to England.[6] Speculation was rife in London concerning new appointments, and Lord George Germain, now Viscount Sackville, gloated at the prospect of ministerial reshuffling. He confided to his old under secretary, Knox, that Lord Temple wanted to become lord lieutenant. Germain liked Temple, which was more than could be said of his feeling toward Burgoyne: "Surely General Burgoyne will return [to London] that he may support his friend Mr. Fox; and, if he does, the command will probably be offered to Lord Cornwallis."[7] As Sackville anticipated, there were new appointments, but not all of them coincided with his predictions.[8] Burgoyne did return to London, but not to assist Fox; he had other reasons.

On July 24, 1782, an actress well known and highly esteemed in the West End for her charming performances in popular comedy gave birth in Queen Street, Soho, to a child fathered by the unwearying Burgoyne. Susan Caulfield, of Bury Street, Westminster, the mother of the child and Burgoyne's mistress, was a friend of the Miss Farren who had beguiled and eventually married the twelfth earl of Derby after his first wife died, and for whom Burgoyne had written "The Maid of the Oaks." Miss Farren probably introduced Burgoyne to Susan Caulfield. The liaison that developed sometime between 1778 and 1783, if not earlier, was a happy one. Burgoyne's affection for the popular singer and actress was unbounded; in his romantic correspondence with her he expressed a profusion of emotion. "My dearest Sue" received regularly love letters, partridges, and other tokens of sentiment. The sixty-two-year-old Burgoyne also delivered playful, fatherly sermons on a variety of subjects, including overindulgence: "Fie! Fie!" he scolded, "to get such colds and pains in the stomach by feasting. If you did but take such care as I do." The first child of the liaison was baptized at Saint Anne's Church in Soho three weeks after birth, and he received the name John Fox Burgoyne.

During the ensuing six years Susan Caulfield provided Burgoyne with three additional children. Maria Burgoyne, the second child, subsequently married Admiral Sir Philip Hornby, rear admiral of England and lord of the Admiralty. Another daughter, Caroline, married twice, the second husband being George Wrottesley, who later wrote a biography of John Fox Burgoyne. Of the fortunes of Edward, a fourth child, nothing is known.

John Fox endured a fitful and unhappy early existence, growing up at "The Oaks" in Surrey and in the Grosvenor Square town house of Lord Derby, who provided for all the Burgoyne children after the general's death. John Fox attended Eton and Royal Military Academy, Woolwich; in later years he became a distinguished officer in the Royal Engineers. He fought in the peninsular campaigns, the Crimean War, and ultimately he received from Queen Victoria the rank of field marshal. His only son, Hugh Talbot Burgoyne, married a daughter of Sir Baldwin Walker, rose to the rank of captain in the Royal Navy, but died in 1870 without issue.

Burgoyne's affair with Susan Caulfield continued until his death, although apparently he did not at any time consider legitimizing the match; perhaps her station as an actress precluded such a step. Whether his ardor for her exceeded his affection for his late wife is an unanswerable question.[9]

Lord Sackville watched and pondered, but he did not have the satisfaction of recording Burgoyne's resignation. However, the duke of Portland was replaced by George Nugent Temple Grenville, the second Earl Temple and first marquess of Buckingham, whose father was prime minister of England during the Stamp Act riots in America, and whose uncle was lord lieutenant of Ireland when the Volunteers began to organize. At the age of thirty, Earl Temple was an industrious, but ill-tempered, haughty aristocrat. His financial ability was recognized by some observers, and his influence upon the crown would soon astonish the British nation. When he arrived in Dublin in September 1782, Temple believed that his task as lord lieutenant would be a desperate one. "No government exists," he told Shelburne, whom he urged to dissolve the Irish legislature and issue writs for new elections. Nor was Temple enthusiastic about his commander in chief, who apparently did not consider resigning upon the death of Rockingham. Burgoyne continued to fulfill his obligations.[10]

Temple wished to name as his own commander in chief Lieutenant General Cunningham, who had obtained some previous experience with the Irish army and who was a personal and political ally of Temple. In December 1782 Temple discovered that Burgoyne was finally contemplating a resignation. Cunningham did not get the plum; in November 1782, Sackville noted that Cunningham was on his way to England and still remained "in the awkward situation of not being out of the staff, though he cannot do the duty of it under the present Commander-in-Chief." Burgoyne did not yet offer to resign.[11]

The general was contemplating at least a return to London, and he cited to Grenville the usual reasons of personal business, health, and attendance at parliamentary debates. Burgoyne was undismayed by the receipt of a blunt letter from Burke at Christmas time, in which that politician indicated his agreement with Portland and Fox that Burgoyne's services would not be needed at that time, even though the House of Commons had split into warring factions. General Burgoyne received an even more negative report from Temple, who informed him that the king had refused to give Burgoyne leave to return to England. Temple believed that the bad news would provoke the commander in chief to resign, and he promised to give Grenville the earliest notice of such action, "that you may apprize Cunningham of it." Burgoyne did write a preliminary draft of a resignation, a copy of which he sent to Portland, who assured Burgoyne that his appointment was purely military, that he could continue to act as commander in chief and carry on "the most violent opposition to the Court at the same time in a political line," and that he should definitely not resign. But Burgoyne could not obtain permission to carry his political opposition to London, and he remained dissatisfied.[12]

Other matters preoccupied British officials during the ensuing weeks; preliminary peace negotiations with France and the United States heralded a reduction in the Irish army, and Temple asked Burgoyne to prepare a paper concerning staff requirements for the following year. The general devoted much time to investigating salary schedules, reviewing the duties of lieutenant and major generals, and airing his opinions concerning the system of rank. "A regular gradation of Rank," he wrote, "is a leading principle in military system; and the more the degrees are Multiplied the more in my Opinion will order be preserved, and emulation which is the very soul of the Service encouraged."[13] He suggested that the principle of rotation in rank would if introduced bring rewarding results. The general reviewed the existing staff arrangements and found that a commander in chief, with two lieutenants and five major generals were sufficient to repel invasion. He concluded that staff arrangements ought to be maintained at the status quo, and that the whole establishment ought to be brought to full strength of fifteen thousand. However, if the government was intent upon saving money, the general urged—perhaps tongue in cheek— that the resignations of Lieutenant General Cunningham and Major General Maxwell could be accepted and their posts abolished. He concluded with a list of the usual platitudes concerning precision in inspections, parade attentions, "and the enforcement of all the minute regulations which are essential in Quarters but apt to fall into disuse in actual Service." Temple's answer to Burgoyne's analysis has not been preserved, but he proposed to Parliament an armed force that resembled the general's specifications in all details of significance.[14]

Temple remained unhappy with Burgoyne, and perhaps intimidated him; Burgoyne's letters to the lord lieutenant were particularly obsequious, even by the standards of the day. Temple wrote angrily to Thomas Townshend, the secretary of state for home and colonial affairs, about the political circumstances of Burgoyne's appointment. Townshend replied that the command of the Irish army was independent of the lord lieutenant. "To that idea," wrote Temple to his brother, "I never will submit." Cunningham was both agreeable to the king and useful to the Irish army, "which he so long, in fact, commanded." As Temple had explained to Shelburne before leaving for Ireland:

It has always been a matter of jealousy, and with reason; for the business of Ireland cannot exist under two masters; and the strongest proof of this is that even Lord Harcourt, under all the circumstances which you well know, first was obligated to force out General Elliott, and then to resign himself.

Early in January 1783, Temple disclosed to his brother that Cunningham seemed to have obtained the king's favor. Perhaps, speculated the lord lieutenant, "there was in reality a wheel within that which is moving according to the language of Townshend." If, however, the king refused to grant Cunningham the post upon Burgoyne's resignation, Temple would reluctantly conclude that the crown had withdrawn its personal patronage.[15]

Burgoyne continued to protest his confinement to Dublin, and he now sent copies of his proposed resignation to Secretary Townshend and to the earl of Derby. If he could not obtain permission to attend Parliament, so Burgoyne argued, then he would resign because the government was not permitting him to fulfill his obligation to support his political friends in the Commons. The secretary replied that Burgoyne ought to remain in Ireland until a new staff assembled for the Irish army, especially since the general had compiled a report on that subject: "You know well," wrote Townshend, "that the frequent interference of the military to support the civil power requires the employment of a person of more attention and temper than may be found upon taking the chance of the rolster [*sic*]." However, if Burgoyne needed to go to England for legitimate reasons of health, he could do so, but only for so long as was necessary. Burgoyne did not trust Townshend, whom he believed to be politically rather than militarily inspired. Nor did Burgoyne's friends trust the secretary. The duke of Portland, who had received additional word by special messenger on January 9 that Burgoyne planned to resign by the end of the month, informed Burgoyne that Lord Derby observed in a conversation with Charles Fox that there was no reason for Burgoyne's "gratifying the spleen of those who directed Townshend's pen." Portland advised against resignation, arguing that neither the business of Parliament nor the state of the army warranted such a step. Moreover, a resignation would indicate determined opposition and hostility to government, and would become an issue that the enemy could easily turn to advantage. In view of the "universal execration and contempt" with which Shelburne was viewed, and in consideration of the possibility of an impending collapse of that ministry, Portland advised Burgoyne to act with caution. When the general shortly thereafter received permission to return to England, he withdrew the proposed resignation. However, he replied to Townshend's letter by stating clearly that health was of secondary consideration and that he wished to go to London for primarily political reasons.

Early in February 1783, Burgoyne got away, for Temple complained to Grenville at that time that he did not know what to do about the army, since Burgoyne was on leave. Without marked success, Temple attempted to work with the general's staff. "Baugh, Lord Rors, Massey, and Gabbit, and not one head between the four!" exploded the temperamental lord lieutenant, who would have been even more upset had he known that Burgoyne later refused under any circumstances to fire Baugh. Temple wanted Cunningham in charge, since as he put it, "he really is the best pen and ink man for the purpose." The lord lieutenant instructed his brother to "try the ground" with Townshend once more. However, other matters intervened shortly thereafter, distracting Temple and Burgoyne from their difficulties.[16]

The War of American Independence was drawing to a close; diplomats in Paris completed preliminary arrangements for peace, and Burgoyne pondered once again the consequences for the Irish army. He began to receive advice from subordinates concerning the feared reductions, and one such prophet of doom in London stated accurately that "with smaller & fewer Possessions abroad and greater notions of Oeconomy we shall certainly not be allowed to keep up a large Army." He wished to know before Parliament reconvened what Temple's recommendations would be. Temple asked Burgoyne to write a report on the proposed reduction of the force. Burgoyne submitted his report on March 15. He concluded that the Irish army ought to remain at full strength—15,000 soldiers—and in addition he recommended that the government augment the cavalry service in Ireland. That force was "smaller than the best writers and Generals establish," he wrote, once again protecting the interests and urging the expansion of the division of army life with which he was most familiar. Since the cavalry service was popular in Ireland and was the great object of patronage in government, Burgoyne suggested that eleven or twelve regiments of cavalry ought to be posted and placed upon equal footing with British cavalry. Although Burgoyne concurred in Temple's opinion that Ireland was the proper repository for regiments of infantry "destined to relieve those abroad in all parts of the World," he urged the government to reserve 2,000 soldiers of the augmentation he recommended for the Irish cavalry.[17]

Burgoyne concluded his voluminous report with the hope that Temple would not consider it "officious" because of length; the lord lieutenant incorporated many of Burgoyne's suggestions within his own report to Parliament, but he was not at all personally interested either in Burgoyne or in his fears concerning officiousness. Temple was not even concerned about Cunningham, except to note caustically that the former favorite was "wonderfully attentive" to him, sending several letters from Brooks Club each day. Cunningham, remarked Temple to his brother, ought to be told that the lord lieutenant was about to resign, especially since Cunningham had been given hope that he would succeed Burgoyne. The earl of Shelburne announced on February 24 that *he* intended to resign, and although Temple claimed that "addresses crowd in thick upon me," he refused to remain in a position "where I do not clearly see my own way." Shelburne did not plan to remain in office after April 1783; Temple would take no risk concerning his tenure under Shelburne's successor—especially since it was not certain that William Pitt the Younger, Temple's favorite, would obtain control. Temple, however, did not hesitate to mislead Burgoyne concerning his successor as commander in chief, as he told Grenville with considerable malicious glee:

> Burgoyne hopes to be Lieutenant-General of the Ordnance in England; but does not open the idea of quitting this kingdom in either contingency. I have taken some pains to countenance gravely an idea that Lord Derby is to be my successor. It is believed, and Burgoyne gravely writes to dissuade him from it.

Temple's comments would seem to indicate that Burgoyne hoped to remain commander in chief, accept the ordnance post in England, and flatter his nephew into accepting the lord lieutenancy of Ireland. Although there is insufficient evidence to indicate that such was his plan, it would not be surprising to discover ambition once again the most obvious characteristic of Burgoyne's personality.[18]

Shelburne formally resigned on April 2, 1783, amidst recriminations and a general lack of appreciation for the work his ministry had accomplished. Temple offered his resignation in mid-March, which was ignored at first, and then accepted with alacrity by Lord North, who had agreed to form a coalition with Charles Fox. North's rudeness caused Temple to spoil for revenge, and several months later the ill-tempered ex–lord lieutenant conspired with the king to destroy the coalition. Although Temple had bruited it about that Burgoyne disliked Dublin and wished to leave, temporarily or permanently, the general remained to serve as commander in chief under yet a third lord lieutenant. He did not obtain his ordnance post; William Howe beat him out once again. Nevertheless, his durability as a politician during a period of ministerial instability was impressive.[19]

During the upheaval that brought about the coalition, Burgoyne devoted much time to pleading for another leave of absence, but George III told him to remain in Ireland until peace negotiations with France and the United States were concluded.[20] Fox was unable to change the king's mind, but he and his colleagues did attempt unsuccessfully to obtain for Burgoyne a permanent cavalry regiment. The support of Fox was clear evidence of his friendship for Burgoyne; indeed, in the course of correspondence he obtained Burgoyne's permission to live in his London town house.[21]

Shortly thereafter, Temple prepared to leave Dublin. The king, forced to accept a coalition of Portland, North, and Fox, wrote bitterly to the outgoing lord lieutenant that he had been thwarted. Temple assured his diary that the monarch spoke of his new ministers in terms of the utmost disgust. Burgoyne, in contrast, could count several friends among the king's new servants. Richard Sheridan became secretary of the treasury and Edmund Burke accepted the post of paymaster of the forces, while Fox assumed the powers of secretary of state. Of more immediate local importance, Thomas Pelham, the earl of Northington, replaced Temple as lord lieutenant of Ireland. Burgoyne wrote on April 29 to Northington, who was still in London, expressing his surprise to discover the coalition in power, and also requesting permission to return to London immediately. The general wished to arrive there before Parliament completed financial arrangements for the staff of the British army in Ireland. He wrote to Northington again on May 7. In the course of a long letter, Burgoyne noted his "precarious Tenure" on the Irish establishment and he also said that he had always believed it proper to retire whenever a new governor arrived "under whom I could not act with Confidence and Zeal." Not wishing to resign now, Burgoyne was "ambitious" to establish a confidential communication with Northington. The king, he said, could not have chosen from "the whole Peerage a Lord Lieutenant so well adapted as your Excellency to make my Continuance in Employment an Object of my Desire." Burgoyne once again requested leave so that he could attend Parliament, which he had desired to do since the previous autumn. He had to consult with General Conway, the commander in chief of the British army, and other officials concerning the strength of the Irish and English army establishments. He had to compare and contrast financial statistics and other long and intricate matters "of more consequence than Detail, I will venture to say." Although he expected to be of invaluable assistance to Northington in many matters that needed explanation and adjustment in Dublin he would ask the king for permission to go to London at once if Northington should discover "any Circumstances Directly or remotely connected with the military Department" that Burgoyne could attend to in London.[22]

Although the king had consistently withheld his permission for leave, he relented on May 16 and in fact saw "great propriety" in Burgoyne's consultation for eight or ten days in the preparation of plans for the new Irish army.[23] North and Conway agreed with the king. On May 22 the general departed, and shortly thereafter spoke in the Commons against any reduction of the Irish establishment.[24] On June 6, he had the satisfaction of informing Northington, who had left for Dublin, that Parliament approved Temple's estimates with little significant alteration.[25] As soon as the debates on the reduction were concluded, Burgoyne told the lord lieutenant, he would work on a settlement for the Irish staff based upon Temple's plan. He further informed Northington on June 27 that he had no doubt the plan of reduction would be adopted, "notwithstanding Lord Temple's changed sentiment." Burgoyne hoped the king would soon consider the Irish staff proposals, the business of Parliament having drawn to a close; George III did so, and favorably, on July 12. Burgoyne also reported that the coalition was gaining in strength and that few dreaded the "day of Embarrasment," when the ministry would be forced to resign. The general's reading of the king's attitude toward the ministry was entirely inaccurate. William Windham, who was Northington's secretary, understood more clearly what was happening, and he sensed that the ministry was in jeopardy.[26] He observed, rightly, to Northington that the king refused to spend additional money for the creation of a new Parliament; moreover, the king's determination "not to contribute to their strength or render them at all independent is manifested without much reserve, for he absolutely refuses to make any English peers."[27] Windham understood what Burgoyne was unable to see: that the king was determined not to cooperate in any substantial way with the coalition. Consequently, the life of the ministry would not be a long one, and Burgoyne's career might well be nearing its end.

Burgoyne would regret the loss of his position for several reasons, not the least of which was the financial consideration involved. He earned £1,460 per year as a regular salary in addition to a per diem allowance of £6 that accumulated at the rate of £2,190 per year—a total of £3,650 annually. During August, the general pondered fiscal matters relating to his salary and the pay of others, for he was required to provide the lord lieutenant with a critique of the army estimates. He labored for the benefit of "those who are to succeed" to his station, he announced, although it can be safely assumed that Burgoyne hoped benefit might accrue to himself for a time. His critique was primarily a plea for higher wages for the commander in chief. No such officer since Lord Rothes, who died in 1767, had received £1,460 per year—or as Burgoyne put it, £4 per day—as a fixed salary. The successor of Lord Rothes, Lieutenant General Dilthes, assumed the command of the army but not the commission of office; after 1767 there ceased to be an officer with the title commander in chief for Ireland. Dilthes was not a privy councillor; he lived by inclination and modestly at the Royal Hospital, Kilmainham. The salary was commensurate with his rank, station, and duties. Just before the commander's death, the king decided to revive the commission, and Lieutenant General Elliott received it.[28] Within a few months he resigned—Burgoyne did not say he resigned for financial reasons, but the implication is clear that his fixed salary was the reason. Lieutenant General Sir John Irwin succeeded Elliott as commander in chief, privy councillor, and president of the barrack board, at which time the £4 salary was supplemented by the £6 daily expense allowance, "the usual stipend of all other Commanders in Chief." Despite that improvement, Irwin's own fortune was "much impaired." In fact, said Burgoyne, he could not find a single instance of a commander in chief in Ireland improving his own fortunes, although he did not wish to insinuate "the most distant idea" that his salary was insufficient. Nevertheless, inflation had pushed up the salary of the lord lieutenant by £4,000 since 1767; the salary of the chancellor had nearly doubled; the judges, bishops, major generals, and household officers had seen their wages almost double. Burgoyne concluded that the commander in chief should not be paid a salary reflecting conditions of 1767.[29] Ten days later Burgoyne, now sixty-one, drew up a will.[30] His child was now a year old.

Late in October 1783, Fox sent Burgoyne a letter urging him to go to London as soon as he could so that the ministry would be fully represented in the House of Commons for the opening of Parliament. Lord Northington refused to permit Burgoyne to go, believing that he would be needed in Dublin at a time when there was widespread fear of dissident uprisings. Later in the month, however, Burgoyne received an express ordering him to depart for London at once to vote upon the ministry's new East India Bill. The general's presence in Parliament was considered of special importance to Fox and North since Burgoyne, Burke, and Henry Dundas were said to have "dominated the house" on the India question throughout the Rockingham and Shelburne ministries. In April 1782 Burgoyne had formed a special committee to investigate the activities of Warren Hastings, successor to Robert Clive's political position as well as to the general's investigative scrutiny. Burgoyne denounced Hastings for his misconduct in India, and the House voted a resolution condemning him for high-handedness. The matter of India became urgent again in May 1783, when the company informed the coalition ministry that it was again bankrupt and therefore required a £1 million loan and a temporary extension of its old charter. The ministry at once moved a bill through Parliament to extend contractual arrangements several more months for the company. Furthermore, Fox and Burke began during the summer of 1783 to prepare a new bill, based in part upon Burgoyne's findings, to provide immediate as well as long-term relief for the company.[31]

Hence, Burgoyne traveled by day and night during November in order to reach Parliament before Fox introduced the revised bill.[32] He would vote for it as a loyal supporter of Fox and also as an interested member who had devoted considerable energy to the business of the India Company. He arrived in time, for the House did not resolve itself into a committee on the Fox bill until December 3. What appeared to be a leisurely debate began to unfold during the ensuing week, and on December 8 William Grenville criticized the bill strongly and censured Burke for endorsing it. Grenville was Temple's brother and represented the line that the noble lord would take concerning this measure; few realized that Temple's hostility toward that legislation was in turn a representation of the king's views. George III remained behind the scenes for another week while Burgoyne replied to Grenville, defending Burke, Fox, and himself. He reminded the house that he had chaired a committee on the India Company sixteen years earlier and had discovered grave delinquency, but no bill was forthcoming at that time. More recently, he read about Fox's bill in a newspaper and at once came away from a country "in which he had the honour to hold a high situation, crossed the sea, and traveled 300 miles post in order to give it his support." Burgoyne approved Burke's observations concerning the conduct of the company, and he described the British torture of Orientals in an elaborate analogy in which British nabobs in India appeared more villainous than the scoundrels seen by Aeneas during his descent into Tartarus. Concluding with a recitation of six lines of Virgil in Latin, Burgoyne expressed indifference to the laughter that greeted the sudden appearance of ministerial supporters in Parliament, including himself.[33]

Burgoyne's speech helped the bill, which passed successfully through the Commons on December 9, as Burgoyne reported jubilantly from Brooks Club in Pall Mall to the lord lieutenant at about nine o'clock that evening.[34] Burgoyne was in high spirits, and, leaping to the conclusion that the ministry had weathered the storm, he asked the lord lieutenant permission to go to Bath for "the dead months of winter." The political atmosphere of London that winter could hardly have remained more alive, as Burgoyne soon learned. Indeed, the king finally found an opportunity to wreak his vengeance upon a ministry he despised. George III, who had called North an ingrate and a traitor, and who had told all and sundry of his contempt for Fox, listened intently to the suggestions of Thurlow, who had been excluded from the coalition, and Temple, who was forced to resign in humiliation upon Shelburne's fall. These two ill-tempered, ambitious politicians goaded the monarch to take action against the India bill, and ultimately against the coalition ministry. The king ought to oppose the reform, they said, on the grounds that it would insure a permanently appointed group of Whig politicians patronage posts in the reconstructed company's legislature. Burgoyne informed Northington, in great surprise, confusion, and fatigue, that the king had invited Temple to his chambers and permitted him to stay for hours, during which time they hatched a plot. When Temple emerged, he announced that he had authority to declare the king's dislike of the entire East India Bill. Burgoyne noted that the monarch during the next day received Portland and Fox kindly, without a word of disapprobation for the India bill. During the weekend, the king departed for Windsor, and the following Monday it was revealed that the monarch had told Temple:

> I think this bill unprecedented, unparliamentary, & subversive of the constitution, as introducing a fourth power which does not belong to it. If this bill passes, I am no more a King—I shall look upon those who support the bill not only as not my friends but as my absolute enemies.[35]

The king confirmed his disapproval to Lord Salisbury, who with Temple managed the fight against it in the Lords. As Burgoyne told Northington, "the opposition is moving Heaven and Earth (not to say Hell) to get a superiority of strength in the Lords." The general concluded, however, in agreement with Fox that ultimately the bill would pass, for "there is not boldness enough to give the negative of the Crown."

Alas for Burgoyne, the negative of the crown prevailed; on December 17 the Lords struck down the bill. Portland and Richmond denounced the interference of the king as unconstitutional meddling in the legislative process. When Richmond alluded to the untoward influence of certain ministers upon the king, reported Burgoyne, "Lord Temple was upon his highest horse; avowed his having had a conference with the King upon the principle of right as a peer to give his opinion and advice to the Crown whenever he thought it useful so to do."[36] After considerable additional debate, the ministry obtained a vote for adjournment, a juncture "of imminent Confusion," wrote Burgoyne, "& pregnant with Consequence, that every lover of his Country must shudder to look to." The coalition was broken; members began to call for William Pitt.[39]

Burgoyne finally realized that his political career was at an end. A week later he informed Northington that he would delay his resignation until it accompanied that of the lord lieutenant, "our Friend Charles" being decidedly of that opinion.[38] On December 24, Burgoyne told Northington of the king's reply to the widespread criticism of his treachery:

> That it had been the study of his reign never to use the prerogatives entrusted to him by the Constitution but for the good of his subjects, that the public revenue, the state of the credit, & the regulations of the affairs of the India Company were objects that required the utmost attention & vigilence of Parliament; that he recommended such an adjournment as might be thought necessary, & promised that no obstruction to their meeting should be given by dissolution or prorogation.[39]

Parliament recessed until January 12. Fox asked Burgoyne to tell Northington that a resignation was in order, but that he should wait until the legislature returned before sending notice. Northington told his son, Pelham, that "Burgoyne had behaved upon this [treason] towards me with particular delicacy & regard, & has withheld his Resignation" until his lordship delivered up his own.[40] Shortly thereafter Northington told Burgoyne that he had sent word of his leaving; "Their manner being full of slight, mine has answered it." Burgoyne officially resigned on January 4 in a letter to Lord Sydney, formerly Thomas Townshend. After the part that he had recently played in opposition, Burgoyne wrote, he could have no pretension to further office, even if his loyalty to the opposition disappeared. Moreover, he felt it his duty to be in the Commons rather than in Ireland.

> At my age, and with a temper that finds no terror in the loss of income, there may be little merit, but there will be solid comfort, in laying up for the close of life this reflection, that at a juncture which I thought a crisis in the fate of

my country I took a decided part, and voluntarily, without a complaint of hardship or anger against any man or power, relinquished a splendid, a profitable, and in many respects a pleasing station, to pursue my parliamentary duty in connection with those men, and in support of those principles, by which alone I believed my country would be redeemed.

Burgoyne's letter of resignation illustrates well his sanctimonious yet charming nature. Unquestionably he found his job in Ireland pleasant; he did betray considerable enthusiasm in his reports concerning the staff, the augmentation, and the budget for the army. He campaigned loyally for the benefit of the cavalry. He exhibited tenacity, durability, and industry in the business of retaining his job during three ministries and three lord lieutenants. He appeared most animated in the matter of a salary adjustment and during the last days of the Fox-North coalition. As for the Irish people, they had not profited by Burgoyne's presence. The distress that he found upon arrival in 1782 still existed in 1784; unemployment, inflation, and food riots continued unabated. Burgoyne was unmoved by such suffering. Nor did he appear to be especially aware of the political activities in London that brought about the fall of the ministry; he wrote of the demise of the coalition in the language of an outsider. He returned in January to London, where he participated occasionally in House debates, wrote several more plays, and fathered three additional children.[41]

Notes

1. April 2, 1782, Richard B. Sheridan to Charles Sheridan, Cecil Price, ed., *The Letters of Richard Brinsley Sheridan*, 3 vols. (Oxford: Clarendon Press, 1966), 1:138–40; April 1782, William Eden to [Lord Carlisle], Historical Manuscripts Commission, *Carlisle MSS.*, pp. 618–20.

2. "John Burgoyne," *DNB;* Barker and Stenning, eds., *Old Westministers*, 1:143; *Army List for 1783*, p. 74; Burgoyne, *Orderly Book*, p. xxxii; Burgoyne, *Dramatic and Poetical Works*, 2 vols. (London: C. Whittington, 1808), introduction, 1:32.

3. January 4, 1784, Burgoyne to Lord Sydney, DeFonblanque, *Episodes*, pp. 434–36.

4. W. E. H. Lecky, *A History of Ireland in the Eighteenth Century*, 5 vols. (London: Longmans, Green, 1892), 2:319–94; for a summary of Anglo-Irish politics, 1782–1784, see also Maurice R. O'Connell, *Irish Politics and Social Conflicts in the Age of the American Revolution* (Philadelphia: University of Pennsylvania Press, 1965).

5. For examples of Burgoyne's activities, see June 1, 1782, Burgoyne to the earl of Charlemont, Historical Manuscripts Commission, *Twelfth Report, appendix, part X, The Manuscripts and Correspondence of James, First Earl of Charlemont* (London: H. M. Stationery Office, 1891), p. 403; June 2, 1782, earl of Charlemont to his son, ibid., pp. 405–6; June 7, 1782, Haliday to Charlemont, ibid., pp. 406–7; June 7, 1782, Burgoyne to Richard Burke, P.R.O. Treasury, 1.572, ff. 139–40; May 1, 1783, Burgoyne to Northington, B. L. Add. MS. 40,178, f. 97; December 4, 1783, Burgoyne to Northington, B. L. Add. MS. 33,100, f. 443.

6. July 17, 1782, Sackville to Irwin, Historical Manuscripts Commission, *Stopford-Sackville MSS.*, 1:142–43.

7. July 13, 1782, Sackville to Knox, Historical Manuscripts Commission, *MSS. in Various Collections*, 6:186–87.

8. July 4, 1782, Portland to Burgoyne, DeFonblanque, *Episodes*, pp. 412–13.

9. "John Burgoyne," *DNB;* Chester, ed., *Registers*, p. 450, note 3; Wrottesley, *Burgoyne*, 1:5 and 2:434. "Talbot" was the heraldic cognizance of the Burgoyne family; Wrottesley, John Fox *Burgoyne*, 1:353, note 1. For a recent appraisal of John Fox Burgoyne, see Jay Luvaas, *The Education of an Army: British Military Thought, 1815–40* (Chicago: University of Chicago Press, 1964), pp. 65–96.

10. Lecky, *Ireland*, 2:330; November 9, 1782, Burgoyne to Townshend, B. L. Add. MS. 40,177, f. 155; November 19, 1782, Burgoyne to Grenville, ibid., f. 155B; December 2, 1782, Burgoyne to Townshend, ibid., f. 156..

11. December 4, 1782, Earl Temple to W. W. Grenville, Historical Manuscripts Commission, *Thirteenth Report, appendix, part 3, the Manuscripts of J. B. Fortescue, Esq. of Dropmore* 10 vols. (London: H. M. Stationery Office, 1892–1927), 1:168–69; November 26, 1782, Sackville to Irwin, Historical Manuscripts Commission, *Stopford-Sackville MSS.*, 1:143.

12. December 7, 1782, Burgoyne to Townshend, B. L. Add. MS. 40,178, f. 36; December 24, 1782, Burke to Burgoyne, DeFonblanque, *Episodes*, pp. 417–21; December 29, 1782, Temple to Grenville, Historical Manuscripts Commission, *Fortescue MSS.*, 1:174–75; December 8, 1782, Portland to Burgoyne, DeFonblanque, *Episodes*, pp. 413–17.

13. December 30, 1782, Burgoyne to Temple, B. L. Add. MS. 40,178, f. 44.

14. Ibid.

15. January 3, 1783, Temple to Grenville, Historical Manuscripts Commission, *Fortescue MSS*, 1:178–79.

16. January 1, 1783, Burgoyne to Portland, and draft, Burgoyne to Derby, DeFonblanque, *Episodes*, p. 424; January 6, 1783, Thomas Townshend to Burgoyne, ibid., pp. 422–23; January 9, 1783, duke of Portland to Burgoyne, ibid., pp. 424–26; January 27, 1783, T. Townshend to Burgoyne, ibid., pp. 426–27; n.d. but c. January 28, 1783, Burgoyne to T. Townshend, ibid., pp. 427–28; February 2, 1783, Temple to Grenville, Historical Manuscripts Commission *Fortescue MSS.*, 1:187–88; June 27, 1783, Burgoyne to Northington, B. L. Add. MS. 33,100, ff. 182–83.

17. "Escorts, Intelligence, Surprises, and improvement of Victory depend upon them. However unfavourable the face of this Country may appear for the Regular Action of Cavalry in extended Line its operations ought to have the greatest effects in every other respect in a Country like this with fortified Posts, it is Cavalry that extends the importance of the Army, and secures obedience where Infantry alone could not enforce it. . . ." February 14, 1783, H.I.C. [Chalmuddy?] to Burgoyne, B. L. Add. MS. 33,100, ff. 140–41; March 15, 1783, Burgoyne to Temple, B. L. Add. MS. 40,178, ff. 64–67.

18. March 20, 1783, Temple to Grenville, Historical Manuscripts Commission, *Fortescue MSS.*, 1:202–3; March 28, 1783, Temple to Grenville, ibid., 1:206; Lecky, *Ireland*, 2:349; W. E. H. Lecky, *A History of England in the Eighteenth Century*, 8 vols. (New York: D. Appleton, 1878–90) 5:218.

19. Lecky, *England*, 5:218.

20. April 4, 1783, the king to North; April 4, 1783, North to the king, Fortescue, ed., *Correspondence*, 6:333–34.

21. April 6, 1783, Temple to Grenville, Historical Manuscripts Commission, *Fortescue MSS.*, 1:208–9; April 15, 1783, North to Temple, B. L. Add. MS. 40,178, f. 122; April 23, 1783, Temple to North, ibid., f. 86; April 24, 1783, Burgoyne to North, DeFonblanque, *Episodes*, p. 430.

22. Lecky, *England*, 1:218–28; April 29, 1783, Burgoyne to Northington, B. L. Add. MS. 33,100, ff. 109–10; May 7, 1783, Burgoyne to Northington, B. L. Add. MS 33,100, ff. 117–19.

23. May 16, 1783, the king to North; May 16, 1783, North to the king, Fortescue, ed., *Correspondence*, 6:387.

24. May 22, 1783, Temple to North, B. L. Add. MS. 33,100, ff. 175–76.

25. June 6, 1783, Burgoyne to Northington, ibid.

26. June 27, 1783, Burgoyne to Northington, ibid., ff. 182–83.

27. July 17, 1783, W. Windham to Northington, ibid., ff. 204–7; July 18, 1783, Windham to

Northington, ibid., ff. 208–9; July, 1783, military letter to Lord North, ibid., ff. 227–30, two enclosures.

28. Elliott later became commander of the British garrison in Gibralter, where he rescued the besieged rock in February, 1783; Nathaniel Wraxall, *The Historical and Posthumous Memoirs of Sir Nathaniel William Wraxall,* ed. Henry B. Wheatley, 5 vols. (London: Bickers & Son, 1884), 2:436, noted some talk of Burgoyne being exchanged for Elliott. The two did exchange letters; DeFonblanque, *Episodes,* p. 432.

29. August 29, 1783, Burgoyne to Northington, B. L. Add. MS. 38,716, ff. 75–78.

30. Chester, ed., *Registers,* p. 450.

31. October 31, 1783, Fox to Burgoyne, DeFonblanque, *Episodes,* p. 430; [October–November] 1783, Northington to Burgoyne, ibid., p. 431.

32. November 23, 1783, Mornington to Grenville, Historical Manuscript Commission, *Fortescue MSS.,* 1:228–35.

33. November 28, 1783, Burgoyne to Northington, B. L. Add. MS. 33,100, ff. 423–24; Cobbett, *Parliamentary History,* 24:29–31.

34. December 9, 1783, Burgoyne to Northington, ibid., ff. 448–50.

35. Cobbett, ed., *Parliamentary History,* 24:29–31; December 15, 1783, Burgoyne to Northington, B. L. Add. MS. 33,100, ff. 464–67.

36. December 16, 1783, Burgoyne to Pelham, B. L. Add. MS. 33,100, ff. 468–70.

37. December 25, 1783, Burgoyne to Northington, B. L. Add. MS. 38,716, ff. 142–43.

38. Hudleston, *Burgoyne,* p. 305 noted that the letter of Burgoyne was blotted and smudged, indicating that Burgoyne and Fox had consumed alcohol that evening.

39. December 24, 1783, Burgoyne to Northington, B. L. Add. MS. 33,100, ff. 486–87.

40. December 29, 1783, Northington to Pelham, B. L. Add. MS. 33,100, ff. 512–15.

41. January 4, 1784, Burgoyne to Sydney, J. Brooke, "Burgoyne" in Namier and Brooke, eds., *Commons,* 2:141–45; Lecky, *Ireland,* 2:382.; John Cannon, *The Fox-North Coalition: Crisis of the Constitution* (Cambridge: At the University Press, 1969).

21

Retirement

The collapse of the Fox-North coalition pleased the king, who ordered new elections. Burgoyne and Houghton again obtained nominations to represent the borough of Preston, and once more they faced a challenge from the corporation of that borough, which attempted for the last time to reverse the decision of 1768 to provide a franchise for "all the inhabitants." The corporation nominated Ralph Clayton and Michael Taylor, two barristers, who attempted to confound Burgoyne with practical jokes—"trotting the general," as it was called. One of them brought Burgoyne a watch and asked him whether he could tell the time of day. Burgoyne did not see the humor of it. He placed the watch on a tray with two pistols and marched with his servant to an inn, where he searched for his opponent. Arriving at the bar of the tavern, the general asked each patron whether he was the owner of the watch. In view of the prominently displayed pistols, no one replied. Burgoyne concluded that "Since the watch belongs to none of you gentlemen it remains my property." Turning to his servant, the general told him to "Take this watch and fob in remembrance of the Swan Inn at Bolton."

Such solemnity did not, fortunately for Burgoyne, lose him the election, and on February 28 both Burgoyne and Houghton were back in the Commons. The general was not pleased with the new ministry, and he declared the newly formed cabinet of William Pitt unconstitutional. Thereafter, Burgoyne consistently supported Fox and ridiculed the highly successful and long-lived Pitt administration in several published collections, including the *Westminster Guide,* and parts of the *Rolliad and Probationary Odes.*[1] In the latter work, Burgoyne severely criticized Thomas Warton, successful candidate for poet laureate.

Both the resignation and the election were events that had an adverse effect upon Burgoyne's bank account. Shortly after his return from Ireland, the general found it necessary to ask an old friend for a loan. Burgoyne wrote to Nathaniel Day, who had served in his Sixteenth Regiment as early as 1763. Day, it will be recalled, was commissary in Canada during the 1777 expedition, and provided Burgoyne with £2,000 upon the occasion of his retirement in 1779. Burgoyne told Day that, having sacrificed fortune to principle in a consistent way throughout his political career, he was in considerable debt and needed £500 immediately. Burgoyne offered as security the diamond ring, known to be worth £1,000, that the king of Portugal had given him, and he promised to repay the loan within either six months or a year. Day replied that the general could have the money without surrendering the ring.[2]

Burgoyne's solvency was restored, at least temporarily. Not so his presence at court. For the balance of 1784 and thereafter, the general's communications with the king were strained. George III apparently resented Burgoyne's resignation because he intrepreted it to be firm evidence of the general's determination to remain in political opposition to the court. By way of apology, Burgoyne informed Lord Sydney, who would presumably tell the king, that he had gone to a levee after his resignation and had noticed that the king no longer looked upon him with kindness. Not wishing to intrude upon the royal displeasure, Burgoyne absented himself from court thereafter. It can readily be inferred that Burgoyne wished Lord Sydney to interpret his absence from court as deference to the king's wish, rather than a sign of political opposition. In the eight years Burgoyne had yet to live, he had no further direct communication with his sovereign. The days of special royal approval were over.[3]

During 1785, the general turned his attention to a new parliamentary investigation. The Pitt ministry appointed a Board of Sea and Land Officers to determine whether Britain retained the ability to repel successfully a foreign invasion. The duke of Richmond, master general of the ordnance, and twenty-two other members of Parliament were appointed to the new committee, including Burgoyne, Cornwallis, and Carleton. The legislators were instructed to prepare a report recommending the proper strategy for defending the British Isles against attack, and to make the royal dockyards at Portsmouth and Plymouth particular subjects of investigation. The report recommended that the government release over £750,000 from the treasury to build effective fortifications at the two seaports. The board adopted the report after marathon sessions during which those who opposed the recommendations united to block supporters of the plan. Carleton and Gray believed that additional defense funds were needed, while Burgoyne opposed the entire scheme, provoking Cornwallis to call him the biggest blockhead and sycophant he had ever seen. Burgoyne, Earl Percy, and the future Lord St. Vincent signed a protest, which was appended to the report, doubting the probability of all the assumptions posited in the instructions and denying that expensive works and large garrisons were necessary to protect the security of Great Britain.

On February 27, 1786, the report was circulated in the cabinet, and Pitt brought it before the House of Commons for debate. Burgoyne and other members of the Whig opposition spoke against the report in strong terms. The general maintained that the army would be weakened elsewhere if 22,000 soldiers were drawn off to support the fortifications at Plymouth and Portsmouth. Instead of such extravagant plans, Burgoyne suggested that the government rely upon the navy for the protection of dockyards. When the duke of Richmond was charged with having erected in the past a battery with badly placed guns that recoiled upon those firing them, Burgoyne came to his rescue, denying that the "inconvenience in question" existed.[4] On March 20, when the debate resumed, Richmond received additional criticism because "the noble Duke's studies had cost the country a great deal of money, more especially as he was always changing his plans." Sheridan branded the report sophistry and charged that the study as circulated among the cabinet members had been trimmed to exclude the dissenting report; he also charged that Richmond packed the committee with supporters, including Sir Guy Carleton, who had been promised a large pension. When the debate concluded, the house divided evenly, with the speaker casting a nay vote to break the tie. Burgoyne had used the traditional British argument against military spending during time of peace, and he had done so successfully. His motivation may be questioned; had Burgoyne remained a member of the military establishment, it is doubtful that he would have cast a vote against such an ambitious and glamorous military project.[5]

The matter of Carleton's pension received additional attention in June 1786, when Pitt presented a message from the king in which Carleton was recommended to receive a stipend of £1,000 per year for his wife and sons. The king had promised Carleton such a reward in 1777, but Germain blocked it, and upon the secretary of state's resignation in 1782 the matter was shelved. Now Burgoyne spoke in support of the man whom he had supplanted in 1777:

I should consider myself as most dishonourable and criminal if I did not take every occasion to declare that had Sir Guy Carleton been personally employed in that important command, he could not have fitted it out with more assiduity, more liberality and zeal, then, disappointed, displeased, and resentful against the king's servants, he employed to prepare it for a junior officer. [I mention] this not only in praise of personal honour, but as a great example of military principle.

Whatever cant and hypocrisy may be found in the passage, Burgoyne cannot be denied credit for supporting another man's pension; he himself received no special emolument from the government.[6]

The general returned to his theatrical endeavors during 1785 and 1786. He had been writing another comedy of manners, most of which was completed during 1785 at Knowsley. *The Heiress* was scheduled to appear during the 1786 season, which Mrs. Sheridan predicted would be a particularly good one, as Londoners were anticipating the pantomime *School for Greyhounds* and an opera, *The Captive*, as well as Burgoyne's offering. The play opened in London on February 4, 1786 at the Theatre Royal, Drury Lane, and ran for thirty performances during its first season. Critical reaction was unanimous; Burgoyne had written a great success. Horace Walpole told Lady Ossory that he "went through [*The Heiress*] twice in one day," and liked it better than any comedy he had seen since *The Provoked Husband.* Horne Tooke called it "the most perfect and meritorious comedy of any on our stage," while the *Pursuit of Literature* said it was "the production of a man of fashion, delicacy, wit and judgment." Burgoyne's Lady Emily, the *Old Playgoer* contended, was "the *only* approach to a fine lady on the modern stage." *The Heiress* soon provoked a discussion of high comedy as a genre. Walpole argued that most high comedy was false because middle-class artists wrote it for middle class performers. Burgoyne, on the other hand, had written "the best modern comedy" because he lived in the best company. It followed that Miss Farren, who was the leading lady of *The Heiress,* acted best in it because she too lived among the best; Mrs. Abingdon, in contrast, could not rise above Lady Teazle, a second-rate character.[7]

A second literary debate occurred when Burgoyne was accused of having stolen the plot for *The Heiress.* Mrs. Tickell advised Mrs. Sheridan that her husband played a part in the plot: "I think your applause much too cold for it, and I'm sure I can find the hand of the Master in several tints—eh?—is it not so?" Burgoyne's sister-in-law told his daughter years later:

> I happen to *know* that your father took the idea of *The Heiress* from Mrs. Lennox's *novel* of *Henrietta* which he reckoned one of the cleverest works of its class that had appeared; and I think what he says in his preface about acknowledging obligations to novelists was aimed at Sheridan, who could never bear to be told (which was, however, perfectly true) that his Sir Oliver Surface and his two nephews were borrowed from his mother's beautiful novel of *Sidney Biddolph.*

Critics in the nineteenth and twentieth centuries have said that *The Heiress* fulfilled many, if not all, of the requirements of high comedy; it cannot, however, be put upon a scale with *The School for Scandal.* The play nevertheless attracted large audiences, and was published in February 1786, by Debrett, who paid Burgoyne £200 for the copyright. The book was printed in ten editions within the first year, achieved translation into four foreign languages, and was adapted for the stage in France and Germany.[8]

If *The Heiress* was Burgoyne's masterpiece, as assuredly it was, remaining popular upon the stage well into the next century and occasionally included in dramatic anthologies in the twentieth, another production of 1786 was the playwright-general's worst effort. Thomas Linley adapted a French opera, Gretry and Sedaine's *Richard Coeur de Lion,* which received its first performance in Paris during 1784, and Burgoyne translated the libretto into English. The play was first presented in London on October 24, 1786, and it was published the same day. A rival production was mounted a week earlier at the Theatre Royal, Covent Garden. Burgoyne's version, which boasted the acting talents of Mrs. Jordan as Mathilda and John Philip Kemble as Richard, was far more popular, and it became a great contemporary success. "Richard's himself again," said Mrs. Tickell. Walpole, however, got to the point immediately, as he often did, when he said that "turning the ferocious Richard into a tender husband is intolerable"; the play "did not answer." Although Sir Gilbert Elliott declared that he was never more highly entertained and delighted in his life, that the story was quite interesting and Mrs. Jordan "divine," the play has not withstood the test of time.[9]

The general frequently penned prologues and epilogues for productions other than his own, one of which was an epilogue for the duke of Richmond's play, *The Way to Keep Him* (1786), which the duke presented in the theater at his estate. Burgoyne's composition was intended to be a salute to George III and his wife, Queen Charlotte, who were in attendance. His address, however, was lugubrious and in part unintelligible:

> Need I here point to virtues more sublime,
> Unchanged by fashion—unimpaired by time?
> To higher duties of connubial ties,
> To mutual blessings that from duties rise?
> Your looks—your hearts the bright assemblage own,
> Which heaven to emulate life has shown,
> And placed in double lustre, on a throne!

The reactions of the sober, middle-aged monarchs have not been preserved, but Burgoyne continued to write such ponderous pieces. In 1787 he offered a prologue for *The Liar*, which Lord Sandwich presented at his estate, and which starred the earl of Derby, among others. Major William Arabin of the Second Life Guards read the prologue, which was received with "great applause," although Burgoyne declined to reveal the authorship. The general also prepared an operatic version of Shakespeare's *As You Like It*, which, fortunately, was never produced. He envisioned a three-act play, in which he would omit— but not alter—portions of the bard's dialogue. He also intended to write new songs, and his revision of the well-known "Hunting Song" was such that the reader may deduce why the play did not appear at Drury Lane, or elsewhere:

> Hark! the hunters' piercing cry,
> See the shafts unerring fly!
> Ah! the dappled fool is stricken
> See him tremble—see him sicken,
> All his worldly comrades flying,
> See him bleeding, panting, dying,
> From his eyelids wan and hollow,
> How the big tears follow—follow
>   Down his face in piteous chace,
> How they follow, follow, follow,
>   Without stop, drop by drop,
> How they follow drop by drop![10]

During his retirement, Burgoyne also found time to join the Society for the Encouragement of Ancient Games, a project that Sheridan and Windham devised in 1787 to investigate various rural games and customs. Such topics had been of interest to Burgoyne since 1774, when he wrote *Maid of the Oaks.*[11]

Burgoyne's attention returned to the politics of empire briefly, for a last time, during 1787. India loomed again upon the rhetorical horizon of the House of Commons. After Warren Hastings was impeached for malpractice as governor general of India, the House appointed a Committee on Management including Burgoyne and almost all of his old friends, to prosecute the errant viceroy. Assisted by Burke, Fox, Sheridan, Windham, and Charles Gray, Burgoyne collected evidence and examined witnesses in preparation for the trial of Hastings. Legal proceedings lasted for eight years, during which time the general did not make any speeches. In December 1787, additional appointments were made to the committee, including that of the controversial Sir Philip Francis, whom Burgoyne defended as an honorable man. If Francis was in fact Junius, Burgoyne's accolade could be considered ironic. After several additional months passed without significant progress concerning the trial, Burke became agitated. He told Burgoyne that Gray was disturbed that the prosecution of Hastings was proceeding at such length and expense. Gray advocated dropping the bulk of the charges against Hastings. Burke disclosed that biased judges, unwilling witnesses, mangled records, and an indifferent public made proper legal hearings difficult. He suggested that Burgoyne might consider permitting a friend to open the proceedings. Burgoyne could reserve himself for the presentation of evidence. As it happened, Burgoyne did not speak at all during the Hastings trial, although several years after it began, he participated in parliamentary debates concerning aspects of it.[12]

During 1788 Spain seized several British ships in China and claimed an exclusive right to trade there. Burgoyne wrote a letter to William Pitt, offering his services in case of war, the subject nearest to his heart. Taking an opportunity to review his entire career, and at the same time dismissing possible objections to his reemployment, Burgoyne noted that he had experienced "the vicissitudes of military life in their extremes: successes, the gracious reception of which by His Majesty highly gratified ambition; reverses, followed by severe persecution of his ministers—extremes in both cases undeserved. I will presume, therefore, upon no merits; I will defend no faults." He took for his example the conduct of General James Wolfe, who once declared that he might commit a hundred additional mistakes before he was a general "so fit for the confidence of my King and country as I aspire to be." He would not discuss at all his political conduct in Parliament, as it was of no importance in the matter of military preference. Reminding the prime minister that his father had given Burgoyne a regiment of dragoons, he claimed to have greeted the younger Pitt's "entrance into public life with a predilection for your talents, and an opinion of your virtues, that your near friends could hardly have exceeded." Consequently, his political opposition was not based upon slight motives.

Twice he had resigned, in 1779 and in 1784, upon "the call of principle," even though he realized his interests "lay directly the contrary way." Rather bluntly, Burgoyne reiterated his opposition to Pitt: "I acknowledge that my partiality gave way to the ideas I conceived in common with most of the opponents of your administration, upon the principles of its formation, the composition of its parts, and the dangerous effects derived from those causes." His objections to the Pitt ministry were based not only upon opposition to the king's intervention in 1784, but also upon affection for Pitt's predecessors in the coalition ministry, and upon agreement with their political principles. However, Burgoyne dismissed fears that he could not work in a military capacity with the present ministry. Burgoyne asked not for "indolent employment," but for assignment to active duty, so that he could devote to his country his "last powers for actual service." Age and approaching infirmities precluded service thereafter. He hoped Pitt would not interpret his letter as a "professional rant" or in any way the "forced sentiment of an old soldier to say that should his period in the destination of Providence be near, he would rather meet it in the duties of the field than amidst the sorrows and afflictions of a sick bed."[13]

Britain and Spain averted war and Burgoyne was not considered for service by the ministry. It is doubtful that Pitt or King George III would have permitted him to volunteer, in view of his advancing age. The general's dramatic and military careers were ended, but he fired several political parting shots during 1789 and 1790 in the House of Commons. In March of the former year, Burgoyne spoke in strong terms during a debate concerning a motion to make the office of commander in chief permanent and responsible exclusively to Parliament. He had supported such a measure two years earlier, which among other things would have prevented "young officers commanding old ones." The bill was defeated. Now he made a second attempt upon the occasion of the removal of the marquis of Lothian from the post of commander in chief because he had voted against the government in Parliament. Burgoyne condemned government by favoritism, and surprisingly, extended his denunciation to the selling of commissions. Officers could reach high rank, he observed, "without ever seeing a soldier, or knowing what a firelock was." In the interests of good government, and perhaps recalling his unpleasant experiences with Germain and Barrington, Burgoyne championed the necessity for a responsible commander in chief. The secretary at war, defending his office, challenged Burgoyne's reasoning; if Parliament appointed a commander in chief, he said, the prerogative might as well not exist. He questioned the need for such an officer during a time of prolonged peace. Fox, however, supported Burgoyne's argument, and urged that Parliament watch carefully the prerogative of the crown. Unfortunately, Burgoyne's proposed change in the army establishment did not take place for many years, until well after the disasters of the Crimean War shocked the nation from its complacency.[14]

Shortly thereafter, Burgoyne joined a debate on the ordnance estimates. As

General John Burgoyne, 1789. Reproduced by permission of the National Army Museum, London.

the House of Commons became a Committee of Supply, the ministry presented an estimate of £218,000 for ordnance expenses for the ensuing year. When Pitt signaled a vote, Burgoyne objected that the house was sparsely attended and that those ministers who would oppose the measure were absent. Pitt replied that Burgoyne had made the wrong inference; the house was poorly attended because there were no objections to the ordnance estimates. The prime minister offered to debate Burgoyne, but the general remained silent. Two days later, however, he criticized another aspect of the estimates. Objecting to a proposal for the fortification of the British West Indies, Burgoyne reminded the House that the climate there was not ideal for British officers, and he urged members to table the estimates until approved by a board of general officers.[15]

Burgoyne's behavior in the Commons was clearly obstructionist. He had not only alienated the Pitt ministry; he had also continued to antagonize the court. In February 1789, Burgoyne and Mrs. Armistead, an actress, conveyed their compliments via Charles Fox to the prince of Wales, surely an accurate reflection of the general's attitude toward the king. Burgoyne may be excused perhaps on account of age for his intransigence, which increased with his gradually declining interest in public life. Charles Fox, in an undated letter, noted that

> Richard Sheridan and you have given up all public concerns (political concerns might be a more correct expression) for Mrs. B. and Miss P., and I was going to write you both a grave remonstrance upon your follies; . . . but I find you expected the remonstrance, and therefore thought to prevent it by an ill-founded attack upon me; but do not think I shall let you off so. I advise you both to read that stanza in the canto of the *Fairy Queen* which contains the Bower of Bliss, and begins with this line—
> "His warlike arms, the idle instruments—" and there you will see yourselves. Shame upon you! Shame upon you![16]

In 1790, Burgoyne was elected for the fifth and last time to represent the borough of Preston. He and Houghton returned without a contest, as the corporation had given up hope of reversing the 1768 franchise judgment. A contemporary cartoon indicates some discontent in Preston concerning Burgoyne, however, for it depicts an elderly woman holding a cup and exclaiming: "I wish to eat the Child I am pregnant with sooner than B–g–ne should be elected member for P–st–n."[17]

Shortly after his reelection Burgoyne returned to the House to observe the continuance of the Hastings trial, although he took no part in the proceedings. Burgoyne did join discussions in the House of Commons concerning the illegal execution of Rajah Mustapha Cawn by a British captain. On March 15, 1790, Burgoyne called it "a cruel and atrocious murder" that was clearly imputable to Hastings. Answering squarely objections that the House was not the proper place for discussion of the matter, Burgoyne recalled a previous military inquiry that "had constituted one of the happiest days of his life." Cutting through an argument that defended the captain for obeying orders, the general stated that the military establishment had to obey the common law as well as the law of humanity. Burgoyne had always obeyed orders, even absurd ones, and he quoted at length from a tract on obedience he had published. But if the order debased the service of a soldier, "an order that my conscience revolts at," said Burgoyne, then the requirements of obedience ceased. Several months later, Burgoyne discovered that Burke and the managers of the Hastings impeachment trial were subjected to attacks by a Major Scott, who questioned and impugned their motivations. Burgoyne spoke again, modestly disclaiming weight and talent that others in the House could display, and denying that he defended Burke and others because of personal prejudices. However, the general charged Scott with libel and breach of privilege. Despite stiff opposition, Burgoyne carried a vote of censure against Scott on the grounds that it was against the law to publish libel or scandal concerning the House of Commons.[18]

Toward the end of 1790, James Boswell proposed Burgoyne's nomination for admittance to the late Dr. Samuel Johnson's renowned circle of artists, scholars, statesmen, and literary giants. On the same day, the bishop of Carlisle and Sir Charles Blagden received nominations, and they were ultimately accepted. Burgoyne was opposed, however, by three members, one of whom was George Stevens, a Shakespeare scholar who may not have been impressed by Burgoyne's treatment of *As You Like It*. Burgoyne took the defeat in his stride, and early in 1791 he received a promise from Sir Joshua Reynolds to submit a painting by one of Burgoyne's friends to an exhibition at the Royal Academy. When the canvas did not appear, Burgoyne sent off a heated, five-page letter to Reynolds, to which he appended the following statement several days later: "After keeping this letter for five days unfinished, I now confess I wrote it in just anger, but upon reflection, I set too high a value on your talents and your virtues not to be placable." Reynolds replied that Burgoyne's letter was inspired by gout; the postscript came from his friend.[19]

In February 1792, Burgoyne gave his last speech in the House of Commons. During a debate on the army estimates, Fox protested against the practice of maintaining skeleton regiments, and Burgoyne agreed with him. In the course of his remarks, the general made a plea for better pay for soldiers:

> I applaud the allowance to the common soldier as equally humane and wise, and I am sure that whoever planned it must be a military man. I only wish that the situation had been considered at the same time. They are still obliged to subsist on their scanty pittance, although every article of substance is at least 30 percent. dearer than when their pay was originally settled.[20]

Although the speech was Burgoyne's last, in the months which followed he continued to attend the House and various social functions in London. On

August 1 and 2 he stayed with Charles Fox at Saint Anne's Hill, complaining of the gout. On the third, the general was in better spirits, and went to London to attend a play at the Theatre Royal, Haymarket. The following morning he was found dead of the gout in his bed at his home on Hertford Street, Mayfair, at the age of seventy years. The king learned of the general's death the next day when Henry Dundas informed him of the event from his home in Wimbledon.[21] Caroline Howe, dipping her pen in vitriol, noted the death in a letter to Countess Spencer: "L[or]d Guilford died yesterday and Gen[era]l Burgoyne is washed off too. I hear he was found dead in his bed. Of course I feel no pity."[22] On August 13, Burgoyne's remains were carried in one coach and four, as he requested, to Westminster Abbey, where he was interred next to Lady Charlotte and his daughter in an unmarked area of the North Cloister. Richard Sheridan purchased his town house for £4,000.[23]

Burgoyne's last will and testament, written in 1783, with a codicil added in 1788, filled seventeen closely written pages, and included a declaration of faith, an admission of sexual transgression, and provision for his mistress and children:

> I therefore declare that from my youth I have lived, and I trust I shall die, in the fullest conviction and truth of the efficacy of the Gospel dispensation; I esteem it a system immediately from God; and I rely upon the merit and oblation of Jesus Christ, as understood by the Church of England, as the only means of salvation.

> During a life too frequently blemished by the indulgence of one predominant passion, it has been a comfort to me to hope that my sensualities have never injured, nor interrupted the peace of, others. Of the greater crimes that originate in the forgetfulness of God, or injustice, or malevolence towards my fellow creatures, my heart is innocent, and upon that ground, though with the deepest consciousness how little my best actions deserve when set against my offences, I commit my soul to the mercy of its Creator.[24]

The general left mementos to Lady Horton and Lady Warburton, two of his late wife's nieces, to his son John as head of the family, to his executors, and to two aides. Each of his servants received a sum of money. The famed diamond ring that Burgoyne obtained from the king of Portugal went to his nephew, Lord Derby; the philanthrophic Nathaniel Day received £2,000. Susan Caulfield, who now lived in Park Street, Dublin, received most of the general's property, valued at £4,000, according to the terms of the original will, with reversion to John Fox Burgoyne for his education to age fifteen, or whenever he entered the navy. Burgoyne strongly recommended to Miss Caulfield and the Derby family that his son train for the navy:

> I recommend the naval profession upon conviction that it is the most proper, the most honourable, and the most promising that a young man in his

circumstances can choose, but I would be no means have his inclination forced.

After he had retired as commander in chief in Ireland, Burgoyne's income was reduced considerably, and his family had multiplied. In the codicil he wrote in 1788, he acknowledged the birth of the three additional illegitimate children, who deserved "equal claims to his care and protection" and were to share his bequests for John Fox Burgoyne equally.[25]

Although Burgoyne made provision for many people, there was little of his personal fortune remaining after his liabilities were paid; indeed, at the time of his death, his private fortune was virtually nonexistent. The *Gentleman's Magazine* in its obituary said that his death would cause lasting regret:

> He has died richer in esteem than in money; in the saving or securing of that he had no talent. Of all the gay, the witty, the fashionable, who eagerly sought his acquaintance, and whose minds were impressed by the elegance of his conversation, and the variety of his talents, very few were present to drop the tear over departed genius. One coach only attended with four gentlemen; a lady was likewise present, whose convulsive agitation showed her to have that within which parted show.[26]

Notes

1. Clemesha, *Preston*, p. 207; P. A. Whittle, *History of Bolton-le Moors* (1856), cited by De-Fonblanque, *Episodes*, p. 89; "John Burgoyne," *DNB;* Pottinger, "John Burgoyne," p. 44. The Westminster Guide and other shorter pieces are collected in Burgoyne, *Dramatic and Poetical Works*, 2:215–48.

2. [January–February] 1784, Burgoyne to Nathaniel Day: [January–February] 1784, Day to Burgoyne, DeFonblanque, *Episodes*, pp. 436–38.

3. October 29, 1784, Burgoyne to Lord Sydney, DeFonblanque, *Episodes*, p. 439.

4. Cobbett, *Parliamentary History*, 25:1116, 1139.

5. DeFonblanque, *Episodes*, pp. 443–44; February 27, 1786, Cobbett, ed., *Parliamentary History*, vol. 25: 1116, 1139; cf. Burgoyne's attitude during the Falkland Islands controversy.

6. June 28, 1786, Cobbett, ed., *Parliamentary History*, 26:194; DeFonblanque, *Episodes*, pp. 444–45.

7. September 5, 1785, Mrs. Sheridan to her father, Rae, *Sheridan*, 2:18–21; February 10, 1786, Walpole to Lady Ossory, *Correspondence*, 33:514. The text of the play is printed in Burgoyne, *Dramatic and Poetical Works*, 2:5–153.

8. January 14, 1786, Mrs. Tickell to Mrs. Sheridan, Rae, *Sheridan*, 2:22; 1823, Lady Warburton to Caroline Parker, De Fonblanque, *Burgoyne*, pp. 6–8.

9. Allardyce Nicoll, *A History of Late Eighteenth Century Drama 1750–1800* (Cambridge: At the University Press, 1927), p. 24; Rae, *Sheridan*, 2:24; October 24, 1786, Mrs. Tickell to ?, in Rae, *Sheridan*, 2:24–25; Walpole, *Correspondence*, 33:546; February 13, 1787, Sir Gilbert Elliott to ?, Rae, *Sheridan* 2:25, note 1. The text of the play is printed in Burgoyne, *Dramatic and Poetical Works*, 2:155–209.

10. October 30, 1787, Major Arrabin to Burgoyne, DeFonblanque, *Episodes*, p. 392.

11. Pottinger, "John Burgoyne," p. 45.

12. November 7, 1787, Burke to Burgoyne, DeFonblanque, *Episodes,* pp. 445–47; May 4, 1788, Burke to Burgoyne, ibid., pp. 447–50.

13. [1788] Burgoyne to William Pitt, DeFonblanque, *Episodes,* pp. 451–55.

14. December 10, 1787, Cobbett, ed., *Parliamentary History,* 26:1288; March 5, 1789, ibid., 27:1310; March 18, 1789, ibid., 37:1318–19.

15. March 20, 1789, ibid., 27:1320–23.

16. February 15, 1789, Fox to the prince of Wales, Arthur Aspinall, ed., *The Correspondence of George, Prince of Wales 1770–1812,* 8 vols. (London: Cassell, 1963–71), 1:490.

17. Dated 1790, copyright reserved, Lancashire Record Office.

18. Clemesha, *Preston,* p. 207; March 15, 1790, Cobbett, ed., *Parliamentary History,* 28:534–37; May 21, 1790, ibid., 28:824; May 27, 1790, ibid., 28:860.

19. Geoffrey Scott and Frederick A. Pottle, eds., *The Journal of James Boswell,* 18 vols. (privately printed, 1930–34), 18:100. Boswell had interviewed Burgoyne in 1778; ibid., 13:117, 123, 303.

20. February, 1792, Cobbett, ed., *Parliamentary History,* 29:811–12.

21. Barker and Stenning, eds., *Old Westminsters,* 1:143; *DNB* lists the date as June 4. Much more likely is the August 4 citation of Lodge, *Peerage,* p. 393, the introduction to Burgoyne, *Dramatic and Poetical Works,* the August 1792 *Gentleman's Magazine;* August 5, 1792, Henry Dundas to the king, in Arthur Aspinall, ed., *The Later Correspondence of George III,* 5 vols. (Cambridge: At the University Press, 1962–70), 1:604. Chester, *Registers,* p. 450, n. 3.

22. August 5, 1792, Caroline Howe to Georgiana, Countess Spencer, Spencer MSS., Althorp.

23. August 7, 1792, Malone to Charlemont, Historical Manuscripts Commission, *Charlemont MSS.,* 2:196–97. This source also records the August 4 date of death.

24. The will Burgoyne wrote on September 10, 1783, added a codicil on June 1, 1788. It was proved August 22, 1792; Chester, ed., *Registers,* p. 450 and note 3.

25. Chester, *Registers,* p. 450, and note 3.

26. August 1792, *Gentleman's Magazine,* 62:771.

22

An Appraisal

Burgoyne personified in many ways the British career officer of the eighteenth and even the nineteenth centuries who continued to win and lose battles, gamble at Brooks Club, and delight his colleagues with witty repartee, sparkling wines, good manners, and devotion to his country and to himself. Another and darker myth of Gentleman Johnny, created by such contemporaries as Baroness Riedesel, Horace Walpole, and Lord George Germain, was sustained and elaborated by George Bancroft, Bernard Shaw, Hoffman Nickerson, and has been most recently examined by George Billias.[1] The latter historian noted, the author believes correctly, that the stereotypes created by those writers concerning bumbling British aristocrats and shrewd American citizen-soldiers were misleading ones. There is no doubt that the caricature of Burgoyne the buffoon and dilettante was based upon hostile contemporary sources.

But he did gamble excessively, drank copiously, and as his will indicated, he was unfaithful to his wife from time to time. A favorite at court, friend of Garrick, Burke, Fox, Sheridan, and Reynolds, Burgoyne indeed desired to shine. He was, as Junius noted, very sensitive concerning his honor, perhaps much more so than the conventional English aristocrat. These personal predilections, eccentricities, and foibles were slightly larger than life even within England's lordly circles.

The general put his varied talents to best advantage when writing plays. He was a perceptive social critic and his *Maid of the Oaks* remains a clever satire, although the maid is a rather lackluster characterization. Lady Bab Lardoon, more carefully developed, is much more intriguing and often amusing. Assuredly, *The Heiress* was Burgoyne's classic. But even that charming play may owe something to Richard Sheridan, Burgoyne's friend and theatrical colleague. It is revealing, perhaps, that in his best work he was concerned with the unmasking of hypocrisy, while at the same time he concealed his identity as author until and unless the play was well received; and that in all probability he did not write the entire play himself. As in Burgoyne's other endeavors, moreover, his theatrical efforts are uneven in quality. *Richard Coeur-de-Lion* is unconvincing, *The Lord of the Manor* even less rewarding, and the projected but never performed adaptation of Shakespeare's *As You Like It* a disaster. In Burgoyne's dramatic failures the characters were virtually stereotypes. He seems to have worked impatiently, not devoting sufficient care and attention to the development of plot and detail, often crossing the line between satire and burlesque. His servants are too servile, his lords more than lords on the surface, less than human beneath it. The desire to please an audience often seems to have distracted Burgoyne from developing motivation or personality. In his poetry Burgoyne left himself open to charges of dilettantism, and in his occasional verse Burgoyne wrote sentimentally rather than eloquently. The literary compositions that he issued on military campaigns were similarly lacking in conviction. The epistles to the Indians and to the American people—melodramatic, sonorous, and whimsical—were based upon a superficial knowledge of the inhabitants of the new world. A careful reading of those proclamations, verses, and theatrical pieces leaves the reader with mixed impressions. While some of the plays contained shrewd analyses of British social life, other contributions are patent examples of what Walpole called rodomontade. Thus the charges of dilettantism and buffoonery were not entirely without substance.

If Burgoyne upon occasion viewed British society with detachment and critical acumen he was not always similarly gifted as a politician. One discovers a careful dependence upon the connections of his wife's family, a ruthless determination to succeed, and a political philosophy of undoubted conventionality. Usually a minor cog in the machinery of state, the general was more a spoilsman that a statesman. His electoral victories were the work of influential friends and relatives, and his conduct at Preston in 1768 was unequaled in brutality, hypocrisy, cynicism, and sheer determination. Voting and debating only occasionally and as a court partisan, Burgoyne delivered sometimes incoherent and often pompous speeches that anyone who dabbled from time to time in the affairs of state could have written. Perhaps desiring more to retrieve his reputation than to institute imperial reform, Burgoyne may have used Clive as a scapegoat for his own misconduct in 1768. The great nabob had plundered on a grander scale than had Burgoyne at Preston, but both men were then acting on similar impulses of self-interest. Burgoyne contributed more to parliamentary confusion and chaos during the investigation than to anything else.

Burgoyne's observations concerning military discipline were perceptive, even advanced. But his mind was not a brilliant one. The evaluations of European armies Burgoyne wrote were not particularly accurate. The criteria that Burgoyne used were applicable in almost every instance to his own forte, the cavalry. Therefore, one discovers that the Austrian army, famous for its horsemen, was among the best in Europe, but that the French were sadly wanting in the general's view. Burgoyne's underestimation of the French army is especially surprising. The general's observations concerning America are likewise unimpressive. It has been suggested that Burgoyne viewed the American Revolution in ideological terms strikingly different from those of his colleagues.

However, his conception of the empire as an indissoluble series of links was not novel, nor was it other than commonplace during Burgoyne's lifetime. At one time urging patience and understanding toward America, Britain's child, Burgoyne later urged forceful conquest. Observing the failure of early campaigns, he then suggested either total war or a British withdrawal. After the catastrophe at Saratoga, Burgoyne opposed the war completely. Although Burgoyne offered competent pragmatic suggestions, his advice was pedestrian: some of it borrowed from the reflections of others, much of it dependent upon his own circumstances.

As a soldier, Burgoyne was more than competent. Displaying courage, daring, and good judgment, he made his mark in France, Portugal, and Spain. He campaigned for promotion successfully. After twelve years of military inactivity between the Peace of Paris and the onset of the American War of Independence, Burgoyne maneuvered to reactivate his military career; he exhibited an ambition greater than it was in 1763; he was jealous of his colleagues, though more impatient, more pompous, and less well controlled than they were. No longer able to rely upon his old connections, Burgoyne attempted to throw his own weight, and he accepted finally a minor post with little grace. The long condemnations of Gage and the obvious attempts to trap Lee recall the ruthless ambitions of 1768. When he received a better appointment in 1776, Burgoyne instigated a campaign to undermine Carleton. Although Burgoyne may have been brighter, bolder, and more direct than many of his contemporaries, he was less intellectually gifted than Carleton and Clinton. He was bolder than Gage, but his boldness often verged upon rashness. Burgoyne was often blunt, but his machinations concerning Carleton were underhanded, and his criticism of Gage deceitful.

Burgoyne's good qualities as a general were not sufficient to overcome the less desirable traits. He did not display ingenuity concerning tactics. Although he encountered remarkably different methods of warfare in America, Burgoyne did not adapt to them. On the contrary, he insisted upon using standard European techniques throughout the campaign. He emphasized the bayonet, formations in line, generous supplies of artillery (but not food or transportation equipment) and conventional foraging expeditions. In fact, he seemed less concerned with tactics than with writing plays, issuing proclamations, and forwarding lengthy dispatches to London. All of which is not to say that Burgoyne was utterly negligent, but he did not display a gifted intellect in the face of the new guerrilla warfare. Moreover, even within his own limited frame of military reference Burgoyne was a careless tactician.[2]

As a field commander, Burgoyne's merits were not conspicuous during the campaign of 1777. The army he met in May did not equal in strength the force that he had recommended, but its quality was beyond dispute. He succeeded admirably in winning the army's affections and loyalty, which remained in great part until the bitter end. His courage on the battlefields during the conflicts of September 19 and October 7 was unquestionable. Burgoyne's indomitable will forced the army through hundreds of miles of virgin forest almost to its destination at Albany. But if the entire operation was jeopardized on the planning boards in Germain's office—where both Burgoyne and Howe influenced strategy—it was doomed to failure and captivity by Burgoyne's ill-considered direction. He neglected to equip the force with a proper supply of transport vehicles before the expedition even began; his early victories were made insignificant when he decided to cut through the forests near Skenesborough, which took a month. The foraging expedition met disaster at Bennington because Burgoyne relied upon the dubious advice of Skene and because he sent too few troops conducted by a commander who could not speak English. When his strength became so low that even his staff objected, Burgoyne continued to plunge toward the enormous force that Gates had collected. After the battle of Freeman's Farm, he had an opportunity to retreat and save his army, but instead Burgoyne chose to await disaster.

The general could have been considered a conventional member of the lesser gentry in almost all respects except the circumstances of his birth and the height of his ambition. An average and at times clever playwright, an unimportant but often ruthless politician, a competent subordinate officer but not an effective field commander, General Burgoyne was a paradoxical personality. He was inordinately sensitive about reputation, yet he sired four children out of wedlock. He desired military glory, but did not make the necessary preparations for victory. He wrote plays to amuse the public, but often hurried through them, thus damaging their ability to endure. Born into the gentry, he overplayed the role and appeared to the public and his enemies as a buffoon. Perhaps because of his birth, Burgoyne displayed a soaring desire to distinguish himself and succeeded only as a playwright. The British general's abilities did not equal his ambition—a judgment confirmed by the greatest test of his talents, the Saratoga expedition. He was nevertheless a colorful, charming, often warm man. His failings were human ones. Without him, Britain in the eighteenth century would have been a less fascinating land. And in North America, her choicest colonies might not have achieved nationhood as rapidly as they did.

Notes

1. George A. Billias, ed., *George Washington's Opponents: British Generals and Admirals in the American Revolution* (New York: William Morrow, 1969), pp. 142–92.
2. John Shy, *A People Numerous and Armed: Reflections on the Military Struggle for American Independence* (New York: Oxford University Press, 1976), p. 10, believes that Burgoyne's previous accomplishments justified his being given high command.

Bibliography

Manuscript Collections

There is no single collection of Burgoyne papers in existence at the present time. Edward B. DeFonblanque consulted and published a portion of the general's personal and official correspondence in 1876, but those manuscripts subsequently disappeared, seemingly without a trace. What follows is a list of Burgoyne manuscripts examined in the course of research for this study.

Alderman Library, University of Virginia, Charlottesville
    Manuscript Division collection

American Philosophical Society, Philadelphia
    Benjamin Franklin papers
    Miscellaneous manuscripts

Bedford County Record Office
    Burgoyne muniments
    Polwarth correspondence

Boston Public Library
    Manuscript collection

British Library, London
    Additional manuscripts series:
    5,847   Cole papers
    21,680–834   Haldimand papers
    24,120   Wotton papers
    24,127   Exchequer papers
    29,475   Auckland papers
    32,913   Newcastle papers
    34,414   Auckland papers
    35,614–36,046   Hardwicke papers
    37,833–35   Robinson papers
    38,200–40,178   Liverpool papers

Buckinghamshire Record Office
    Howard Vyse papers

Chicago Historical Society
    Gates papers

Clements Library, University of Michigan, Ann Arbor
    Clinton papers
    Gage papers
    Germain papers
    Miscellaneous manuscripts

Edinburgh University Library
    Manuscripts collection

Houghton Library, Harvard University, Cambridge
    Burgoyne letter

House of Lords Record Office, London
    Papers relating to the Burgoyne expedition

Lancashire Record Office, Preston
    Petitions, indentures, and memoranda concerning elections in Preston 1768,
        1774, 1780, 1784, 1790

Library of Congress, Washington, D.C.
    Schuyler letters

Liverpool Record Office
    Derby papers

Massachusetts Historical Society, Boston
    Heath papers

New-York Historical Society
    Gates papers

New York Public Library
    Adams papers
    Bancroft manuscripts
    Emmett collection
    Schuyler papers

Nottingham University Library
    Newcastle manuscripts

Perkins Library, Duke University, Durham
    Revolutionary War Collection

Public Record Office, London
   Audit Office papers
   12.30–12.101 accounts, various

   Carleton papers
   30.55

   Colonial Office papers
   5.91–96   Military correspondence, America and the West Indies
   5.182–183   Miscellaneous military correspondence
   5.236   Military entry books
   5.243   Dispatches to commanding officers
   5.253   Colonial office précis
   5.254–256   Colonial secretary departmental correspondence
   42.36   Canada; letters to the secretary of state
   324.44   Plantations general

   Foreign Office
   4.1

   Treasury Office
   1.387–605   Treasury board papers, original correspondence

   War Office
   1.1   Officers in America to secretary of state, correspondence
   1.2   Letters and dispatches to Secretary Barrington
   1.11   Letters from Generals Carleton and Haldimand
   1.616   Amherst-Barrington correspondence
   1.682   Germain and Barrington to Treasury
   1.890   Statistics relative to forces in America and West Indies
   1.1001–4   Barrington-Amherst-Burgoyne correspondence
   4.55–79   Secretary at war, general letters
   4.108   Secretary at war, general letters
   4.273   American letterbooks (secretary at war to commanders)
   4.274   Saratoga convention correspondence
   17.1317–1494   Monthly returns
   28.4   Headquarters records, America
   72.103   Judge advocate general's records: courts martial correspondence
   81.13   Judge advocate general's records: letter books

Sheffield City Libraries
   Wentworth Woodhouse muniments

South Carolina Historical Society, Charleston
   Laurens papers

Spencer Muniments, Althorp, Northamptonshire
   Papers of Georgiana, Countess Spencer

Printed Primary Source Material

Adams, John. *Familiar Letters of John Adams and His Wife Abigail during the Revolution.* Edited by Charles F. Adams. New York: Hurd and Houghton, 1876.

Almon, John, ed. *The Parliamentary Register: History of the Proceedings and Debates of the House of Commons 1774–1780.* 17 vols. London: J. Almon, 1775–80.

Anburey, Thomas. *Travels through the Interior Parts of America. In a Series of Letters.* 2 vols. London: W. Lane, 1789.

————. *With Burgoyne from Quebec: An Account of the Life at Quebec and of the Famous Battle of Saratoga.* Edited by Sydney Jackman. Toronto: Macmillan, 1963.

Annual Register; or, A View of the History, Politics, and Literature. 34 vols. London: Longmans, 1758–92.

Balderston, Marion, and David Syrett, eds. *The Lost War: Letters from British Officers during the American Revolution.* New York: Horizon, 1975.

Beresford, John. *The Correspondence of the Right Honourable John Beresford.* Edited by William Beresford. 2 vols. London: Woodfall and Kinder, 1854.

Boswell, James. *The Journal of James Boswell.* Edited by Geoffrey Scott and Frederick A. Pottle. 18 vols. N.p., 1930–34.

Bradford, S. Sydney, ed. "Lord Francis Napier's Journal of the Burgoyne Campaign." *Maryland Historical Magazine* (December 1962) 57:285–333.

Burgoyne, John. *Dramatic and Poetical Works.* 2 vols. London: Whittingham, 1808.

————. *The Heiress.* London: J. Debrett, 1786.

————. *A Letter from Lieutenant-General Burgoyne to His Constituents upon His Late Resignation.* Manchester: Manchester Mercury, 1779.

————. *The Lord of the Manor.* London: Evans, 1781.

————. *The Maid of the Oaks.* London: Beckett, 1774.

————. *Orderly Book of John Burgoyne from his Entry into the State of New York until his Surrender at Saratoga, 16th Oct., 1777.* Edited by Edmund B. O'Callaghan. Albany, N.Y.: Munsell, 1860.

————. *The Speech of a General Officer in the House of Commons, February 20th 1775.* London: n.p., 1775.

————. *A State of the Expedition from Canada, as Laid before the House of Commons by Lieutenant General Burgoyne, and Verified by Evidence with a Collection of Authentic Documents and an Addition of Many Circumstances Which Were Prevented from Appearing before the House by the Prorogation of Parliament Written and Collected by Himself.* 2d ed. New York: Arno Press, 1969.

————. *The Substance of General Burgoyne's Speeches.* London: J. Almon, 1778.

————. *A Supplement to A State of the Expedition from Canada Containing*

General Burgoyne's Orders, Respecting the Principal Movements, and Operations of the Army to the Raising of the Siege of Ticonderoga. London: Robson, 1780.

Burke, Edmund. *The Correspondence of Edmund Burke*. Edited by Thomas W. Copeland et al. 10 vols. Chicago: University of Chicago Press, 1958–78.

Burnett, Edmund C., ed. *Letters of Members of the Continental Congress*. 8 vols. Washington, D.C.: Carnegie Institution of Washington, 1921–36.

Chester, Joseph, ed. *The Marriage, Baptismal and Burial Registers of the Collegiate Church or Abbey of St. Peter, Westminster*. London: Harleian Society, 1876.

Clark, Jane, ed. "The Convention Troops and the Perfidy of Sir William Howe." *American Historical Review* (1932) 37:721–23.

Clinton, Henry. *The American Rebellion: Sir Henry Clinton's Narrative of His Campaigns, 1775–1782*. Edited by William B. Willcox. New Haven: Yale University Press, 1954.

Cobbett, William, ed. *The Parliamentary History of England from the Earliest Period to the Year 1803*. 36 vols. London: Hansard, 1806–20.

Coke, Lady Mary. *The Letters and Journals of Lady Mary Coke*. 4 vols. Bath, Eng.: Kingsmead Reprints, 1970.

Commager, Henry S., Morris, Richard B., eds. *The Spirit of 'Seventy-Six*. 2 vols. Indianapolis, Ind.: Bobbs-Merrill, 1958.

Davies, Kenneth G., ed. *Documents of the American Revolution, 1770–1783—Colonial Office Series*. 21 vols. Shannon: Irish University Press, 1972–80.

Dearborn, Henry. *The Revolutionary Journals of Henry Dearborn*. Edited by Lloyd A. Brown and Howard H. Peckham. Chicago: Caxton Club, 1939.

Digby, William. *The British Invasion from the North: The Campaigns of Generals Carleton and Burgoyne from Canada 1776–1777, with the Journal of Lieutenant William Digby of the 53rd or Shropshire Regiment of Foot*. Edited by James P. Baxter. Albany, N.Y.: J. Munsell, 1887.

"An Englishman." *A Letter to Lieut. Gen. Burgoyne, on His Letter to His Constituents*. London: n.p., 1779.

Force, Peter, ed. *American Archives: A Documentary History of the Origin and Progress of the North American Colonies*. 9 vols. Washington, D.C.: St. C. Clarke and Force, 1837–53.

Foster, Joseph, ed. *London Marriage Licenses 1521–1869*. London: Quaritch, 1887.

Ford, Worthington C., ed. *Journals of the Continental Congress 1774–1789*. 34 vols. Washington, D.C.: United States Government Printing Office, 1904–37.

Franklin, Benjamin. *Letters to the Press, 1758–1775*. Edited by Verner W. Crane. Chapel Hill, N.C.: University of North Carolina Press, 1950.

Gentleman's Magazine. 70 vols. London: n.p., 1732–92.

George III. *Additions and Corrections to Sir John Fortescue's Edition of the*

Correspondence of King George III. Edited by Sir Lewis Namier. Manchester: Manchester University Press, 1937.

―――. *Correspondence of King George III from 1760 to December 1783.* Edited by Sir John W. Fortescue. 6 vols. London: Macmillan, 1927–28.

―――. *Correspondence of King George III with Lord North from 1768–1783.* Edited by W. B. Donne. 2 vols. London: Murray, 1867.

―――. *The Later Correspondence of George III.* Edited by Arthur Aspinall. 5 vols. Cambridge: At the University Press, 1962–70.

George IV. *The Correspondence of George, Prince of Wales, 1770–1812.* Edited by Arthur Aspinall. 8 vols. London: Cassell, 1963–71.

Glover, John. *General John Glover's Letterbook 1776–1777.* Edited by Russell W. Knight. Salem, Mass.: Essex Institute, 1976.

Grenville, George. *Additional Grenville Papers, 1763–1765.* Edited by John R. G. Tomlinson. Manchester: Manchester University Press, 1962.

―――. *The Grenville Papers.* Edited by William J. Smith. 4 vols. London: Murray, 1853.

Hadden, James M. *Hadden's Journal and Orderly Book.* Edited by Horatio Rogers. Albany, N.Y.: J. Munsell, 1884.

Harcourt, Edward W., ed. *The Harcourt Papers.* 14 vols. Oxford: n.p., n.d.

Heath, William. *The Heath Papers: Collections of the Massachusetts Historical Society,* fifth series, vol. 4. Boston: Massachusetts Historical Society, 1878.

―――. *Memoirs of Major-General William Heath.* Edited by William Abbatt. New York: Abbatt, 1901.

Herbert, Sydney C., ed. *Henry, Elizabeth and George, 1734–80. Letters and Diaries of Henry, Tenth Earl of Pembroke and his aide.* London: Cape, 1939.

―――, ed. *Pembroke Papers (1780–1794). Letters and Diaries of Henry, Tenth Earl of Pembroke and his Circle.* London: Cape, 1950.

Historical Manuscripts Commission. *Report on the Manuscripts of the Marquess of Abergavenny.* London: H. M. Stationery Office, 1887.

―――. *Report on the American Manuscripts in the Royal Institution of Great Britain.* 4 vols. London and Dublin: H. M. Stationery Office, 1904–9.

―――. *The Manuscripts and Correspondence of James, First Earl of Charlemont.* London: H. M. Stationery Office, 1891.

―――. *Report on the Manuscripts of the Earl of Carlisle.* London: H. M. Stationery Office, 1897.

―――. *The Manuscripts and Correspondence of James, First Earl of Charlemont.* London: H. M. Stationery Office, 1891.

―――. *Report on the Manuscripts of the Earl of Dartmouth.* 3 vols. London: H. M. Stationery Office, 1887–96.

―――. *The Manuscripts of J. B. Fortescue, Esq., of Dropmore.* 10 vols. London: H. M. Stationery Office, 1892–1927.

―――. *Report on the Manuscripts of the late Reginald Rawdon Hastings, Esq., of the Manor House, Ashby de la Zouch.* 4 vols. London: H. M. Stationery Office, 1928–47.

———. *Report on the Manuscripts of Lord Kenyon.* London: H. M. Stationery Office, 1894.

———. *Report on the Manuscripts of the Marquess of Lothian.* London: H. M. Stationery Office, 1905.

———. *The Manuscripts of His Grace the Duke of Rutland, K.G., preserved at Belvoir Castle.* 4 vols. London: H. M. Stationery Office, 1888–1905.

———. *Report on the Manuscripts of Mrs. Stopford-Sackville of Drayton House, Northamptonshire.* 2 vols. London: H. M. Stationery Office, 1904–10.

———. *Report on the Manuscripts in Various Collections.* 8 vols. London, Dublin and Hereford: H. M. Stationery Office, 1901–14.

Howe, William. *Lieutenant General Sir William Howe's Orderly Book.* Edited by Benjamin F. Stevens. London: Stevens, 1890.

Hutchinson, Thomas. *The Diary and Letters of Thomas Hutchinson.* Edited by Peter O. Hutchinson. 2 vols. London: Sampson Low, 1883–86.

"A Journal of Carleton's and Burgoyne's Campaigns." *Bulletin of the Fort Ticonderoga Museum* 11 (December 1964):234–69; 11 (September 1965): 306–35; 12 (March 1966):5–62.

Junius. *The Letters of Junius.* Edited by John Cannon. Oxford: Clarendon Press, 1978.

The Kemble Papers. New York: New-York Historical Society, 1884.

Lamb, Roger. *An Original and Authentic Journal of Occurrences during the Late American War from Its Commencement to the Year 1783.* Dublin: Wilkinson and Courtney, 1809.

———. *Memoir of His Own Life.* Dublin: Jones, 1811.

LaPrade, William T., ed. *Parliamentary Papers of John Robinson 1774–1781.* London: Royal Historical Society, 1922.

Lee, Charles. *The Lee Papers.* 4 vols. New York: New-York Historical Society, 1872–75.

Lesser, Charles H., ed. *The Sinews of Independence: Monthly Strength Reports of the Continental Army.* Chicago: University of Chicago Press, 1976.

A List of the General and Field Officers, As They Rank in the Army. 24 vols. London: J. Millan, 1754–78.

London Chronicle.

London Morning Herald.

London Public Advertiser.

Montagu, John. *The Private Papers of John Earl of Sandwich, First Lord of the Admiralty, 1771–1782.* Edited by G. R. Barnes and J. H. Owen. 4 vols. London: Navy Records Society, 1932–38.

Montresor, James. *Journals of Col. James Montresor.* Edited by G. O. Scull. New York: New-York Historical Society, 1882.

Pausch, Georg. *Journal of Captain Pausch, Captain of the Hanau Artillery during the Burgoyne Campaign.* Edited by William L. Stone. Albany, N.Y.: J. Munsell, 1886.

Peckham, Howard H., ed. *Sources of American Independence: Selected Manuscripts from the Collections of the William L. Clements Library.* 2 vols. Chicago: University of Chicago Press, 1978.

Pell, Joshua. *Diary of Joshua Pell, III, an Officer of the British Army in America, 1776–1777.* New York: n.p., 1934.

Pettengill, Ray W., ed. *Letters from America, 1776–1779, Being Letters of Brunswick, Hessian and Waldeck Officers with the British Armies during the Revolution.* Boston: Houghton Mifflin, 1924.

Pitt, William. *The Correspondence of William Pitt.* Edited by W. S. Taylor and J. H. Pringle. 4 vols. London: Murray, 1838–40.

A Reply to Lieutenant General Burgoyne's Letter to His Constituents. London: J. Wilkie, 1779.

Riedesel, Friedrich A. von. *Memoirs and Letters and Journals of Major General Riedesel during his Residence in America.* Translated by William L. Stone. Edited by Max Von Eelking. 2 vols. Albany, N.Y.: J. Munsell, 1868.

Riedesel, Friederike C. von. *Baroness von Riedesel and the American Revolution: Journal and Correspondence of a Tour of Duty, 1776–1783.* Edited by Marvin L. Brown, Jr. Chapel Hill, N.C.: University of North Carolina Press, 1965.

————. *Letters and Journals relating to the War of the American Revolution, and the Capture of the German Troops at Saratoga.* Edited by William L. Stone. Albany, N.Y.: J. Munsell, 1867.

————. *Letters and Memoirs relating to the War of Independence and the Capture of the German Troops.* New York: Carvill, 1827.

St. Clair, Arthur. *The St. Clair Papers. The Life and Public Services of Arthur St. Clair, with His correspondence.* 2 vols. Cincinnati: Clark, 1882.

Sedaine, M. J. *Richard Coeur de Lion.* Translated by John Burgoyne. London: Debrett, 1786.

Searle, Ambrose. *The American Journal of Ambrose Searle, Secretary to Lord Howe, 1776–1778.* San Marino, Calif.: The Huntington Library, 1940.

Sheridan, Richard. *The Letters of Richard Brinsley Sheridan.* Edited by Cecil Price. 3 vols. Oxford: Clarendon Press, 1966.

Sparks, Jared, ed. *The Correspondence of the American Revolution, Being Letters of Eminent Men to George Washington.* 4 vols. Boston: Little, Brown, 1853.

Stanley, George F., ed. *For Want of a Horse.* Sackville, New Brunswick: Tribune Press, 1961.

Stevens, Benjamin F., ed. *Facsimiles of Manuscripts in European Archives relating to America 1773–1783.* 25 vols. London: Malby and Sons, 1889–98.

Stuart Wortley, Emmaline, ed. *A Prime Minister and His Son.* London: Murray, 1925.

Thacher, James. *A Military Journal of the American Revolution from 1775 to 1783*. Hartford, Conn.: American Subscription Publishing House, 1862.

Walpole, Horace. *Journal of the Reign of King George III from the year 1771 to 1783*. Edited by D. Doran. 2 vols. London: Bentley, 1859.

————. *The Last Journals of Horace Walpole during the Reign of George III, from 1771 to 1783*. Edited by A. Francis Steuart. 2 vols. London: Lane, 1910.

————. *Memoirs of the Reign of King George the Third*. Edited by G. F. R. Barker. 4 vols. London: Lawrence and Bullen, 1894.

————. *The Yale Edition of the Correspondence of Horace Walpole*. Edited by Wilmarth S. Lewis et al. 40 vols. New Haven: Yale University Press, 1937–74.

Washington, George. *The Writings of George Washington from the Original Manuscript Sources, 1745–1799*. Edited by John C. Fitzpatrick. 39 vols. Washington, D.C.: United States Government Printing Office, 1931–44.

Wilkinson, James. *Memoirs of My Own Times*. 3 vols. Philadelphia: Abraham Small, 1816.

Secondary Sources

Abbott, Wilbur C. *New York in the American Revolution*. New York: Scribner, 1929.

Adams, Charles F. *Studies Military and Diplomatic, 1775–1865*. New York: Macmillan, 1911.

Adams, James T. "The Burgoyne Expedition." *North American Review* 224 (September 1927):374–80.

Alden, John R. *The American Revolution 1775–1783*. The New American Nation Series, edited by Henry S. Commager and Richard B. Morris. New York: Harper, 1954.

————. *General Charles Lee: Traitor or Patriot?* Baton Rouge, La.: Louisiana State University Press, 1951.

————. *General Gage in America: Being Principally a History of His Role in the American Revolution*. Baton Rouge, La.: Louisiana State University Press, 1948.

————. *A History of the American Revolution*. New York: Knopf, 1969.

Anderson, Troyer S. *The Command of the Howe Brothers during the American Revolution*. New York: Oxford University Press, 1936.

Baker, Charles H. and Muriel I. Baker. *Life and Circumstances of James Brydges, First Duke of Chandos*. Oxford: Clarendon Press, 1949.

Baker, Norman. *Government and Contractors: The British Treasury and War Supplies 1775–1783*. London: University of London Athlone Press, 1971.

Bakshian, Aram, Jr. "General John Burgoyne." *History Today* 22 (July 1972):470–80.

Bancroft, George. *A History of the United States from the Discovery of the American Continent.* 6 vols. Boston: Little, Brown, 1837–85.

Barger, Bradley D. *Lord Dartmouth and the American Revolution.* Columbia, S.C.: University of South Carolina Press, 1965.

Barker, George F. R. and A. H. Stenning, eds. *The Record of Old Westminsters.* 2 vols. London: Chiswick, 1928.

Barrington, Shute. *The Political Life of William Wildman, Second Viscount Barrington, Compiled from Original Papers by his Brother Shute, Bishop of Durham.* London: Bulmer, 1814.

Batchelder, Samuel F. *Burgoyne and His Officers in Cambridge, 1777–1778.* Cambridge, Mass.: Cambridge Historical Society, 1926.

Bayse, A. H. "The Secretary of State for the Colonies, 1768–1782." *American Historical Review* 28 (October 1922):12–23.

Bell, Whitfield J., Jr. "Thomas Anburey's Travels through America: A Note on Eighteenth Century Plagiarism." *Papers of the Bibliographical Society of America* 37 (1943):23–36.

Bellot, Leland J. *William Knox: The Life and Thought of an Eighteenth Century Imperialist.* Austin, Tex.: University of Texas Press, 1977.

Billias, George. A. *General John Glover and his Marblehead Mariners.* New York: Holt, 1960.

———, ed. *George Washington's Opponents: British Generals and Admirals in the American Revolution.* New York: Morrow, 1969.

Bird, Harrison. *March to Saratoga: General Burgoyne and the American Campaign, 1777.* New York: Oxford University Press, 1963.

Boswell, James. *Life of Samuel Johnson.* Edited by George B. Hill and L. F. Powell. 6 vols. Oxford: Clarendon Press, 1950.

Boulton, William B. *The History of White's.* 2 vols. London: Bourke, 1892.

Bowler, R. Arthur. *Logistics and the Failure of the British Army in America 1775–1783.* Princeton, N.J.: Princeton University Press, 1975.

Brooke, John. *The Chatham Administration 1766–1768.* London: Macmillan, 1956.

———. *King George III.* New York: McGraw-Hill, 1972.

Brown, Gerald S. *The American Secretary: the Colonial Policy of Lord George Germain 1775–1778.* Ann Arbor, Mich.: University of Michigan Press, 1963.

Brydges, Egerton, ed. *Collins' Peerage of England, Genealogical, Biographical, and Historical.* 9 vols. London: Rivington, 1812.

Burke, Sir Bernard, and Ashworth P. Burke, eds. *A Genealogical and Heraldic History of the Peerage and Baronetage, the Privy Council, and Knightage.* 3 vols. London: Burke's Peerage, 1931.

Burt, Alfred L. *Guy Carleton: Lord Dorchester.* Ottawa: Canadian Historical Association, 1955.

———. *The Old Province of Quebec.* Minneapolis, Minn.: University of Minnesota Press, 1933.

Bush, Martin. *Revolutionary Enigma: A Re-appraisal of General Philip Schuyler of New York*. Port Washington, N.Y.: Friedman, 1969.

Cannon, John. *The Fox-North Coalition: Crisis of the Constitution*. Cambridge: At the University Press, 1969.

Carter, Clarence E. "The Office of Commander in Chief." *Era of the American Revolution: Studies Inscribed to Evarts Boutall Greene*. Edited by Richard B. Morris. New York: Columbia University Press, 1939.

————. "Significance of the Military Office in America." *American Historical Review* 38 (1923):475–88.

Cavanagh, John C. "The Military Career of Major General Benjamin Lincoln in the War of the American Revolution, 1775–1781." Ph.D. dissertation, Duke University, 1969.

Christie, Ian R. *The End of the North Ministry 1780–82*. London: Macmillan, 1958.

————. *Myth and Reality in Late Eighteenth-Century British Politics, and Other papers*. London: Macmillan, 1970.

Clapp, William W. *A Record of the Boston Stage*. Boston: Munroe, 1853.

Clark, Jane. "The Command of the Canadian Army for the Campaign of 1777." *Canadian Historical Review* 10 (June 1929):129–35.

————. "Responsibility for the Failure of the Burgoyne Campaign." *American Historical Review* 35 (April 1930):542–59.

Clemesha, H. W. *History of Preston*. Manchester: Manchester University Press, 1912.

Coburn, Frank W. *The Centennial History of the Battle of Bennington*. Boston: Littlefield, 1877.

Cone, Carl B. *Burke and the Nature of Politics: the Age of the American Revolution*. Lexington, Ky.: University of Kentucky, 1957.

Corbett, Julian S. *England in the Seven Years' War*. 2 vols. London: Longman, 1907.

Creasy, Edmund S. *The Fifteen Decisive Battles of the World*. London: Bentley, 1851.

Cullum, George W. "The Struggle for the Hudson." In *Narrative and Critical History of America*, edited by Justin Winsor. 8 vols. Boston: Houghton Mifflin, 1887–89.

Curtis, Edward E. *The Organization of the British Army in the American Revolution*. New Haven, Conn.: Yale University Press, 1926.

Dabney, William M. *After Saratoga: the Story of the Convention Army*. Albuquerque, N.M.: University of New Mexico Press, 1954.

Dawson, Henry B. *Battles of the United States*. 2 vols. New York: Johnson, Fry, 1858.

Debrett, John, ed. *Debrett's Peerage, Baronetage, Knightage and Companionage.* 5 vols. London: Debrett, 1932.

DeFonblanque, Edward B. *Political and Military Episodes in the Latter Half of the Eighteenth Century derived from the Life and Correspondence of the Rt. Hon. John Burgoyne, General, Statesman, Dramatist.* London: Macmillan, 1876.

Donoughue, Bernard. *British Politics and the American Revolution: the Path to War 1773–1775.* New York: St. Martin's Press, 1964.

Ernst, Robert. *Rufus King: American Federalist.* Chapel Hill, N.C.: University of North Carolina Press, 1968.

Fitzmaurice, Lord Edmond. *The Life of William, Earl of Shelburne, Afterwards First Marquis of Lansdown.* 3 vols. London: Macmillan, 1875–76.

Foord, Archibald S. *His Majesty's Opposition 1714–1830.* Oxford: Clarendon Press, 1964.

Forbes, Esther. *Paul Revere and the World He Lived In.* Boston: Houghton Mifflin, 1942.

Forster, Cornelius. *The Uncontrolled Chancellor: Charles Townshend and His American Policy.* Providence, R.I.: Rhode Island Bicentennial Foundation, 1978.

Fortescue, Sir John W. *A History of the British Army.* 13 vols. London: Macmillan, 1899–1930.

Foster, Herbert D. and Thomas D. Streeter. "Stark's Independent Command at Bennington." *Proceedings of the New York Historical Association* 5 (1905):29–96.

Freeman, Douglas S. *George Washington: A Biography.* 7 vols. New York: Scribner, 1948–57.

French, Allen. *The First Year of the American Revolution.* Boston: Houghton Mifflin, 1934.

Frothingham, Richard. *A History of the Siege of Boston.* Boston: Little, Brown, 1851.

Frothingham, Thomas G. *Washington, Commander in Chief.* Boston: Houghton Mifflin, 1930.

Furneaux, Rupert. *The Battle of Saratoga.* New York: Stein and Day, 1971.

Gee, Clive. "The British War Office in the Later Years of the American War of Independence." *Journal of Modern History* 26 (June 1954):123–26.

Gerlach, Don R. "After Saratoga: The General, His Lady, and 'Gentleman Johnny' Burgoyne." *New York History* 52 (January 1971):5–30.

———. *Philip Schuyler and the American Revolution in New York, 1733–1777.* Lincoln, Nebr.: University of Nebraska Press, 1964.

Gerson, Noel [Paul Lewis, pseud.] *The Man Who Lost America.* New York: Dial, 1973.

Glover, Michael. *General Burgoyne in Canada and America: Scapegoat for a System.* London: Gordon and Cremonsi, 1976.

Gore-Browne, Robert. *Chancellor Thurlow: The Life and Times of an Eighteenth Century Lawyer.* London: Hamilton, 1953.

Graham, Henry. *History of the Sixteenth, the Queen's Light Dragoons (Lancers).* N.p., 1912.

Gruber, Ira D. *The Howe Brothers and the American Revolution.* New York: Atheneum, 1972.

Guttridge, George H. "Lord George Germain in Office, 1775–1782." *American Historical Review* 33 (October 1927):23–43.

Haiman, Miecislaus. *Kosciuszko in the American Revolution.* New York: Polish Institute, 1943.

Hargreaves, Reginald. "Burgoyne and America's Destiny." *American Heritage* 7 (June 1957):4–7, 83–85.

Hargrove, Richard J. "Young John Burgoyne: Child of the Eighteenth Century." *Eighteenth Century Life* 3 (September 1976):12–16.

Higginbotham, R. Don. *Daniel Morgan: Revolutionary Rifleman.* Chapel Hill, N.C.: University of North Carolina Press, 1961.

———, ed. *Reconsiderations on the Revolutionary War: Selected Essays.* Westport, Conn.: Greenwood Press, 1978.

———. *The War of American Independence: Military Attitudes, Policies, and Practice, 1763–1789.* The Macmillan Wars of the United States, edited by Louis Morton. New York: Macmillan, 1971.

Hoffman, Ross J. S. *The Marquis: A Study of Lord Rockingham, 1730–1782.* New York: Fordham, 1973.

Howson, Gerald. *Burgoyne of Saratoga.* New York: Times Books, 1979.

Hudleston, Francis J. *Gentleman Johnny Burgoyne: Misadventures of an English General in the Revolution.* Indianapolis, Ind.: Bobbs-Merrill, 1927.

———. "The Misfortune at St. Cas." *United Services Magazine* 29 (January 1908):421–26.

Jones, Eldon L. "General Guy Carleton and the Close of the American War of Independence." Ph.D. dissertation, Duke University, 1968.

Judd, Gerrit P. *Members of Parliament 1734–1832.* New Haven: Yale University Press, 1955.

Knepper, George W. "The Convention Army, 1777–1783." Ph.D. dissertation, University of Michigan, 1954.

Lecky, William E. H. *A History of England in the Eighteenth Century.* 8 vols. New York: Appleton, 1878–90.

———. *A History of Ireland in the Eighteenth Century.* 5 vols. London: Longman, 1892.

Leslie, Charles R. and Tom Taylor. *Life and Times of Sir Joshua Reynolds.* 2 vols. London: Murray, 1865.

Lodge, Edmund, ed. *Lodge's Peerage, Baronetage, Knightage and Companionage of the British Empire for 1912.* London: Kelly's Directories, 1912.

Lowell, Edward J. *The Hessians and Other German Auxiliaries of Great Britain in the Revolutionary War.* New York: Harper, 1884.

Lunt, James. *John Burgoyne of Saratoga*. London: Macdonald and Janes, 1976.

Luvaas, Jay. *The Education of an Army: British Military Thought 1815–1940*. Chicago: University of Chicago Press, 1964.

Mackesy, Piers G. *The War for America 1775–1783*. Cambridge, Mass.: Harvard University Press, 1964.

Mahoney, Tom. "Saratoga: the Turning Point." *American Legion Magazine* 105 (August, 1978):20–43.

Mark, Irving. *Agrarian Conflicts in Colonial New York, 1711–1775*. New York: Columbia University Press, 1940.

Martelli, George. *Jemmy Twitcher: A Life of the Fourth Earl of Sandwich, 1718–1792*. London, Cape, 1962.

Matthews, William and Dixon Wecter. *Our Soldiers Speak*. Boston: Little, Brown, 1963.

Montross, Lynn. *Rag, Tag, and Bobtail: The Story of the Continental Army*. New York: Harper, 1952.

Morton, Doris B. *Philip Skene of Skenesboro*. Granville, N.Y.: Grastorf Press, 1959.

Namier, Sir Lewis. *The Structure of Politics at the Accession of King George III*. London: Macmillan, 1929.

————, and John Brooke, eds. *The History of Parliament: The House of Commons 1754–90*. 3 vols. London: Oxford University Press, 1964.

Neilson, Charles. *An Original, Compiled, and Corrected Account of Burgoyne's Campaign, and the Memorable Battles of Bemis Heights*. Albany, N.Y.: J. Munsell, 1844.

Nelson, Paul D. "British Conduct of the American Revolutionary War: A Review of Interpretations." *Journal of American History* 65 (December 1978):623–53.

————. "The Gates-Arnold Quarrel, September 1777." *New-York Historical Society Quarterly* 55 (July 1971):235–52.

————. *General Horatio Gates: A Biography*. Baton Rouge, La.: Louisiana State University Press, 1976.

————. "Legacy of Controversy: Gates, Schuyler and Arnold at Saratoga, 1777." *Military Affairs* 37 (April 1973):41–46.

Nicoll, Allardyce. *A History of Late Eighteenth Century Drama, 1750–1800*. Cambridge: At the University Press, 1927.

Nickerson, Hoffman. *The Turning Point of the Revolution; or, Burgoyne in America*. Boston: Houghton Mifflin, 1928.

O'Connell, Maurice R. *Irish Politics and Social Conflicts in the Age of the American Revolution*. Philadelphia: University of Pennsylvania Press, 1965.

Olson, Alison G. *The Radical Duke: Career and Correspondence of Charles Lennox, Third Duke of Richmond*. Oxford: Oxford University Press, 1961.

Palmer, Dave R. *The River and the Rock: the History of Fortress West Point, 1775–1783*. New York: Greenwood, 1969.

Pancake, John S. *1777: The Year of the Hangman.* University, Ala.: University of Alabama Press, 1977.

Patterson, Samuel W. *Horatio Gates: Defender of American Liberties.* New York: Columbia University Press, 1941.

Peckham, Howard H. *The War of Independence: A Military History.* University of Chicago History of American Civilization Series, edited by Daniel J. Boorstin. Chicago: University of Chicago, 1958.

————, ed. *The Toll of Independence: Engagements and Battle Casualties of the American Revolution.* Chicago: University of Chicago Press, 1974.

Perry, Eugene L. "Sir Guy Carleton as a Military Leader during the American Invasion and Repulse in Canada, 1775–1776." Ph.D. dissertation, Ohio State University, 1960.

Pottinger, David T. "John Burgoyne: Politician, Dandy and Man of Letters." *Proceedings of the Cambridge Historical Society* 22 (1937):29–45.

Procter, Winifred. "The Preston Election of 1768." *Transactions of the Historical Society of Lancashire and Cheshire* 3 (1960):93–116.

Rae, William F. *Sheridan: A Biography.* 2 vols. London: Bentley, 1896.

Ritchieson, Charles R. *British Politics and the American Revolution* Norman, Okla.: University of Oklahoma Press, 1954.

Robson, Eric. *The American Revolution in Its Military and Political Aspects.* Edited by Sir Lewis Namier and T. H. McGuffie. New York: Oxford University Press, 1956.

Ropp, Theodore. *War in the Modern World.* Durham, N.C.: Duke University Press, 1959.

Rose, John H. *William Pitt and the Great War.* London: Bell, 1911.

Royster, Charles. *A Revolutionary People at War: the Continental Army and American Character, 1775–1783.* Chapel Hill, N.C.: University of North Carolina Press, 1979.

Scheer, George F., and Hugh F. Rankin. *Rebels and Redcoats.* Cleveland: World, 1957.

Shaw, George Bernard. *The Devil's Disciple: A Melodrama. Being the First of Three Plays for Puritans.* London: Richards, 1901.

Sherrard, Owen A. *Lord Chatham and America.* London: Bodley Head, 1958.

Shy, John. *A People Numerous and Armed: Reflections on the Military Struggle for American Independence.* New York: Oxford University Press, 1976.

Smith, Justin H. *Our Struggle for the Fourteenth Colony.* 2 vols. New York: Putnam, 1907.

Smith, Paul H. *Loyalists and Redcoats: A Study in British Revolutionary Policy.* Chapel Hill, N.C.: University of North Carolina Press, 1964.

Stanhope, Philip H. *History of England from the Peace of Utrecht to the Peace of Versailles 1713–1783.* 7 vols. London: Murray, 1836–54.

Stone, William L. *The Campaign of Lieut. Gen. John Burgoyne and the Expedition of Lieut. Col. Barry St. Leger.* Albany, N.Y.: J. Munsell, 1877.

Sutherland, Lucy S. *The East India Company in Eighteenth-Century Politics.* Oxford: Clarendon Press, 1952.

Syrett, David. *Shipping and the American War, 1775–1783: A Study of British Transport Organization.* London: University of London Athlone Press, 1970.

Tanner, Lawrence. *Westminster School: A History.* London: Country Life, 1934.

Tharp, Louise H. *The Baroness and the General.* Boston: Little, Brown, 1962.

Thomas, P. D. G. "Votes in the House of Commons, 1768–1774." *Bulletin of the Institute of Historical Research* 35 (November 1962):220–26.

Trevelyan, Sir George O. *The American Revolution.* 4 vols. New York: Longmans, Green, 1899–1907.

————. *George the Third and Charles Fox.* 2 vols. New York: Longmans, Green, 1912–14.

Turberville, Arthur S., ed. *Johnson's England: An Account of the Life and Manners of His Age.* 2 vols. Oxford: Clarendon Press, 1933.

Tyler, Moses C. *The Literary History of the American Revolution, 1763–1783.* New York: Putnam, 1897.

Upham, George B. "Burgoyne's Great Mistake." *New England Quarterly* 3 (October 1930): 657–80.

Van Tyne, Claude H. *The War of Independence: American Phase 1775–77* Boston: Houton Mifflin, 1929.

Von Eelking, Max. *The German Allied Troops in the North American War of Independence 1776–1783.* Edited by J. G. Rosengarten. Albany, N.Y.: J. Munsell, 1893.

Von Ruville, Albert. *William Pitt, Earl of Chatham.* Translated by H. J. Chaytor. 3 vols. London: Heineman, 1907.

Wallace, Willard M. *Appeal to Arms: A Military History of the American Revolution.* New York: Harper, 1951.

————. *Traitorous Hero: The Life and Fortunes of Benedict Arnold.* New York: Harper, 1954.

Ward, Christopher L. *The War of the Revolution.* Edited by John R. Alden. 2 vols. New York: Macmillan, 1952.

Wickwire, Franklin B. *British Subministers and Colonial America, 1763–83.* Princeton, N.J.: Princeton University Press, 1966.

————, and Mary Wickwire. *Cornwallis: the American Adventure.* Boston: Houghton Mifflin, 1970.

Willcox, William B. *Portrait of a General: Sir Henry Clinton in the War of Independence.* New York: Knopf, 1964.

Wright, Esmond. *Fabric of Freedom, 1763–1800.* New York: Hill and Wang, 1978.

Wrottesley, George. *Life and Correspondence of Field Marshal Sir John Burgoyne, Bart.* 2 vols. London: Bentley, 1873.

Index

287